W9-AJJ-765

ATLA BIBLIOGRAPHY SERIES
Jack Ammerman, Series Editor

25. *A Bibliography of Christian Worship*, by Bard Thompson. 1989.
26. *The Disciples and American Culture: A Bibliography of Works by Disciples of Christ Members, 1866–1984*, by Leslie R. Galbraith and Heather F. Day. 1990.
27. *The Yogacara School of Buddhism: A Bibliography*, by John Powers. 1991.
28. *The Doctrine of the Holy Spirit: A Bibliography Showing Its Chronological Development* (2 vols.), by Esther Dech Schandorff. 1995.
29. *Rediscovery of Creation: A Bibliographical Study of the Church's Response to the Environmental Crisis*, by Joseph K. Sheldon. 1992.
30. *The Charismatic Movement: A Guide to the Study of Neo-Pentecostalism with Emphasis on Anglo-American Sources*, by Charles Edwin Jones. 1995.
31. *Cities and Churches: An International Bibliography* (3 vols.), by Loyde H. Hartley. 1992.
32. *A Bibliography of the Samaritans*, 2nd ed., by Alan David Crown. 1993.
33. *The Early Church: An Annotated Bibliography of Literature in English*, by Thomas A. Robinson. 1993.
34. *Holiness Manuscripts: A Guide to Sources Documenting the Wesleyan Holiness Movement in the United States and Canada*, by William Kostlevy. 1994.
35. *Of Spirituality: A Feminist Perspective*, by Clare B. Fischer. 1995.
36. *Evangelical Sectarianism in the Russian Empire and the USSR: A Bibliographic Guide*, by Albert Wardin Jr. 1995.
37. *Hermann Sasse: A Bibliography*, by Ronald R. Feuerhahn. 1995.
38. *Women in the Biblical World: A Study Guide. Vol. I: Women in the World of Hebrew Scripture*, by Mayer I. Gruber. 1995.
39. *Women and Religion in Britain and Ireland: An Annotated Bibliography from the Reformation to 1993*, by Dale A. Johnson. 1995.
40. *Emil Brunner: A Bibliography*, by Mark G. McKim. 1996.
41. *The Book of Jeremiah: An Annotated Bibliography*, by Henry O. Thompson. 1996.
42. *The Book of Amos: An Annotated Bibliography*, by Henry O. Thompson. 1997.
43. *Ancient and Modern Chaldean History: A Comprehensive Bibliography of Sources*, by Ray Kamoo. 1999.
44. *World Lutheranism: A Select Bibliography for English Readers*, by Donald L. Huber. 2000.
45. *The Christian and Missionary Alliance: An Annotated Bibliography of Textual Sources*, by H. D. (Sandy) Ayer. 2001.
46. *Science and Religion in the English-Speaking World, 1600–1727: A Bibliographic Guide to the Secondary Literature*, by Richard S. Brooks and David K. Himrod. 2001.
47. *Jurgen Moltmann: A Research Bibliography*, by James L. Wakefield. 2002.

48. *International Mission Bibliography: 1960–2000*, edited by Norman E. Thomas. 2003.
49. *Petra and the Nabataeans: A Bibliography*, by Gregory A. Crawford. 2003.
50. *The Wesleyan Holiness Movement: A Comprehensive Guide* (2 vols.), by Charles Edwin Jones. 2005.
51. *A Bibliography of the Samaritans: Third Edition: Revised, Expanded, and Annotated*, by Alan David Crown and Reinhard Pummer. 2005.
52. *The Keswick Movement: A Comprehensive Guide*, by Charles Edwin Jones. 2007.
53. *The Augustana Evangelical Lutheran Church in Print: A Selective Union List with Annotations of Serial Publications Issued by the Augustana Evangelical Lutheran Church and Its Agencies and Associates, 1855–1962, with Selected Serial Publications after 1962*, by Virginia P. Follstad. 2007.

The Augustana Evangelical Lutheran Church in Print

A Selective Union List with Annotations of Serial Publications Issued by the Augustana Evangelical Lutheran Church and Its Agencies and Associates, 1855–1962, with Selected Serial Publications after 1962

Virginia P. Follstad

ATLA Bibliography Series, No. 53

The Scarecrow Press, Inc.
Lanham, Maryland • Toronto • Plymouth, UK
2007

SCARECROW PRESS, INC.

Published in the United States of America
by Scarecrow Press, Inc.
A wholly owned subsidiary of
The Rowman & Littlefield Publishing Group, Inc.
4501 Forbes Boulevard, Suite 200, Lanham, Maryland 20706
www.scarecrowpress.com

Estover Road
Plymouth PL6 7PY
United Kingdom

British Library Cataloguing in Publication Information Available

Library of Congress Cataloging-in-Publication Data

Follstad, Virginia P., 1935–
    The Augustana Evangelical Lutheran Church in print : a selective
union list with annotations of serial publications issued by the
Augustana Evangelical Lutheran Church and its agencies and
associates, 1855–1962, with selected serial publications after 1962
/ Virginia P. Follstad.
        p. cm. — (ATLA bibliography series ; no. 53)
    Includes bibliographical references and indexes.
    ISBN-13: 978-0-8108-5831-2 (pbk. : alk. paper)
    ISBN-10: 0-8108-5831-2 (pbk. : alk. paper)
    1. Augustana Evangelical Lutheran Church—Bibliography.
I. Title.

    Z7776.7.F65 2007
    [BX8049]
    016.2841'333—dc22

                                                    2006031650

♾️™ The paper used in this publication meets the minimum requirements
of American National Standard for Information Sciences—Permanence of
Paper for Printed Library Materials, ANSI/NISO Z39.48-1992.
Manufactured in the United States of America.

Contents

Foreword

The Augustana Evangelical Lutheran Church, founded in 1860, was the Lutheran Church of Swedish origins in the United States and Canada. It merged with Lutheran churches of other ethnic traditions to form the Lutheran Church in America in 1962. The latter merged with still other Lutheran churches to form the Evangelical Lutheran Church in America in 1988.

The persons who emigrated from Sweden to America came from a country that had a high rate of literacy. Early on they founded Swedish-language newspapers and magazines, published books, and recorded their memories and aspirations. In time the transition was made to English. During the same time, Swedish-Americans also established publishing houses, colleges, seminaries (particularly, Lutheran, Baptist, and Evangelical Covenant), literary societies, and various interest groups. All of these sponsored publications. During the nineteenth and twentieth centuries, Swedish-Americans were among the most productive of ethnic groups within North America in terms of literary output.

The Augustana Evangelical Lutheran Church was the largest organization founded by persons of Swedish heritage in America. Its people wrote, debated, and recorded events through hundreds of periodicals and books.

The present volume stands within the stream of the Augustana heritage. It has been commissioned by the Augustana Heritage Association as a tool for research in the years to come. It is a guide to the periodical publications of the Augustana Church, giving detailed information on what was published and where those publications can be found. As the subtitle indicates, some publications came into existence prior to the founding of the church itself (as early as 1855). The researcher will also discover that publications have continued after the merger of 1962, most notably, the *Augustana Heritage Association Newsletter*.

The researcher will also want to obtain books that have been published. A complete bibliography would take up another entire volume of its own. Quick entrée can be gained through four volumes in particular (all with bibliographical helps): G. Everett Arden, *Augustana Heritage: A History of the Augustana Lutheran Church* (Rock Island, IL: Augustana Press, 1963); Arland J. Hultgren and Vance L. Eckstrom, eds., *The Augustana Heritage: Recollections, Perspectives, and Prospects* (Chicago: Augustana Heritage Association, 1999); Hartland H. Gifford and Arland J. Hultgren, *The Heritage of Augustana: Essays on Its Life and Legacy* (Minneapolis: Kirk House, 2004); and a forthcoming new history of the church by Maria Erling and Mark Granquist. Many more essays concerning the church are available in electronic format at the website of the Augustana Heritage Association (www.augustanaheritage.org). Additional materials are kept in special archival collections at the Archives of the Evangelical Lutheran Church in America; the Lutheran School of Theology at Chicago; Augustana College, Rock Island, Illinois (including its Swenson Center); Bethany College, Lindsborg, Kansas; and Gustavus Adolphus College, St. Peter, Minnesota.

The author of this volume, Virginia Follstad, has carried out a labor of love, dedication, and skill. Anyone interested in doing research on Swedish-American history and culture, the history of the Lutheran Church in the United States and Canada, Swedish-American church history more broadly, and particularly the history and inner life of the Augustana Evangelical Lutheran Church, will find this volume an exceedingly generous and helpful guide. All who have interests in these areas will be grateful to the author, and all who share the Augustana heritage in particular are in her debt.

The Rev. Paul Cornell, President
Augustana Heritage Association
The Day of Pentecost
June 4, 2006

Preface

Considering that the printed word is an influential and powerful part of the total ministry of the Church, the Augustana Heritage Association Board felt that a record of the periodicals issued by the Augustana Evangelical Lutheran Church was needed in order to facilitate research about the church and its institutions, organizations, and leading personalities. Such a record should also serve as a union list indicating the holdings of these serial publications in Augustana institutions, archives, and other libraries owning files. Thus this publication was born.

For more than a century, from 1855 through 1962, a legacy of the printed word has developed. Through the years, many editors and writers planned and prepared their paragraphs. Parish pastors, scholars, and church leaders were joined by reporters and church members, all with gifts of written expression, to create publications as messengers of the church. Printers and publishers set words on paper. Many worked to promote and distribute all manner of publications from extensive magazines and newspapers to modest newsletters. Many persevered under challenging circumstances. Librarians and archivists have faithfully acquired and preserved the written word on paper and microfilm, thereby preserving yesterday for tomorrow. All have persistently and successfully pursued their goal of informing, educating, and inspiring people of the Augustana Evangelical Lutheran Church and others of the religious faith. Each has provided a thread that has woven the total fabric of what is the Augustana heritage of the printed word.

The Augustana Evangelical Lutheran Church in Print is offered with the prayer that it will assist those who seek to find information about the Augustana Evangelical Lutheran Church. May the vision held by the Augustana Heritage Association Board be realized.

Acknowledgments

A publication of this kind can be prepared only with the cooperation of many resourceful, helpful, and willing individuals offering their assistance on behalf of the institutions they serve. In doing so, they have made it possible for the Augustana Heritage Association to provide this resource for Augustana Evangelical Lutheran Church serial publications.

These resourceful, helpful, and willing individuals are:

Sara Mummert at the Lutheran Theological Seminary, A. R. Wentz Library, in Gettysburg, Pennsylvania, whose early encouragement and support by loaning a copy of the SEPTLA union list and the Voigt serials list and by her e-mail messages were more helpful than one can ever expect or adequately acknowledge.

Iris Doksansky at Midland Lutheran College, Luther Library Archives, in Fremont, Nebraska, whose thorough search and reports of archival materials from Luther College and Academy are invaluable for this list and for preservation of the importance of Luther College and Academy in Augustana history.

Joel Thoreson at the Evangelical Lutheran Church in America Archives in Chicago, Illinois, whose timely and thorough responses to many different questions indicate his admirable professional dedication to his work. His assistance clarified many details about the history of the Augustana Evangelical Lutheran Church and its publications.

Jeannine Strunk at the Evangelical Lutheran Church in America Archives in Chicago, Illinois, who accepted the challenge of researching existing lists and producing new lists with historical data along with holdings of the archives, thus providing bibliographic information in a useful format.

Bruce Eldevik and Kate Rattenborg at Luther Seminary Library, St. Paul, Minnesota, whose professional dedication to thorough accuracy in reporting holdings is exemplary.

Monica Knutsson at Lund University in Lund, Sweden, who introduced LIBRIS, the national database of Sweden. Her e-mail message influenced significantly the content, accuracy, and broad thoroughness of this publication. Numerous holdings reports from four libraries in Sweden are included herein from that introduction.

Edi Thorstensson at Gustavus Adolphus College, Folke Bernadotte Library, in St. Peter, Minnesota, who, under severe time limitations, persevered to locate files and complete her reports from an institution that had been heavily damaged by a tornado, leading to a variety of challenging storage and verification issues. Her dedication to the project is exemplary.

Anne Jenner at the Swenson Swedish Immigration Research Center at Augustana College in Rock Island, Illinois, who shared her early enthusiasm about the project and indicated her willingness to assign priority to reporting items at the SSIRC for the project within the limits of her available time.

Sharon Baker at the Lutheran Theological Seminary, Krauth Memorial Library, in Philadelphia, Pennsylvania, who sent early reports and correspondence.

Vicki Eckhardt at the Texas Lutheran University, Blumberg Memorial Library, in Seguin, Texas, who sent early reports.

Clay E. Dixon at the Graduate Theological Union in Berkeley, California, who, by introducing the GRACE website, opened a new research tool and extended support for the project on behalf of the Pacific Lutheran Theological Seminary.

Patricia Hilker at the California Lutheran University, Pearson Library, in Thousand Oaks, California, who shared their serials list, making it possible to include holdings in that collection.

Jeanette Brandell at the Evangelical Lutheran Church in Canada Archives who, as a volunteer, gave many hours to research and reporting Canadian holdings.

Jeannette Bergeron at the Evangelical Lutheran Church in America Region 9 Archives, the James R. Crumley, Jr. Archives in Columbia, South Carolina, who sent a report.

Sara Fox Roth at the Tri-Synod Archives at Thiel College in Greenville, Pennsylvania, who provided a thorough report of holdings there.

Jean Peterson and Robert Wiederaenders at the Evangelical Lutheran Church in America Region 5 Archives in Dubuque, Iowa, whose reports included special titles.

Susan Ebertz at the Wartburg Theological Seminary, Reu Memorial Library, in Dubuque, Iowa, who shared her professional interest and forwarded reports for the project.

Individuals at the following libraries and regional ELCA archives who sent correspondence: Carla Tracy and Brent Etzel at Augustana College, Thomas Tredway Library, in Rock Island, Illinois; Christine Wenderoth and the reference librarian at the Lutheran School of Theology, Jesuit-Krauss-McCormick Library in Chicago, Illinois; reference librarian at Trinity Lutheran Seminary, Hamma Library, in Columbus, Ohio; Arvid Anderson for the Augustana Heritage Association; Mary Krieger for the Evangelical Lutheran Church in Canada; A. John Pearson at the ELCA Region 4 Archives in Lindsborg, Kansas; Ellen Engseth at North Park University, Chicago, Illinois; Kerstin Ringdahl at the ELCA Region 1 Archives in Tacoma, Washington; Carol Schmalenberger at the ELCA Region 2 Archives in Berkeley, California; and Jeanene Letcher at the ELCA Region 6 Archives in Columbus, Ohio.

Individuals at libraries who responded to specific requests: Steve Nielsen at the Minnesota Historical Society; Christopher Lieske at the Concordia Historical Institute; Susan Forbes at the Kansas State Historical Society; Ann Billesbach at the Nebraska State Historical Society; Sharon Adler at the University of Iowa; Vicki Glasgow and Carla Pfahl at the University of Minnesota; Travis Westly at the Library of Congress; Kathleen Kern and Ron B. at the University of Illinois at Urbana-Champaign; Marti Alt at Ohio State University; Kenneth Lohrentz at the University of Kansas; and the reference librarian at the Seattle, Washington Public Library.

Individuals at the following regional ELCA archives who responded that there either were no Augustana holdings in their custody or that archived materials were not available: Suzanne Hequet at the ELCA Region 3 Archives in St. Paul, Minnesota; Linda Landsberg at the ELCA Region 4 Archives in Omaha, Nebraska; John E. Peterson at the ELCA Region 7 Archives in Philadelphia, Pennsylvania; Elwood W. Christ at the ELCA Region 8 Archives in Gettysburg, Pennsylvania; Raymond M. Bost at the ELCA Region 9 Archives in Salisbury, North Carolina.

Interlibrary loan and reference librarians at each of the twenty libraries that graciously loaned print materials from their collections for research and documentation. Refer to the list of those libraries in the appendix.

Staff at the Dwight Foster Public Library in Fort Atkinson, Wisconsin, who extended a variety of professional courtesies.

Staff at the Hedberg Public Library, Reference Department, in Janesville, Wisconsin, who extended a variety of professional courtesies.

The University of Wisconsin–Whitewater, Harold Andersen Library, in Whitewater, Wisconsin, which permitted access to the OCLC First Search database and access to the WorldCat database. Many entries in this publication are based on bibliographic information contained in WorldCat. Access to print reference sources and other professional courtesies were also extended.

Sally Mason, assistant director and reference librarian at the Irvin L. Young Memorial Library in Whitewater, Wisconsin, who, with her consistent perseverance and knowledge of the state interlibrary loan system in Wisconsin, made certain that requested items arrived during the research portion of the project. This publication could not have been what it is without her professional dedication to bringing these items to my desk.

Ruth Ann Deppe, office manager for the Augustana Heritage Association at the Lutheran School of Theology in Chicago, Illinois, who kept a supply of correspondence materials and encouragement coming to my desk.

My family: Linda, Brian, Tim, Tyler, and Alex, who shared their steady encouragement; and my husband, Merle, who gave patiently of his time as my chauffeur, errand person, and paper and ink shopper, and shared his tolerance of my efforts. His faithful encouragement has endured all the way to the end of the project.

John Foust, whose professional expertise in computer technology and his endless patience made possible the final electronic version of all project files.

Arland J. Hultgren, professor of New Testament at Luther Seminary in St. Paul, Minnesota, and chair of the Augustana Heritage Association Projects and Publications Committee, who graciously shared his guidance, suggestions, and assistance.

And finally, the Augustana Heritage Association Board who considered their vision of the need for this union list, who supported their desire that it be published to facilitate research in subjects related to the Augustana Evangelical Lutheran Church, and who shared their encouragement throughout the time required for its completion.

Sincere gratitude and appreciation to all for their assistance.

Virginia P. Follstad, Project Coordinator
Whitewater, Wisconsin
May 2006

Introduction

From the initial list of 20 titles available for inclusion in this union list of Augustana Evangelical Lutheran Church serial publications the entries presented herein increased to number more than 330 titles. Certainly many more unique titles and files exist in archives, in library storage cartons, and even possibly in trunks and boxes in attics and basements of homes and churches. Thus, this present list is to be considered as only a beginning for the identification and location of information about Augustana Evangelical Lutheran Church serial publications.

Indeed, gathering information for this union list has been an international treasure hunt extending from the United States to Canada and then to Sweden. The search has been overflowing with surprises, moments of amazement, and expressions of gratitude for the diligence evident among those who have acquired and preserved print and microfilm.

Holdings statements are as current as possible at the moment of publication. However, admittedly, holdings change. A library may purchase something on this list and add the publication to its collection. A benefactor may present a gift of material that includes items in this list. Perhaps an estate was dissolved and those precious trunks and boxes revealed their contents to be valuable publications. A library may decide to discard an incomplete file or to donate it to another library that welcomes it to help complete its file. And an archives staff person may find time to sort and catalog items held in storage. In summary, holdings of an institution may change over time.

In the interest of maintaining as much accuracy as possible, the Augustana Heritage Association as sponsor of this publication solicits notice of any errors and omissions. Notices of any corrections that should be made are welcome and can be forwarded to the Augustana Heritage Association headquarters at 1100 East 55th Street, Chicago, Illinois 60615.

CRITERIA FOR CONTENTS

Even though this union list originally was planned to include only serial publications issued by the Augustana Evangelical Lutheran Church, it became clear as research continued that additional criteria for inclusion should be considered.

These selective criteria for inclusion are:

1. Publications issued by the Augustana Evangelical Lutheran Church at large.
2. Publications issued by an agency or division of the Augustana Evangelical Lutheran Church such as the Women's Missionary Society, the Lutheran Brotherhood, and the several boards of missions.
3. Publications issued by a regional Conference of the Augustana Evangelical Lutheran Church or by agencies of a regional conference.
4. Publications issued by an institution supported by the Augustana Evangelical Lutheran Church such as colleges and social service agencies.
5. Publications not of Augustana Evangelical Lutheran Church background or origin, but which became part of a merger with an Augustana Evangelical Lutheran Church publication. (For example, *Valkyrian*, which merged with *Ungdoms-Vännen* [1895])

Criteria for excluding titles that may have been considered eligible entries under the inclusion criteria are:

1. Publications issued by an individual parish or congregation, such as a newsletter or anniversary booklet. These should be in local files.
2. Publications from an individual regional social service institution, such as a newsletter from a home for the aged. These may be in local or regional archives.
3. Publications whose bibliographic information could not be verified in more than one source, with the exception of citations in the Lundeen bibliography.
4. Monographs that are not part of a series.
5. Publications issued after 1962, with the exception of items issued by the original affiliated institutions.
6. Publications issued by the LCA (Lutheran Church in America) or by the ELCA (Evangelical Lutheran Church in America).

TITLE ENTRY FORMAT AND CONTENTS

Titles and "See" references in this union list are arranged in alphabetical order in a single A to Z arrangement. In filing titles, initial articles such as *A, An, Den, Det,* and *The* are ignored. Whenever possible, each segment in a family of titles is treated as a distinct unit. Each of such entries provides its own genealogy.

Filing of the three additional letters in the Swedish alphabet (ä, å, and ö) is done as though the special marks are ignored, rather than arranging these letters in the traditional Scandinavian order at the end of the English alphabet. For example, *Österns Härold* is filed after *One* and before *Our Church* rather than at the end of the list.

Some additional liberties have been taken to depart from certain standard practices regarding the citation and description of serials. Such deviations were considered acceptable for the purposes of this publication, which is intended as a history as well as a union list.

A complete title entry includes:

1. Complete title.
2. Subtitle, whenever such exists.
3. Translation of title and subtitle from Swedish into English.
4. Place of publication; if not known, s.l. is shown.
5. Publisher; if not known, s.n. is shown.
6. Volume numbers, with beginning and ending single issue numbers when known. The Swedish årg., n:r. notations have been changed to volume and number.
7. Dates of publication, with specific month, day, and year indicated in complete format, when known. If specifics are uncertain, followed by a "?". Swedish spellings have been changed to English.
8. "Formed by the union of:" statement when applicable.
9. "Merged with . . . to form . . ." statement when applicable.
10. "Continues:" statement when applicable.
11. "Continued by:" statement when applicable.
12. "Other titles:" statement when applicable. Frequently these are added in the union list as "See" references.
13. "Sometimes referred to as:" statement when applicable. Frequently these are added in the union list as "See" references.
14. ISSN numbers, when available.
15. Narrative essay about the history, development, genealogy, general content, editors, and intended readership, with commentary and interesting information about the title, when known.
16. Primary sources of information. Refer to lists of Works Consulted for complete citations.

17. Holdings at named institutions in the following order:
    a. Institutions that reported holdings directly by correspondence or included holdings in their local online catalog.
    b. Institutions listed in the Erickson bibliography, the Lundeen bibliography, the Setterdahl microfilm list, or the Union List of Serials (ULS).
    c. Institutions listed in the OCLC FirstSearch WorldCat database, selected according to criteria outlined in "Libraries Included in Holdings Listings" section below.
    d. Institutions listed in LIBRIS.
    Note that names of institutions are spelled out in full, rather than using a code system. This presentation makes the list easier to use with less concern regarding the interpretation of codes.

    Holdings at institutions in (b) and (c) above could not be verified in an online catalog but were considered worthy of mention. Frequently a library indicates in a note accompanying its online catalog that publications or holdings prior to a specific date may not be online, may not be cataloged, may be recorded only in a card file, or may be in storage with specific information uncertain. Inasmuch as such titles are mentioned in these sources it was considered appropriate to include them in this union list.

18. Information about holdings format. Every effort has been extended to report accurate holdings statements, based on relevant available information. The format used to indicate holdings is as follows:
    a. A complete file indicates volume numbers and years:
       Vols. 1–5; 1874–1878
       Note that for clarity, years are indicated in full:
          1874–1878 (not 1874–78)
    b. An incomplete file is shown using brackets:
       Vol. 1– [8, 10–12]; 1952– [1959, 1961–1963]
       This library reports that it owns a complete file of volume 1 through volume 7; an incomplete file of volume 8; volume 9 is lacking; volumes 10 through 12 are incomplete.
    c. The classification or call number or shelf location for a file is also indicated, when known.
    d. Microfilm files are so designated.

Not all title entries contain all elements listed above. Some titles do not have a subtitle. The translation from Swedish to English is literally from a dictionary. The place of publication and the publisher are sometimes unknown or uncertain as indicated in bibliographic records. The various genealogical statements are not available for or applicable to some titles, due to sparse information in available resource material. No ISSN number has been assigned for many titles. Because of little information, a few titles are without a narrative descriptive essay. Unfortunately, no holdings listings in United States or Canada or Sweden were available for a few titles. Are these forever lost to historical research?

A "See" reference has been made from many of the "Other titles" and "Sometimes referred to as" entries. These title statements were found in reference sources and are offered for clarity and greater ease of use. All "See" references are interfiled alphabetically with the title entries.

In some of the essays accompanying entries in the union list, several phrases are used interchangeably. Phrases such as Augustana Lutheran Synod, Augustana Synod, Augustana Lutheran, the Synod, Lutheran Augustana Synod and the Augustana Church may be found. Numerous reference sources use this terminology. The word Augustana is also used as an adjective to accompany words such as clergy, pastor, congregation, news, missionaries, children, men, and women. All have reference to the organized religious group that in its later years (1948–1962) was known officially as the Augustana Evangelical Lutheran Church. A list of both official and unofficial names is included in the appendix.

LIBRARIES INCLUDED IN HOLDINGS LISTINGS

Libraries associated with each of the theological seminaries of the Evangelical Lutheran Church in America (ELCA) were invited to participate in this union list of Augustana Evangelical Lutheran Church serial publications project. These theological seminaries are:

Luther Seminary
Lutheran School of Theology at Chicago
Lutheran Theological Seminary at Gettysburg
Lutheran Theological Seminary at Philadelphia
Lutheran Theological Southern Seminary
Pacific Lutheran Theological Seminary
Trinity Lutheran Seminary
Wartburg Theological Seminary

Libraries associated with each of the academic institutions supported, in whole or in part, by the Augustana Evangelical Lutheran Church were invited to participate in this union list. These academic institutions are:

Augustana College
Augustana College Swenson Center
Bethany College

California Lutheran University
Gustavus Adolphus College
Gustavus Adolphus College Archives
Midland Lutheran College
Pacific Lutheran University
Texas Lutheran University

In addition, the Evangelical Lutheran Church in America (ELCA) archives and each of its regional archives were invited to participate. These regional archives are:

Region 1: Tacoma, WA
Region 2: Berkeley, CA
Region 3: St. Paul, MN
Region 4: Tulsa, OK
          Lindsborg, KS
          Seguin, TX
          Omaha, NE
Region 5: Dubuque, IA
Region 6: Columbus, OH
Region 7: Philadelphia, PA
          Staten Island, NY
Region 8: Greenville, PA
          Gettysburg, PA
Region 9: Salisbury, NC
          Columbia, SC
          Salem, VA
Canada: Evangelical Lutheran Church in Canada

Other libraries considered to own Augustana holdings include North Park University and four libraries in Sweden: the Royal Library of Sweden, the Swedish Emigrant Institute, Lund University, and Uppsala University.

Several sources used for verification of serial publication titles, dates, volume numbers, and genealogy are also union lists themselves. These are the OCLC FirstSearch WorldCat electronic database, the LIBRIS national database of Sweden, the *Union List of Serials, Swedish-American Periodicals* by Erickson, and the microfilms list of Swedish-American newspapers by Setterdahl.

In each instance, when a library listed above was shown as holding either a complete or an incomplete file of a title, that information is included in the present list. In some instances, either very few libraries on the above lists or even none of these libraries invited to participate were shown as owning holdings. Then other libraries that did indicate holdings were added to the present union list so that individuals seeking a file of a title would be able to locate it. Consequently, the present union list of Augustana Evangelical Lutheran Church serial publications includes holdings from a total of seventy-six locations and archives. Some institutions are cited very few times or possibly only once, but it was considered important that users of this list be aware of the existence of a file in a non-Augustana or non-ELCA location.

In some bibliographic sources, the list of institutions owning a file of an Augustana Evangelical Lutheran Church serial publication was quite extensive. Selection for the present list was then based on criteria including completeness or extent of the file, with the most complete files chosen for the list; the geographical location of the institution, so as to represent different areas of the country; and availability.

In each of the instances where an extensive list of institutions with relevant holdings was listed, as in the OCLC FirstSearch WorldCat database, all those institutions originally invited to participate in the present union list project were included, regardless of the extent of the holdings shown. Whenever possible, this information was verified with the institution as the owner, either by direct correspondence or by the library online catalog of that institution.

Following are those institutions that were not a part of the original Augustana-associated or ELCA-associated list but are shown at least once as owning a specific Augustana Evangelical Lutheran Church serial publication file in the present list:

American Theological Library Association
Augustana Heritage Association office
Brown University
Center for Research Libraries
Chicago Historical Society
Concordia Historical Institute
Connecticut Historical Society
Connecticut State Library
Duke University
East Orange, New Jersey Library
Free Public Library of Newark, New Jersey
Fuller Theological Seminary
Harvard University
Harvard University Divinity School
Illinois State Historical Library
Iowa State Historical Society
Kansas State Historical Society

Legislative Library, Winnipeg, Manitoba, Canada
Library of Congress
Library of Michigan
Luther College (Iowa)
Minnesota Historical Society
National Library of Canada
Nebraska State Historical Society
New Jersey Historical Society Library
New York Public Library Research Library
Ohio State University
Princeton Theological Seminary
Princeton University
Rhode Island Historical Society
Seattle Public Library
Southwestern Baptist Theological Seminary
Texas State Library
Union Theological Seminary
United Libraries (Illinois)
University of Chicago
University of Illinois–Urbana Champaign
University of Iowa
University of Michigan
University of Minnesota–Minneapolis
University of Nebraska
University of North Dakota
University of Texas at Austin
University of Washington
University of Wisconsin
Wheaton College
Wisconsin Historical Society
Wisconsin Lutheran Seminary
Yale University

The primary goal has been to include holdings of those institutions originally invited to participate in the union list project. However, when it was considered that other institutions owning files of Augustana serial publications could make a significant contribution to the completeness of the present list, these were added in order to make this union list more useful and comprehensive. Even though the OCLC WorldCat database is quite comprehensive in its holdings reports, there are some collections shown in this Augustana Heritage Association union list that are not included in WorldCat.

Policies regarding access to materials vary among libraries. Some locations indicate the necessity for an appointment prior to a visit in order to use archival materials. Frequently, a library website indicates relevant information for visitors regarding hours, fees, and policies. Communication with library staff prior to a visit is recommended.

Names of the Augustana Evangelical Lutheran Church institutions and their affiliated libraries are shown with addresses, telephone numbers, and Web addresses for the online catalog in a separate list included in the appendix of this publication. This information is offered for the convenience of users of this union list and is current as of the date of publication.

Chapter 1

Union List of Titles A–Z

– A –

Academica

Lindsborg, KS: Bethany Academy
Vol. 1, nos. 1–2
December 1884–January 1885
Continued by: *Pedagogen*
Sometimes referred to as: *Academia*

According to Lindquist, this was a "modest publication produced by hand" (168). It was issued by Rector Edward Nelander and supported by Carl Swensson. Both men were associated with Bethany Academy. Devoted to the interests of Bethany Academy, *Academica* was in the Swedish language. It seems to have been planned as a monthly but lasted for only two issues. In February of 1885 it became *Pedagogen*. *Sources:* Lindquist 1953, 168; Setterdahl 15.

Augustana College Swenson Center: Vol. 1, no. 2, Microfilm
Bethany College: Microfilm
Setterdahl: Kansas Historical Society: Microfilm

Advance

Minneapolis, MN: Minnesota Conference of the Augustana Lutheran Church
Vol. 7, no. 1–vol. 20, no. 6
January 1949–November/December 1962

Continues: *Minnesota Conference Advance*
Other titles:
  Advance (Minneapolis, MN)
  Minnesota Conference Advance
Sometimes referred to as: *The Advance*

The *Advance* was a modification of the title of its predecessor, effective in 1949. Issued bimonthly, it continued its status as the official organ of the Lutheran Minnesota Conference of the Augustana Evangelical Lutheran Church until the end of 1962. *Source:* WorldCat

  Augustana College Swenson Center: Vol. 7, no. 1–vol. 8, nos. 1–6; 1949–1950
  Evangelical Lutheran Church in America Archives: 1949–1962
  Gustavus Adolphus College Archives: Vols. 7–20; 1949–1962
  Harvard University Divinity School: Vols. 7–20; 1949–1962
  Minnesota Historical Society: BX8049.1 .A34 1949–1962

Advocate

See *Luther College Advocate.*

AHA Newsletter

See *The Augustana Heritage Newsletter.*

All Yours

  Minneapolis, MN: Augustana Luther League
  1950–?

This was a magazine published for young people in the Augustana Luther League organization. Issued bimonthly, it was the means by which league members and local pastors and sponsors of the youth organization could keep informed about the program and projects of the league. Illustrated articles featured what other leagues were doing, which then assisted them in local project and program planning. *Sources: Augustana Annual* 1952, 83 and 1953, 91; WorldCat.

  No holdings reported.

Almanac for the Year . . .

  Rock Island, IL: Augustana Book Concern
  1911–1947
  Merged with: *My Church* to form *Augustana Annual*

The English language edition of the Swedish *Almanack*, the *Almanac* appeared as a yearbook of the Evangelical Lutheran Augustana Synod of North America in 1911.

The *Almanac* was published by the Augustana Book Concern in Rock Island, Illinois, as an annual through 1947, when publication ceased. It followed a format similar to the Swedish *Almanack* but did not always include all of the Swedish contents of its counterpart. Advertisements differed also, in consideration of the reading audience. Each volume contained a congregational directory, clergy roster, directory of synod officers and leaders, and information on the structure of the synod.

Editors included E. W. Olson (1921, 1923), G. A. Fahlund (1922, 1928–1929), E. F. Bergren (1924–1927), and Birger Swenson (1930–1947). Prior to 1921 the annual was edited anonymously. The *Almanac* was continued in the *Augustana Annual* beginning in 1948. *Sources:* Hultgren 2001; Nystrom 81; WorldCat.

Augustana College Swenson Center: AY75 .A4 1927, 1930, 1931
Gustavus Adolphus College Archives: 1924, 1941–1945
Lutheran Theological Seminary at Gettysburg: BX8009.A88 1912, 1919–1920, 1922–1929, 1931–1933, 1939–1946
Lutheran Theological Seminary at Philadelphia: BX8049.A2 1920–1933, 1937, 1939–1947
Midland Lutheran College: 284.1 Au45a Vols. 3, 6, 10, 15
Minnesota Historical Society: BX8049.2 .A43rs 1945–1947
Trinity Lutheran Seminary: 1928–1938, 1940–1947
Wartburg Theological Seminary: 1945–1947

Almanack: för året efter Jesu Kristi födelse . . .

[*Almanac: for the Year after Jesus Christ Birth . . .*]
Rock Island, IL: Lutheran Augustana Book Concern
Vols. 1–52
1894–1947
Superseded by: *Augustana Annual*

The Swedish language yearbook of the Evangelical Lutheran Augustana Synod of North America was issued by the Lutheran Augustana Book Concern in Rock Island, Illinois, beginning in 1894.

Each volume included a congregational directory, clergy roster, directory of synod officers and leaders, and information on the structure of the synod. Some of the articles were translated and concurrently published in the English language *Almanac*. Publication ceased in 1947. Issues for leap years have the title *Almanack för skottåret efter Kristi födelse . . .*

Editors included E. W. Olson (1920–1923), E. F. Bergren (1924–1927), G. A. Fahlund (1928–1929), and Birger Swenson (1930–1947). Prior to 1920 it was edited anonymously. The *Almanack* was succeeded by the *Augustana Annual* beginning in 1948. *Sources:* http://tomos.oit.umn.edu/F/; Hultgren 2001; LIBRIS; Nystrom 81; WorldCat.

Augustana College Swenson Center: BX8049 .A13 1895–1902, 1904–1947

Bethany College: 030.97 A445 E Lindq. 103

Evangelical Lutheran Church in America Archives: AUG 14/3 1894–1945, 1947

Gustavus Adolphus College Archives: 1899, 1914–1921, 1925, 1933, 1934, 1936, 1944, 1946, 1947

Lutheran Theological Seminary at Gettysburg: BX8009.A8816 1894, 1911, 1913–1916, 1918, 1920–1925, 1927

Lutheran Theological Seminary at Philadelphia: BX8049.A217 1914–1929, 1931–1939

Minnesota Historical Society: BX8049.2 .A43r 1894–1934, 1938–1943, 1945

University of Illinois: 284.1 AU45A 1922–1947

University of Minnesota–Minneapolis: BX8049 .A47x 1895–1897, 1903, 1905–1908, 1910–1911, 1914–1919, 1923–1927, 1930; Also: 284.1 Au45 al S 1906, 1913, 1918–1922, 1925–1929, 1931, 1933–1947

Wisconsin Historical Society: BX8049 .A22 1894–1895, 1915–1933, 1938–1947

LIBRIS: Swedish Emigrant Institute: 1895, 1905, 1907–1908, 1910, 1917–1920, 1924–1927, 1930–1932, 1936–1939, 1942–1943, 1945–1947

The Alumnus

Rock Island, IL: Alumni Association of Augustana College

Vol. 1, no. 1–vol. 2, no. 8 (issues for November 1893–June 1894, also called whole no. 13–whole no. 20)

September 1892–June 1894

Merged with: *Young Observer* to form *Augustana Journal*

Other title: *Alumnus* (Rock Island, IL)

Sometimes referred to as: *Alumnus*

Several professors and students at Augustana College in the early 1890s felt that an English-language publication was needed. Published by the Alumni Association of Augustana College, the first number of *The Alumnus* was issued in September 1892. It was described as an educational magazine for young people. In regular octavo format, it was illustrated and available for a subscription price of fifty cents per year. Issued monthly, it continued through June 1894 for a total of twenty numbers. Faculty and alumni contributed articles. P. G. Sjöblom served as editor. During its short life, *The Alumnus* ran competition with the *Young Observer*. The two publications merged in July 1894 to form the *Augustana Journal*. *Sources:* Nystrom 62; Swan 70–71; WorldCat.

Augustana College Swenson Center: Vols. 1–2; 1892–1894

Evangelical Lutheran Church in America Archives: AUG 14/6 Vols. 1–2; 1892–1894, Paper and Microfilm

Harvard University Divinity School: Vol. 1, nos. 1–12; September 1892–August 1893

Illinois State Historical Library: IX896 AU .Ya

Luther Seminary: LH1.A9 Vol. 1, nos. 1–12; September 1892–August 1893, BX8001.L93 Vol. 1, no. 1–vol. 2, no. 8; September 1892–June 1894, Microfilm

Lutheran School of Theology at Chicago: BX8001 .L4510 Vols. 1–2; 1892–1894, Microfilm

Pacific Lutheran Theological Seminary: September 1892–June 1894, Microfilm

WorldCat: American Theological Library Association: Microfilm
    Gustavus Adolphus College: Vols. 1–2; 1892–1894
    Minnesota Historical Society: Vols. 1–2; 1892–1894

Anchor

See *Luther College & Academy Yearbook.*

Annual Messenger

St. Peter, MN: Gustavus Adolphus College
May 1891
Continued by: *Vox Collegi*

The Literary Circle issued this first printed student publication at Gustavus Adolphus College for the 1891 commencement. It was a sixteen-page pamphlet. In a sense, it could be considered the first Gustavus Adolphus College annual.

Prior to this time, but also including this period, literary societies were important student organizations. Meetings were a popular Friday-evening activity, as there were no intercollegiate activities or other clubs or societies. The Philomathian Society, the Weekly Spelling and Debating

Society, the Irenian Society, and the Literary Circle all offered opportunity for literary discussions, debates, and socializing. Programs were alternately in English and Swedish.

Peterson writes that "the first college paper was the manuscript weekly read at these society meetings. These papers furnish interesting illustrations of student life, student ideas and student humor of the time." *Source:* Peterson 49, 58.

Gustavus Adolphus College: Paper and Microfilm

Arkivfynd

St. Peter, MN: Gustavus Adolphus College
Nos. 1–4
May 1979–November 1984
ISSN 0277–6472

Published by the Archives of Gustavus Adolphus College and the Archives of the Minnesota Synod of the Lutheran Church in America, this series of occasional papers focuses on historical subjects directly related to Minnesota.

1. Norberg, first Swede at Chisago Lake/Emeroy Johnson. May 1979.
2. Social Ministry by Lutherans in Minnesota/Emeroy Johnson. November 1980.
3. The Printed Word in the Service of the Minnesota Conference/ Emeroy Johnson. July 1984.
4. The Beginnings of English Lutheranism in Minnesota/Emeroy Johnson. November 1984.

Sources: LIBRIS; WorldCat.

Augustana College Swenson Center: 977.6 Ar48 Nos. 1–4
Gustavus Adolphus College
Minnesota Historical Society: BX8049.8.M6 A74 Nos. 2–4
University of Minnesota: BX8049.1.M6 J65 Nos. 1–4
Wisconsin Historical Society 82–431 Nos. 1–4
WorldCat: Lutheran School of Theology at Chicago
LIBRIS: Royal Library of Sweden: Nos. 1–4

Årsbok/Svenska Litterära Sällskapet De Nio

Svenska Litterära Sällskapet De Nio (Upsala College, East Orange, NJ) [Yearbook: Swedish Literary Society the Nine]

Kenilworth, NJ: De Nios Förlag (1918–1924)
East Orange, NJ: De Nios Förlag (1925–1930)
Vols. 1–13
1918–1930
Other titles:
Nios Årsbok
Svenska Litterära Sällskapet De Nios Årsbok

This literary annual was issued by the Swedish student literary society at Upsala College. It was published from 1918 through 1930 in the Swedish language. The emphasis was on including Swedish-American literature in the yearbook and promoting an interest in literature for readers. *Sources:* LIBRIS; WorldCat.

Augustana College Swenson Center: PT9990 .S86 1919, 1928; 839.7808 .Up7n 1918–1930
Bethany College: 839.7 S968 E Lindq. 159 1930
Minnesota Historical Society: PT9990 .S86 1926
New York Public Library Research Library: Vols. 1, 9; 1918, 1926
University of Minnesota–Minneapolis: LD5491 .U385 A77x Vols. 1–13; 1918–1930
LIBRIS: Swedish Emigrant Institute: Årg 1–13

Augustana: Tidskrift för Swenska Lutherska Kyrkan i Amerika (1868)

[*Augustana: Journal for Swedish Lutheran Church in America*]
Chicago, IL: Svenska Lutherska Tryckföreningen
Vol. 1, nos. 1–11
October 1868–July/August 1869
Merged with: *Rätta Hemlandet och Missionsbladet* to form *Rätta Hemlandet och Augustana*
Sometimes referred to as: *Augustana* (Chicago, IL: 1868)

After the organization of the Augustana Lutheran Synod, there was a felt need for a paper that would serve as the official organ of the Church. Such a paper should be primarily concerned with the affairs of the synod. Even at this time, *Hemlandet*, the first paper that had an association with the synod, was developing into more of a political and general news publication than a religious publication.

In 1868, the synod leaders decided to publish such an official paper in Swedish. The synod commissioned the Swedish Lutheran Publication Society (Svenska Lutherska Tryckföreningen) in Chicago as the publisher.

The first number was published in October 1868 with T. N. Hasselquist as editor. Issued monthly, it contained sixteen pages in magazine format (15 cm. × 23 cm.) with continuous paging. Beginning with number 4 until its end with number 11 it was issued bimonthly for the subscription price of fifty cents.

As *Hemlandet* took up more of a secular program, *Augustana* continued to take its place among Augustana Synod readers. However, at the end of 1869 the two Swedish papers—*Rätta Hemlandet och Missionsbladet* and *Augustana*—combined to form *Rätta Hemlandet och Augustana*. *Sources:* Erickson 3; LIBRIS; Matthews 21; Nystrom 55; WorldCat.

Augustana College Swenson Center: BX8001.A9

Center for Research Libraries: Vol. 1, nos. 4/5–10/11; 1869

Gustavus Adolphus College: Vol. 1, nos. 1–11; October 1868–July/ August 1869

Harvard University Divinity School: Vol. 1, nos. 1–10/11; October 1868–July/August 1869, Microfilm

Lutheran School of Theology at Chicago: BX8001 .A810 Vol. 1; 1868–1869, Microfilm

Lutheran Theological Seminary at Gettysburg: nos. 1–7, 10–11; 1868–1869 October 1868–April 1869; July–August 1869

Minnesota Historical Society: BX8049.1 .R23 Vol. 1, nos. 1–11

Erickson: Royal Library of Sweden: Vol. 1, nos. 1–12; October 1868– December 1869 [NB The only library that lists no. 12; December 1869]

WorldCat: American Theological Library Association: Microfilm

LIBRIS: Swedish Emigrant Institute: Årg. 1:1–11 (1868–1869)

Augustana: Kyrklig Tidskrift för Swenska Lutherska Kyrkan i N. Amerika (1874)

[*Augustana: Ecclesiastical Journal for Swedish Lutheran Church in North America*]

Rock Island, IL: A. C. F. de Remee (1874–1875)

Moline, IL: A. C. F. de Remee (January–July 1876)

Moline, IL: Swedish Printing Co. (August 1876–1877)

Moline, IL: Wistrand & Thulin Bok–och Accidenstryckeri (1878)

Vol. 1, no. 1–vol. 5, no. 12 (i.e., 19–23)

January 1874–December 1878

Formed by the union of: *Rätta Hemlandet och Augustana* and *Missionären* (Chicago, IL) and *Luthersk Kyrkotidning* (Red Wing, MN) and *Nytt och Gammalt*

Merged with: *Missionären* (Moline, IL) to form *Augustana och Missionären*

Sometimes referred to as: *Augustana* (Rock Island, IL: 1874)

Concerned that so many papers being published at several different places in the Augustana Synod could become a disservice to the Church, and even divisive, the respective editors decided to merge their publications for the sake of unity in the synod. On October 28, 1873, the following papers combined to form a new *Augustana: Rätta Hemlandet och Augustana, Missionären* (Chicago, IL); *Luthersk Kyrkotidning* (Red Wing, MN); and *Nytt och Gammalt.*

The editors of the new paper during 1874 and 1875 were T. N. Hasselquist, Eric Norelius, and Olof Olsson. Hasselquist served alone from January through September 1876. O. Olsson assisted him from October 1876 through 1878.

Beginning publication in January 1874, *Augustana* was issued as a semimonthly for two years (1874–1875) and as a monthly from 1876 to its last issue in December 1878. In 1874 and 1875 it was published in Rock Island, moving to Moline in 1876. As of January 1879, *Augustana* joined *Missionären* (Moline, IL) to form *Augustana och Missionären.*

An index for *Augustana* (1874) is included in an index also for *Rätta Hemlandet* (Vols. 1–7; 1856–1862) and also for *Rätta Hemlandet och Missionsbladet* (Vols. 8–14; 1863–1869) and also for *Rätta Hemlandet och Augustana* (Vols. 14–18; 1869–1873). This index is printed in volume 22 (1877) of *Augustana* (1874), it being a cumulative index for volumes 1–22 (1856–1877). *Sources:* Erickson 3; http://jkm.ipac; LIBRIS; Matthews 21; Nystrom 55; WorldCat.

Augustana College Swenson Center: BX8001 .A9 K9 Vols. 1–5; 1874–1878
Center for Research Libraries: Vols. 1–5; 1874–1878
Evangelical Lutheran Church in America Archives: AUG14/7, Paper and Microfilm
Gustavus Adolphus College: 1874–1878
Harvard University Divinity School: Vols. 1–5; 1874–1878, Microfilm
Luther Seminary: 1874–1878, Microfilm
Lutheran School of Theology at Chicago: BX8001 .A810 Vols. 19–23; 1874–1878, Microfilm
Lutheran Theological Seminary at Gettysburg: Vols. 1–5; 1874–1878
Minnesota Historical Society: BX8049.1 .A91 Vols. 1–5; 1874–1878
New York Public Library Research Library: Vols. 19, 21–23 (i.e., Vols. 1, 3–5)
WorldCat: American Theological Library Association: Microfilm
LIBRIS: Swedish Emigrant Institute: Årg. 1–5 (1874–1878)

Augustana: Tidning för den Swenska Luterska Kyrkan i Amerika **(1889)**

[*Augustana: Newspaper for the Swedish Lutheran Church in America*]
Rock Island, IL: Lutheran Augustana Book Concern; Augustana Book Concern

Vol. 34, no. 127–vol. 94, no. 52
December 5, 1889–December 26, 1949
Formed by the union of: *Hemvännen* and *Augustana och Missionären*
Merged with: *Lutheran Companion* (Rock Island, IL: 1911) to form *Augustana Lutheran*
Continued by: *Augustana Lutheranen*
Sometimes referred to as: *Augustana* (Rock Island, IL: 1889)

Another major stage in the development of *Augustana* occurred on November 19, 1889, when the Lutheran Augustana Book Concern Board and leaders of the Augustana Synod decided that the official church paper should again take the name *Augustana*. Furthermore, it should be enlarged after absorbing the weekly *Hemvännen* and changing the name from *Augustana och Missionären*. Some sources indicate that *Vårt Land och Folk* was absorbed in this merger.

The first issue of this new, but also revived, title was dated December 5, 1889, thus providing a smooth and unbroken transition in date and numbering from its predecessors. As a weekly in quarto size with sixteen pages, it sold for $2.00 per year from 1889 to 1896, for $1.75 from 1897 to 1926, and $2.00 thereafter. For all years it was published at the Augustana Book Concern in Rock Island, Illinois.

Eric Norelius was selected as the editor in 1889 but had to resign in June 1890 due to ill health. S. P. A. Lindahl served as editor then from July 1890 until his death in March 1908. C. J. Bengston was the editor from April through June 1908. L. G. Abrahamson then began his long tenure as editor in July 1908 until 1939, when he retired at the age of 82 years. A. T. Lundholm took over the position in 1940. Associate editors included A. Rodell (1892–1897), C. J. Bengston (December 1900–March 1908), M. J. Englund (1909–1912), C. Kraft (who wrote occasional editorials with Abrahamson) until 1941, and C. E. Nelson after 1940.

Some of the most prominent men of the synod served as editors, from this position directing the paper to become more conservative or more progressive according to the personal views of the editor. As an example, Lindahl was opposed to secret societies and let this be known through the paper. Under Lindahl and Abrahamson, *Augustana* wielded a powerful influence on synodical solidarity. It was committed to the American cause during the World War.

The average weekly circulation of 13,000 during the period 1890 to 1908 held firm even though the church membership had almost doubled. The highest mark of 21,600 subscribers came in 1914. Three years later in 1917 circulation was on a downward trend at 20,925. In 1926 circulation was 18,584; in 1935 it was 10,535; by 1940 it was 9,000; and in 1945 it was 7,681. In 1948 the paper was reduced from twenty-four pages to twelve pages.

Due to the increasing use of English by readers and the deaths of faithful readers who preferred the Swedish text, popularity continued to decline. However, in spite of this language transition in every area of synod activity, *Augustana* still remained an influential force, as it served those who held fast to the Swedish text.

The era of the synod's general paper in the Swedish language ended with the December 26, 1949, issue when it merged with the synod's English-language periodical *The Lutheran Companion* to form the *Augustana Lutheran*. However, it continued also in Swedish as the *Augustana Lutheranen*, beginning this title in January 1950.

Several historians summarize the influence of *Augustana*. Backlund writes: "Throughout the years *Augustana* has been faithful to its purpose to support the Lutheran faith and serve as a mouthpiece for the Augustana Synod and promote its activities, providing news of its church activities, devotional reading and doctrinal guidance" (80).

Capps states that *Augustana* was the "most prominent spokesman for the Lutheran viewpoint among Swedish–Americans" (32).

Dowie states that "while such a paper was not likely to be impartial on subjects closely related to the Augustana Church, it represents a vast source of historical data on the Swedish Lutheran Church, institutions, and its leaders" (247). Others have named it a major Swedish-American periodical because of its longevity, quality of content, and ability to survive the rapid process of Americanization of the synod. *Sources:* Backlund 80; Capps 32, 233; Dowie 247; Erickson 3; LIBRIS; Nystrom 59; Olson 1933, 44–50; Stephenson 350–52; ULS; WorldCat.

Augustana College: 1889–1949
Center for Research Libraries: Vols. 34–64; 69:32–vol. 94; December 1889–1919, August 1924–1949
Evangelical Lutheran Church in America Archives: AUG 14/7 Vols. 37, 39, [56]; 1892,1894, [1921]; vols. 34–94; 1889–1949, Microfilm
Gustavus Adolphus College: 1889–1949
Harvard University Divinity School: Vol. 35, nos. 5–22, 24–49, 51–56; vol. 36–vol. 37, nos. 1–39, 41–44; vols. 38–43; vol. 44, nos. 1–38, 40–52; vols. 45–67; vol. 68, nos. 1–6, 8–52; vols. 69–94; 1890–1949, Microfilm
Library of Congress: December 5, 1889, no. 1 [pp. 5–14 only]–March 28, 1895, no. 13; vols. 50–55; 69–87; 1905–1910; 1924–December 29, 1942
Luther Seminary: BX8001.A9 Vols. 34–94; 1889–1949, Paper and Microfilm
Lutheran School of Theology at Chicago: BX8001 .A810 Vol. 35, no. 5–vol. 94, no. 52; 1889–1949, Microfilm
Lutheran Theological Seminary at Gettysburg: Vols. 44, [45], 46–47, [48–49], 50, 52–54, [55–57], 58–73, 91; 1899–1946

Lutheran Theological Seminary at Philadelphia: Vols. 53–94; 1908–1949
Midland Lutheran College: August 1922; May 11, 1933
Minnesota Historical Society: BX8049.1 .A93 1889–1949
New York Public Library Research Library: Vols. 34–39, 41–42, 45, 48–94
Pacific Lutheran University: BX8001 .A8 Vol. 48; 1903
University of Minnesota–Minneapolis: Microfilm; also BX8049 .A94x
    Vol. 35; 1889–1890
WorldCat: American Theological Library Association: Microfilm
LIBRIS: Swedish Emigrant Institute: Årg. 35–75, 78–94 (1889–1930,
    1933–1949)

Augustana (1956)

Rock Island, IL: Augustana Book Concern
Vol. 102, nos. 1–12
January 1956–December 1956
Continues: *Augustana Lutheranen*
Sometimes referred to as: *Augustana* (Rock Island, IL: 1956)

In spite of a dwindling subscription list to the *Augustana Lutheranen*, the
Swedish language edition of the *Augustana Lutheran*, the former *Augustana* reappeared in 1956 as a monthly independent publication. When the
decision to end publication of *Augustana Lutheranen* in 1955 was made, a
decision that had long been delayed, there were so many requests for the
continuance of a Swedish paper, it was considered to try to answer those
requests in 1956. This 1956 publication was called the official organ of
Evangelisk Lutherska Augustanakyrkans. A. T. Lundholm was the editor.
    However, due to ever continuing financial losses and fewer subscribers
able to read the Swedish language, it was finally decided to end *Augustana* with the December 1956 issue, number 12 of volume 102. It had continued far beyond its years as a financial asset to the Augustana Book
Concern, having been published for at least twenty years at a loss.
    In summary, Nystrom writes: "But keeping the paper going was a
grateful tribute to the old constituency of the church. It was considered a
service due them, and it was surely a policy that paid dividends in good
will and in profit, intangible but none the less real" (62). *Sources:* Erickson
3; LIBRIS; Nystrom 61–62; WorldCat.

Center for Research Libraries: Vol. 102; 1956
Evangelical Lutheran Church in America Archives: AUG 14/7 Vol. 102;
    1956, Paper and Microfilm
Gustavus Adolphus College: 1956
Harvard University Divinity School: Vol. 102; 1956

Luther Seminary: BX8001.A9 Vol. 102; 1956, Paper and Microfilm
Lutheran School of Theology at Chicago: BX8001 .A810 Vol. 102; 1956,
  Microfilm
WorldCat: American Theological Library Association: Microfilm
LIBRIS: Swedish Emigrant Institute: Årg. 102; (1956)

Augustana Annual

Augustana Annual: Yearbook for the Evangelical Lutheran Augustana Synod
  (1948)
Augustana Annual: Yearbook for the Augustana Evangelical Lutheran Church
  (1949)
Augustana Annual: Yearbook of the Augustana Evangelical Lutheran Church
  (1950–1962)
Rock Island, IL: Augustana Book Concern
Vols. 1–14
1948–1962
Supersedes: *My Church* and *Almanack.* and *Almanac.*
Continues: *Korsbaneret*
Variant titles:
  Recording a Year's Progress—1951
  Parish Speaks—1952
  Responsible Church—1953
  Advance for Christ—1954
  Lines o'Type—1955
  Century of the Church Press—1956
  Advance for Christ—1957
  Share Christ with Your Neighbor—1958
  Christ Calls You—1959
  His Kingdom Is Forever—1960
  Teach Us to Pray—1961
  Family of God—1962
Merged with: *Report to the . . . Annual Convention of American Evangel-
ical Lutheran Church*, issued by the Church, and *Directory*, issued by
Suomi Synod, and *Yearbook*, issued by the United Lutheran Church
in America, to form *Yearbook*, issued by the Lutheran Church in
America.

This English edition, serving as a directory and yearbook for the Augustana Evangelical Lutheran Church, first appeared in 1948 published
by the Augustana Book Concern in Rock Island, Illinois. Birger Swenson
served as editor for all fourteen volumes, sharing that work with Sigfrid
Engstrom (1948–1955) and then with E. E. Ryden until 1962.

Augustana Annual may be rightly considered a continuation of the earlier *Almanack* and *Almanac* and perhaps even of *My Church* and *Korsbaneret*. For its yearbook, the Augustana Evangelical Lutheran Church was now issuing exclusively an English-language edition. By the mid-1950s, it was published in an edition of 12,000 copies.

Nystrom presents an excellent summary regarding the importance of the *Augustana Annual*:

> Over the years *Augustana Annual* became in increasing measure a work and re-source book for pastors and lay workers. It served to keep church members abreast of the events and developments of each year and offered clear interpre-tations of them. In it they found both a clerical and church register, a church-centered almanac, and much useful and interesting information about their church. The volumes of *Augustana Annual* will prove a veritable mine of source material for future historians who may delve into the story of the closing years of the Augustana Church. (81)

Sources: http://207.56.64.20/; LIBRIS; Nystrom 81; WorldCat.

Augustana College: BX8009 .A8 1948–1962
Bethany College: 1948–1962
Evangelical Lutheran Church in America Archives: AUG 14/4 1948–1962
Evangelical Lutheran Church in America Archives Region 5—IA: 1948–1962
Evangelical Lutheran Church in America Archives Region 8—PA (Greenville): 1959–1962
Evangelical Lutheran Church in America Archives Region 9—SC: 1949; 1958
Gustavus Adolphus College: BX8009 .A8 1948–1962
Harvard University Divinity School: 906 Luth A923 an 1948–1962
Luther Seminary: BX8049 .A27 1948–1962
Lutheran School of Theology at Chicago: BX8009 .A8 1951
Lutheran Theological Seminary at Gettysburg: BX8009.A9 H Vols. 1–14; 1948–1962
Lutheran Theological Southern Seminary: BX8049 .A95 1948–1962
Minnesota Historical Society: BX8049 .A95 1948–1962
Trinity Lutheran Seminary: BX8049 .A5 1948–1962
Wartburg Theological Seminary: 1948–1949; 1951–1962
Wisconsin Historical Society: BX8049 .A95 1948–1962
LIBRIS: Royal Library of Sweden: 1948–1962

Augustana Bulletin

Rock Island, IL: Augustana College
Ser. 1–54

April 1905–1959
Continued by: *Augustana College Bulletin*

In 1905, the series *Augustana Bulletin* was introduced. Originally a quarterly, the title changed to a bimonthly schedule in 1921. After 1927, special issues were distributed, particularly related to fund-raising appeals.

The annual catalog was included in this series. Augustana Theological Seminary contributed a number regularly, after 1927. Beginning in 1936/37 the academic year report of the college president was a part of this series. Other numbers were devoted to a college department or division.

Many issues include significant articles related to college history and individuals who were important to the school. The cornerstone laying and dedication of the Denkmann Memorial Library in 1911 was featured in Series VIII, number 1 in 1912. A significant publication in 1917 was prepared by Marcus Skarstedt, librarian at Augustana College, in which the books in the library of Augustana College and Theological Seminary were listed. (Series XIII, no. 1) "Science at Augustana College" edited by F. M. Fryxell was issued in 1922 as Series XVII, no. 4. The October 1925 issue (Series 20, no. 5) had the title "L. P. Esbjorn and the Pilgrim Fathers of 1849," written by Gustav Andreen. *Sources:* Bergendoff 204; http://lms01.harvard.edu/F/; Matthews 21.

Augustana College
Bethany College: Series 20, no. 5; 1925
Harvard University: Series: 8, no. 1, series 13, no. 1; 1912, 1917
Lutheran Theological Seminary at Gettysburg: Series [2, 4, 6, 8, 11–13, 15–18, 20, 23–24, 30, 32–54]; [1906–1959]
New York Public Library Research Library: Series 13 no. 1; 1917

Augustana Churchmen

Rock Island, IL: Augustana Brotherhood
Vol. 7, no. 1–vol. 9, no. 4
First Quarter 1954–July–August 1957?
Continues: *Augustana-Men*
Continued by: *Augustana Lutheran Churchmen*

This periodical is the continuation of *Augustana-Men*, published as a news and devotional item for members of the Augustana Brotherhood. It was issued on an irregular basis and perhaps ended publication in mid-1956 under this title. The WorldCat record indicates that the July–August 1956 issue was probably the last. However, two libraries report holdings dated 1957. It was continued by *Augustana Lutheran Churchmen*. *Sources:* Lundeen, group 6; WorldCat.

Gustavus Adolphus College Archives: 1953–1957 scattered issues
Lutheran School of Theology at Chicago: BV4525 .A8 Vols. 7–9;
    1954–1956
Lundeen: Evangelical Lutheran Church in America Archives: 1954–1957

Augustana College Bulletin

Rock Island, IL: Augustana College
Ser. 55–72
1960–July 1979
Some issues called: *Augustana Story*
Continues: *Augustana Bulletin*
Continued by: *Augustana College Magazine*
Sources: LIBRIS; Matthews 21.

Augustana College
Lutheran Theological Seminary at Gettysburg: Series [55–57, 62–63,
    65–72]; [1960–1977; 1978–1979]
LIBRIS: Royal Library of Sweden: Series 58–72; 1963–April 1979

Augustana College Catalog

Rock Island, IL: Augustana College
1876/1877–
Continues: *Student–Katalog*
Sometimes referred to as: *Catalogue*

An official catalog of Augustana College has been published regularly
beginning with the Swedish text *Student–Katalog* in 1871/1872. The English-
language publication began with the 1876/1877 catalog from the new campus in Rock Island, Illinois.

At unspecified intervals, early catalogs included supplementary information such as names of board members, graduates, and honorary de-
grees awarded. In 1905, the *Augustana Bulletin* series began. The annual
catalog was then one issue of this series.

Some catalogs were issued annually and others issued biennially, with
some variations in the title. All include descriptions of courses offered,
lists of faculty, and general information about the school for current and
prospective students. *Source:* Bergendoff 203; WorldCat.

Augustana College
Lutheran Theological Seminary at Philadelphia: LD271 .A665 Nos. 1–9
University of Illinois–Urbana, Champaign: C AU 45 H 1895–96

University of Minnesota–Minneapolis: LD271 .A665 A2 1924/25
University of Texas–Austin: 378.73 AU45 1926/27

Augustana College Library Occasional Paper

Rock Island, IL: Augustana College Library
Nos. 15–18
1986–1988
Continues: *Occasional Paper/Augustana College Library*

The following four titles were issued with this series name from 1986
through 1988:

A Pioneer Lutheran Ministry: L. P. Esbjörn and His Family in Andover, Illinois, by Lilly Setterdahl. 1986.
The Problem of the Third Generation Immigrant: a Republication of the 1937 Address, by Marcus Lee Hansen. 1987.
Letters from Andover to Högarp, Sweden, 1858–1898, edited and translated from Swedish by Conrad Bergendoff. 1988.
The Parkander Papers: A Festschrift Honoring Dr. Dorothy J. Parkander, edited by Jane Telleen, Ann Boaden, Roald Tweet. 1988.

Sources: Augustana College Library Occasional Papers Inventory as of
11/03; LIBRIS; WorldCat.

Augustana College: 15–18
Lutheran School of Theology at Chicago: 15–16, 18
WorldCat: Bethany College: 15–18
   California Lutheran University: 15, 17–18
   Evangelical Lutheran Church in America Archives: 15
   Gustavus Adolphus College: 15–16
   North Park University: 15
LIBRIS: Lund University: 15–18
   Royal Library of Sweden: 15, 17–18
   Uppsala University: 15–18

Augustana College Library Publications

Rock Island, IL: Augustana College Library
Nos. 36–
1992–
Published irregularly
Continues: *Augustana Library Publications*

Beginning in 1992 with number 36, *Earth Interpreters: F. M. Fryxell, Geology, and Augustana*, edited by David A. Schroeder and Richard C. Anderson, 1992, this series continues the earlier *Augustana Library Publications* series. *Sources:* LIBRIS; WorldCat.

Augustana College: 36
Gustavus Adolphus College: 36
WorldCat: Bethany College: 36
   California Lutheran University: 36
LIBRIS: Lund University: 36
   Royal Library of Sweden: 36
   Uppsala University: 36

Augustana College Magazine

Rock Island, IL: Augustana College
Vols. 73 ?–
November 1979–
Continues: *Augustana College Bulletin*

This illustrated quarterly is published in the interests of Augustana College for students, alumni, friends, and supporters of the college. *Source:* LIBRIS.

Augustana College
Lutheran Theological Seminary at Gettysburg: November 1979–
LIBRIS: Royal Library of Sweden: November 1979–

Augustana Foreign Missionary

Rock Island, IL: Board of Foreign Missions of the Lutheran Augustana
   Synod
Vol. 24, no. 1–vol. 36
January 1926–December 1938
Continues: *Kina Missionären*
Other title: *Augustana Hednamissionstidning*
Sometimes referred to as: *The Augustana Foreign Missionary*

News and articles about the Augustana Synod's world missions activity provided the contents for the *Augustana Foreign Missionary* magazine, the English-language continuation of the former *Kina Missionären* paper. It continued its predecessor's volume numbering, with its first issue dated January 1926.

Sponsored by the Board of Foreign Missions of the Lutheran Augustana Synod, the monthly magazine was not limited only to news of Augustana but offered articles about other church-sponsored world mission activity. It included letters and reports from missionaries as human interest material, along with reports on missions support.

A separate Swedish language edition with the name *Augustana Hednamissionstidning* was issued beginning with the January 1927 issue and continued through 1938.

Special issues about China were published in June 1927 and September 1931. An issue about the first decade in Tanganyika came in November 1937.

Fred Wyman served as editor from 1926 to 1933; A. F. Almer from 1933 to 1934; and Anton Lundeen from 1934 to 1938. The *Augustana Foreign Missionary* ceased publication in December 1938. *Source:* WorldCat.

Augustana College Swenson Center: 1926, 1929, 1933

Evangelical Lutheran Church in America Archives: AUG 24/1/9/1 Vols. 24–36; 1926–1938

Gustavus Adolphus College Archives: Swedish edition: Vols. 25–36; January 1927–December 1938; English edition: Vol. 26, no. 3–vol. 36; March 1928–December 1938; scattered issues

Lutheran School of Theology at Chicago: Swedish edition: BV2540 .A1 A9319 Vols. 35–36; 1937–1938; English edition: BV2540 .A1 A930 Vols. 25–36; 1927–1938

Augustana Hednamissionstidning

See *Augustana Foreign Missionary.*

Augustana Heritage Newsletter

Chicago, IL: Lutheran School of Theology
Vol. 1–vol. 4, no. 2 os
1995–January 1999
Continued by: *The Augustana Heritage Newsletter* (1999)
Other titles:
　Augustana Heritage Newsletter (1995)
　The Augustana Heritage Newsletter

Prior to the official organization of the Augustana Heritage Association, the Lutheran School of Theology sponsored publishing of the *Augustana Heritage Newsletter*. Donovan J. Palmquist served as editor of this series, which ended with the January 1999 issue.

As stated in the publication, "The *Augustana Heritage Newsletter* is established to remember and honor the heritage of the Augustana Lutheran Church and Augustana Seminary." Included are articles relevant to Augustana Synod history, reminiscences, and news reports.

The association began a new series of its newsletter with the July 1999 issue. *Source:* Deppe.

Augustana Heritage Association office

The Augustana Heritage Newsletter

Chicago, IL: Augustana Heritage Association
Vol. 1, no. 1–vol. ns
July 1999–
Continues: *Augustana Heritage Newsletter* (1995)
Other titles:
  AHA Newsletter
  Augustana Heritage
  Augustana Heritage Newsletter

Issued on a semiannual schedule, this newsletter is published in the spring and fall of each year on behalf of members and friends of the Augustana Heritage Association. The first issue of this new series states the purpose of the newsletter: "This newsletter will be the voice of the Augustana Heritage Association. It will report on current programs and activities of AHA, serve as a means of reflecting on the gifts of Augustana and help to network former Augustana institutions and agencies with the people for whom Augustana is an important part of their lives."

Significant feature articles are provided by historians, clergy, and laypersons knowledgeable about Augustana Synod subjects. News of members and organization events are included. Arvid Anderson and Nancy Anderson have served as editors of this new series.

Volumes are numbered according to the two-year period between the AHA Gatherings with a new volume beginning following a Gathering. This policy began with volume 2 and the Fall 2000 issue. Therefore, volume 1 has only three numbers from July 1999 through May 2000. The first number in 1999 has the title *Augustana Heritage*. *Sources:* Anderson; Deppe; http://jkmlibrary.org/ie/resources/catalog.

Augustana Heritage Association office
Lutheran School of Theology at Chicago: Current year only

Augustana Historical Society Newsletter

See *Newsletter/Augustana Historical Society.*

Augustana Historical Society Publications

Rock Island, IL: Augustana Historical Society
Nos. 1–[4]; nos. 5–19
1931–1962
ISSN 0882–6102
Published irregularly; each number has a distinctive title
Continued by: *Publication/Augustana Historical Society*; beginning with
No. 20 in 1963

A group of distinguished individuals associated with the Augustana Evangelical Lutheran Church organized the Augustana Historical Society in 1930. The group included well-known historians and writers such as Gustav Andreen, Conrad Bergendoff, E. W. Olson, L. G. Abrahamson, George M. Stephenson, G. N. Swan, O. Fritiof Ander, I. O. Nothstein, and O. L. Nordstrom, among many others.

The objective of the Augustana Historical Society, as written in its original Constitution, "shall be to collect and preserve documents, publications, correspondence, and objects of historical interest of the Scandinavians in America and of the religious movements among them, especially of the Augustana Synod, and of the Evangelical Lutheran Church in general; likewise to encourage historical research and publication" (Constitution, 86).

An ambitious publishing program was launched in 1931 with the printing of volume 1 of the Society's *Publications* series. This book was written by O. F. Ander on the life and work of T. N. Hasselquist. This was also designated as number 14 of the *Augustana Library Publications* series.

Issued on an irregular basis, each volume or number has a distinctive title and individual author. Each is listed following this narration. There are 19 numbers in the series. *Sources:* Constitution 86–87; LIBRIS; Wiscat; WorldCat.

1. *T. N. Hasselquist: The Career and Influence of a Swedish–American Clergyman, Journalist, and Educator,* by O. Fritiof Ander, 1931.
2. *The Early Missionary Work of the Augustana Synod in New York City, 1865–1866,* by Gustav Andreen; *The Iowa Synod's Attempt at Missionary Work among the Indians, 1859–1864,* by Henry F. Staack; *Thomas Moran's Journey to the Tetons in 1879,* by Fritiof Fryxell; *The Historical and Cultural Background of Swedish Immigrants of Importance to their*

Assimilation in America, by Albert F. Schersten; *Swedish–American Newspapers and the Republican Party, 1855–1875,* by O. Fritiof Ander, 1932.

3. *Augustana Book Concern: Publishers to the Augustana Synod: History of Its Activities since 1889, with an Introductory Account of Earlier Publishing Enterprises,* by Ernst W. Olson; *Christina Nilsson's Visit to Brockton, Mass., in November, 1870. Pages from the Early History of the Oldest Swedish Lutheran Church in New England,* by Evald B. Lawson, 1933.

4. *Early Life of Eric Norelius (1833–1862): Journal of a Swedish Immigrant in the Middle West by Eric Norelius,* rendered into English by Emeroy Johnson; *Guide to the Material on Swedish History in the Augustana College Library,* by O. F. Ander, 1934.

5. *Diary Kept by L. P. Esbjörn: When Making the Trip from Gefle to New York on the Steamship Cobden in the Summer of 1849,* translated by Oscar L. Nordstrom; *Reports to the American Home Missionary Society, 1849–1856,* by Conrad J. I. Bergendoff; *The Sources of the Original Constitution of the Augustana Synod, 1860,* by Conrad J. I. Bergendoff; *Early Letters to Erland Carlsson: from a File for the Years 1852 to 1857,* translated by Ernst W. Olson; *Sources on Revolutionary Europe; a Selected List from the Charles XV Collection,* by George G. Andrews; *The Augustana Historical Society, 1930–1935,* by O. L. Nordstrom, 1935.

6. *Swedish–American Literary Periodicals,* by G. N. Swan, 1936.

7. *Letters Relating to Gustaf Unonius and the Early Swedish Settlers in Wisconsin,* translated and edited by George M. Stephenson, assisted by Olga Wold Hansen, 1937.

8. *The Problem of the Third Generation Immigrant,* by Marcus Lee Hansen, 1938.

9. *The American Origin of the Augustana Synod: from Contemporary Lutheran Periodicals, 1851–1860: A Collection of Source Material,* gathered and edited by O. Fritiof Ander and Oscar L. Nordstrom, 1942.

10. *Selected Documents Dealing with the Organization of the First Congregations and the First Conferences of the Augustana Synod and their Growth until 1860,* Part I, translated and edited by I. O. Nothstein, 1944.

11. *Selected Documents Dealing with the Organization of the First Congregations and the First Conferences of the Augustana Synod and their Growth until 1860,* Part II, edited by I. O. Nothstein, 1946.

12. *The Swedish Theatre of Chicago, 1868–1950,* by Henriette C. K. Naeseth, 1951.

13. *Smoky Valley People: A History of Lindsborg, Kansas,* by Emory K. Lindquist, 1953.

14. *Olof Christian Telemak Andren: Ambassador of Good Will,* by Oscar N. Olson, 1954.

15. *Swärd–Johnston: Biographical Sketches of Augustana Leaders*, by Oscar N. Olson, 1955.
16. *Anders Jonasson Lindström: First Augustana Student Sponsored by the Church for Study Abroad in Preparation for Augustana Seminary Professorship*, by Oscar N. Olson, 1957.
17. *Two Primary Sources for a Study of the Life of Jonas Swensson*, by Evald B. Lawson, 1957.
18. *Prairie Grass Dividing*, by James Iverne Dowie, 1959.
19. *Pioneering Adventures of Johan Edvard Lilljeholm in America, 1846–1850*, translated by Arthur Wald, 1962.

Augustana College: F536 .A96 3–19
Augustana College Swenson Center: 2–11; 1932–1946
Gustavus Adolphus College: F536.A96 2–3, 5, 10–15, 18
Luther Seminary: E184.S4A8 2–7
Lutheran School of Theology at Chicago: 13–14
Lutheran Theological Seminary at Gettysburg: F536.A96 nos. 1–6, 8–19
Lutheran Theological Seminary at Philadelphia: F536.A96 Vols. 10–11
Pacific Lutheran Theological Seminary: 1–3, 5, 10–11, 18–19
Trinity Lutheran Seminary: 1, 4, 9, 14
Wartburg Theological Seminary: 1–9, 13, 17, 18
WorldCat: Bethany College: 1–6, 8–19
   California Lutheran University: 1, 3–4, 6, 8–9, 12, 14, 17–19
   Evangelical Lutheran Church in America Archives: 1, 4, 6–19
   Lutheran Theological Southern Seminary: 9
   Midland Lutheran College: 10–13, 18
   North Park University: 1, 3, 6–9, 12–14, 18–19
   Pacific Lutheran University: 3, 6, 8–19
   Texas Lutheran University: 1
LIBRIS: Lund University: 18–19
   Royal Library of Sweden: 1–19
   Swedish Emigrant Institute: 2–3, 5–6, 9–12, 16–19
   Uppsala University: 1–19

Augustana Home Altar

See *The Home Altar*.

Augustana Journal

Rock Island, IL: Alumni Association of Augustana College. Evangelical Lutheran Augustana Synod of North America
Vol. 2, no. 9–vol. 14, no.52 (whole no. 21–whole no. 329)
July 1894–December 29, 1906

Formed by the union of: *Alumnus* (Rock Island, IL) and *Young Observer*
Continued by: *Young Lutheran's Companion*
Sometimes referred to as: *The Augustana Journal*

This new English-language monthly magazine came into existence in
July 1894 when the *Alumnus* changed its name to the *Augustana Journal*
and absorbed the *Young Observer* (sometimes called *The Observer*). It continued the format, paging, serial numbers, and price of the *Alumnus*. Editors were O. Olsson and C. W. Foss until July 1895. E. W. Olson was appointed editor through October of that year.

Even at this time the *Augustana Journal* began to include news items
about the Augustana Synod and its churches, suggesting that it was on
the way to becoming something like an official synodical organ. Because
of financial difficulties, the Alumni Association of Augustana College
turned over control of the *Augustana Journal*, issued monthly in 1895, so
that it became the property of the Lutheran Augustana Book Concern.

In January 1896, A. Rodell, also associated with *Augustana*, the Swedish
organ of the Augustana Synod, became its editor. Early in 1897, G. A.
Brandelle was appointed the editor and served through 1905. Now published in a larger newspaper format, twice monthly, for seventy-five cents
per year, it continued to the end of 1905. In 1906 it was issued weekly as
a paper for the more Americanized element of the synod. O. V. Holmgrain
was editor during 1906. Gradually more space was given to Augustana
Church news items and articles of interest to its members.

Beginning in 1907 it became the *Young Lutheran's Companion*. Other editors and associates had been C. L. E. Esbjörn, C. J. Södergren, A. P. Fors,
and Adolf Hult. Some Augustana clergy and members now considered it
the official English organ of the Augustana Synod. *Sources:* Nystrom 62;
Swan 71–72; WorldCat.

Augustana College: 1895–1897, 1904
Evangelical Lutheran Church in America Archives: AUG 14/6 Vols.
    2–3, [4–6], 7, [8–11], 12, [13–14]; 1894–1895, [1896–1898], 1899,
    [1900–1903], 1904, [1905–1906] Paper; AUG 14/6 Vols. 2–14;
    1894–1906, Microfilm
Luther Seminary: BX8001.L93 Vol. 2, no. 9–vol. 14; July 1894–1906, Mi-
    crofilm
Lutheran School of Theology at Chicago: BX8001 .L4510 Vols. 4–14;
    1896–1906, Microfilm
Lutheran Theological Seminary at Gettysburg: Vols. [7–14], [1899–1906]
Lutheran Theological Seminary at Philadelphia: Vols. 4–14; 1895–1906
Pacific Lutheran Theological Seminary: July 1894–December 1906, Mi-
    crofilm

Wisconsin Lutheran Seminary: Vol. 4, no. 1–vol. 11, no. 24; vol. 14, nos. 1–52; January 1, 1896–December 29, 1906
WorldCat: American Theological Library Association: Microfilm
Minnesota Historical Society: Vols. 4–14; 1896–1906

Augustana Library Publications

Rock Island, IL: Augustana College and Theological Seminary, Augustana College
Nos. 1–35
1898–1981
ISSN 0894–0053
Published irregularly; each number has a distinctive title
Other titles:
    Augustana Library Publications (Augustana College and Theological Seminary, Denkman Memorial Library, Rock Island, IL)
    Augustana Library Publications (Augustana College Library, Rock Island, IL)
    Publications/Augustana College (Augustana College, Rock Island, IL)
Succeeding title: *Augustana College Library Publications*; in 1992

As early as 1898, the library at Augustana College and Theological Seminary began issuing a series of publications on a variety of subjects. Published irregularly, each number has a distinctive title and individual author. The series includes thirty-five numbers, ending in 1981. Early issues were used in an exchange program with other libraries and academic institutions, thus bringing gifts into the college and seminary library collection. In 1992, the series continued as the *Augustana College Library Publications* series. Titles and authors are listed as follows:

1. *The Mechanical Composition of Wind Deposits*, by Johan August Udden, 1898.
2. *An Old Indian Village*, by Johan August Udden, 1900.
3. *Studies in the Idyl in German Literature*, by Gustav Andreen, 1902.
4. *On the Cyclonic Distribution of Rainfall*, by Johan August Udden, 1905.
5. *A Preliminary List of Fossil Mastodon and Mammoth Remains in Illinois and Iowa*, by Netta C. Anderson; *On the Proboscidean Fossils of the Pleistocene Deposits in Illinois and Iowa*, by Johan August Udden, 1905.
6. *Scandinavians Who Have Contributed to the Knowledge of the Flora of North America: A Memoir Prepared for the Celebration at Augustana*

College and Theological Seminary of the 200th Anniversary of the Birth of Linne, by Per Axel Rydberg; *Report on a Geological Survey of the Lands Belonging to the New York and Texas Land Company, Ltd., in the Upper Rio Grande Embayment in Texas*, by Johan August Udden, 1907.

7. *Genesis and Development of Sand Formations on Marine Coasts*, by Pehr Olsson-Seffer; *The Sand Strand Flora of Marine Coasts*, by Pehr Olsson-Seffer, 1910.

8. *Alternative Readings in the Hebrew of the Books of Samuel*, by Otto Henry Boström, 1918.

9. *On the Solutions of the Differential Equations of Motion of a Double Pendulum*, by William E. Cederberg, 1923.

10. *The Danegeld in France*, by Einar Joranson, 1923.

11. *Sedimentation in the Mississippi River between Davenport, Iowa, and Cairo, Illinois*, by Alvin L. Lugn, 1927.

12. *The Development of Commerce between the United States and Sweden, 1870–1925*, by Frederick Tilberg, 1929.

13. *Glacial Features of Jackson Hole, Wyoming*, by Fritiof M. Fryxell, 1930.

14. *T.N. Hasselquist: The Career and Influence of a Swedish-American Clergyman, Journalist, and Educator*, by Oscar Fritiof Ander, 1931. (Issued as No. 1 of *Augustana Historical Society Publications*.)

15. *The Relation of the Swedish-American Newspaper to the Assimilation of Swedish Immigrants*, by Albert Ferdinand Schersten, 1935.

16. *The Structural Geology and Physiography of the Teton Pass Area, Wyoming*, by Leland Horberg, 1938.

17. *The Mexican Revolution of Ayutla, 1854–1855: An Analysis of the Evolution and Destruction of Santa Anna's Last Dictatorship*, by Richard A. Johnson, 1939.

18. *The Structural Geology of the Cache Creek Area, Gros Ventre Mountains, Wyoming*, by Vincent E. Nelson, 1942.

19. *The Planting of the Swedish Church in America: Graduation Dissertation of Tobias Eric Biörck*, translated and edited by Ira Oliver Nothstein, 1943.

20. *Regional Conflicts Around Geneva: An Inquiry into the Origin, Nature, and Implications of the Neutralized Zone of Savoy and of the Customs-Free Zones of Gex and Upper Savoy*, by Adda B. Bozeman, 1949.

21. *Geology of the Northwest Flank of the Gros Ventre Mountains, Wyoming*, by Frank Albert Swenson, 1949.

22. *The Swedish Theatre of Chicago, 1868–1950*, by Henriette C. K. Naeseth, 1951.

23. *Structural Geology and Physiography of the Northern End of the Teton Range, Wyoming*, by Rudolph William Edmund, 1951.

24. *The Resistance of the Air to Stone-Dropping Meteors*, by Harry E. Nelson, 1953.

25. *The Port of Milwaukee,* by Edward Hamming, 1953.
26. *The John H. Hauberg Historical Essays,* compiled and edited by O. Fritiof Ander, 1954.
27. *The Cultural Heritage of the Swedish Immigrant: Selected References,* by O. Fritiof Ander, 1956.
28. *The Building of Modern Sweden: The Reign of Gustav V, 1907–1950,* by O. Fritiof Ander. 1958.
29. *Lincoln Images: Augustana College Centennial Essays,* edited by O. Fritiof Ander, 1960.
30. *Nazi War Aims: The Plans for the Thousand Year Reich,* by John Robert Bengtson, 1962.
31. *In the Trek of the Immigrants: Essays Presented to Carl Wittke,* edited by O. Fritiof Ander. Contents: Preface, by C. W. Sorenson; Introduction, by O. F. Ander; "Carl Wittke, Historian," by H. Wish; "Four Historians of Immigration," by O. F. Ander; "Immigration, Emigration, Migration," by C. C. Qualey; "Bibliography of Works by Carl Wittke," by C. H. Cramer; "A Forgotten Theory of Immigration," by E. P. Hutchinson; "Agrarian Myths of English Immigrants," by C. Erickson; "A Brief History of Immigrant Groups in Ohio," by F. P. Weisenburger; "The Germans in American Fiction," by J. T. Flanagan; "English Migration to the American West, 1865–1900," by O. O. Winther; "Saga in Steel and Concrete," by K. O. Bjork; "Finnish Immigrant Farmers in New York, 1910–1960," by A. W. Hoglund; "The Immigrant and the American National Idea," by W. O. Forster; "British Backtrailers: Working–Class Immigrants Return," by W. S. Shepperson; "Exodus U. S. A.," by T. Saloutos; "The Negro in the Old Northwest," by J. H. Rodabaugh; "The American Negro: An Old Immigrant on a New Frontier," by J. I. Dowie, 1964.
32. *Kierkegaard's Authorship: A Guide to the Writings of Kierkegaard,* by George E. Arbaugh and George B. Arbaugh, 1967.
33. *Augustana . . . A Profession of Faith: A History of Augustana College, 1860–1935,* by Conrad Bergendoff, 1969.
34. *The Masks of Comedy: Papers Delivered at the Humanities Festival, 1978, Augustana College,* edited by Ann Boaden, 1980.
35. *Swedish–American Newspapers: A Guide to the Microfilms Held by Swenson Swedish Immigration Research Center, Augustana College, Rock Island, Illinois,* compiled by Lilly Setterdahl, 1981.

Sources: Augustana College Library Publications Inventory as of 11/03; LIBRIS; WorldCat.

Augustana College: Z881.A93 R62 P8 1–35
Gustavus Adolphus College: 1, 3–12, 14–19, 21–35
Luther Seminary: 8, 14, 19, 22, 26–27, 29, 31–32, 35

Lutheran School of Theology at Chicago: 8, 32, 34
Trinity Lutheran Seminary: 14, 32
WorldCat: Bethany College: 1–2, 14, 19, 22, 27, 31, 33–35
    California Lutheran University: 1, 4–5, 7–11, 14–26, 28–29, 31–35
    Evangelical Lutheran Church in America Archives: 14, 19, 22, 27–28,
    31–32, 33, 35
    North Park University: 1–3, 5, 7–8, 10–17, 19, 22, 26–29, 31–33
    Lutheran Theological Seminary at Gettysburg: 8, 14, 22, 32
    Lutheran Theological Seminary at Philadelphia: 8, 14–20, 22, 27, 33
    Lutheran Theological Southern Seminary: 19
Midland Lutheran College: 19, 22, 32–33
    Pacific Lutheran Theological Seminary: 8, 14, 19, 22, 32
Pacific Lutheran University: 22, 28, 31–32, 35
    Texas Lutheran University: 14
    Wartburg Theological Seminary: 14
LIBRIS: Lund University: 1–35
    Royal Library of Sweden: 1–35
    Swedish Emigrant Institute: 22
    Uppsala University: 1–35

Augustana Library Publications. Occasional Paper

Rock Island, IL: Augustana College Library
Nos. 1–4
1957–1958
Continued by: *Occasional Paper/Augustana College Library*

The following four titles were issued with this series name in 1957 and
1958:

1. *Notable Advances in the Understanding and Treatment of Mentally Hand-
   icapped Children,* by J. E. Wallace Wallin, 1957.
2. *One Hundred Years of British Colonial Policy,* by Edgar L. Erickson,
   1958.
3. *The United States and Lafayette: Les Etats-Unis et Lafayette,* by Louis
   Gottschalk, 1958.
4. *Obligations of the Educated Man,* by Charles H. Whitmore, 1958.

Sources: Augustana College Library Occasional Papers Inventory as of
11/03; LIBRIS; WorldCat.

Augustana College: 1–4
Gustavus Adolphus College: 2, 4
LIBRIS: Lund University: 1–4

Augustana Luther Leaguer

Chicago, IL: [s.n.]
1923–?

Ander writes that this was "a young people's journal of the Augustana Synod." *Source:* Ander 1956, 151.

No holdings reported.

Augustana Lutheran

Rock Island, IL: Augustana Book Concern
Vols. 95–96
January 4, 1950–December 26, 1951
Formed by the union of: *Augustana* (Rock Island, IL: 1889) and *Lutheran Companion* (Rock Island, IL: 1911)
Also in Swedish-language edition as: *Augustana Lutheranen*
Continued by: *Lutheran Companion* (Rock Island, IL: 1952)
Sometimes referred to as: *The Augustana Lutheran*

As the official organ of the Augustana Evangelical Lutheran Church, the *Augustana Lutheran* became the new name of the former *Lutheran Companion* as of January 4, 1950. It was formed by the union of *Augustana* (Rock Island, IL: 1889) and *Lutheran Companion* (Rock Island, IL: 1911). It continued the volume numbering of *Augustana* (Rock Island, IL: 1889) rather than the volume numbering of the *Lutheran Companion*.

In January 1952, after only two years with this title, the weekly periodical again took the former name of its predecessor *Lutheran Companion*. *Source:* WorldCat.

Augustana College: Vols. 95–96; 1950–1951
Bethany College: Vols. 95–96; 1950–1951
Evangelical Lutheran Church in America Archives: AUG14/6 Vols. 95–96; 1950–1951, Paper and Microfilm
Gustavus Adolphus College: Vols. 95–96; 1950–1951
Luther Seminary: BX8001.L93 Vols. 95–96; 1950–1951, Paper and Microfilm
Lutheran School of Theology at Chicago: BX8001 .L4610 Vols. 95–96; 1950–1951, Microfilm
Lutheran Theological Seminary at Gettysburg: Vols. 95–96; 1950–1951
Lutheran Theological Seminary at Philadelphia: Vols. 95–96; 1950–1951
Midland Lutheran College: Vols. 95–96; 1950–1951

Pacific Lutheran Theological Seminary: Vols. 95–96; 1950–1951, Micro-
film
Trinity Lutheran Seminary: 1950–1951
WorldCat: Texas Lutheran University: Vol. 95; 1950

Augustana Lutheran Churchmen

Rock Island, IL: Augustana Book Concern for Augustana Lutheran
Churchmen
Autumn 1957 ?–1962
Continues: *Augustana Churchmen*

At the 1956 convention of the Augustana Brotherhood, the delegation
voted unanimously to change the name of the organization to Augustana
Lutheran Churchmen, with a new constitution and revised structure.

Thus the title of the organization's newsletter became *Augustana
Lutheran Churchmen*. It continued to publish program suggestions, news,
and devotional items. Publication ended in 1962 with the LCA merger.
Source: Augustana Annual 1957.

Gustavus Adolphus College Archives: 1958–1962 scattered issues

Augustana Lutheranen: den Svenska Upplagen av Augustana Lutheran

[*Augustana Lutheran: the Swedish edition of Augustana Lutheran*]
Rock Island, IL: Augustana Book Concern
Vol. 95, no. 1–vol. 100/101, no. 26
January 2, 1950–December 26, 1955
Continued by: *Augustana* (Rock Island, IL: 1956)

Even though the *Augustana Lutheran*, formed by combining the *Lutheran
Companion* (1911) and *Augustana* (1889) at the end of 1949, was the new title
of the official English-language periodical of the Augustana Evangelical
Lutheran Church, there was still considerable sentiment for a Swedish paper.

Consequently, the *Augustana Lutheran* was also issued as the *Augustana
Lutheranen*, its Swedish-language edition. This publication continued
from 1950 through 1955. It was issued biweekly, being designated as the
official organ of the Evangelisk Lutherska Augustanakyrkans. In 1951
there were 5,121 subscribers and in 1954 there were 5,080 subscribers.
Even though these were relatively small numbers, it was felt that the paper was fulfilling a need for those church members who wished to be informed about church activities through the Swedish language.

In January 1955, the one-hundredth anniversary of *Augustana*, now evolved into the *Augustana Lutheranen*, was recognized. This date was based on the 1855 inauguration of *Hemlandet, det Gamla och det Nya*, the first paper with a relationship to the Augustana Evangelical Lutheran Church and the first Swedish-language newspaper in the Midwest.

Yet another change related to Augustana Evangelical Lutheran Church publications took place at the end of 1955, when a separate monthly in the Swedish-language, *Augustana*, appeared in 1956. *Sources: Augustana Annual* 1954, 74; Erickson 3; Nystrom 61; WorldCat.

> Center for Research Libraries: Vol. 95, no. 1–vol. 99, no. 26; January 2, 1950–December 26, 1954 (Lacks: vol. 95, no. 9; vol. 97, nos. 16, 23; vol 98, no. 12)
>
> Evangelical Lutheran Church in America Archives: AUG14/7 Vols. 99–101; 1954–1955 Paper; Vols. 95–101; 1950–1955, Microfilm
>
> Gustavus Adolphus College: 1950–1955
>
> Harvard University Divinity School: Vols. 95–100/101; 1950–1955, Microfilm
>
> Luther Seminary: BX8001.A9 Vols. 95–101; 1950–1955, Paper and Microfilm
>
> Lutheran School of Theology at Chicago: BX8001 .A810 Vols. 95–100/101; 1950–1955, Paper and Microfilm
>
> WorldCat: American Theological Library Association: Microfilm

Augustana Men

> Rock Island, IL: Brotherhood of the Lutheran Augustana Synod
> Vol. 1, no. 1–vol. 6, no. 2
> January 1948–April/July 1953
> Continued by: *Augustana Churchmen*
> Other title: *Augustana-Men*

The Augustana Brotherhood issued this monthly periodical for its members beginning in January 1948. The first issues through February 1949 were mimeographed sheets. After that the publication, through the April–July 1953 issue, was printed. The title was then changed to *Augustana Churchmen*. *Source:* WorldCat.

> Gustavus Adolphus College Archives: scattered issues
> Lutheran School of Theology at Chicago: BV4525 .A8 Vols. 1–6; 1948–1953

Augustana Missions

Minneapolis, MN: Board of Home Missions and Board of Foreign Missions of the Augustana Evangelical Lutheran Church
Rock Island, IL: Augustana Book Concern
Vol. 1, no. 1–vol. 2, no. 6
October 1948–May 1951
Formed by the union of: *Augustana Overseas* (Minneapolis, MN: 1947) and *Pastor's Paragraphs*
Other title: *Augustana Missions* (Minneapolis, MN: 1948)

The Board of Home Missions and the Board of Foreign Missions jointly began publication of a new periodical, *Augustana Missions*, with the first issue in October 1948. This monthly was actually a union of the earlier *Augustana Overseas* and a paper called *Pastor's Paragraphs*, which had been prepared by the Board of Home Missions.

This Augustana Evangelical Lutheran Church publication was devoted entirely to news and articles about home and foreign missions. The ELCA Archives notes that *Augustana Missions* "was produced in conjunction with a special free-will missionary ingathering, known as the Augustana Mission Advance, that was to be taken up in 1949 for foreign and home missions" (http://lrc.elca.org:8080/webcat/).

Publication was suspended from July 1949 to January 1950. Then it reappeared in a new format, again publicizing the special Augustana Mission Advance financial appeal for 1950. The January issue was referred to as volume 1, number 1, even though the October 1948 issue had the same designation. The revised plan was for it to be published monthly from January through June. The 1951 monthly issues were published from December through May. Marion Pillman was the editor. Devoted to news about and requesting support for mission efforts in the United States and overseas by the Augustana Evangelical Lutheran Church, it ended with the May 1951 issue. *Sources:* http://lrc.elca.org:8080/webcat/; WorldCat.

Evangelical Lutheran Church in America Archives: AUG 24/1/9/3 1948–1951
Gustavus Adolphus College Archives: 1948–1949 scattered issues
Harvard University Divinity School: Vol. 1, nos. 1–9; 1948/1949, Microfilm
Lutheran School of Theology at Chicago: BX8001 .A930 Vol. 1; 1948
Southwestern Baptist Theological Seminary: Vol. 1, nos. 1–4, 6–9; October 1948–June 1949
WorldCat: Augustana College: Vol. 1, nos. 1–9; 1948–1949

Augustana Missions

Minneapolis, MN: Board of American Missions and Board of Foreign
  Missions, Augustana Evangelical Lutheran Church
Rock Island, IL: Augustana Book Concern
Vols. [1]–5
1956–1961
Continues: *Augustana Overseas* (Minneapolis, MN: 1951)
Other title: *Augustana Missions* (Minneapolis, MN: 1956)

Several years earlier (1948–1951), a publication with the same title had
been issued by the same boards in order to promote the synod-sponsored
Augustana Mission Advance appeal for support for home and foreign
missions.

Continuing the annual publication *Augustana Overseas* which had been
issued by the Board of Foreign Missions, this new annual *Augustana Missions* was again a joint project of the Boards of American and Foreign Missions. It was published in yearbook format from 1956 through a report for
1960. As the Augustana Mission Advance program continued, this yearbook for home and foreign mission work did include promotional information for the special offering. Editors were R. C. Burke and Thomas
Wersell (1956–1959) and Burke and T. E. Matson (1959–1961). *Sources:*
http://lrc.elca.org:8080/webcat/; WorldCat.

Augustana College: BV2540 .A13 A8my 1956–1961
Evangelical Lutheran Church in America Archives: AUG 24/1/9/3
  1956–1961
Gustavus Adolphus College Archives: 1956–1961
Harvard University Divinity School: 817.083 A923.3am Vols. 1–5;
  1956–1960
Lutheran Theological Seminary at Gettysburg: BV2540 .A82 1956–1960
Lutheran Theological Seminary at Philadelphia: BV2540 .A7 A2 Vols.
  1–5; 1956–1960
Lutheran Theological Southern Seminary: BX8001 .A84 1956–1960
Pacific Lutheran Theological Seminary: 1956–1961
Princeton Theological Seminary: BX8001 .A84 1956; BX8065.2 .A93 1958
Southwestern Baptist Theological Seminary: Vols. 1–3, 5; 1956–1958,
  1960
Trinity Lutheran Seminary: BV2540 .A9 1956–1960

Augustana Observer (1881)

Philadelphia, PA: [s.n.]
New York: C. E. Lindberg, C. J. Petri, Albert Rodell

Vol. 1, no. 1–vol. 2, no. 12
December 15, 1881–November 15, 1883

The *Augustana Observer* was originally launched in Philadelphia in 1881 by three Augustana pastors: C. E. Lindberg, C. J. Petri, and Albert Rodell. All served as editors. In the first number, the following statement justifying the new venture read: "Although there are six Swedish papers published within our Synod, this is the first English paper, and everybody who is impartial must admit that we need an English paper" (Augustana ELC 36). Its editors stated that their purpose was "to observe and report the work and interests of the Augustana Synod" among the English-speaking population. In December 1882 the paper moved to New York.

Soon this experiment of publishing an English paper on a weekly basis failed due to the lack of subscribers. Its last issue from New York was dated November 15, 1883 (according to WorldCat).

However, Backlund writes that in 1884 the paper moved to Rock Island. Söderstrom also indicates its location in Rock Island from May through September 1884. The Lutheran Theological Seminary at Gettysburg reports 1884 issues in its holdings. Also, LIBRIS indicates publication through September 1884 with a separate special number. *Sources: After Seventy-Five Years* 99; Augustana ELC 36; Backlund 81; http://tomos.oit.umn.edu/; LIBRIS; Söderstrom 24; WorldCat.

Evangelical Lutheran Church in America Archives: AUG 14/14 Vols. 1–2; 1881–1883
Lutheran Theological Seminary at Gettysburg: Vols. [2, 4]; [1883, 1884]
University of Minnesota–Minneapolis: BX8049 .A95x Vol. 2, no. 12; November 15, 1883
LIBRIS: Royal Library of Sweden: December 1883–September 1884

Augustana Observer (1902)

Rock Island, IL: Augustana College
Vol. 1, no. 1–vol. 70, no. 28
December 2, 1902–May 17, 1972
Continued by: *Observer*
Sometimes referred to as: *Observer*

The official college paper published by and for the students of Augustana College was born in November 1902, when President Gustav Andreen presented a petition from the Lyceum to the faculty. The request for a paper was then granted. A sixteen-page publication, its first editor was S. G. Hägglund. The *Augustana Observer* was issued on a monthly schedule during the academic year from December 1902 through May 1921.

From 1906 through 1909, the June number served as an annual. Then in 1910, the senior class produced *The Jubilee* as its annual.

In the earlier years, some of the best essays written for English classes were printed alongside articles of general interest. These general articles reported athletics, musical, cultural, and social events, giving a broad view of the many activities that occupied students and faculty.

Beginning with the September 9, 1921, issue, the paper was published weekly during the academic year through May 17, 1972. This 1921 venture produced a large size (16" × 22") paper which was reduced to 12" × 18" the following year. Literary pieces, both essays and verse, were printed then only in an end-of-the-year supplement. Regular space was devoted to campus news and events. During the 1920s, the paper received several regional awards, as it did in the 1930s also. In spite of economic hardships, the paper thus was ably edited.

Through the years it continued to be the official organ, published by students, of the Augustana College campus for its students, staff, faculty, and friends. *Sources:* Bergendoff 125, 168; LIBRIS; WorldCat.

Augustana College: LH1.A9 A9 1902–1972

Illinois State Historical Library: IX896 Au.7a

Wisconsin Historical Society: September 9, 1921–December 18, 1946, Microfilm

LIBRIS: Royal Library of Sweden: May 17, 1934–1972

Augustana och Missionären: Weckotidning för Kyrka och Mission

[*Augustana and Missionary: Weekly Paper for Church and Mission*]

Moline, IL: Wistrand & Thulin's Bok–och Accidenstryckeri (January 1879–September 17, 1884)

Rock Island, IL: Augustana Book Concern (September 24, 1884–November 1889)

Vol. 24, no. 1–vol. 34, no. 48

January 1, 1879–November 28, 1889

Formed by the union of: *Missionären* (Moline, IL) and *Augustana* (Rock Island, IL: 1874)

Merged with: *Hemvännen* to form *Augustana* (Rock Island, IL: 1889)

As of January 1879, *Augustana* combined with its competitor *Missionären* (Moline, IL), which had appeared in 1876, to form *Augustana och*

Missionären. Through early September 1884 it was published in Moline, Illinois. The Augustana Book Concern, the private stock company, assumed its publication in September 1884 at Rock Island, Illinois.

By official action of the Augustana Synod in 1885, this paper was designated the official organ of the church. It was devoted to the affairs of the church and especially to the mission program, with substantial space given to the subject of foreign missions.

Continuing his editorial responsibilities for the synod, T. N. Hasselquist served until his resignation in 1889. Associates included O. Olsson (1879–June 1882), A. R. Cervin (1879–June 1882), C. P. Rydholm (1879–1880), Erl. Carlsson (August 1882–July 11, 1883), A. O. Bersell (July 18, 1883–September 7, 1885), C. M. Esbjörn (November 19, 1884–May 5, 1886), and L. G. Abrahamson (July 15, 1885–November 1889). For a subscription price of $1.50 per year readers received weekly copies.

It seems that at about this time there developed a sense of competition with *Hemvännen,* a family paper also published by the Augustana Book Concern, but showing a loss of readership and some financial instability. By the end of 1888, *Augustana och Missionären* showed a loss of one-third of its subscribers. Finally it was decided that the best approach to saving both papers would be to consolidate them. Thus the November 1889 issue was the last independent one for both *Hemvännen* and *Augustana och Missionären.* The new combined paper, again taking the name *Augustana,* appeared with its first issue dated December 1889. Some sources indicate that *Vårt Land och Folk* was also a part of the merger.

Thus also ended the editorial career of T. N. Hasselquist. Andreen pays tribute to Hasselquist and his contribution to the synod: "By the church paper he [Hasselquist] continued to reach the rank and file of the people, to direct them in their religious development, to exhort them to penitence, faith, hope and assurance, to instruct them in the doctrine and fellowship of the Master, Jesus Christ." *Sources:* Andreen 1931, 94; Dowie 214; Erickson 3; http://mnhs.mnpals.net; LIBRIS; Stephenson 333; ULS; WorldCat.

Augustana College: 1879–1889

Bethany College: Vols. 24–34; 1879–1889

Center for Research Libraries: Vols. 24–34, no. 48; 1879–November 28, 1889

Evangelical Lutheran Church in America Archives: AUG 14/7 Vols. [24], 25–31; [1879], 1880–1886, Paper; Vols. 24–33; 1879–1888, Microfilm

Gustavus Adolphus College Archives: Vol. 24, no. 1–vol 34, no. 48; January 1879–November 1889

Harvard University Divinity School: Vol. 24–vol. 34, nos. 1–48; 1879–1889, Microfilm

Luther Seminary: BX8001.A9 Vols. 24–34; 1879–1889, Microfilm
Lutheran School of Theology at Chicago: BX8001 .A810 Vols. 24–34; 1879–1889, Microfilm
Lutheran Theological Seminary at Gettysburg: Vols. 24–29, [33]; 1879–1888
Lutheran Theological Seminary at Philadelphia: 1879–1889
Midland Lutheran College: [1883]; 1884–1886
Minnesota Historical Society: BX8049.1 .A92 Vols. 24–34; 1879–1889
New York Public Library Research Library: Vols. 24–29, 32–34
University of Minnesota–Minneapolis: Vol. 34, no. 8; February 21, 1889
WorldCat: American Theological Library Association, Microfilm
LIBRIS: Swedish Emigrant Institute: Årg. 24–34 (1879–1889)

Augustana Overseas

Minneapolis, MN: Board of Foreign Missions of the Lutheran Augustana Synod
Vol. 1, no. 1–vol. 2, no. 3
January 1947–July 1948
Merged with: *Pastor's Paragraphs* to form *Augustana Missions* (Minneapolis, MN: 1948)
Other title: *Augustana Overseas* (Minneapolis, MN: 1947)

The Board of Foreign Missions of the Augustana Synod attempted to sponsor a quarterly periodical with an issue beginning in January 1947. Its emphasis was to provide news and articles about Augustana missions worldwide. However, it ceased publication with the July 1948 issue and merged with *Pastor's Paragraphs* to form *Augustana Missions* (Minneapolis, MN: 1948). S. Hjalmar Swanson was the editor, assisted by C. Vernon Swanson in 1948. *Sources:* http://lrc.elca.org; WorldCat.

Evangelical Lutheran Church in America Archives: AUG 24
Gustavus Adolphus College Archives: Vol. 1, no. 1–vol. 2, no. 2; 1947–1948
Lutheran School of Theology at Chicago: BV2540 .A1 A8 Vols. 1–2; 1947–1948
WorldCat: Augustana College: Vol. 1–vol. 2, nos. 1–3; 1947–1948

Augustana Overseas

Minneapolis, MN: Board of Foreign Missions, Augustana Lutheran Church
1951–1955

Continued by: *Augustana Missions* (Minneapolis, MN: 1956)
Other title: *Augustana Overseas* (Minneapolis, MN: 1951)

The Board of Foreign Missions issued an annual publication from 1951 through 1955 that reported information about its work with missions worldwide. It was continued by *Augustana Missions* (Minneapolis, MN: 1956). *Source:* WorldCat.

Augustana College: BV2540 .A13 A8oy 1951–1954
Evangelical Lutheran Church in America Archives: AUG 24/1/9/2 1951, 1953–1954
Gustavus Adolphus College Archives: 1951–1954
Harvard University Divinity School: 817.083 A923.3 ao 1953–1954
Southwestern Baptist Theological Seminary: Vols. 1, 3–4; 1951, 1953–1954

Augustana Quarterly: The Church Quarterly of the Augustana Lutheran Church

Rock Island, IL: Augustana Book Concern
Vol. 1, no. 1–vol. 27, no. 4
March 1922–October 1948
Merged with: *Lutheran Church Quarterly* to form *Lutheran Quarterly* (Gettysburg, PA: 1949) (0024–7499)
Other title: *Augustana Quarterly* (Rock Island, IL: 1922)

Officially published by the Augustana Synod, the *Augustana Quarterly* in a sense was a continuation of the *Augustana Theological Quarterly*, which had ceased publication five years earlier in 1917. Text is in both Swedish and English for the first twelve volumes. After that, text is only in English.

This is primarily a theological journal or a theological review with appropriate articles related to Augustana theological subjects. Book reviews are also included and tables of contents are provided. For some time A. F. Almer and O. N. Olson were editors.

At the end of 1948, the *Augustana Quarterly* merged with the *Lutheran Church Quarterly* to form a new theological journal *Lutheran Quarterly* beginning in 1949. *Sources:* Hultgren 2001; Wiscat; WorldCat.

Augustana College: Vols. 1–27; 1922–1948
Evangelical Lutheran Church in America Archives: AUG 14/13 Vols. 1–2, [3], 4–5, [6], 7–12, [13–14], 15–25, [26–27]; 1922–1923, [1924], 1925–1926, [1927], 1928–1933, [1934–1935], 1936–1946, [1947–1948] Paper. AUG 14/13 Vols. 1–27; 1922–1948, Microfilm

Gustavus Adolphus College: Vols. 1–25, 27; 1922–1946; 1948
Harvard University Divinity School: Vols. 1–27; 1922–1948
Luther Seminary: BX8001.A93 Vols. 1–27; 1922–1948
Lutheran School of Theology at Chicago: BX8001 .A8310 Vols. 1–27; 1922–1948, Microfilm
Lutheran Theological Seminary at Gettysburg: Vols. 1–27; 1922–1948
Lutheran Theological Seminary at Philadelphia: Vols. 1–27; 1922–1948
Midland Lutheran College: Vols. 3–27; 1924–1948
Pacific Lutheran Theological Seminary: Vols. 1–27; 1922–1948
Pacific Lutheran University: BX8001 .A63 Vols. 1–2, 7–27; 1922–1923, 1928–1948
Trinity Lutheran Seminary: Vols. 1–27; 1922–1948, Microfilm
University of Chicago: BX8001 .A9 Vols. 1–10, 13–15, 18–19, 22–23, 24:4, 25–27; 1922–1931, 1934–1936, 1939–1940, 1943–1948
Wartburg Theological Seminary: Vols. 1–27; 1922–1948
WorldCat: American Theological Library Association: Microfilm California Lutheran University

Augustana Seminary Review

Rock Island, IL: Augustana Theological Seminary
Vol. 1, no. 1–vol. 14, no. 3
1949–3rd Quarter 1962
Continued by: *The Seminary Review*

Issued on a quarterly schedule, the *Augustana Seminary Review* journal was published at Augustana Theological Seminary during its later years. Seminary faculty members, Augustana Evangelical Lutheran Church leaders and theologians, as well as leaders of other denominations provided articles. The first issue of each volume was the seminary catalogue.

The journal ceased publication with this title in 1962 at the time of the Lutheran Church in America merger. It was continued by *The Seminary Review*. *Sources:* Hultgren 2001; WorldCat.

Augustana College: BV4070 .A81 Vols. 1–14:3; 1949–1962
Evangelical Lutheran Church in America Archives: Vols. [1], 2, [3], 4–5, [6–14]; [1949], 1950, [1951], 1952–1953, [1954–1962]
Evangelical Lutheran Church in America Archives Region 5—IA: Vols. [6–8, 10]; [1954–1956, 1958]
Gustavus Adolphus College: Vols. 1–14; 1949–1962
Harvard University Divinity School: Vols. 1–14; 1949–1962
Luther Seminary: BV4070.A972 Vols. 1–2, [3], 4, [5], 6–14; 1949–1950, [1951], 1952, [1953], 1954–1962

Lutheran School of Theology at Chicago: BV4070.L791 .S471 Vols. 1–14; 1949–1962
Lutheran Theological Seminary at Gettysburg: Vols. 1–2, [3], 4–5, [6], 7–14, no. 3; 1949–1950, [1951], 1952–1953, [1954], 1955–1962
North Park University: Vols. 10–14; 1958–1962
Pacific Lutheran Theological Seminary: Vols. 1–14; 1949–1962
Princeton Theological Seminary: BR1 .A83 Vols. 1–14; 1949–1962
Trinity Lutheran Seminary: 1949–1962
Wartburg Theological Seminary: Vols. 1–14; 1949–1962

Augustana Story

See *Augustana College Bulletin*.

Augustana Theological Quarterly

Rock Island, IL: Lutheran Augustana Book Concern
Vols. 2–19
January 1900–October 1917
Variant title: *Tidskrift för Teologi och Kyrkliga Frågor* [*Journal for Theology and Ecclesiastical Questions*]
Continues: *Tidskrift för Svensk. Ev. Luth. Kyrkohistoria i N. Amerika och för Teologiska och Kyrkliga Frågor*
Sometimes referred to as: *Teologisk Tidskrift*

Described as "a religious periodical with unusual historical merits as a source on the early period of the Swedish Lutheran Church in America" (Ander 1956, 182), the *Augustana Theological Quarterly* was published for seventeen years from 1900–1917. It was also known by its Swedish title *Tidskrift för Teologi och Kyrkliga Frågor*. Volume 1 was issued with a complete Swedish title, *Tidskrift för Svensk. Ev. Luth. Kyrkohistoria i N. Amerika och för Teologiska och Kyrkliga Frågor* in 1898–1899.

Articles are in both Swedish and English, with Swedish the predominant language in the early volumes and English more predominant in the later volumes. The journal was issued quarterly with approximately two hundred sixty pages comprising each complete volume, or sixty-four pages in each issue of octavo format. Tables of contents were provided.

As founders of the journal, various members of the Augustana Seminary Faculty of Theology edited volumes 2 through 4 dated 1900–1902. E. Norelius and N. Forsander served as editors for volumes 5 through 11 (1903–1909), Forsander alone for volumes 12 through 14 (1910–1912) and S. G. Youngert for volumes 15 through 19 (1913–1917). Assistants during the later years included C. A. Blomgren, J. G. Dahlberg, Adolph Hult, and Emil Lund.

The journal included scholarly articles on church history, biographies, and theological literature especially related to the Lutheran Church and Augustana Synod. Aspiring to reach a place among learned journals, it ended publication in 1917. Following an interval of five years, it was revived as the *Augustana Quarterly. Sources:* Ander 1956, 182; Andreen 1905, 176; Erickson 7; Hultgren 2001; LIBRIS; Stephenson 357; WorldCat.

Augustana College Swenson Center: Vols. 2–19; 1900–1917
Evangelical Lutheran Church in America Archives: AUG 14/15 Vol. 2; 1900 Paper; AUG 14/15 Vols. 2–19; 1900–1917, Microfilm
Gustavus Adolphus College: Vols. 2–19; 1900–1917
Harvard University Divinity School: Vols. 2–19; 1900–1917, Microfilm
Luther Seminary: BX8001.T5 Vols. 2–17, [18], 19; 1900–1917
Lutheran School of Theology at Chicago: BX8001 .A84 Vols. 2–19; 1900–1917
Lutheran Theological Seminary at Gettysburg: Vols. [5–9], 10–12, [13]; 1903–1911
Lutheran Theological Seminary at Philadelphia: Vols. 11–19; 1909–1917
Minnesota Historical Society: BX8049.1 .T5
Trinity Lutheran Seminary: 1903–1911, 1916
University of Chicago: BX8001 .T55 Vols. 2–16; 1900–1914
University of Minnesota–Minneapolis: Vols. 2–19; 1900–1917
WorldCat: American Theological Library Association, Microfilm
Pacific Lutheran University Vols. 17–19; 1915–1917
LIBRIS: Royal Library of Sweden
Swedish Emigrant Institute Årg. 2–19

Axplockerskan

Omaha, NE: Immanuel Deaconess Institute
1900–1904?

According to Ander, this publication was issued on a quarterly schedule by the Immanuel Deaconess Institute from 1900 to a possible ending in 1904. *Source:* Ander 1956, 152.

Augustana College Swenson Center: Vol. 4, no. 1; 1904

– B –

Balder: A Literary Annual

Rock Island, IL: Augustana College and Theological Seminary; Lutheran Augustana Book Concern

Vols. 1–2
1890–1891
Continued by: *Lyceum Annual*

This literary annual produced by the Lyceum student organization at
Augustana College was first issued in 1890. At that time, the Lyceum was
a combination of two groups, the Phrenokosmian Society and the Adelphic Society. The 1891 volume was issued by only the Lyceum.

The annual included stories, poems, and essays. Entries were in both
Swedish and English text.

Bergendoff provides an interesting portrait of the Lyceum group on the
Augustana College campus:

> Next to music the literary societies claimed the student's extra–curricular in-
> terests. Meeting weekly the Adelphic and the Phrenokosmian societies gave
> their members practice in debate, oratory, declamation and parliamentary
> procedure. A good deal of rivalry existed between the two, each seeking the
> more gifted students as members, each claiming excellence in programs. Yet
> they could unite in a common effort, establishing the Lyceum. This arranged
> a lecture and concert course which brought featured personalities to the cam-
> pus. The community was invited to these events. (96–97)

After the 1891 annual, the title was changed to *Lyceum Annual,* which existed from 1892 to 1894. *Sources:* Ander 1956, 152; Bergendoff 96–97, 205;
ULS.

Augustana College: 1890–1891
Library of Congress: LD271 .A6655 L9
University of Minnesota–Minneapolis: LD271 .A665 B35x 1890–1891

Banner (Omaha, NE)

Omaha, NE: Immanuel Medical Center
Vol. 52–?
Spring 1973–?
Continues: *Immanuel Medical Center Banner*

The newsletter of the Immanuel Medical Center continued to inform
readers of the diversified services provided to patients. *Source:* Matthews
1985, 32.

Lutheran Theological Seminary at Gettysburg: Vol. 52– ; 1973–

Barn Vännen

See *Barnvännen.*

Barnens Tidning

[*Children's Paper*]
Chicago, IL: Lindahl och Quist (1886–1889)
Rock Island, IL: Lutheran Augustana Book Concern (1890–1932)
Vol. 1, no. 1–vol. 47, no. 24
January, 1886–December 1932
Absorbed: *Barnvännen*

In January 1886, S. P. A. Lindahl and H. P. Quist began publishing a Swedish-language paper with the name *Barnens Tidning* for Sunday School children. As a private enterprise, they donated the proceeds of $200 in 1886 to Augustana College and Theological Seminary. *Barnens Tidning* was a semiofficial Sunday School paper, but it received synod-wide circulation. In 1890, 25,000 copies of each issue were distributed throughout Augustana Synod member congregations.

In 1888, Lindahl and Quist were asked to turn over *Barnens Tidning* to the Lutheran Augustana Book Concern so that it could be merged with *Barnvännen*. Lindahl chose not to follow this plan but instead in 1889 purchased *Barnvännen* and discontinued it. In 1890, *Barnens Tidning* was taken over from Lindahl, who was paid $1,000 for his rights and title and was also chosen as its editor. It was then a publication of the Lutheran Augustana Book Concern.

Originally issued on a monthly schedule until 1898, its success let it become a semimonthly in 1899. The annual subscription price was thirty-five cents in 1886, which was increased to forty cents in 1899 and finally to fifty cents in 1928. This illustrated four-page paper printed children's stories, inspirational articles, and poems of interest to children.

By 1917 circulation increased to 37,538 copies. However, soon the downward trend in readership was obvious as the English-language steadily replaced interest in Swedish. In 1920, the circulation was at 24,237 copies. In 1926 distribution had fallen to 9,916 copies. By 1931, only 2,110 copies were distributed. *Barnens Tidning* was continued until the end of 1932 when it was decided that there was no longer a need for a juvenile paper in the Swedish language. *Sources:* Arden 1963, 204; Erickson 8; Hamrin 74; Johnson 186; LIBRIS; Olson 1933, 26–27, 44, 78; Stephenson 350; ULS.

Augustana College Swenson Center: April 1904–May 1916
Evangelical Lutheran Church in America Archives: AUG 25/5/1 Vols.
1–18, [19], 20–24, [25, 32–34], 43–47; 1886–1903, [1904], 1905–1909, [1910, 1917–1919], 1928–1932

Lutheran Theological Seminary at Gettysburg: Vols. 8–13, [14], 15–17,
[18–19], 20, [21–25], 26, [27–28], 29–31, [32], 33–38, [39], 40, [41–47];
1893–1932

Erickson: Gustavus Adolphus College: Vols. 1–14, [15–23, 28–34]
Lutheran School of Theology at Chicago: Vols. [1–25, 32–34, 43–47];
[1886–1910, 1917–1919, 1928–1931]

ULS: Minnesota Historical Society: Vols. [8–9, 11, 21, 23–24, 27–47]

LIBRIS: Swedish Emigrant Institute: Vols. [9, 28–29, 32, 34–36, 41];
[1894, 1913–1914, 1917, 1919–1921, 1926]

Barnvännen: Illustrerad Månadstidning för Söndagsskolan och Hemmet

[*Children's Friend: Illustrated Monthly Paper for Sunday School and Home*]
also: *Illustrerad månadsskrift för barn och ungdom*
[*Illustrated monthly paper for children and youth*]
New York: Osborn, Nilsson & Co. (January–June 1874)
New York: A. Hult och J. G. Princell (July 1874–August 1875)
Boston: A. Hult och J. G. Princell (September 1875–February 1876)
Boston: A. Hult (March 1876–October 1878)
Chicago: A. Hult och C. O. Lindell (November 1878–June 1879)
Chicago: A. Hult (July 1879–January 1880)
Chicago: C. O. Lindell (February 1880)
Chicago: Engberg–Holmberg Pub. Co. (March 1880–November 1888)
Vol. 1, no. 1–vol. 15, no. 11
January 1874–November 1888
Absorbed by: *Barnens Tidning*
Sometimes referred to as: *Barn vännen* or *Barn–Vännen*

With the thought that a Swedish language paper supplementary to the basic educational materials used in the Sunday church school should be provided for Augustana children, Joseph E. Osborn started *Barnvännen* in New York in January 1874. He was the son of L. P. Esbjörn, the pioneer Augustana Lutheran pastor from Sweden.

This little monthly paper contained stories, brief articles, devotional reading, and poems of interest to children. Contents were of literary quality. Illustrations added interest to the four-page leaflet. Its price was fifty cents per year until the end of 1882 and forty cents thereafter.

Very soon Anders Hult and J. G. Princell entered upon private sponsorship of the venture in July 1874, with publication in New York and then in Boston from September 1875 through October 1878. In 1876, Princell left the paper, with C. O. Lindell taking his place when it moved to

Chicago late in 1878. Finally in March 1880, the Engberg-Holmberg Publishing Company in Chicago took it over to its final issue in November 1888, with C. A. Evald and C. O. Lindell the editors. In 1889 it was absorbed by *Barnens Tidning*. Erickson related the complicated publishing history as noted above (10).

Originally a private venture, *Barnvännen* received official notice from the Augustana Synod in 1876 when it was recommended to all pastors and congregations. The synod was not otherwise issuing an official paper for its Sunday church school children.

The Board of Directors of the Augustana Book Concern (the private stock company) in 1884 offered $2,000 for *Barnvännen* so that the company would sponsor a children's paper. The resolution read that if the offer was rejected, then steps should be taken immediately toward publishing a Sunday church school paper. Anders Hult, long associated with *Barnvännen*, was offered $1,000 a year to take charge of such a new paper, beginning in January 1885. The pending transaction failed, leading to the birth of *Barnens Tidning*, a competitor, in 1886.

Ultimately, in 1889 S. P. A. Lindahl, who started *Barnens Tidning* as a private enterprise in 1886, purchased *Barnvännen* and discontinued it. *Sources:* Arden 1963, 204; Erickson 10; LIBRIS; Olson 1933, 25; WorldCat.

> Evangelical Lutheran Church in America Archives: AUG 25/5/2 Vols. 1–6, [7–15]; 1874–1879, [1880–1888]
> Gustavus Adolphus College Archives: Vols. 1–5; January 1874–December 1878
> Lutheran Theological Seminary at Gettysburg: Vols. 1–3, [4, 7–9], 10–11, [12–15]; 1874–1888
> Minnesota Historical Society: BR6 .B37 Vol. 1, no. 1–vol. 5, no. 12; January 1874–December 1878
> Erickson: Augustana College: Vols. 1–11
> Lutheran School of Theology at Chicago: Vols. 1–15
> Royal Library of Sweden: Vols. 1–15, with few missing numbers
> LIBRIS: Swedish Emigrant Institute: Årg. [1–2]; [1874–1875]

Beacon

> Rock Island, IL: Augustana Book Concern
> 1930–1933

Ander reports that this was a newsletter for the New York Conference. *Source:* Ander 1956, 152.

No holdings reported.

Betania: Luthersk Månadstidning

[*Betania: Lutheran Monthly Newspaper*]
Rock Island, IL: Augustana Book Concern
Vols. 1–9 ?
April 1905–1913

Ander writes that this was "a monthly publication of the LaPorte District of the Illinois Conference of the Augustana Synod." D.A. Lofgren served as editor. *Sources:* Ander 1956, 152; LIBRIS.

Augustana College Swenson Center: Vols. 1–9; 1905–1913
LIBRIS: Swedish Emigrant Institute: Vols. [4–5, 8]; [1908–1909, 1912]

Bethania: Evangelisk Luthersk Uppbyggelsetidning

[*Bethany: Evangelical Lutheran Edification Paper*]
Chicago, IL: Enander & Bohman (1881)
Burlington, IA: J. G. Erlander (1882–February 1884)
Des Moines, IA: [s.n.] (March 1884–December 1885)
Vols. 1–5
January 1881–December 1885

Associated with the Iowa Conference of the Augustana Lutheran Synod, *Bethania* was planned by a group of clergymen who began its publication with the January 1881 issue. That year it was issued weekly from the Enander and Bohman printers in Chicago. In 1882 it moved to Burlington, Iowa, until March 1884 when it moved to Des Moines, Iowa. Late in 1881 the Iowa Conference made it the official newspaper. At times news about church work in Nebraska also appeared in *Bethania*.

This Swedish-language paper was issued semimonthly after the first year, usually in sixteen pages. Subscription price in 1881 was fifty cents per year, in 1882 it was seventy-five cents and after that fifty cents. Olson states that "those [pastors] in Iowa sought to build a tract society around their paper, *Bethania*" (Olson 1933, 40).

Several individuals served as editors, including O. J. Siljeström, N. Forsander, N. E. Dahlstedt, O. Olson, J. E. Erlander, and L. A. Johnston. *Sources:* Bengston 460; Dowie 248; Erickson 11; Lundeen, group 6; Olson 1933, 40; ULS.

University of Iowa: BX8001 .B4 Vols. 1–2; 1881–1882
University of Minnesota–Minneapolis: BX8049 .B48x Vol. 1, nos. 7, 18, 20, 21/22; vol. 2, no. 18; vol. 3, nos. 20–21; vol. 4, nos. 3, 10, 12, 14–15, 23; [1881–1884]

Erickson: Augustana College: Vols. 1–2 (ULS: Vols. 1–[5])
   Gustavus Adolphus College: Vols. 1–2
   Lutheran School of Theology at Chicago: Vol. 1
   Royal Library of Sweden: Vols. 1–5
Lundeen: Evangelical Lutheran Church in America Archives: 1881–1884

Bethania

Lindsborg, KS: Bethany College
May–October 1891

With a brief appearance in 1891, *Bethania* was designed to gather support for the young and struggling Bethany College and to promote the educational mission there. It was sponsored by the Kansas Conference of the Augustana Synod. *Sources:* Lindquist 1953, 168; Lindquist 1975, 248.

No holdings reported.

Bethanian

Lindsborg, KS: Bethany College
1959–
Continues: *The Daisy*

The Bethany College annual changed its name in 1959 from *The Daisy* to the *Bethanian*.
The annual continues to record important events and activities as well as information about campus organizations, students, faculty, and staff, giving a complete picture of that year at Bethany College. It continues to serve as an important source for the history of the college. *Source:* Lindquist 1975, 251.

Bethany College: 1959–

Bethany Academy Catalogue

See *Catalogue of Bethany Academy at Lindsborg, Kansas.*

Bethany Annual

Lindsborg, KS: Bethany College
Vol. 1–vol. ?
1896–?

The first number with this title included a section *The Story of Bethany* by Gustav A. Andreen. Volume I was issued in 1896. *Source:* http://library .bethanylb.edu.

Bethany College: 378.19 A558s

Bethany College Bulletin

Lindsborg, KS: Bethany College
1886–?
Continued by: *Bethany College Catalog*

Published periodically during the early years of Bethany College, this also served as the catalog. It offered a description of the college, degree requirements, course offerings, and registered students for the years covered.

A special "Alumni number" dated October 20, 1911, was numbered volume 5, no. 12. This special issue contains a historical sketch of the college and addresses delivered at the thirtieth anniversary of the college in 1910. *Sources:* http://library.bethanylb.edu/; WorldCat.

Bethany College: 378.1542 B562 ca E Lindq. 1886/1887–1890/1891; October 20, 1911

Bethany College Bulletin/Alumni News

Lindsborg, KS: Bethany College
Vols. 49–60
1954–1965
Continued by: *Bethany College Bulletin/Bethany Magazine*
Source: http://library.bethanylb.edu.

Bethany College: Vols. 49–60; 1954–1965

Bethany College Bulletin/Bethany Magazine

Lindsborg, KS: Bethany College
Vols. 60–78
1965–1983
Continues: *Bethany College Bulletin/Alumni News*
Continued by: *Bethany Magazine*
Source: http://library.bethanylib.edu.

Bethany College: Vols. 60–78; 1965–1983

Bethany College Catalog

Lindsborg, KS: Bethany College
1886/1887–
Continues: *Bethany Academy Catalogue*
Other titles:
Annual Catalogue of Bethany College and Normal Institute
Bethany College Academic Catalog
Bethany College Announcements
Bethany College Annual Catalog
Catalog of Bethany College
Catalogue of Bethany College

As the general catalog of Bethany College, this has, through the years, presented a description of the college; outlined courses of study, degree requirements, and major divisions of the school; listed faculty; and in general portrayed the college to prospective students. *Source:* Lindquist 1975, 289–99.

Augustana College Swenson Center
Bethany College

Bethany College Messenger

Lindsborg, KS: Bethany College
Vol. 84–
1988–
Continues: *Bethany Messenger* (1902)

The student publication took this revised title, *Bethany College Messenger*, in 1988. As the student newspaper, it continues to report campus news and activities. *Source:* http://library.bethanylb.edu.

Bethany College: Vol. 84– ; 1988–

Bethany Daisy

See *Daisy*.

Bethany Magazine

Lindsborg, KS: Bethany College
Vol. 79–
1984–
Continues: *Bethany College Bulletin/Bethany Magazine*

This periodical is issued quarterly on behalf of Bethany College. It is distributed by free subscription to alumni and friends of the college as a means of communicating news of interest to its readers. *Source:* http:// library.bethanylb.edu.

Bethany College: Vols. 79– ; 1984–

Bethany Messenger (1892)

Lindsborg, KS: Bethany College
Vols. 1–5
December 1892–1897
Sometimes referred to as: *Bethany's Messenger*

This first *Bethany Messenger* series was launched by C. A. Swensson in 1892. Its purpose was the promotion of Bethany College, especially to describe the college program and to seek financial support for the young school. Members of the college faculty served as editors. Early issues were published bimonthly but at times only four times a year in English. Later again the paper appeared bimonthly and occasionally monthly, as editorial time allowed.

A special feature at times was the translation of Swedish hymns into English. After 1897, publication was suspended until the student publication of the same title began in 1902. *Sources:* LIBRIS; Lindquist 1975, 248–50; Swan 71.

Bethany College: Vols. 1–5; 1892–1897, Microfilm
LIBRIS: Royal Library of Sweden: 1894–1896

Bethany Mesenger (1902)

Lindsborg, KS: Bethany College
Vols. 6–83
October 1902–1989
Continued by: *Bethany College Messenger*
Sometimes referred to as: *Bethany's Messenger* or *Messenger*

The student publication with the title *Bethany Messenger* appeared in October 1902. The Lyceum Society and the Adelphic Society, both student literary organizations, were responsible for early issues. Some issues were edited by a class.

First a monthly and later a biweekly, the paper was normally a twenty-two-page magazine format. The first editors were Alma Luise Olson, Oscar Freeburg, and Carl O. Olson.

In September 1908, the *Bethany Messenger* became a weekly in newspaper format. Since then, the paper has continued regularly in each academic year by reporting campus news and activities, in providing a place for students to express opinions, and in general promoting the mission of the school. *Sources:* http://library.bethanylib.edu; LIBRIS; Lindquist 1975, 251.

Bethany College: 1908–1909, 1918–1926, 1930–1969, 1974–1989, Paper; Vols. 6–83; 1902–1989, Microfilm
LIBRIS: Royal Library of Sweden: 1908–1909, 1912–1913

Bethany's Budbäraren

[*Bethany's Messenger*]
Lindsborg, KS: Bethany College
Vols. 1–2
January 1895–June 1896
Sometimes referred to as: *Budbäraren*

As the Swedish edition of the *Bethany Messenger*, this was issued on an occasional basis beginning in 1895. It was suspended in 1896 with the June issue. *Source:* Lindquist 1953, 168.

Bethany College: Vols. 1–2; 1895–1896, Microfilm

Bethphage Messenger

Axtell, NE: Bethphage Mission
[Minden, NE: Emal–Strine Printing]
Vol. 28, no. 2–vol. ?
February 1940–
Continues: *Guldax*
Other title: *Mosaic: Opening Doors to Extraordinary Lives*

Continuing the Swedish text publication *Guldax*, the *Bethphage Messenger* appeared in early 1940 with English and Swedish text combined. In 1941, English was used exclusively. From 1981 to 1985, ten issues were published each year.

More recently, beginning in 1986 it has been issued with a quarterly publication schedule. The paper has continued to report news and activities at the Bethphage Mission. *Sources:* http://www.niclc.org/; Matthews 25; WorldCat.

Augustana College Swenson Center: 1958–1983

Gustavus Adolphus College Archives: Vol. 28, no. 4; vol. 29, no. 3; vol. 32, no. 2; vol. 34, nos. 2, 6–8, 10–12; vols.35–36; vol. 37, nos. 1–3, 5–12; vol. 38; vol. 39, nos.1–5, 8–12; vol. 40, nos. 1–4, 6, 8–12; vols. 41–46; vol. 47, nos. 1, 4–12; vols. 48–50; vol. 51, nos. 1–8, 10–11; vols. 52–53; vol. 54, nos. 1–8, 11; vol. 55, nos. 1, 3, 5, 6, 11; vols. 56–68; vol. 69, nos. 1–11; vol. 70, nos. 1–5, 7–12; vol. 71-Winter 1987; [1940–1941, 1944, 1946], 1947–1948, [1949], 1950, [1951–1952], 1953–1958, [1959], 1960–1962, [1963], 1964–1965, [1966–1967], 1970–1980, [1981–1982], 1983–1987

Lutheran Theological Seminary at Gettysburg: Vols. [47–48], 49–51, [52–55], 56– ; 1959–1967, 1968–

Midland Lutheran College: 1954–2004

WorldCat: University of Nebraska

Bethphagebiblioteket

Axtell, NE: Bethphage Inner Mission Association
1915–?

This appears to be a series title intended to include special publications from the Bethphage Inner Mission Association.

Only one title has been identified, *F. N. Swanberg: in Memoriam,* which was issued in 1915. This recognized the Swedish-American clergyman, F. N. Swanberg (1853–1913), who was active in the establishing of Augustana Lutheran congregations in Nebraska. *Sources:* http://jkm.ipac ; LIBRIS.

Lutheran School of Theology at Chicago: BV4253 .S9
LIBRIS: Royal Library of Sweden: Vol. 1

Bible Banner

St. Paul, MN; Minneapolis, MN: Lutheran Bible Institute
Vols. 1–66
1920–1985
Sometimes referred to as: *The Bible Banner*

The Lutheran Bible Institute opened in St. Paul, Minnesota, in the fall of 1919 at the First Lutheran Church. Ten years later it was moved to its Minneapolis campus. In 1920, the official organ of the school began publication as *The Bible Banner* on a monthly schedule. In 1925, it had three thousand paid subscriptions. In 1963 it became a bimonthly publication. The periodical contained news and reports about activities at LBI, Bible studies, and inspirational articles and meditations. It was edited by the faculty.

Frequently referred to as LBI, the Institute was not strictly an Augustana institution. However, it was largely an enterprise of Augustana individuals in its early years and supported by Augustana through the following years.

Arden writes that "the general stance taken by the leadership of the Institute, and enunciated in the columns of the official organ of the school, *The Bible Banner*, has usually been that of fundamentalistic Lutheran orthodoxy" (Arden 1963, 316). He continues: "A strain of fundamentalistic Puritanism is also evident in the social attitudes expressed in *The Bible Banner*" (319). LBI appealed to the conservative and pietistic spirit among young Lutherans.

Over the years, many students came from the Augustana Lutheran Church and a good percentage of faculty members were Augustana men. The governing board was composed of men selected without consideration of synodical affiliation. Readers frequently expressed gratitude for the enrichment of their own spiritual life through the study of scripture inspired by LBI. Publication ceased in 1985. *Sources:* Arden 1963, 316, 319; http://jkm.ipac; Hultgren 2001; Peterson 169; Stephenson 394; ULS; WorldCat.

Evangelical Lutheran Church in America Archives: [1950, 1952, 1953, 1955], 1956, [1957, 1962]

Gustavus Adolphus College: Vol. 31, no. 5; vol. 32, no. 12; vol. 33, nos. 1–12; vol. 34, nos. 1–8, 10–11; vol. 35, nos. 5, 7; vols. 36–38; vol. 39, nos. 1, 3–6; vol. 40, nos. 1, 2, 6; vols. 41–42; vol. 43, nos. 1–5; vols. 44–55; vol. 56, nos. 1–3, 5, 6; vols. 57–65; vol. 66, nos. 1–2; [1955–1959], 1960–1962; [1963–1964], 1965–1966; [1967], 1968–1979; [1980], 1981–1984; [1985]

Luther Seminary: BX8001.B49 Vols. [1–3], 4, [5]; ns, Vols. [1–4], 5–42, [43], 44–60, [61]; 1920–1985

Lutheran School of Theology at Chicago: BS603 .B520 Vols. [14, 39–56], [1938, 1963–1980]

Lutheran Theological Seminary at Gettysburg: Vols. 27–41, [42–43, 59]; 1951–1983

Minnesota Historical Society: BX8001 .B58 Vol. [1]+

North Park University: Vols. 15–29, 31–38

Trinity Lutheran Seminary: 1937–1968, 1984–1985

Wartburg Theological Seminary: 1935–1985

The Bible Study Quarterly

Rock Island, IL: Augustana Book Concern
Vol. 1, no. 1–vol. 9, no. 5
January 1920–December 1928
Continued by: *The Bible Study Quarterly: Teacher's Edition* and *The Bible Study Quarterly: Student's Edition*

Based on the International Uniform Lesson Texts, *The Bible Study Quarterly* was designed to serve the adult Bible classes in the Sunday school. The material was written by Augustana clergy so that laypersons could use the lessons for local adult classes. It was issued every three months.

Beginning in 1929, it was published in separate teacher's and student's editions. *Source:* WorldCat.

Evangelical Lutheran Church in America Archives: AUG 25/5/3 Vols. [1–9]; [1921–1928; only issue no. 4 of each vol.]
Minnesota Historical Society: BS410 .B5 Vols. 1–9; 1920–1928

The Bible Study Quarterly: Student's Edition

Rock Island, IL: Augustana Book Concern
Vols. 10–42
October 1929–1961
Continues in part: *The Bible Study Quarterly*

Continuing in part *The Bible Study Quarterly*, the student's edition was issued separately beginning with volume 10 in 1929. A new study guide appeared every three months. It was designed to be used by students participating in adult Bible classes.

Produced by the Board of Parish Education, in the 1950s it was edited by Daniel Nystrom. Lessons were written by J. W. Kempe, R. S. Nelson, Roland Swanson, and John Breck. *Sources: Augustana Annual* 1954, 72; WorldCat.

Evangelical Lutheran Church in America Archives: AUG/25/5/3 Vols. 10–17, 19–42; 1929–1936, 1938–1961
Gustavus Adolphus College Archives: [1931], 1933, 1936–1938, 1945–1946, 1961
Minnesota Historical Society: BS410 .B52 Vols. 10–42; 1929–1961

The Bible Study Quarterly: Teacher's Edition

Rock Island, IL: Augustana Book Concern
Vols. 10–42

October 1929–1961
Continues in part: *The Bible Study Quarterly*

Continuing in part *The Bible Study Quarterly*, the teacher's edition was issued separately beginning with volume 10 in 1929. A new issue appeared every three months. It was designed, as its predecessor, to be used by laypersons in leading adult Bible classes.

Produced by the Board of Parish Education, in the 1950s it was edited by Daniel Nystrom. Lessons were written by J. W. Kempe, R. S. Nelson, Roland Swanson, and John Breck. *Source: Augustana Annual* 1954, 72; WorldCat.

Evangelical Lutheran Church in America Archives: AUG/25/5/3 Vols. 10–17, 19–42; 1929–1936, 1938–1961
Gustavus Adolphus College Archives: [1932], 1933, 1936–1938, 1946
Minnesota Historical Society: BS410 .B51 Vols. 10–42; 1929–1961

Blommor vid Vägen

[*Roadside Flowers*]
Rock Island, IL: Lutheran Augustana Book Concern
1886–1921

A series published in Swedish for the enjoyment of young children, *Blommor vid Vägen* contained stories written in fairly simple vocabulary for children. The content was "heavily religious" (Blanck 158).

Edited and mainly written by S. P. A. Lindahl, the series began in 1886 (40 pages) as number 1/2. Number 3 appeared in 1887 (64 pages), number 4 in 1893 (63 pages), number 5 in 1894 (64 pages), and number 7 later with 111 pages. These all are identified in LIBRIS.

Naming this as a literary serial, Blanck states that he identified these volumes in the Augustana Book Concern publications list. The series was "published mainly before the turn of the century in total editions between 9,000 and 14,000" (158).

WorldCat indicates the series began in 1900 with Lindahl as the author. Its ending date is shown as 1921. There is no indication who took responsibility for it after Lindahl's death in 1908. *Sources:* Blanck 1997, 158; LIBRIS; WorldCat.

Augustana College Swenson Center: PT9995 .L48 B3 Vols. 1–9
Bethany College: 839.7 L742b Vol. 5
Minnesota Historical Society: PT9995 .L48 B3 Vols. 5–7
University of Minnesota–Minneapolis: PT9990 .B5x Vol. 7

LIBRIS: Royal Library of Sweden: Vols. 1–4
Swedish Emigrant Institute: Vols. 3, 5

The Bond (1924)

Mount Morris, IL: Kable Brothers Co. for the Lutheran Brotherhood
Vol. 1–vol. 29, no. 2
May 1924–June 1952
Continued by: *The Lutheran Brotherhood Bond*
Sometimes referred to as: *Bond* (Mount Morris, IL)

Published in the interests of insurance policy holders with the
Lutheran Brotherhood insurance firm, *The Bond* enhanced its title in
1952 to include the firm's name. It was considered the official publication of the Lutheran Brotherhood. *Sources:* http://mnhs.mnpals.net/F/;
LIBRIS; ULS.

Lutheran Theological Seminary at Gettysburg: Vols. 7–20, [21–22],
    23–26, [27], 28; 1930–1952
Minnesota Historical Society: BX8001 .B6 Vols. 6–29; 1930–1952
Wartburg Theological Seminary: Vols. 7–29; 1930–1952
ULS: University of Illinois: Vol. [14] +
LIBRIS: Royal Library of Sweden: Vols. 12–22; 29; 1935–1946, 1952

Breidablick: Jubilee Annual

St. Peter, MN: Gustavus Adolphus College
1912
Continues: *Valkyria* (1909)
Continued by: *The Gustavian* (1917–)

In commemoration of the fiftieth anniversary of Gustavus Adolphus
College, the senior class of 1912 published a jubilee annual *Breidablick*.
The title was taken from Norse mythology. The majority of the text
was in English, with some Swedish articles. *Sources:* Lund 1987, 30;
WorldCat.

Gustavus Adolphus College: LD2091.G62G65 1912
Minnesota Historical Society: LD2091 .G6 G8799 1912

Brotherhood News Bulletin

See *News Bulletin*.

Budbäraren

See *Bethany's Budbäraren.*

Bulletin/Lutheran Bible Institute

Minneapolis, MN: Lutheran Bible Institute
Vol. 1–?
June 1955–?
Continues: *L.B.I. Bulletin*
Other title: *Let's Be Intercessors*

Published quarterly by the Lutheran Bible Institute, this bulletin presented news and feature articles. *Source:* http://mnhs.mnpals.net.

Minnesota Historical Society: BS603.L9

– C –

Calendar

Rock Island, IL: Kvinnornas Hem- och Hedna-Missionsförening Augustana-Synoden; Augustana Evangelical Lutheran Church Women's Missionary Society
1894–1927
1894, 1910, 1913, 1915
1917: *Calendar* 5, 1892–1917; Also referred to as *Silfver Jubileums Minneskrift: Kalendar*
1919: *Calendar* 6, 1918–1919
1922: *Calendar* 7, 1919–1922
1924: *Calendar* 8, 1923–1924
1927: *Calendar* 9, 1892–1927

The Evangelical Lutheran Church in America Archives provides the following description of *Calendar*:

Calendar was the Women's Missionary Society/Augustana Lutheran Church Women's (WMS/ALCW) earliest publication. The first issue appeared in 1894. It was published eight more times: 1910, 1913, 1915, 1917, 1919, 1922, 1924, and 1927. *Calendar*'s primary purpose was to provide specific information pertaining to the work of the Women's Missionary Society for a particular time period. Items contained in the publication include yearly reports from WMS President Emmy Evald, conference reports, statistical reports, reports pertaining to foreign and home mission work, conference listings of life members and annual members, and a list of people memorialized through the In Memoriam program. Later issues include listings of synodical and conference officers, treasurer's reports, reports from WMS Departments of Work, and listings of Augustana missionaries and the locations where they were serving." (WorldCat)

The first four issues are in Swedish. Beginning with *Calendar 7*, some reports are in English. *Source:* WorldCat.

Augustana College Swenson Center: BX8049 .E93 1917
Evangelical Lutheran Church in America Archives: AUG 40/8/3/1

Calendar/Minnesota College

Minneapolis, MN: Minnesota College
1913–1930 ?
Continues: *College Calendar/Minnesota College*

With a slight title change, this item continued to publish information for students and prospective students at Minnesota College. *Source:* WorldCat.

Minnesota Historical Society: LD7514.M55C64; Spring 1913

Canada

Winnipeg, Manitoba, Canada: [s.n.]
Vol. 3, no. 45–vol. 15 ?
November 16, 1895–June 12, 1907
Continues: *Väktaren*
Became: *Svenska Canada Tidningen*
Sometimes referred to as: *Canada* (Winnipeg, Manitoba)

In August of 1895, K. Fleming, who had been a partner with Svante Udden in the publication of *Väktaren*, purchased the paper, thus becoming the sole owner. For a brief time it had the title *Canada Väktaren*. However, in the winter of 1896 Fleming sold the paper to J. E. Forslund. Even by this time the weekly title had been changed to *Canada*. Fleming became editor and partner again, when he resumed partial ownership of the paper in 1905. Finally in 1906, Fleming sold the paper to the Canada Weekly Publishing Company when P. M. Dahl became the leader. The new owners adopted a new title *Svenska Canada Tidningen*.

Gradually, following the departure of Udden and as the paper changed ownership, it became more secular in content. Baglo claims that by 1906 "it actually had become antagonistic to the Church" (Baglo 1962, 35). *Sources:* Backlund 74; Baglo 1962, 35; LIBRIS; Setterdahl 34.

Augustana College Swenson Center: November 16, 1895–December 23, 1896
Evangelical Lutheran Church in Canada Archives: July, 1896
LIBRIS: Royal Library of Sweden: January 1902–June 1907; October 25, 1905–June 12, 1907: Microfilm

Canada Härold

[*Canada Herald*]
Calgary, Alberta, Canada: [s.n.]
Winnipeg, Manitoba, Canada: [s.n.]
Vol. 1, no. 1–vol. ?
April 1, 1914–1917

Augustana clergy in Canada were concerned that Svante Udden's early paper *Väktaren* had evolved through several business transactions into a political paper, *Svenska Canada-Tidningen*.

L. P. Bergstrom reported to the 1910 Minnesota Conference convention the need for a church publication specifically of interest to members in Canada. He made the same plea in 1911 and also in 1912. In 1913, he reported that he had contracted with *Svenska Canada-Tidningen* for a page of church news. A committee of pastors had even offered to purchase the paper, to no avail as the owners were not willing to sell.

Pressing ahead on the issue, in 1914 V. J. Tengwald from Calgary was named head of the publication committee of the newly organized Canada Conference. Immediately, the committee began planning a journal like the old *Augustana* to be named *Canada Härold*. P. Nelson of Winnipeg was the manager. A printer at Wetaskiwin, Alberta, received the contract. Advertising space was sold.

The first issue of April 1, 1914, received general approval. A tabloid-size newspaper, it grew to sixteen pages. As the paper was gaining in subscribers, advertising declined, with a deficit in 1915. Rising cost of production, censorship, and recession were problems for the young paper. Tengwald persevered to continue the paper. Format was increased to full newspaper size. Pages had been reduced from sixteen to six but were now increased to eight. Secular news was added as an appeal to more subscribers. The paper was issued twice monthly. There were five hundred new subscribers in 1915–1916. In 1916, the Canada Conference established a publishing board. However, in 1917 the *Canada Härold* ended publication due to lack of financial support.

The Canada Conference then arranged a plan to revive the newspaper with the establishment of a joint stock company. Shares were offered and congregations would receive stock for their earlier investment. However, the plan failed. Then the committee again tried to purchase *Svenska Canada-Tidningen*, but again to no avail. *Sources:* Baglo 1962, 36; Setterdahl 34.

Augustana College Swenson Center: April 1914–April 15, 1916, Microfilm
Evangelical Lutheran Church in Canada Archives: 1914–1915

Canada News

[s.l.]: Canada News Company
December 18, 1919–September 1920?
Sometimes referred to as: *Canada Times*

Following the demise of *Canada Härold* in 1917, the executive committee of the Canada Conference continued its efforts to provide a newspaper for the Swedish Lutheran population. J. E. Lindberg of Kenora accepted the appointment to work on the matter for three months for a salary of $125 plus travel expenses. Thus was born *Canada News* on December 18, 1919. Lindberg was named the editor.

All appeared to be working well. However, already in September 1920 there was trouble due to faulty business transactions. The Canada Conference claimed the publishing firm owed the Conference in excess of a thousand dollars. This financial situation led to disillusioned investors and a quick end for the paper. It was the last publication attempt of the Canada Conference for more than thirty years. *Source:* Baglo 1962, 36.

No holdings reported.

Canada Times

See *Canada News*.

Canada Väktaren

See *Canada* and *Väktaren*.

Canadian Crusader

[Saskatoon, Saskatchewan]: Evangelical Lutheran Church of Canada
Vols. 1–14
1946?–1960
Sources: http://ruth.luthersem.edu; WorldCat.

Archives of Evangelical Lutheran Church in Canada: 1956–1957
Luther Seminary: BX8001.C3 Vols. [6]–14; [1952]–1960

Catalog of Upsala College

See *Upsala College Catalog*.

Catalogue

See *Augustana College Catalog*.

Catalogue of Bethany Academy at Lindsborg, Kansas

Lindsborg, KS: Bethany Academy; News Book and Job Printing House
1882/1883–1884/1885
Continued by: *Bethany College Catalog*
Sometimes referred to as: *Bethany Academy Catalogue*

As the annual catalog of Bethany Academy, this presented a description
of the academy, courses of study offered, and a list of the registered students and officers. This catalog was published for three academic years
under the *Catalogue of Bethany Academy at Lindsborg, Kansas* title. It was always in the English language.

Bethany Academy became Bethany College in 1886. In the immediately
following years, the annual catalog was issued under varying titles and
by various publishers. *Source:* WorldCat.

Bethany College: 1882/1883, 1883/1884, 1884/1885

Catalogue of Gustavus Adolphus College

St. Peter, MN: Gustavus Adolphus College
1877/1878–1986
Continued by: *Gustavus Adolphus College Academic Catalog*
Sometimes referred to as: *Gustavus Adolphus College Catalog*

The first annual *Catalogue of Gustavus Adolphus College* was issued in
1878 at the initiative of the 1877–1878 college faculty. It was printed at the
Tribune Office in St. Peter.

Publication has continued on an annual schedule with slight variations
in the title. Through the years, it has presented a description of the college,
outlined courses of study and major divisions of the school, listed faculty,
and in general portrayed the college to prospective students. *Sources:* http://
mnpals.gustavus.edu; LIBRIS; Lund 1987, 23; Peterson 36.

Gustavus Adolphus College: LD2091.G62 G63
LIBRIS: Royal Library of Sweden: 1877/78, 1884/85, 1888/89, 1890/91

Catalogue of Hope Academy, Moorhead, Minnesota

Moorhead, MN: Hope Academy
1888/1889–1894/1895?

Published to promote the high school for Lutheran youth established as Hope Academy, the catalog provided basic information about the program and mission of the school. It was issued in English. *Sources:* http:// www.mnpals.net/F/; WorldCat.

Minnesota Historical Society: 1888/1889–1890/1891, 1893/1894–1894 /1895

Challenger

Rock Island, IL: Augustana Book Concern
1935–?

Ander writes that "this was a publication of the Iowa Conference Luther League of the Augustana Synod and the monthly periodical was undoubtedly published in Rock Island." *Source:* Ander 1956, 154.

Evangelical Lutheran Church in America Archives Region 5, IA: July– August 1943

Children's Friend

Chicago, IL: Engberg–Holmberg Pub. Co.
Vols. 1–3
January 1886–November 1888

A children's paper published monthly in English, the *Children's Friend* was issued as a rival of the *Olive Leaf*, which was published at that time by the Augustana Book Concern, the private stock company. The Chicago firm issued a Swedish children's paper, *Barnvännen*, at the same time as the *Children's Friend. Sources:* Lundeen, group 7; Olson 1933, 35; Söderström 19.

Lundeen: Evangelical Lutheran Church in America Archives: Vols. [1–3]; [1886–1888]

Christian Messenger

Lindsborg, KS: [s.n.]
1912–1914
Continues: *Kansas Young Lutheran*

This paper was published monthly by the Kansas Conference Luther League of the Augustana Lutheran Synod as a continuation of the *Kansas Young Lutheran*. *Source:* Ander 1956, 154.

Augustana College Swenson Center: January 1912–October 1914

Church Paper for the Cleveland District

Rock Island, IL: Augustana Book Concern
1930–1934
Continues: *Kyrkotidning för Cleveland-Distriktet*

This was a monthly paper for the Lutheran churches of the Augustana Synod in the Cleveland District of the New York Conference. In addition to the areas of Cleveland, Ashtabula, Erie, Youngstown, and Akron included in its predecessor, it added the area of New Castle. The paper continued to report district news items and also print inspirational articles. *Sources:* Ander 1956, 154; Erickson 57.

Evangelical Lutheran Church in America Archives: [1930–1934]

Church School Teacher

Rock Island, IL: Augustana Book Concern; Columbus, OH: Wartburg Press
Vol. 1, no. 1–vol. 28, no. 6
1932–June 1959
Superseded in part by: *Lutheran Teacher* and *Resource*
Sometimes referred to as: *The Church School Teacher*

As a periodical for teachers and officers of the Sunday school, the *Church School Teacher* was published monthly beginning in 1932 except in July and August of each year. The paper was issued jointly by the Board of Parish Education (earlier named the Board of Christian Education and Literature) of the Augustana Evangelical Lutheran Church and the Board of Parish Education of the American Lutheran Church. Helps for teachers included Bible background materials, articles on the Catechism, facts of church history, and worship suggestions. In the 1950s, Lael Westberg served as editor. The final issue was dated June 1959.

After the June 1958 issue, the American Lutheran Church joined the Evangelical Lutheran Church in the joint publication of the *Lutheran Teacher*. It then no longer participated in the *Church School Teacher* project. *Sources: Augustana Annual* 1954, 72; LIBRIS; WorldCat.

Augustana College Swenson Center: 1932–1959
Evangelical Lutheran Church in America Archives: AUG 25/5/4 Vols. 1–24, [25], 26–27, [28]; 1932–1955, [1956], 1957–1958, [1959]
Gustavus Adolphus College Archives: Vols. [1]–[3–5, 7–8, 10], 12–28; [1932], 1933, [1934–1936, 1938–1939, 1941], 1943–1959
Lutheran School of Theology at Chicago: BV1460 .C5 Vols. 1–28; 1932–1959
Pacific Lutheran Theological Seminary: Vols. [12–16], 17, [18], 19, [20–22], 23–27, [28]; [1943–1947], 1948, [1949], 1950, [1951–1953], 1954–1958, [1959]
Texas Lutheran University: Vols. [13–27]; [1944–June 1958]
Wartburg Theological Seminary: 1932–June 1959
LIBRIS: Lund University: Vols. 1–28; 1932–1959

City Missionary

Chicago, IL: [s.n.]
1925–1955?
Continues: *Stadsmissionären*

Ander states that this publication was the "official organ of the Chicago Lutheran Inner Mission Society" (Ander 1956, 154). Its predecessor was the Swedish *Stadsmissionären*. *Sources:* Ander 1956, 154; Lundeen, group 6.

Lundeen: Evangelical Lutheran Church in America Archives: [1925–1955]

Class Annual

Rock Island, IL: Augustana College
1900
Continued by: *The Garnet and Silver-Gray*

This first college annual issued by Augustana College was published by the Senior class in 1900. Editors were A. L. Hallquist, C. G. Carlton, and W. E. Cederberg. *Source:* http://library.ilcso.illinois.edu/aug.

Augustana College LD271.A6655 R597 1900

College Breezes

St. Peter, MN: Gustavus Adolphus College
Vol. 11, no. 1–vol. 25, no. 8
October 1905–May 1920
Continues: *Gustavus Journal*
Continued by: *Gustavian Weekly*

Published as the monthly student newspaper during the academic year from September through May, *College Breezes* was the new title of the *Gustavus Journal* as of 1905. However, both Peterson and Söderström indicate that the title *College Breezes* was used as of 1902. If so, the volume numbering was not continued until 1905, and then volume 11 was repeated from 1901. According to the Gustavus Adolphus College catalog, apparently there was no student paper during the intervening years from 1901 to 1905.

In the autumn of 1919, a college forum was organized to serve as a general literary society, a socializing opportunity, and a means of expressing student opinion. From this effort, in 1920 the *College Breezes* became the *Gustavian Weekly*. Peterson writes that the "change necessarily meant a loss of literary quality but a gain in news value" (Peterson 88). *Sources:* Peterson 58, 88; Söderström 32; WorldCat.

Gustavus Adolphus College: Vol. 11, no. 1–vol. 25, no. 8; 1905–1920, Paper and Microfilm

College Calendar/Minnesota College

Minneapolis, MN: Minnesota College
1904/1905?–1912
Continued by: *Calendar*

This item was issued for the use of students and prospective students at Minnesota College, the academy that opened on October 4, 1904, in Minneapolis. *Source:* WorldCat.

Minnesota Historical Society: LD7514.M55 C64; Fall 1912

Columbia

LaConner, WA: N. J. W. Nelson (July 1900–April 1901)
Rock Island, IL: Augustana Book Concern (for Sv. Ev. Luth. Church, Moscow, ID: May 1901–December 1908)
Vol. 1, no. 1–vol. 9, no. 12
July 1900–December 1908

This paper for the Columbia Conference of the Augustana Lutheran Synod was a project initiated by N. J. W. Nelson. It was intended as a means to provide information to and to link the Columbia Conference congregations. Originating in LaConner, Washington, the paper moved with its editor to Moscow, Idaho, in 1901. In 1902, at its annual meeting, the Columbia Conference designated *Columbia* as the official Conference organ. In 1905, Gustaf Bergman was elected the chief editor. Responsibility for the paper came back to Nelson in 1906. He continued to edit the paper through its final issue in December 1908.

For the most part, the paper was issued monthly, but at times only quarterly. In large format, it consisted of twelve to twenty pages, increasing to twenty-eight to thirty-four pages in 1908. Starting at twenty-five cents per year, the subscription price increased to seventy-five cents in 1908. In addition to conference news items, it also included religious and inspirational articles and poetry. *Sources:* Bengston 472; Erickson 17.

Augustana College: March 1903
Erickson: Gustavus Adolphus College: Vols. 1–9; 1900–1908
    Royal Library of Sweden: Vol. 1, no. 2–vol. 8, no. 12; August 1900–December 1907

Columbia Lutheran

Tacoma, WA: E. C. Bloomquist
Vol. 19, no. 2–vol. 27?
February 1927–1935
Merged with: *Pacific Lutheran Herold* to form *Western Lutheran*
Continues: *Sions-Bladet*

The new paper *Columbia Lutheran* was designated as the official organ of the Columbia Conference of the Lutheran Augustana Synod when it began publication in February 1927. It continued to carry the designation as a paper for the Swedish Lutheran people in the Pacific Northwest. Text was in both English and Swedish.

When the *Western Lutheran* began publication in 1937, the *Columbia Lutheran* was one of the titles included in this new merger. *Sources:* http://catalog.lib.washington.edu; WorldCat.

University of Washington: [February 1927–May 1933], Microfilm A7062

Companion

See *Lutheran Companion* and *Young Lutheran's Companion*.

Conference Messenger: Spokesman for
Illinois Conference Missions and Welfare Work

Chicago, IL: [s.n.]
Vols. 1–15
1932/1933–1947
Sometimes referred to as: *The Conference Messenger*
Source: LIBRIS.

LIBRIS: Royal Library of Sweden: Vols. 1–15; 1932/33–1947
No United States holdings reported.

– D –

Daisy

Lindsborg, KS: Bethany College
1908–1958
Continued by: *Bethanian*
Sometimes referred to as: *Bethany Daisy* or *The Daisy*

In 1908, the first edition of the Bethany College annual, *The Daisy*, appeared. The "Jolly Juniors" accepted responsibility for launching the series, with George Anderson the first editor. Since then it has been published regularly, with only a few exceptions, through the years.
In 1959, the name was changed to the *Bethanian*. Most likely the *Daisy* took its name from the lovely flowers that so abundantly flourished in the park adjacent to the campus.
Through the years the *Daisy* recorded important events and activities as well as information about campus organizations, students, faculty, and staff. It is an important source for the history of the college. *Source:* Lindquist 1975, 251.

Augustana College Swenson Center: scattered issues
Bethany College: 1908–1958

Deaconess Banner

Omaha, NE: Immanuel Deaconess Institute
Vol. 4–vol. 44, no. 2
1924–April 1965
Continues: *Diakoniss-Baneret*
Continued by: *The Immanuel Banner*

This publication of the Immanuel Deaconess Institute is the English text of the bulletin designed to promote the interests of the institute and its ministry of mercy. News of events and activities at each division of the institute was included. It was issued bimonthly when possible, but more often on an irregular basis. Among editors were Emil G. Chinlund and F. A. Linder. In 1965, the *Deaconess Banner* took the title *The Immanuel Banner*. *Sources:* Ander 1956, 155; LIBRIS; Matthews 75; WorldCat.

Augustana College Swenson Center: Vols. 6, 17; 1926, 1937
Gustavus Adolphus College Archives: 1929–1958 scattered issues
Luther Seminary: BV4424 .L9085 Vols. [27, 29–30]; [1947–1951]
Lutheran Theological Seminary at Gettysburg: Vols. [5, 20, 27], 28–30, [31, 39], 40, [41], 42–43, [44]; 1926–1965
Pacific Lutheran Theological Seminary: Vols. [42–43]; [1963–1964]
Trinity Lutheran Seminary: 1948–1952
University of Minnesota–Minneapolis: BV4424 .L8 D43x Vol. 4, nos. 2–3; vol. 5, nos. 1–3 [1924–1925]
LIBRIS: Royal Library of Sweden: Årg. 6–30; 1926/27–1951

Diakoniss-Baneret

[*Deaconess Banner*]
Omaha, NE: Immanuel Deaconess Institute
Vols. 1–3
1921–1924
Continues: *Dorkas*
Continued by: *Deaconess Banner*

This publication of the Immanuel Deaconess Institute was designed to promote the interests of the institute and its ministry of mercy. Text was in Swedish.

In 1924, it changed to English text and the English title *Deaconess Banner. Sources:* Ander 1956, 155; Voigt 23.

No holdings reported.

Dorkas: en hälsning från Diakonissanstalten i Omaha; Dorkas: en julhälsning från Diakonissanstalten i Omaha

[*Dorkas: A Greeting from the Deaconess Institute in Omaha*]
[*Dorkas: A Christmas Greeting from the Deaconess Institute in Omaha*]
Rock Island, IL: Lutheran Augustana Book Concern
Omaha, NE: Diakonissföreningens Forlag; Immanuel Hospital and Deaconess Institute

Vols. 1–7

1893–1919

1893 title: *Kalender för qvinlig diakoni och barmhertighetsverksamhet* [Calendar for Female Diaconate and Works of Mercy]

Continued by: *Diakoniss-Baneret*

Intended as an annual publication for the benefit of the Diakonissanstalten or Immanuel Deaconess Institute in Omaha, Nebraska, *Dorkas* appears to have existed from 1893 to 1919. However, it also appears that it was published intermittently and not regularly each year. Volume 5 consisting of 108 pages is dated 1914 and volume 7 is dated 1919, for example. Both English and Swedish texts were used.

The 1893 title was *Kalender för qvinlig diakoni och barmhertighetsverksamhet*. It was written by E. A. Fogelström, the energetic and faithful founder of the Immanuel Deaconess Institute and an Augustana Lutheran pastor in Omaha.

The next issue appeared in 1910 with the *"en julhälsning . . ."* subtitle, which was used through the 1919 publication. Those volumes were published in Omaha, Nebraska, by the Immanuel Hospital and Deaconess Institute. It was not published between 1893 and 1910.

The purpose of *Dorkas* was to promote the institute's ministry of mercy on behalf of orphaned children, the sick, infirm, and aged and to promote the female diaconate. *Sources:* http://tomos.oit.umn.edu; LIBRIS; Lundeen, group 9; WorldCat.

Augustana College Swenson Center: BX8009 .D67 J84 Vols. 2–7; 1910–1919

Bethany College: 361.75 D699 E Lindq. 479 1914

Harvard University Divinity School: BV4424 .L8 D6 Nos. 1–5, 7; 1893–1914, 1919

University of Minnesota–Minneapolis: BV4424 .L8 D67x 1893, 1910–1912, 1914–1919

Lundeen: Evangelical Lutheran Church in America Archives: 1893, 1910–1919

LIBRIS: Royal Library of Sweden: Vols. 1–7; 1893–1919

Swedish Emigrant Institute: Vols. 1–3, 5, 7; 1893, 1910–1911, 1914, 1919

A Drop of Ink

Rock Island, IL: Augustana Book Concern

Spring 1952–?

Lundeen reports that this was the house organ of the Augustana Book Concern.

Source: Lundeen, group 9.

Lundeen: Evangelical Lutheran Church in America Archives: Spring 1952–Summer 1957 with scattered issues thereafter

– E –

Ebenezer

San Francisco, CA: [s.n.]
Vol. 1, nos. 1–2
October, November 1886
Continued by: *Vestkusten*

As a local Augustana Lutheran parish paper, *Ebenezer* existed for only two monthly issues in late 1886. At the beginning of 1887 its name was changed to *Vestkusten* and enlarged considerably. *Sources:* Ander 1956, 185; Setterdahl 6.

Augustana College Swenson Center: Vol. 1, nos. 1–2; October–November 1886, Microfilm

Ev. Luth. Barntidning

See *Evangelisk Luthersk Barntidning*.

Ev. Luthersk Tidskrift

[*Evangelical Lutheran Periodical*]
Red Wing, MN: De Remee & Romo; A. C. F. De Remee
Vol. 1, no. 1–vol. 1, no. 20
December 1877–December 1878
Continued by: *Skaffaren* (Red Wing, MN: 1878)
Sometimes referred to as: *Evangelisk Luthersk Tidskrift* or *Tidskrift*

In December of 1877, Eric Norelius, together with P. E. Sjöblom, started a Swedish-language newspaper in Red Wing, Minnesota, which they named *Ev. Luthersk Tidskrift*. Sometimes this paper is referred to as *Evangelisk Luthersk Tidskrift* or simply *Tidskrift*.

The paper was issued twice each month, with a few exceptions. It included sixteen pages, each in one column (15 cm. × 23 cm.). The annual subscription price was one dollar.

As an effort to inform readers of Minnesota Conference news, it was an early contact with Augustana Synod clergy and members. Devotional articles and sermonlike material were included.

A supplement after number 20 written by Norelius, with the title "Pastor J. Auslunds lefwerne och werksamhet: korteligen tecknade," was issued in the fall of 1878 as a free bonus, the equivalent of two issues (numbers 21–22), to subscribers. Jonas Auslund (1843–1878) was an Augustana Synod pastor in Illinois and Minnesota.

With the December 1878 issue it became *Skaffaren*, a large format newspaper also edited and published by Norelius in Red Wing, Minnesota. *Sources:* Erickson 25; http://jkm.ipac; http://library.ilcso.illinois.edu/aug; *Minnesskrift* 459; WorldCat.

Augustana College Swenson Center: BX8001 .E9 1877–1878 and BX8080 .A9 N6; Nos. 21–22; 1878

Evangelical Lutheran Church in America Archives: Vol. 1; 1877–1878

Gustavus Adolphus College Archives: Vol. 1, nos. 1–20, 22; December 1877–December 1878, Paper and Microfilm

Harvard University Divinity School: Vol. 1, nos. 1–20; December 1877–December 1878, Microfilm

Luther College (Iowa): BX8001 .E93 Vol. 1; 1877–1878

Lutheran School of Theology at Chicago: BX8001 .L95 Vol. 1, nos. 1–20; 1877–1878

Midland Lutheran College: Vol. 1, nos. 1–20; December 1877–December 1878

Minnesota Historical Society: December 1877–December 1878, Microfilm

Erickson: Royal Library of Sweden

Evang. Luth. Barntidning

See *Evangelisk Luthersk Barntidning*.

Evangelisk Luthersk Barntidning

[*Evangelical Lutheran Children's Paper*]
Chicago, IL: [s.n.]
January 1880?
Sometimes referred to as: *Ev. Luth. Barntidning* or *Evang. Luth. Barntidning*

In January of 1880, C. O. Lindell started a small newspaper for children. It was published in Chicago, Illinois, to be issued monthly. This was at the same time as his association with the children's paper *Barnvännen*.

Apparently, no file of the paper exists in the United States. It is uncertain how long the paper was issued. Sources indicate only the year

1880; it may have been only the January issue that was printed. *Sources:* Ander 1956, 156; LIBRIS; *Minnesskrift* 460.

LIBRIS: Royal Library of Sweden: 1880:1
No United States holdings reported.

Evangelisk Luthersk Tidskrift

See *Ev. Luthersk Tidskrift* and *Evangelisk Luthersk Tidskrift för Kyrkan Skolan och Hemmet: var den Enda Svenska Tidning i New England.*

Evangelisk Luthersk Tidskrift för Kyrkan Skolan och Hemmet: var den Enda Svenska Tidning i New England

[*Evangelical Lutheran Paper for Church, School and Home: the only Swedish Paper in New England*]
Boston, MA: J. A. Dahleen
Vol. 1, nos. 1–?
June 25, 1875–November 19, 1875
Continued by: *Fridens Härold*
Sometimes referred to as: *Evangelisk Luthersk Tidskrift*

For several months in 1875, J. A. Dahleen edited and published this weekly four-page paper in Boston. By the August 13, 1875, issue it increased to eight pages. After the November 19, 1875, issue it moved to Brooklyn with a new name *Fridens Härold.*

Announcements of Lutheran church news and church services in Boston, Brooklyn, and several other cities in the Northeast were included, along with brief news items from Sweden and America, short religious articles, and some instructional material. *Sources:* Erickson 35; LIBRIS.

LIBRIS: Royal Library of Sweden: 1875
No United States holdings reported.

Excelsior

St. Peter, MN: Gustavus Adolphus College: Irenian Society/Association
1883–?

In 1883, the Irenian Society was organized as a literary society for women, since they were excluded from other campus literary societies. The group issued a manuscript paper on a semimonthly basis for a subscription price of fifty cents a year. The newspaper was handwritten in English and Swedish. The usual procedure was that it be read aloud at weekly meetings. It included essays, news, and various notices. *Source:* Lund 1987, 17.

Gustavus Adolphus College

– F –

Folkvännen

[*People's Friend*]
Moorhead, MN; Fargo, ND: Folkvännen Pub. Co.
Vol. 1, no. 1–vol. ?
September 1891–December 1892
Other title: *People's Friend*

Published in the interest of promoting Hope Academy, this monthly newspaper in the Swedish language existed for only two years—1891 and 1892. *Sources:* Ander 1956, 158; Setterdahl 20; WorldCat.

Augustana College Swenson Center: 1891–1892, Microfilm
Minnesota Historical Society: Vol. 1, nos. 1–4; September 1891–December 1891, Microfilm
University of North Dakota: Vol. 1, nos. 1, 3–[4]; September, November–[December] 1891, Microfilm AN2 .F64
WorldCat: Library of Michigan: 1891–1892

Förgät-Mig-Ej: Fosterländsk och Luthersk
Ungdomskalender för Jubelåret 1893 (1892)

[*Forget–Me–Not: Patriotic and Lutheran Youth Calendar for Jubilee Year 1893*]
Chicago, IL: [Alfred Lindell & Co.]
1892
Other title: *Jubelkalendar 1893*

This Christian annual for the jubilee year 1893, was published by C. A. Swensson in collaboration with other contributors. A substantial volume of 282 pages with illustrations and portraits, it advocated Swedish nationalism in America. *Sources:* Larsson and Tedenmyr 40; LIBRIS; Swan 58.

Augustana College: BV4515 .S99
Augustana College Swenson Center: BV4515 .S99
Bethany College: 839.7 F721 E Lindq. 618
Minnesota Historical Society: AY19 .F6
University of Minnesota–Minneapolis: BV4535 .F67x 1892; 839.5 F684
   1892
Yale University: MiL60 Au4 Sw43
LIBRIS: Swedish Emigrant Institute

Förgät-Mig-Ej: Årskalender (1902)

[*Forget-Me-Not: Annual Calendar*]
Lindsborg, KS: Bethany College; Rock Island, IL: Lutheran Augustana
   Book Concern
1902
Other title: *Forget Me Not: the Annual of Bethany College, Lindsborg,
   Kansas, 1902.* Salina, KS: Central Kansas Pub. Co.

In 1902, Carl A. Swensson was a major contributor to this volume dealing largely with Christian education and Bethany College.

This illustrated volume of 174 pages was in Swedish. A companion volume, *Forget-Me-Not*, was published at the same time in English in an edition of 159 pages. The book also contains the program of the twentieth anniversary of Bethany College.

It appears that even though this may have been intended as an annual
publication, only the 1902 volume was published. *Sources:* http://tomos
.oit.umn.edu; LIBRIS; Lindquist 1975, 37.

Augustana College Swenson Center: LD433 .F6 S9 1902
Bethany College: 371.8976 B562f E Lindq.
University of Minnesota–Minneapolis: L426 .F67x 1902
LIBRIS: Royal Library of Sweden
   Swedish Emigrant Institute

Förgät-Mig-Ej: Kristlig, Osekterisk Månadstidning,
den Svensk-Amerikanska Ungdomen och Familjen Tillegnad

[*Forget–Me–Not: Christian Monthly Paper, the Swedish-American Youth and
   Family*]
Minneapolis, MN: Carl G. Bohmansson
Vol. 1, no. 1–vol. 2, no. 3
March 1897–May 1898?

Beginning in 1897, a group in Minneapolis published this monthly paper dedicated to Swedish American youth and family. Carl Bohmansson was the leader. He was assisted by Leonard Strömberg, L. A. Sahlstrom, Signe Ankarfelt, and Eric Sandell.

Contents of the magazine were divided into several departments such as "Woman's," "Children's," "Temperance," "Everybody's," and "Literary." The magazine included stories, poetry, and inspirational pieces. The magazine also carried Swedish lyrics and articles from Swedish papers. The sixteen-page magazine was entirely in Swedish. Its subscription price was one dollar per year. Advertisements were printed in order to help supplement cost of the venture.

Bohmansson's dream of publishing a quality family magazine ended quickly. Having sacrificed his savings and after devoting so much time and talent to the venture, he became ill and died in July 1898. Thus ended this short-lived magazine, not directly related to the Augustana Synod but certainly of interest to its members. Swan suggests, however, that possibly three additional numbers were issued. *Sources:* Erickson 29; Swan 76–77; WorldCat.

Minnesota Historical Society: AP49 .F72 Vol. 1, no. 1–vol. 2, nos. 12, 14; March 1897–February, April 1898
WorldCat: University of Minnesota–Minneapolis

Forget-Me-Not

See *Förgät-Mig-Ej* (1902).

Församlingsvännen: Evangelisk–Luthersk Illustrerad Tidning för Pittsburgh-Distriktet

[*Congregation Friends: Evangelical Lutheran Illustrated Paper for Pittsburgh District*]
Duquesne, PA: [s.n.] (May 1905–September 1906)
Erie, PA: [s.n.] (October 1906–?)
Rock Island, IL: Augustana Book Concern
Vol. 1, no. 1–vol. 11?
May 1905–1916

This monthly magazine was issued for the Swedish Evangelical Lutheran congregations in Braddock, Duquesne, Greensburg, Irwin, McKeesport, Monessen, Munhall-Homestead, Pittsburgh, Wilson, and Windber, Pennsylvania. All were in the Pittsburgh District of the New York Conference of the Augustana Lutheran Synod.

The publication contained news and inspirational articles in editions of twenty to thirty-two pages. N. Ebb was the first editor, followed by O. Chillen until early 1912, when a committee edited the magazine. *Sources:* Erickson 31; Lundeen, group 6; Söderström 48.

Augustana College Swenson Center: 1905–1908
Erickson: Gustavus Adolphus College: Vols. 1–3; 1905–1908
   Royal Library of Sweden: 1905–1912
Lundeen: Evangelical Lutheran Church in America Archives: [1906–1916]

Forward

See *Framåt* (Lindsborg, KS: 1887).

Fosterlandet

[*The Native Country*]
Chicago, IL: Framåt Pub. Co.
Vol. 7, no. 44–vol. 23, no. 356
November 4, 1891–September 25, 1907
Merged with: *Framåt* (Chicago, IL)
Continued by: *Fylgia*

As the continuation of *Pedagogen* and *Framåt*, the weekly Swedish-language paper *Fosterlandet* was sympathetic to the Augustana Synod, even though some readers considered it a political paper. Carl A. Swensson, who was editor and contributor to the earlier papers, continued his frequent contributions to its columns. Editor was J. A. Nyvall while J. E. Norling was the publisher. Ordinarily the paper consisted of eight pages, each with seven columns.

In October 1907, *Fosterlandet* merged with *Fylgia* in Chicago. *Sources:* Andreen 1905, 169; Erickson 33; LIBRIS; Setterdahl 8; WorldCat.

Augustana College Swenson Center: Vols. 7–23; November 1891–September 1907
Center for Research Libraries: 1896–October 1900; 1901–1906
Chicago Historical Society: PN4885 .S8F82 [1891: vol. 11, no. 4–vol. 12, no. 30]; [1892: vol. 1, no. 6–vol. 11, no. 23; vol. 12, nos. 7–28]; [1893: vol. 4, no. 26; vol. 6, nos. 7–14; vol. 9, no. 13; vol. 10, no. 4; vol. 11, no. 1]; [1894: vol. 1, no. 3; vol. 2, no. 21; vol. 3, nos. 7–21; vol. 4, no. 4–vol. 6, no. 13; vol. 6, no. 27–vol. 8, no. 1; vol. 9, no. 5–vol. 12, no. 26]; [1895: vol. 1, no. 2–1907: vol. 9, no. 25], Microfilm

University of Minnesota–Minneapolis: F548.9 .S23 F67x Vol. 9, no. 4; January 25, 1893
LIBRIS: Royal Library of Sweden: 1891–1907

Framåt (Lindsborg, KS: 1887)

[*Forward*]
Lindsborg, KS: [s.n.] (March 1887–May 1888; November 1888–December 1889)
Kansas City, MO: [s.n.] (June–October 1888)
Chicago, IL: Framåt Pub. Co. (January 1890–October 28, 1891)
Vol. 3, no. 24–vol. 7, no. 43
March 16, 1887–October 28, 1891
Continues: *Pedagogen*
Continued by: *Fosterlandet*
Other titles:
   Framåt (Chicago, IL)
   Forward

Framåt, a weekly Swedish-language newspaper, succeeded *Pedagogen* in 1887. First published in Lindsborg, Kansas, from March 1887 through May 1888, it moved to Kansas City, Missouri in June 1888. In November 1888 it returned to Lindsborg through December 1889. It finally then moved to Chicago as of January 1890. The paper consistently maintained strong ties with the Augustana Synod, even though it became more of a political newspaper.

At first edited by Carl A. Swensson and published in the interests of Bethany College, *Framåt* also carried news of the Swedes in Kansas, encouraging new settlers to make their home there. Occasionally, it included news items from Luther Academy in Nebraska. Swensson wrote a column under the pen name "Leopold." Stephenson calls them "breezy columns from Kansas" (334). He also indicates that *Framåt* was one of the papers aggressively engaging in "bitter polemics with the synodical organ" [*Augustana*] (334).

Editorial duties were later taken by C. G. Norman. Late in 1891, *Framåt* merged with *Fosterlandet* in Chicago. *Sources:* LIBRIS; Setterdahl 9, 16; Söderström 38, 41; Stephenson 334; WorldCat.

Augustana College Swenson Center: 1887–1891
Bethany College: Microfilm
Chicago Historical Society: PN4885 .S8 F84 [1890: vol. 1, no.8–vol. 2, no. 19; vol. 3, no. 5–vol. 12, no. 30]; [1891: vol. 1, no. 7–vol. 3, no. 4; vol. 3, no. 25–vol. 7, no. 1; vol. 7, no. 22–vol. 10, no. 28], Microfilm

Setterdahl: Kansas Historical Society: Microfilm
LIBRIS: Royal Library of Sweden: 1887–1890; January 7–February 18,
  1891

Framåt (Providence, RI: 1892)

[*Forward*]
Providence, RI: M. Hulting & Co.
Vol. 1, no. 1–vol. 2, no.?
July 2, 1892?–December 1893?
Continued by: *Framåt* (Brooklyn, NY: 1894)

In 1892 C. G. Norman, who was then the pastor of the Swedish
Lutheran Church in Providence, Rhode Island, started *Framåt* with the
plan that it be a Swedish-language political news sheet issued weekly. In
1893 a stock company was organized, taking over the new paper. Shortly
after, it was moved to Brooklyn as of January 24, 1894. The plan was that
it should become the official organ of the New York Conference of the Augustana Synod. Note, regarding the dates in the list above, that the Royal
Library of Sweden reports microfilm beginning with a February 12, 1892,
issue. *Sources:* Backlund 47; LIBRIS: Setterdahl 29; WorldCat.

Augustana College Swenson Center: 1892–1893, Microfilm
University of Minnesota–Minneapolis: F89 .P9 F73x No. 28; January 18,
  1893
WorldCat: Chicago Historical Society: 1892
  Rhode Island Historical Society: 1892
LIBRIS: Royal Library of Sweden: 1892–1893; February 12–December
  28, 1892, Microfilm

Framåt (Brooklyn, NY: 1894)

[*Forward*]
Brooklyn, NY: [s.n.]
January 26, 1894–December 25, 1895
Continues: *Framåt* (Providence, RI: 1892)
Continued by: *Österns Härold*

The paper of the same name, which C. G. Norman started in 1892 in Providence, Rhode Island, was moved to Brooklyn, New York, in January 1894.
The plan was that it should become the official organ of the New York Conference of the Augustana Synod. Norman continued as editor until 1895. In
1896 the name was changed to *Österns Härold*. *Sources:* LIBRIS; WorldCat.

Augustana College Swenson Center: 1894–1895
WorldCat: University of Minnesota–Minneapolis
  Rhode Island Historical Society
LIBRIS: Royal Library of Sweden: 1894–1895; January 26, 1894–December 25, 1895, Microfilm

Fridens Härold: är den enda Religiost Politiska Tidning Öster om Chicago

[*Peace Herald: Is the Only Religious Political Paper East of Chicago*]
Brooklyn, NY: J. A. Dahleen
Vol. 2, no. 1–vol ?
December 10, 1875–March 10, 1876
Continues: *Evangelisk Luthersk Tidskrift för Kyrkan Skolan och Hemmet*

Announcements of Lutheran Church news and church services in Boston, Brooklyn, and several other cities in the Northeast comprised partial contents of *Fridens Härold*. It also included brief news from Sweden and America, short religious articles, and instructional material. J. A. Dahleen was the editor and publisher of this short-lived publication. Note that Söderström indicates the dates in the above list as January–October 1876. *Sources:* Erickson 35; LIBRIS; Söderström 34.

LIBRIS: Royal Library of Sweden: 1876
No United States holdings reported.

From Luther: Newsletter from Luther College— the Junior College of the Augustana Lutheran Church

Wahoo, NE: Luther College
1958?–1962
Vols. 1–3

This newsletter for general distribution was issued during the final years of Luther College in Wahoo, Nebraska, before the merger with Midland Lutheran College in Fremont, Nebraska. *Source:* Midland Lutheran College Archives.

Midland Lutheran College: Vols. 2–3; 1959–1962

Fylgia

Chicago, IL: C. F. Erikson
Vol. 23, no. 40–no. 1189

October 4, 1907–September 10, 1909
Merged with: *Svenska Tribunen Nyheter*
Continues: *Fosterlandet*

Fylgia was a continuation of *Fosterlandet*. Ander writes that "it aimed to be a family journal and not a weekly newspaper," (158) as *Fosterlandet* had been. Therefore, even though its goals were a bit less ambitious, it survived for only two years from 1907 to 1909. As a Swedish-language paper, it then was absorbed by *Svenska Tribunen Nyheter* in Chicago. *Sources:* Ander 1956, 158; LIBRIS; Setterdahl 9; WorldCat.

Setterdahl: Augustana College: Microfilm
WorldCat: Chicago Historical Society: 1907–1909
LIBRIS: Royal Library of Sweden: 1907–1909

Fyrbåken: Månadsblad för Församlingarna inom New Jersey-Distriktet

[*Monthly Paper for Congregations in New Jersey District*]
Rock Island, IL: Augustana Book Concern
July 1907–May 1908

This paper was issued for the congregations in the New Jersey District of the New York Conference of the Augustana Lutheran Synod. *Sources:* Ander 1956, 159; Lundeen, group 6.

Lundeen: Evangelical Lutheran Church in America Archives: 1907–1908

– G –

Gamla och Nya Hemlandet

[*Old and New Homeland*]
Chicago, IL: Svenska Lutherska Tryckföreningen
Vol. 16, no. 21–vol. 60, no. 39
May 24, 1870–September 24, 1914
Continues: *Hemlandet det Gamla och det Nya*
Merged with: *Svenska Amerikanaren* (Chicago, IL: 1885) to form *Svenska Amerikanaren Hemlandet*

As a variant title of the Swedish-language newspaper established in 1855 with the title *Hemlandet, det Gamla och det Nya*, this title *Gamla och Nya Hemlandet* seems to be more consistently used as of mid-1870.

Literature about the paper regularly uses the short title *Hemlandet*, thus including this variant. At times it appears that each title or a slight variant is used interchangeably in the literature citing the paper.

For example, the issues of *Hemlandet det Gamla och det Nya* for August 8–28, 1855, and November 3, 1855–January 28, 1857, were published as: *Gamla och det Nya Hemlandet*. Also, the issues of *Gamla och Nya Hemlandet* for May 24, 1870–October 3, 1871, have the publisher's block title as: *Hemlandet, Gamla och Nya*. In other issues the imprint varies.

A narrative history of the paper is herein printed under the entry for *Hemlandet, det Gamla och det Nya. Sources:* LIBRIS; WorldCat.

Augustana College Swenson Center
Bethany College: 1870–1914, Microfilm
Center for Research Libraries: [1907–September 24, 1914]
Chicago Historical Society: [1876: vol. 9, no. 8], [1882: vol. 8, no. 2]
Concordia Historical Institute: 1870–1914, Microfilm
New York Public Library Research Library: [1899: vol. 11, no. 29]
University of Minnesota–Minneapolis: F548.9.S23 G36x Vol. 39, no. 41;
    October 12, 1893
WorldCat: Illinois State Historical Library
    Wisconsin Historical Society: October 1898–September 24, 1914
LIBRIS: Royal Library of Sweden: 1870–1899, 1901–1914 Paper;
    1870–1914, Microfilm

The Garnet and Silver-Gray

Rock Island, IL: Augustana College
1905
Continues: *Class Annual*
Continued by: *Jubilee 1910*

This annual was edited and published by the senior class of Augustana College in 1905. Editors were J. E. A. Alexis, A. V. Anderson, A. J. Anderson, and E. W. Carlson. *Sources:* Bergendoff 131; http://library.ilcso.illinois .edu/aug.

Augustana College: LD271.A6655 R598 1905
Augustana College Swenson Center: LD271.A6655 R598

The Gazette

East Orange, NJ: Upsala College
Vol. 85, no. 1–vol. 87, no. 3

September 9, 1991–May 5, 1994
Continues: *Upsala Gazette*

After suspension of the student newspaper during the 1990–1991 academic year, *The Gazette* resumed publication in September 1991; however, issues appeared sporadically during the academic year. There were 11 issues from 1991 to 1992 (volume 85), 8 issues from 1992 to 1993 (volume 86), and only 3 issues from 1993 to 1994 (volume 87). No issues appeared after 1994. Upsala College closed in May 1995. *Source:* WorldCat.

Augustana College Swenson Center: LH1.U67 U67 Vol. 85:1–vol. 87:3; September 9, 1991–May 5, 1994

Glimpses from Central Honan

See *Honan Glimpses.*

God Jul: Illustrerad Jultidning för Svenskarna i Amerika

[*A Merry Christmas: Illustrated Christmas Magazine for Swedes in America*]
Rock Island, IL: Augustana Book Concern
1916

Amid discussions about the appropriate quality of Christmas literature from Sweden being promoted in America, the Augustana Book Concern Board of Directors in 1916 took on the matter. The group felt that a Christmas magazine produced by the Augustana Book Concern was "urgently needed" in order to "obviate the evil influence of certain Swedish Christmas magazines with very offensive contents" which were annually imported.

In further action, the board resolved to publish such a Christmas magazine, designating E. W. Olson as its editor. It was to be "adapted to the needs of the Swedish Americans in general without regard to their church affiliation." It would be "a literary publication of good moral tendency" (Blanck 1997, 147, quoting from Augustana Book Concern Board Minutes, April 11, 1916).

Following through on this resolve, the editor chose authors Jakob Bonggren, Ernst Skarstedt, Leonard Strömberg, David Nyvall, and Mauritz Stolpe to provide literary contributions. Birger Sandzen, G. N. Malm, Henry Reuterdahl, and Olof Grafström provided quality artwork.

However well intended this project was, this effort survived for only one year—1916. *Sources:* Blanck 1997, 147; LIBRIS; WorldCat.

Minnesota Historical Society: GT4985 .G63 1916
University of Minnesota–Minneapolis: GT4985 .G63x 1916
LIBRIS: Royal Library of Sweden
    Swedish Emigrant Institute

Golden Ear

See *Guldax*.

Greater Gustavus Association Quarterly

See *Greater Gustavus Quarterly*.

Greater Gustavus Quarterly

[Minneapolis, MN: Gustavus Adolphus Association] (1944–May 1947)
St. Peter, MN: Gustavus Adolphus College (June 1947–Spring 1994)
Vol. ?–vol. 51, no. 3
October 31, 1944–Winter 1995
Continued by: *Gustavus Quarterly*
Other title: *Greater Gustavus Association Quarterly*

In 1944, the Gustavus Adolphus College Alumni Association reorganized to become the Greater Gustavus Association. Its new quarterly publication began with the October 31, 1944, issue and continued through
1980/81. After that time it was issued bimonthly. In 1995, this title was
succeeded by the *Gustavus Quarterly*. *Sources:* http://mnhs.mnpals.net;
Peterson 131; WorldCat.

Gustavus Adolphus College: LD2091.G65G7 1944–1995
Lutheran Theological Seminary at Gettysburg: Vols. [33, 35], 36–49;
    1972–1985
Minnesota Historical Society: LD2091 .G662 1945–1969, [1969–1971],
    1971–1979, [1979–1982], 1982–1994

Guldax: ett Månadsblad i Guds Rikes Tjänst
Guldax: Organ för Bethphage Inre Missionsförening
Guldax: Organ för de Sv. Ev. Luth. Församlingarna i Kearney–Distriktet af Nebraska Konferensen

[The Golden Ear: Monthly Paper in God's Kingdom Service]
[Organ for Bethphage Inner Mission Association]

[Organ for the Swedish Evangelical Lutheran Congregations in Kear-
ney District of Nebraska Conference]
Axtell, NE: [K. G. Wm. Dahl]; Bethphage Mission (1919–)
Vol. 1, no. 1–vol. 28, no. 1
January 1913–January 1940
Continued by: *Bethphage Messenger*
Other title: *Golden Ear*

The official organ for the Bethphage Mission began publication in 1913
with Swedish text through 1920. From 1921 to 1940, *Guldax* was published
in double issues, Swedish and English. In 1940–1941, English and
Swedish were combined in the *Bethphage Messenger*, with English-only following. Ordinarily, it was issued monthly with some exceptions when
two numbers were combined into one.

K. G. William Dahl, the founder of the Bethphage Mission, was the original editor through August 1917. C. A. Lonnquist continued editorial
work until June 1937. Arthur A. Christenson succeeded him.

From its original eight-page format, *Guldax* expanded to twelve pages, but
during the 1930s, it was reduced to four pages. Subscription price was fifty
cents per year. For the most part, *Guldax* reported news and activities at the
Bethphage Mission. Some meditations, articles on religious subjects, and poetry were also included. With the February 1940 issue, *Guldax* took on its
English title, *Bethphage Messenger*. *Sources:* Erickson 41; http://tomos.oit
.umn.edu/F/; LIBRIS; Lundeen, group 9; Matthews 25; ULS.

Augustana College Swenson Center: January 1935–February 1936
Lutheran Theological Seminary at Gettysburg: Vols. 6–18; 1918–1931
Gustavus Adolphus College Archives: Vols. 6–9; vol. 17, no. 3;
  1918–1921, [1930]
University of Minnesota–Minneapolis: BX8049.1 .N2 G85x Vol. 1, 3–4, 7,
  12; 1913, 1915–1916, 1919, 1925
Erickson: Lutheran School of Theology at Chicago
  University of Wisconsin: Vols. 8, 10–11, 13
  Royal Library of Sweden: Vols. 1–6, 8–10, 13, 15, 17–18, 20–24, 26–28
Lundeen: Evangelical Lutheran Church in America Archives: 1913–
ULS: Minnesota Historical Society: Vol. 17+
LIBRIS: Swedish Emigrant Institute: Årg. [1–3], 4–5, [6–7], 8, [9], 10,
  [11–13, 15–16]: 1913–1926, 1928–1929

Gustaf Adolfs Journalen

See *Gustavus Journal.*

The Gustavian

St. Peter, MN: Gustavus Adolphus College
1917–1989; 1991–
Continues: *Breidablick* (1912)
Other titles:
  Gustavian Yearbook (1948)
  Gustavian Annual (1953)
  Gustavian for . . . (1956)
  Best of Life at G.A.C. (1976)
  G.A.C. Gustavian (1979–1980)
  Significant Pursuit (1985)
Sometimes referred to as: *Gustavian*

The title *The Gustavian* was first given to the Gustavus Adolphus College annual in 1917. Beginning in 1920, the publication was issued on a biennial schedule. In 1924, it was published by the junior and senior classes together. The same publication plan continued in following years until 1946 when *The Gustavian* became an annual published by the senior class alone.

An interesting sidelight was the cartoon contributions of Eben Lawson from 1909 until 1930, especially illustrating the Swedish-American characteristics of the school.

At various times, the annual was published with slight variations in the title. *The Gustavian* continues to record important events and activities as well as information about campus organizations, students, faculty, and staff, giving a complete picture of that year at Gustavus Adolphus College. It continues to serve as an important source for the history of the college. *Sources:* http://mnhs.mnpals.net; Lund 1987, 50; Peterson 89, 133.

Gustavus Adolphus College: LD2091.G62G65
Minnesota Historical Society: LD2091 .G6 G88 1953–1987

Gustavian Weekly (1920)

St. Peter, MN: Gustavus Adolphus College
Vol. 26, no. 1–vol. 82, no. 26
September 18, 1920–May 21, 1971
Continues: *College Breezes*
Continued by: *Junction*
Sometimes referred to as: *Gustavian Weekly* (Saint Peter, MN: 1920)

During 1919, a college forum at Gustavus Adolphus College was organized to serve as a general literary society, a socializing opportunity, and a means of expressing student opinion. From this effort, the new title for the student newspaper was born—the *Gustavian Weekly*. Peterson writes that the "change necessarily meant a loss of literary quality but a gain in news value" (Peterson 88).

The first issue with this new title came in September 1920, and was published weekly during the school year. It enjoyed a lengthy tenure under this title until the end of the 1971 school year. *Sources:* LIBRIS; Peterson 58, 88; WorldCat.

Gustavus Adolphus College: Vols. 26:1–82:26; 1920–1971 and Index, Paper and Microfilm

Minnesota Historical Society: Vol. 26, no. 3–vol. 32, no. 14, vol. 32, no. 18–vol. 82, no. 26; October 2, 1920–December 15, 1925; January 12, 1926–May 21, 1971, Microfilm

LIBRIS: Royal Library of Sweden: May 1935–September 1960

The Gustavian Weekly (1973)

St. Peter, MN: Students of Gustavus Adolphus College
Vol. 85, no. 1(?)–
September 1973–
Continues: *None of the Above*
Sometimes referred to as: *Gustavian Weekly* (Saint Peter, MN: 1973)

At the beginning of the 1973–1974 academic year, the student newspaper at Gustavus Adolphus College returned to the title it had held from 1920 through May 1971—*The Gustavian Weekly*. *Source:* http://www.mnpals .net/F/.

Gustavus Adolphus College: Vols. 85–114; 1973–2003/2004, Paper and Microfilm

Minnesota Historical Society: February 18–22, 1977; September 10, 1993–May 10, 2002. Some issues lacking.

Gustaviana

St. Peter, MN: Gustavus Adolphus College
Vol. 1, no. 2–vol. 5, no. 9
December 1891–May 1895
Continues: *Heimdall*
Continued by: *Gustavus Journal*

Gustavus Adolphus College students edited and prepared this paper beginning in December 1891. It appeared monthly during the academic year until 1895. Both Ander (159) and Voight (38) cite 1893 as the ending year. Both Lund and Peterson use 1895 as the ending year. Both English and Swedish texts were used.

In 1896, *Gustaviana* was replaced by the *Gustavus Journal*. *Sources:* LIBRIS; Lund 1987, 30; Peterson 58.

Gustavus Adolphus College: Paper and Microfilm
LIBRIS: Swedish Emigrant Institute: Vols. [1–5]; [1892–1895]

Gustavus Adolphus College Catalog

See *Catalogue of Gustavus Adolphus College*.

Gustavus Adolphus Journal

See *Gustavus Journal*.

Gustavus Journal

St. Peter, MN: Gustavus Adolphus College
Vol. 6, no. 1–vol. 11, no. 9
December 1896–May 1901
Continues: *Gustaviana*
Continued by: *College Breezes*
Other title: *Gustaf Adolfs Journalen*
Sometimes referred to as: *Gustavus Adolphus Journal* and numbered
vols. 1:1–5:17; December 1896–May 1901

As the continuation of *Gustaviana*, the *Gustavus Journal* began publication with the December 1896 issue. From then through April 1, 1899, there were two issues monthly, the second being in the Swedish language. This edition carried the title *Gustaf Adolfs Journalen*.

With the May 1899 issue, this policy changed when it became an English-language monthly only. During the bilingual years the paper enjoyed a number of off-campus subscribers, sometimes printed in editions of two thousand copies. Profits were used to help support the growing college library.

This student monthly continued until May 1901. It became *College Breezes* in 1905. Apparently, there was no student paper during the intervening years. *Sources:* Peterson 58; WorldCat.

Gustavus Adolphus College
Minnesota Historical Society: Microfilm 370

The Gustavus Quarterly

St. Peter, MN: Gustavus Adolphus College
Vol. 51, no. 3–
Winter 1995–
Continues: *Greater Gustavus Quarterly*
Sometimes referred to as: *Gustavus Quarterly*

This periodical is issued quarterly on behalf of Gustavus Adolphus College. It is distributed by free subscription to alumni and friends of the college as a means of communicating news of interest to its readers. *Source:* http://mnpals.gustavus.edu.

Gustavus Adolphus College: LD2091.G65 #b G7
Minnesota Historical Society: LD2091 .G6622 Vols. 51– ; 1995–

– H –

Heimdall

St. Peter, MN: Gustavus Adolphus College
Vol. 1, no. 1
November 1891
Continues: *Vox Collegi*
Continued by: *Gustaviana*
Sometimes spelled: *Heimdal*

In November 1891, there appeared volume 1, number 1 of *Heimdall* following the single issue of *Vox Collegi* in September 1891. This also proved to be a single issue, primarily due to some objections to the name. In Norse mythology, Heimdall is the guardian of the bridge of the gods.

Therefore, in December 1891, the *Gustaviana* appeared as the student newspaper. *Sources:* Lund 1987, 30; Peterson 58.

Augustana College Swenson Center: Vol. 1, no. 1; 1891
Gustavus Adolphus College: Paper and Microfilm

Hem Missionären

[*Home Missionary*]
Chicago, IL: [s.n.]

1888
Became: *Home Missionary*

Ander states that "this is an Augustana Lutheran Home Missionary publication" (160). The Swedish edition existed for only one year when in 1889 it took the English title. *Source:* Ander 1956, 160.

Augustana College Swenson Center: 1888 scattered issues

Hem-Vännen

See *Hemvännen*.

Hemåt: Luthersk Traktat-Tidning

[*Homeward: Lutheran Tract Paper*]
San Francisco, CA: [s.n.]
June 1900–December 1904

This Swedish-language paper was issued for the Swedish Lutheran congregations in California from 1900 to 1904. It was designated the official paper for the California Conference in February 1903. *Sources:* Ander 1956, 160; Lundeen, group 6; Söderström 39.

Lundeen: Evangelical Lutheran Church in America Archives: 1900–1904

Hemlandet

See *Hemlandet, det Gamla och det Nya*; *Gamla och Nya Hemlandet*; *Rätta Hemlandet*; *Rätta Hemlandet och Augustana*; *Rätta Hemlandet och Missionsbladet*.

Hemlandet, det Gamla och det Nya

[*The Homeland, the Old and the New*]
Galesburg, IL: T. N. Hasselquist
Chicago, IL: Svenska Lutherska Tryckföreningen; Enander & Bohman
Vols. 1–60
January 3, 1855–September 24, 1914
Absorbed: *Minnesota Posten*
Merged with: *Svenska Amerikanaren* (Chicago, IL: 1885) to form *Svenska Amerikanaren och Hemlandet*

Sometimes referred to as: *Det Gamla och det Nya Hemlandet* or *Gamla och Nya Hemlandet* or *Hemlandet*

One of the most influential and perhaps the most widely read Swedish-language newspaper in America during the last half of the nineteenth century was born in humble circumstances in Galesburg, Illinois, in 1854. The first issue of *Hemlandet, det Gamla och det Nya* was dated January 3, 1855. This was the second Swedish-language newspaper published in the United States, outliving its predecessor (*Skandinaven* in New York) and many others published during its sixty years.

T. N. Hasselquist, along with his pioneer Augustana pastor colleagues Erland Carlsson and L. P. Esbjörn, had discussed the need for a Swedish-language newspaper to serve the ever-expanding Swedish immigrant population. New settlements and new congregations were being organized. The need for a Swedish-language newspaper that could speak to this growing population was imperative. In 1854 such a paper, to be named *Svenska Posten*, was earnestly planned, but more pressing responsibilities of the three men kept the project from becoming reality.

Hasselquist was determined. The need was urgent. The responsibility was all-consuming. The task was daunting. Hasselquist pressed on with vision, perseverance, and a plan, resulting in the first issue coming off the press on January 3, 1855. By some standards, it was not an impressive paper, only four pages (10x14 in.) and devoted completely to church news and devotional articles. Subscription price was two dollars a year.

During the preceding months, Hasselquist had faced major challenges to his plan. A typographer who could set Swedish type was finally located in Boston. N. P. Armstrong, a native of Sweden, came to Galesburg as compositor, printer, and foreman of the planned paper.

Securing necessary equipment, including types and cases, was another problem. An old German printing office in New York sold such to Hasselquist. But when it was time to work on the new paper, the equipment had not yet arrived. Not giving up or postponing his plan, Hasselquist asked the publishers of the *Galesburg Free Democrat* if they could set up his paper. They agreed.

Very soon the Swedish typographer realized that these cases were lacking an adequate supply of important letters such as *k*. The letter *c* is used in English where many times *k* is used in Swedish. Still undaunted, Hasselquist sent his typesetter, carrying copy and type that had already been set, to Knoxville, Illinois, where another publisher cooperated and finished the work. Thus was born the first issue of *Hemlandet* in January 1855.

The frustrations experienced by Hasselquist are evident in his letter to Erland Carlsson, dated February 2, 1855:

Dear Brother: Long have I been expecting a few lines from you, especially after the first number of *Hemlandet* reached you. You have not sent me any news from Sweden, nor any other article for the paper. I can not possibly single-handed write all that is required for the paper, although it is not large; you too must contribute, furnishing historical information about your congregations, articles on practical matters, etc.; Swedish letters would also be good materials. Now, however, the publication of the paper is interrupted temporarily, possibly for quite a while. The type has not arrived, and I don't know when it will come; the first issue was printed in Knoxville under difficulties and at a cost almost twice what it ought to be if the enterprise is to carry itself. Nevertheless, I decided to print one issue per month, despite the expense, until the type arrives. I had everything in readiness last Monday, but the printer answered me that he could not possibly let me use his type; the case was the same here in Galesburg. So here I stand helpless, not knowing what to do. You must exert yourself to the utmost to get an issue printed in Chicago; I have plenty of manuscripts on hand. The whole newspaper enterprise is jeopardized, and a failure would mean an equally great loss to each one of us. The paper will no doubt be a success, just so it can be issued regularly. The number of subscriptions, paid and unpaid, is not far below 500. Help me bear my cares, Brother! May the Spirit of the Lord guide you in all your undertakings, so that many blood-bought souls through you be saved. That is what we are chiefly called to accomplish. Greetings to all! Your affectionate, T. N. Hasselquist. (Olson 1935, 127–29)

On March 1, 1855, the material purchased in New York arrived in Galesburg. The third issue of the new paper had been half set, so the new equipment was immediately put to use. Consequently, the March issue was printed using two different types.

Needing space for this enterprise, Hasselquist moved the printing work from his modest residence to a small building that he erected on the premises of his home. The print shop filled the basement there. He purchased a small hand press from the Galesburg paper so all composing and printing could be done in one place, small and primitive as it may have been. After six months there were more than four hundred subscribers, and after a year there were a thousand. Because of its Swedish Lutheran leanings, the paper depended upon Augustana members and clergy as potential subscribers. During 1855–1858 the paper was issued every other week.

In a letter dated April 8, 1856, which was his last report to the American Home Missionary Society, the group sponsoring his work, Hasselquist wrote:

Dear Christian Friends and Brethren in Christ!: My first duty is to beg you excuse me in not writing to you before now, but my work has been more manifold and arduous than at any time before. The preaching stations are about as many as they have been, yet more people everywhere. The Swedish newspaper, *Hemlandet* of which I am editor, has put me in connection with almost every part of the United States and already on that account gives much to do receiving and answering letters, besides the care of the paper itself. I hope the merciful God will bless this little sheet, that it may do its work to his praise and to direct the thoughts of my countrymen to the heavenly home! The paper has about twelve hundred subscribers at present. (Reports, 82–83)

In July of 1856, Hasselquist began issuing another paper, *Det Rätta Hemlandet*, also from the Galesburg shop. Both papers were the endeavor of Hasselquist through 1858. A. R. Cervin assisted him until 1857. Already *Hemlandet* had become more of a political journal, so *Det Rätta Hemlandet* was devoted exclusively to religious subjects. The two were issued biweekly, on alternate weeks.

In 1859 the operation was moved to Chicago, where the Svenska Lutherska Tryckföreningen took it over. This Swedish Lutheran Printing Company (or Swedish Lutheran Publication Society) was a stock company owned and controlled by a group of clergy and laymen in the Mississippi Conference of the Synod of Northern Illinois. Erland Carlsson was the influential leader of this group.

Also in 1859 the *Minnesota Posten*, the short-lived paper edited by Eric Norelius at Red Wing, Minnesota, was absorbed by *Hemlandet*. During its short life, the *Minnesota Posten* was considered by some to be an unwelcome rival of *Hemlandet*. This enlarged paper then became a weekly and the church paper, *Det Rätta Hemlandet*, became a monthly. E. Norelius and J. Engberg were editors in 1859. E. Carlsson and J. Engberg served from 1860 to 1868, and Engberg alone in 1863 and 1864. Then A. R. Cervin served until 1868. In early 1869 J. G. Princell and in late 1869 P. A. Sundelius were editors.

Various changes, particularly in editorial policy, shaped the future of *Hemlandet*. By the 1860s other Swedish-language papers, both religious and secular, were appearing in various areas of the country, but especially in Chicago. Competition for readership was everywhere. Papers were sometimes short-lived, as financial support dwindled.

Hemlandet began to concentrate more on general news and political matters, in fact becoming more and more a purely political paper. Its columns and sixteen pages were filled with discussion concerning economic and political issues. Correspondence from readers was published, along with information about Swedish settlements in Illinois, Iowa, Kansas, and Nebraska. Letters and editorials in *Hemlandet* encouraged the establishing of new Swedish rural Lutheran communities. Railroads advertised in *Hemlandet* in an attempt to attract settlers by reaching farmers. Editorials and correspondence reflected a pro-Union and antislavery sentiment during the war years, urging support of the newly formed Republican Party.

In December 1869, Johan A. Enander was asked to become the editor. During his able leadership and long tenure, *Hemlandet* grew in popularity and was considered one of the leading weekly Swedish-American papers. The paper gradually became secularized, but the editorial opinions were similar to attitudes of the Augustana Synod.

In 1872, a newly organized company, Enander and Bohman (J. A. Enander and G. A. Bohman) purchased *Hemlandet* from the Swedish Lutheran Printing Company. This firm continued to publish *Hemlandet* until 1891. Enander left for other work then, but returned in 1896 and remained with *Hemlandet* until his death in 1910. A. E. Johnson and J. N. Söderholm served as editors during the 1891–1896 interim. Although it became a secular newspaper, its editors continued to be sympathetic to the cause of Swedish Lutheranism and friendly to the Augustana Synod.

With Enander's death, the future of *Hemlandet* took a downward turn. Anders Schön was editor. In 1913 the paper was purchased by C. S. Peterson. Schön was joined by P. G. Norberg and E. Westman in editorial duties. The struggle for subscribers against feverish competition from other newspapers seemed insurmountable. In October 1914, Peterson sold *Hemlandet* to its old political rival *Svenska Amerikanaren*, with which it was merged.

Regarding its significance to Augustana readers in its early years, C. W. Foss quoted by Arden (1963) wrote:

> *Hemlandet* became a welcome visitor in many homes. It served as a bond of union among the Swedes, who, though separated by hundreds of miles, still felt drawn toward one another by kindred ties. It also became a means of communication between them and the friends and kindred forever left behind in the dear old "homeland." Again it served to instruct the newcomers in the political, social, and religious questions of their "new homeland." . . . On the great moral and political questions of the day—slavery, know-nothingism, and temperance—*Hemlandet* gave no uncertain sound. The most complicated questions were discussed by the editor in that clear and simple style which was so peculiar to him. (112)

In further tribute, an anonymous writer in 1935 wrote:

> Dr. T. N. Hasselquist's venture in starting a Swedish newspaper in 1855, entitled "*Hemlandet, det Gamla och det Nya*," not only served an urgent need, but was an act of far-reaching cultural importance. It served to cement together the rapidly increasing numbers of immigrants. Through it a connection was also maintained with relatives and interested persons in Sweden. While its aim was partly religious, the broad interests and strong convictions of Dr. Hasselquist on political and other questions were powerful factors in forming

opinions which have guided the Synod to the present day. When "*Hemlandet*" became a secular weekly and secured as its editor so able a man as Dr. J. A. Enander, it became an ardent exponent of Swedish literature and culture and at the same time an interpreter to the newcomers of the principles of true Americanism." (*After Seventy-Five Years* 115)

Sources: After Seventy-Five Years 115; Arden 1963, 112; Backlund 15–18, 35–38; Benson 1938, 184; Griswold 37; Olson 1933, 4–9; Olson 1935, 127–29; Reports 82–83; WorldCat.

Augustana College Swenson Center
Bethany College: Vols. 1–13; 1855–1870, Microfilm
Center for Research Libraries: January 4, 1860–December 24, 1866, Microfilm
Concordia Historical Institute: 1855–1870, Microfilm
Gustavus Adolphus College Archives: January 3, 1855–September 24, 1914, Microfilm
Lutheran Theological Seminary at Gettysburg: Vols. [1, 10–12]; [1855, 1864–1866]
University of Minnesota–Minneapolis: F549 .G35 H46x Vol. 1, no. 1; January 3, 1855 (reprint 1878)
WorldCat: Chicago Historical Society: 1855–1870
Illinois State Historical Library
For additional holdings see: *Gamla och Nya Hemlandet*.
LIBRIS: Royal Library of Sweden: 1855–1870, Paper and Microfilm

Hemvännen

[*Friend of the Home*]
Chicago, IL: [s.n.]; Rock Island, IL: Augustana Book Concern
Vol. 9, no. 7–vol. 11, no. 48 (1887–1888)
June 25, 1887–November 30, 1889
Absorbed: *Ungdomsvännen*, June 25, 1887; *Vårt Land och Folk*, December 1888
Merged with: *Augustana och Missionären* to form *Augustana* (1889)
Sometimes referred to as: *Hem-Vännen*

In 1887, the Augustana Book Concern Board decided to publish their monthly *Ungdomsvännen* as a weekly with a new name *Hemvännen*, intended as a Christian magazine for the entire family, thus with a wider program planned than what was intended for *Ungdomsvännen*.

Published in Chicago, the first issue was dated June 25, 1887. Its four pages in large quarto were illustrated each week. The initial announcement read:

This is not a new periodical, but it is the already nine-year-old *Ungdoms-Vännen* that has taken a step forward and now presents itself in new garb and with a somewhat altered name and an enlarged program. This change has been made to meet a very generally expressed wish on the part of its readers, that the magazine might appear once a week. (Swan 43–44)

Editors included A. Rodell, C. A. Bäckman, N. Forsander, S. P. A. Lindahl, and A. O. Bersell. O. Olsson was a regular contributor. In 1888 C. L. E. Esbjörn became an editor until 1889 when H. O. Lindeblad and J. A. Udden took on editorship, with Lindahl still being a dominant partner in the venture. In late 1888, the periodical *Vårt Land och Folk*, published in Chicago, was absorbed by *Hemvännen*.

Hemvännen, as a religious paper, had excellent editing and included a variety of contents. However, financially it was not stable and readership not as large as expected. In the final issue, dated November 30, 1889, the announcement from the editors read: "With this number the editors of *Hem-Vännen* must bid their readers farewell." At that time it had been decided to expand *Augustana* so *Hemvännen* ended its individual identity with the merger. Swan makes the same comment about its demise as he did about the end of *Ungdomsvännen*: "that it was altogether too religious for some people and not religious enough for others" (Swan 42). *Sources:* Erickson 44; LIBRIS; Swan 42–44; WorldCat.

Gustavus Adolphus College Archives: Vol. 9, no. 7–vol. 11, no. 48; June 25, 1887–December 30, 1888
WorldCat: Chicago Historical Society: 1889
LIBRIS: Royal Library of Sweden: 1887–1889

The Home Altar: A Guide for Daily Home Devotions

Rock Island, IL: Augustana Book Concern
Vol. 1, no. 1–vol. 22, no. 4
January/March 1940–November 1962/January 1963
Continues: *The Augustana Home Altar*
Sometimes referred to as: *Home Altar*

The original title *The Augustana Home Altar* in 1940 was revised in 1941 to *The Home Altar*. Planned as a resource for families to use in their daily devotions in the home, it enjoyed a long life and staunch popularity. In 1952, each edition numbered ninety thousand copies.

An advertisement for *The Home Altar* read: "For the whole family. *The Home Altar* stands ready to aid you in the important phase of Christian living—daily devotions. Available by individual subscription or in bulk for distribution to your entire congregation, *The Home Altar* encourages the important foundation of daily Bible reading" (*Augustana Annual* 1956, 191).

Nystrom writes about this devotional quarterly: "Containing daily devotions for family and individual use, prepared under the editorial supervision of the secretaries of literature by pastors and lay people of the Augustana Church, this publication has had a remarkable growth in circulation and has performed a blessed ministry . . . by 1960 it had reached nearly 200,000" (81). *Sources: Augustana Annual* 1956, 191; Nystrom 81; WorldCat.

Lutheran School of Theology at Chicago: BV4810 .H58 Vols. [1]–22; [1940]–1962

Home Mission News

Minneapolis, MN: Board of Home Missions, Augustana Synod
1946?–19?

Issued by the Board of Home Missions of the Augustana Synod, this quarterly news sheet apparently was a companion to *Pastor's Paragraphs*, issued also by the Board of Home Missions. *Source:* Thorstensson.

Gustavus Adolphus College Archives: Spring 1946, Spring 1948

Home Missionary

Chicago, IL: [s.n.]
1889–1904
Continues: *Hem-Missionären*

Ander states that this was "an English tract of the Augustana Synod on home missions." It supersedes the Swedish title *Hem-Missionären*. *Sources:* Ander 1956, 160; Söderström 19.

Augustana College Swenson Center: 1889–1892 scattered issues

Honan Glimpses

Shekow and Hankow, China: Board of Foreign Missions and China Mission Board, Evangelical Lutheran Augustana Synod in North America
December 1923–March 1927
Continues: *Glimpses from Central Honan*

This publication "included missionary letters and stories, reports from the stations and institutions [in Honan Province] and photographs."

The description provided by the Evangelical Lutheran Church in America Archives continues:

> *Honan Glimpses* was a publication of the Augustana Synod Mission, based in the Honan Province of China. It began publication in March of 1922 under the name *Glimpses from Central Honan,* changing to *Honan Glimpses* in December of 1923. Although it began as a mimeographed publication, by March of 1923 it was appearing as a printed paper. It was published ten times per year, with no issues during July and August when the missionaries came together for their annual conferences.
>
> The paper was started as a newsletter between mission stations. As such, a reporter was assigned from each station, with the editorship taken by Gustav Carlberg for the life of the paper. Though it began with a modest printing of 60 copies, within a year it had expanded its subscription list to 1000, including many from the United States interested in the Chinese mission work. Publication was abruptly ended when missionaries were evacuated in 1927. What was to have been their March issue of that year was printed in the June issue of the *Augustana Foreign Missionary,* and subscriptions to *Honan Glimpses* were completed by the *Augustana Foreign Missionary* as well. . . . An explanatory note about the change stated, "Hereafter our missionaries will write for the A.F.M."

Source: WorldCat.

Augustana College Swenson Center: March 1927
Evangelical Lutheran Church in America Archives: AUG 24/3/5

– I –

The Immanuel Banner

Omaha, NE: Immanuel Medical Center
Vol. 44, no. 3–vol. 49
August 1965–Winter 1970
Continues: *Deaconess Banner*
Continued by: *Immanuel Medical Center Banner*
Sometimes referred to as: *Immanuel Banner*

This publication of the Immanuel Medical Center (formerly the Immanuel Deaconess Institute) was a newsletter regarding the services of the center. *Sources:* Matthews 1985, 135; Thorstensson.

Gustavus Adolphus College Archives: Vol. 44, no. 3–vol. 45, no. 4; August 1965–December 1966

Lutheran Theological Seminary at Gettysburg: Vols. 45–49; 1966–1970

Immanuel Medical Center Banner

Omaha, NE: Immanuel Medical Center
Vols. 50–51
Spring 1971–Winter 1972
Continues: *The Immanuel Banner*
Continued by: *Banner* (Omaha, NE)

This publication was the newsletter of the Immanuel Medical Center with a new title to highlight the work and services of the medical center. *Source:* Matthews 1985, 135.

Lutheran Theological Seminary at Gettysburg: Vols. 50–51; 1971–1972

Inner Mission Herald

Minneapolis, MN: [s.n.]
1917–1920

Lundeen states that this was a publication of the Minnesota Conference of the Augustana Lutheran Synod. *Source:* Lundeen, group 6.

Lundeen: Evangelical Lutheran Church in America Archives: 1917–1920

– J –

Jubelkalendar (1893)

See *Förgät-Mig-Ej* (1892).

The Jubilee

Rock Island, IL: Augustana College and Theological Seminary
1910
Continues: *The Garnet and Silver-Gray*
Continued by: *Rockety-I*

This illustrated annual was edited and published by the senior class of 1910 of Augustana College in commemoration of the fiftieth anniversary of Augustana College and Theological Seminary. Editors were R. A. Jacobson and E. E. Ryden. *Sources:* Bergendoff 131; http://library.bethanylb .edu; LIBRIS.

Augustana College: LD271 .A6655 R599 1910
Augustana College Swenson Center: LD271 .A6655 R599 1910
Bethany College: Rare Bk. 378.73 J91
LIBRIS: Royal Library of Sweden

Julklockorna: en julbok för de unga

[*The Christmas Bells: A Christmas Book for the Young*]
Rock Island, IL: Lutheran Augustana Book Concern
No. 1–no.?
1890–1921?

A Christmas annual for young readers, *Julklockorna* was issued in rather simple Swedish-language text. Its religious content was included in a typical edition of only twenty-four pages. These illustrated collections of Swedish stories made a thoughtful holiday gift for children. *Sources:* Blanck 1997, 158; LIBRIS; WorldCat.

Augustana College Swenson Center: PN6071 .C6 J86 "some volumes"
Minnesota Historical Society: PN6071 .C6 J86 1890 and PN6071 .C6 J861
    [189–?]
University of Minnesota–Minneapolis: PN6071 .C6 J85x 1890z
LIBRIS: Royal Library of Sweden: Nos. 1–2
    Uppsala University: No. 1

Julrunan: Illustrerad Tidning utgifven af Svenska Vitterhetssälskapet vid Augustana College och Teologiska Seminarium, Rock Island, IL

[*The Christmas Rune: Illustrated Paper Published by the Swedish Literary Society at Augustana College and Theological Seminary*, Rock Island, IL]
Rock Island, IL: Augustana College and Theological Seminary
1905; 1911; 1912

The student Swedish literary society, Svenska Vitterhetssälskapet, issued a Christmas publication in 1905. Later in 1911 and 1912, there was a

successful student effort to revive the literary publication. Also, Bergendoff cites the existence of a 1906 volume, but Blanck does not. *Julrunan* ac-
companied the group's regular publication, *Runan*. All were ambitious
projects for the student organization.

In its 1911 publication, the society indicated "that the goal of the society
was to work for the preservation of 'Swedishness and the Swedish language and literature among the Swedish Americans,' and added that
Svenska Vitterhetssällskapet seeks to be to American Swedes what the
[Swedish] Academy is to the people of Sweden" (Blanck 1997, 103).

All three issues of *Julrunan* "show how Swedish-American cultural concerns were important to the society [. . . and] included many literary contributions—poems and short stories—the majority authored by Swedish-
American authors connected with the Augustana Synod" (Blanck 1997,
106). Such writers as C. W. Andeer, K. G. William Dahl, Ludvig Holmes,
Carl Kraft, C. A. Lonnqvist, Anna Olsson, and E. W. Olson were contributors. *Sources:* Bergendoff 206; Blanck 1997, 103, 106.

Augustana College Swenson Center

Junction

St. Peter, MN: Gustavus Adolphus College
Vol. 83, no. 1–vol. 85, no. 3
September 17, 1971–May 17, 1972
Continues: *Gustavian Weekly* (1920)
Continued by: *None of the Above*

At the beginning of the 1971–1972 academic year, the student newspaper at Gustavus Adolphus College took this new title. It continued with
the title *Junction* for only that year. Note that volume 84 was assigned to
None of the Above. *Source:* http://www.mnpals.net/F/.

Gustavus Adolphus College: Vol. 83, no. 1–vol. 85, no. 3; September 17,
    1971–May 17, 1972
Minnesota Historical Society: Vol. 83, no. 1–vol. 85, no. 3; September 17,
    1971–May 17, 1972

Junior Life

Rock Island, IL: Augustana Book Concern
Vol. 72, no. 40–vol. 81, no. 34
October 3, 1954–August 25, 1963
Continues: *Olive Leaf*

The weekly Sunday church school paper for the intermediate grades, the *Olive Leaf*, was replaced in 1954 by *Junior Life*. It was considered that this new title would be more descriptive of and appealing to its intended readership.

An advertisement for *Junior Life* read: "A new four-page illustrated paper for boys and girls of the Junior department, (ages 9–11) packed with fiction, nature and science stories and also containing puzzles, jokes and games. *Junior Life* both attracts and holds the interest of this critical age group. Printed in two colors" (*Augustana Annual* 1957, 205). A single subscription was ninety cents or seventy-five cents for five or more.

Another advertisement read: "edited so as to have not only an interesting design or 'eye appeal' but to contain materials that the children will enjoy reading and, more important, that will aid in Christian development" (*Augustana Annual* 1956, 182).

Designed to aid teachers in the parish education program, it was correlated with the Christian Growth series widely used in local congregations. As an Augustana Synod publication of the Parish Education Department, its final issue was published in August 1963. *Sources: Augustana Annual* 1956, 182; 1957, 205; Lundeen, group 7; WorldCat.

Augustana College Swenson Center: 1960, 1963
Evangelical Lutheran Church in America Archives: AUG 25/5/5 Vols. 72–80, [81]; 1954–1962, [1963]
Gustavus Adolphus College Archives: Vols. 73–81; 1955–1963

Juvelskrinet: berättelser för barn

[*The Jewel Box: Short Stories for Children*]
Rock Island, IL: Augustana Book Concern
1890–1930?

A publication for young readers, *Juvelskrinet* printed religious stories in Swedish that were of interest to children. Several of the titles included were:

Genom den lilla smala dörren
Stäng dörren
Lilla Tina
En liten julvisa
Bertrands trumma
Han har sagt det
En svår läxa
Öppna ögon

Sources: Blanck 1997, 158; http://mnhs.mnpals.net/F/.

Augustana College Swenson Center
Minnesota Historical Society: PT9993.C5 J8 Nos. 16–19

– K –

Kalender för Qvinlig Diakoni och Barmhertighetsverksamhet

See *Dorkas.*

Kansas Conference Lutheran

Lindsborg, KS: [s.n.]
January 1931–June 1958
Supersedes: *Lindsborgs–Posten*
Became: *West Central Lutheran*

Following the long life of the *Lindsborgs–Posten* which ended in 1930, this monthly publication printed entirely in English succeeded it. Its mission was to report news and items of interest to parishioners in the Kansas Conference of the Augustana Lutheran Synod. Among its editors were Hans J. Hoff (1931–May 1941), N. E. Olson (1941), and Philemon Smith (1941–1945). The June 1958 issue was the final one bearing this title. It then became the *West Central Lutheran. Sources:* Capps 233; LIBRIS; Lindquist 1953, 168.

LIBRIS: Royal Library of Sweden: June 1935–June 1958
No United States holdings reported.

Kansas Missions Tidning

[*Kansas Missions Paper*]
Lindsborg, KS: [s.n.]
October 1902–1912

Lindquist writes that this Swedish-language journal concerned with missions was published from July 1904 to 1912 and that it was edited by D. Brunström. Söderström indicates that it began publication in October 1902. *Sources:* Lindquist 1953, 168; Söderström 42.

Augustana College Swenson Center: Vol. 8, no. 2; 1909

Kansas Posten

Lindsborg, KS: Svensk–Amerikanska Tryckföreningen
Vol. 1, no. 1–?

October 4, 1882–October (?) 1883
[Bengston reports that the first issue was dated April 10, 1882. Lindquist and WorldCat report the first issue was dated October 4, 1882]
Absorbed by: *Gamla och Nya Hemlandet*
Sometimes referred to as: *Kansasposten* or *Kansas–posten*

Sponsored by C. A. Swensson, this new Swedish-language weekly newspaper appeared in 1882 in Lindsborg, Kansas. It was introduced in the first issue as "A Journal devoted to political, general and local news, Tidings from the Swedish-American Settlements and the Development of the great West and Southwest." Assisting Swensson in this new venture were J. A. Udden and Edw. Nelander, both associated with Bethany Academy.

Another Lindsborg paper, the *Lindsborg Localist*, commented about it: "A neat little paper it is. May it grow; grow, grow and still grow. It is spicy, full of news, Republican and a friend of temperance" (Lindquist 1953, 167). At that time it was the only Swedish paper in Kansas. The October 3, 1883, issue included a supplement in English with the title "Proceedings of the State Temperance Convention."

The paper was abandoned in 1883 with an autumn issue. Then it was absorbed by *Gamla och Nya Hemlandet. Sources:* Bengston 461; http://ksuc-agent.auto-graphics.com/; LIBRIS; Lindquist 1953, 167; WorldCat.

Augustana College Swenson Center: 1882–1883
Bethany College: 1882–1883, Microfilm
Kansas State Historical Society: 071.81 M24 1882–1883
WorldCat: Chicago Historical Society: 1882
LIBRIS: Royal Library of Sweden: 1882–1883

Kansas Stats Tidning

[*Kansas State Newspaper*]
Lindsborg, KS: Skarstedt & Lundqvist
Vol. 1, nos. 1–10
December 24, 1879–February 25, 1880
Sometimes referred to as: *Kansas Statstidning*

Ernst Skarstedt and Emil Lundqvist started a Swedish language weekly newspaper in Lindsborg, Kansas, with its first issue on December 24, 1879.

Skarstedt, the celebrated Swedish writer, had arrived from Sweden in the spring of 1879 to work as a farmhand and carpenter in the Lindsborg area. Yearning to write, he intended the *Kansas Stats Tidning* to be a liberal independent political paper. He applied "high literary and cultural ideals" to his seven-column paper (Lindquist 1953, 167). However, he soon realized that there were not enough liberals among the Swedish pioneers in central Kansas to support his newspaper. After publishing ten issues, he gave up his enterprise with the February 25, 1880, issue.

While not an Augustana publication, the paper was important as the beginning of the Swedish press in Lindsborg, being launched by one who became a well-known Swedish newspaperman and journalist in America. *Sources:* Kastrup 464; LIBRIS; Lindquist 1953, 167; Setterdahl 16; WorldCat.

Augustana College Swenson Center: 1879–1880, Microfilm
Kansas State Historical Society: 071.81 M24m 1879–1880
LIBRIS: Royal Library of Sweden: December 24, 1879–January 4, 1880

Kansas Young Lutheran

Lindsborg, KS: [s.n.]
Vol. 1, no. 1–vol. 4, no. 12
January 1908–December 1911
Became: *Christian Messenger*

This paper was the organ of the Kansas Conference Luther League of the Augustana Lutheran Synod. It was issued monthly, using both English and Swedish text. *Sources:* Ander 1956, 162; ULS.

Augustana College Swenson Center: Vols. 1–4; 1908–1911
ULS: Kansas State Historical Society: Vols. 1–4
    Minnesota Historical Society: Vols. [1–3]

Kansasposten

See *Kansas Posten.*

The Key

See *Luther College & Academy Yearbook.*

Kina Missionären: Luthersk Tidskrift

[*China Missionary: Lutheran Periodical*]
St. Paul, MN: Foreign Mission Society
Rock Island, IL: China Mission Society
Vol. 6, no. 1–vol. 23, no. 12

March 1908–December 1925
Continues: *Luthersk Tidskrift för Hednamission och Diakoni*
Continued by: *Augustana Foreign Missionary*

Interest in providing mission assistance in China was supported by *Kina Missionären*, the new name for its predecessor *Luthersk Tidskrift för Hednamission och Diakoni*. Publication was moved from St. Paul, Minnesota, to Rock Island, Illinois. The volume numbering was continued from the previous title except that the March 1908 issue should have been number 3.

This Swedish-language monthly included general articles about world missions. However, the emphasis was on mission work in China, so letters and reports from Augustana Synod missionaries in China were regularly included. Reports of contributions were also printed.

A. F. Almer continued as editor with the assistance at various periods of time from C. A. Hultkrans, Carl E. Nelson, A. W. Edwins, and J. N. Brandelle. It was a sixteen-page paper in a single column with a 15 cm. × 24 cm. format. The price was twenty-five cents per year.

In its final issue (December 1925) the editor of *Kina Missionären* announced that a new mission newspaper, the *Augustana Foreign Missionary* to be published in both Swedish and English, would replace it. *Sources:* Erickson 51; LIBRIS; WorldCat.

Augustana College Swenson Center: 1913, 1914, 1924
Evangelical Lutheran Church in America Archives: AUG 24/4/2 Vols. 6–23; 1908–1925
Erickson: Lutheran School of Theology at Chicago: Vols. 6–23; 1908–1925
Minnesota Historical Society: Vols. 7–23; 1909–1925
Royal Library of Sweden
LIBRIS: Swedish Emigrant Institute: Årg. [7, 9–11, 14–22], 23; [1909, 1911–1913, 1916–1924], 1925

Korsbaneret: Kristlig Kalender för . . .

[*The Banner of the Cross: Church Calendar for . . .*]
Chicago, IL: Enander & Bohman (1880–1881)
Moline, IL: Wistrand & Thulin (1882)
Moline, IL: Thulin & Anderson (1883–1884)
Rock Island, IL: Augustana Book Concern (1885–1950)
Vols. 1–71
[1879] 1880–1950
Continued by: *Augustana Annual*

Volume 50 includes index for Vols. 1–50 (1880–1929); Volume 71 includes index for Vols. 51–71 (1930–1950)

Korsbaneret was an illustrated annual publication of the Augustana Lutheran Synod. It contained historical sketches, church and congregational news, biographical articles and obituaries of clergy and other leaders, articles about the various synod schools, information about ordinands, religious articles, and poetry.

Olof Olsson and Carl A. Swensson in 1879 began planning *Korsbaneret* as a Christmas book. *Korsbaneret* started its long life in Chicago, being published at the Enander & Bohman printing establishment. In 1880, it was taken over by the Föreningen Ungdomens Vänner, a publication society at Augustana College in Rock Island, Illinois. The group continued publishing *Korsbaneret* for three more years. In 1884 it was published by the Augustana Tract Society. The Augustana Book Concern then accepted responsibility for its publication when through its long life *Korsbaneret* made solid its place as the Swedish yearbook of the Augustana Synod. Each annual yearbook contained 250 to 300 pages. Many readers considered *Korsbaneret* as the synod's devotional manual. Its popularity was partly based on its "homely fare" and appeal to Swedish-speaking readers.

Many capable individuals served as editors and associate editors over the years. That list includes O. Olsson, C. A. Swensson, A. O. Bersell, C. A. Bäckman, C. M. Esbjörn, S. P. A. Lindahl, E. Norelius (1893, 1896), O. J. Siljestrom (1899–1900), J. G. Dahlberg (1903–1906), C. J. Bengston, P. Thelander, O. H. Ardahl (1915), O. N. Olson, A. W. Lindquist, C. A. Lindevall, H. P. Johnson, A. T. Lundholm, S. G. Hägglund, and G. A. Fahlund.

As the trend toward use of the English language heightened and moved forward, *Korsbaneret* held its own as "a treasured synodical annual" (Nystrom 71). When in 1929 the Augustana Book Concern discontinued publishing new Swedish-language materials, only *Korsbaneret* along with *Augustana* survived. It continued through its seventy-first volume in 1950, when the Augustana Book Concern Board decided that *Korsbaneret* should become a part of the *Augustana Annual*, "the publication having set a record for popularity and its readers one for loyalty." (Olson 1933, 64) It is now considered a valuable record of and one of the most important references for Augustana Lutheran Synod history. *Sources:* http://tomos.oit.umn.edu/F; Larsson & Tedenmyr 49; LIBRIS; Nystrom 71, 80; Olson 1933, 64; WorldCat.

Augustana College Swenson Center: BX8009 .K6 1880–1950
Bethany College: 839.7 K84 1880–1950
Evangelical Lutheran Church in America Archives: AUG 14/2 Vols. 1–71; 1880–1950

Evangelical Lutheran Church in America Archives Region 8—PA (Greenville): 1883, 1892, 1894–1896, 1898–1944, 1946–1949
Gustavus Adolphus College: AY75.K7 1880–1950
Luther Seminary: BX8049.A26K6 1880–1883; 1885–1886; 1888–1894; 1896–1946; 1948–1950
Lutheran School of Theology at Chicago: BX8009 .K6 Vols. 1–60, 62–71; 1880–1939, 1941–1950
Lutheran Theological Seminary at Gettysburg: BX8009 .K6 H 1880–1892, 1899, 1911–1912, 1914, 1922–1924, 1927–1928, 1935
Lutheran Theological Seminary at Philadelphia: BX8049 .A18 1880–1881, 1883, 1885–1944, 1946–1950
Midland Lutheran College: 1890–1922
Minnesota Historical Society: BX8049.2 .K84 1880–1950
Pacific Lutheran Theological Seminary: BX8049 K844 1903–1904, 1906–1907, 1909–1911, 1913–1914, 1916–1919, 1921–1922, 1926–1948, 1950
Pacific Lutheran University: SIE AY75 .K7 1881–1939, 1941–1949
Trinity Lutheran Seminary: 1885, 1888–1890, 1893–1934
University of Minnesota–Minneapolis: BX8049 .K67x Vols. 1–69, 71; 1880–1948, 1950; Also: 839.5 K844 Vols. 1–71; 1880–1950
LIBRIS: Royal Library of Sweden
Swedish Emigrant Institute: 1880–1950
Uppsala University: 1880–1950

Kyrkobladet: Kyrko-Tidning för Warren-Distriktet

[*Church Leaflet: Church Paper for the Warren, PA District*]
Rock Island, IL: Augustana Book Concern
Vol. 1, no. 1–vol. 12? [Erickson records 1911 as volume 7 and also as volume 12.]
January? 1905–December 1911 [Söderström indicates that the first issue was August 1905.]

This monthly paper was issued for the congregations in the Warren, Pennsylvania District of the Augustana Lutheran Synod. It contained news from member churches in the district and articles of a religious nature. Editors included J. A. Rinell, C. A. Hallberg, and E. F. Bergren. *Sources:* Ander 1956, 162; Erickson 55; Söderström 48.

Augustana College Swenson Center: Vols. 1–7 ; 1905–1911
Erickson: Royal Library of Sweden: Vols. 1–12; January 1905–December 1911

Kyrkohärolden: Svenska Lutherska South St. Paul Pastoratets Tidning

[*Church Herald: Paper for Swedish Lutheran Pastors of South St. Paul*]
St. Paul, MN: [s.n.]
Vols. 1–12?
June 1907–1918
Sometimes referred to as: *Kyrko-Härolden*

This was an Augustana Lutheran publication for the clergy in the St. Paul and South St. Paul, Minnesota, area. *Sources:* Ander 1956, 162; Söderström 27.

Augustana College Swenson Center: Vols. 1–2, 4–7, 9, 11; 1907–1909, 1910–1913, 1915, 1917

Kyrkosången: Musiktidning för Församlingskörer inom den Evang. Lutherska Augustana–Synoden

[*The Church Song: Music Journal for Church Choirs of the Evangelical Lutheran Augustana Synod*]
Minneapolis, MN: Kyrkosången Publishing Co. (1906–1908)
St. Peter, MN: Kyrkosången Publishing Co. (1909–1911)
Minneapolis, MN: Peter R. Melin, Inc. (1912–?)
Vol. 1, no. 1–vol. 11?
November, 1906–1917?

Planned for the use of Augustana Synod parish musicians, the periodical *Kyrkosången* appeared in November 1906. Its contents included anthems for church choirs and articles on music, emphasizing church music and pipe organs. The major portion of each issue was devoted to anthems.

R. Lagerström, a professor of music at Gustavus Adolphus College, and Peter R. Melin, the organist at Center City, Minnesota, were the editors. Published entirely in Swedish, it was issued quarterly until 1911 when it was published three times a year—the first, second, and fourth quarters. Music and text were paged separately with continuous paging for the separate sections. Subscription price was $1.25 per year through 1911, then $1.00 and finally 80 cents in January 1916. The ending date is uncertain; however, holdings are recorded through 1917. *Sources:* Erickson 56; Hendrickson 7; WorldCat.

Augustana College Swenson Center: M2126 .K97x Vols. 1–11; 1906–1917
Luther Seminary: Vol. 11; November 1917
University of Minnesota–Minneapolis: Vol. 1, no. 1; November 1906

Erickson: Gustavus Adolphus College: Vols. [1, 3], [1907, 1909]
    Minnesota State Historical Society: Vols. 1–7, [9], 10, [11]; 1906–1913,
    [1915], 1916, [1917]

Kyrkotidning för Cleveland Distriket

[*Church Paper for Cleveland District*]
Rock Island, IL: Augustana Book Concern for the Cleveland District
Vol. 1, no. 1–vol. 25
February 1904–1930
Became: *Church Paper for the Cleveland District*

This was a monthly paper for the Lutheran churches of the Augustana
Synod in the Cleveland District of the New York Conference. The areas of
Cleveland, Ashtabula, Erie, Youngstown, and Akron were included. Contents were devoted to district news items and schedules of church services. Inspirational articles and poems were also included. *Sources:* Ander
1956, 163; Erickson 57; ULS.

Evangelical Lutheran Church in America Archives: [1904–1930]
Erickson: Minnesota Historical Society: Vols. [5–7], 8, [9–10, 13], 14,
    [15–16], 17–19, [20]; [1908–1910], 1911, [1912–1913, 1916], 1917,
    [1918–1919], 1920–1922, [1923]
    Royal Library of Sweden: Vols. [1–12, 23–27]; [1904–1915, 1926–1930]
    ULS: Augustana College: Vols. 1–14, 21, [23–25]

Kyrkotidning för Jamestown-Distriket
af Svenska Lutherska New York Konferensen

[*Church Paper for the Jamestown District of the Swedish Lutheran New York
    Conference*]
Rock Island, IL: Augustana Book Concern
December 1905?–1916? [Ander used 1907 as the beginning date.]
Sometimes referred to as: *Kyrko Tidning* or *Kyrko-Tidning*

This monthly publication was issued for the congregations in the
Jamestown District of the New York Conference of the Augustana
Lutheran Synod. It carried district and local church news. *Sources:* Ander
1956, 163; Lundeen, group 6.

Augustana College Swenson Center: Vols. 1–3; 1906–1916
Lundeen: Evangelical Lutheran Church in America Archives:
    1905–1907

– L –

L.B.A. Bulletin

Des Moines, IA: Lutheran Brotherhood of America
Vols. 1–5
January 1920–December 1924
Continued by: *Lutheran Brotherhood*

Issued quarterly for men interested in the Lutheran Brotherhood organization, the *L.B.A. Bulletin* carried news, convention proceedings, and inspirational articles. All material was written in English. As of 1925 the title changed to *Lutheran Brotherhood*.

The ELCA Archives provides information about the organization:

Begun in 1917 in Des Moines, Iowa, the LBA [Lutheran Brotherhood of America] was formed by local church leaders to provide a religious center for the many Lutheran soldiers stationed at Camp Dodge while training for service in World War I. The LBA was very successful, gaining sixty thousand members within its first few months of existence and establishing centers at military sites and colleges around the country.

The first biennial convention was held in 1919, in Chicago, Illinois. After the war the LBA continued to support Lutherans who were members of the armed forces but also had to shift its focus to other areas. The LBA began to support existing men's Lutheran organizations, to promote the formation of new Synodical Brotherhoods, and support Lutheran Brotherhood centers. It also endeavored to provide insurance as part of its program. In 1920 the Luther Union, an insurance provider, agreed to work along with the LBA. Luther Union changed its name to Lutheran Brotherhood. While the two organizations were separate, they endeavored to affiliate their members with each other. In 1927 the LBA dissolved and reorganized.

Sources: http://lrc.elca.org:8080/webcat/; Matthews 142; WorldCat.

Evangelical Lutheran Church in America Archives
Lutheran Theological Seminary at Gettysburg: Vols. 1–5; 1920–1924
Wisconsin Historical Society: Vol. 3, no. 3; November 1922

L. B. I. Bulletin

St. Paul, Minneapolis, MN: Lutheran Bible Institute
19??–May 1955
Continued by: *Bulletin/Lutheran Bible Institute*

Published quarterly by the Lutheran Bible Institute, this bulletin presented news and feature articles. *Source:* http://mnhs.mnpals.net.

Minnesota Historical Society: BS603.L88

Lekkamraten: bilder för de små

[*The Playmate: Pictures for the Small*]
Rock Island, IL: Augustana Book Concern
1887?–?
Sometimes referred to as: *Lek–kamraten*

A publication for young children, *Lekkamraten* included illustrations accompanying the Swedish text. Its content was religious and in simple language. Editions contained twenty-four pages. *Sources:* Blanck 1997, 158; LIBRIS.

LIBRIS: Royal Library of Sweden: 1887
No United States holdings reported.

Let's Be Intercessors

See *Bulletin/Lutheran Bible Institute.*

Lille Barnvännen

[*The Friend of Little Children*]
Omaha, NE: Immanuel Deaconess Institute
October 1898–1913
Sometimes referred to as: *Den Lille Barnvännen*

Ander lists this as an annual publication of the Immanuel Deaconess Institute, issued from 1898 to 1913 just prior to Thanksgiving Day. It consisted of four pages.

Andreen writes that the paper was founded in 1901 by E. A. Fogelström for promotion of the children's home at the Immanuel Deaconess Institute. Fogelström was the founder and strong force in the organization of the institute. *Sources:* Ander 1956, 163; Andreen 1905, 177; Söderström 40.

Augustana College Swenson Center: October 1902

Lille Missionären: Illustrerad Missionstidning för de unga

[*The Little Missionary: Illustrated Missions Paper for the Young*]
Rock Island, IL: Augustana Book Concern
Vol. 1, no. 1–vol. 4?
January 1893–1896?
Sometimes referred to as: *Den Lille Missionären*

A mission paper for children in Sunday church school, *Den Lille Missionären*, appeared in January 1893 as a publication edited by O. Olsson. It was issued monthly as a four-page illustrated paper featuring articles about missions in foreign lands. Format was three columns on 22 cm. × 29 cm. paper. Subscription price was twenty cents per year.

Olsson served as editor through 1894. A. Rodell then edited the paper from 1895 to 1896 when it ceased publication.

Most sources indicate 1893 as the first year of publication. However, Bengston claims that the first issue was dated July 19, 1892 (465). All holdings reported show the 1893 date as the first volume. *Sources:* Ander 1956, 163; Bengston 465; Erickson 60.

Lutheran Theological Seminary at Gettysburg: Vols. 1, [2–3], 4; 1893–1896
Erickson: Augustana College: Vol. 1: nos. 1, 3–4, 6; January, March, April, June 1893
Royal Library of Sweden: Vol. 1; 1893

Lindsborg Mail

See *Lindsborgs-Posten*.

Lindsborgs-Posten

Lindsborg, KS: Bethany Book & Printing Co.
December 1897–December 1930 [LIBRIS reports that separate occasional numbers were published during the period of 1889–1896.]
Continued by: *Kansas Conference Lutheran*
Sometimes referred to as:
Lindsborgs Posten
Lindsborg Posten
Lindsborg Mail
Linsborg Mail

Another effort to establish a Swedish-language weekly newspaper in Lindsborg, Kansas, came with the first issue of the *Lindsborgs-Posten* in December 1897. Founded by C. A. Swensson, he was its first editor and publisher. The Lindsborg Land Company provided the financial support with a donation of a lot and a house on it in Lindsborg.

Even though it was designed for general news reporting, the eight-page paper was a semiofficial organ for the Kansas Conference of the Augustana Synod. During his tenure at Bethany College as its president, Swensson made the paper an organ of the school. He used the paper "to gain the goodwill of the businesses of Lindsborg. He generally wrote brief laudatory notices of each businessman along the street, and after applying that softening process he never failed to call on each one of them for a good-sized ad" (Bergin in Backlund 69).

Because of the press of Swensson's responsibilities with the young college, in 1899 he turned over the editor position to G. G. Peterson. Other editors during the lifetime of the paper were A. Bergin, G. A. Dorf (1919–October 17, 1928), J. P. Leaf (1928–January 8, 1930), and Hans J. Hoff (1930).

Some portions were written in English until later all material was in English. It continued to serve as the organ of the Swedish community of Lindsborg and its surrounding territory, but also regularly generating support for Bethany College. In 1925 there were twelve hundred subscribers. When it ended publication in December 1930, it was succeeded by the *Kansas Conference Lutheran*, a monthly paper. *Sources:* Backlund 69; Capps 233; Lindquist 1953, 167–168; LIBRIS; *Newspapers* 2:115; Setterdahl 16; WorldCat.

Augustana College Swenson Center: 1897–1930 scattered issues, Microfilm
Bethany College: 1898–1930, Microfilm
University of North Dakota: AN49 .L55x 1909–1913, Microfilm
Wisconsin Historical Society: January 1, 1908–January 15, 1930, Microfilm; Lacks: 1917: July 11–September 5, 19–October 17, 31–November 21
LIBRIS: Royal Library of Sweden: 1898–1930, Microfilm

Linsborg Mail

See *Lindsborgs-Posten*.

Little Folks

Rock Island, IL: Augustana Book Concern
Vol. 1, no. 1–vol. 27, no. 39
January 1, 1928–September 26, 1954
Continued by: *'til 8 Stories*
Sometimes referred to as: *The Little Folks*

A leaflet designed for the youngest children attending Sunday church school began weekly publication in January 1928 with the name *The Little Folks*. It was issued in the English language in response to the growing interest in providing Augustana children with such materials. In its later years, Mrs. C. Vernon Swenson served as the editor. Beginning in October 1954, the name was changed to '*til 8 Stories*. *Sources: Augustana Annual* 1954, 72; Lundeen, group 7; WorldCat.

Augustana College Swenson Center: 1931–1953
Evangelical Lutheran Church in America Archives: AUG 25/5/7 Vols. 1–26; 1928–1953
Gustavus Adolphus College Archives: Vols. 15–27, no. 39; 1942–September 26, 1954

L Q

See *Lutheran Quarterly.*

Lutersk Kvartalskrift: för Behandling af Teologiska och Krykliga, Pedagogiska, Literära, och Sociala Frågor

[*Lutheran Quarterly Review: for Treatment of Theological and Christian, Educational, Literary and Social Questions*]
Rock Island, IL: Alumni-Föreningen vid Augustana College
Vol. 1, no. 1–vol. 3, no. 1
January 1887–January 1889
Parallel title: *Lutheran Quarterly Review*
Sometimes referred to as: *Luthersk Qvartalsskrift*
Title frequently misspelled as: *Luthersk Kvartalskrift*

Published by the Alumni Association of Augustana College, *Lutersk Kvartalskrift* existed for two years from January 1887 through January 1889. Apparently, it ceased publication abruptly. Issued quarterly, it appeared each January, April, July, and October.

As the subtitle indicates, the periodical contained scholarly articles related to theology and discussions of questions on education, literature, and social matters. Text was in both Swedish and English. Each issue was of substantial size, being sixty-four pages (15 cm. × 22 cm.). The price of $2.00 per year applied to the first two issues. Then the price was lowered to $1.50 per year.

Serving as editors at various times were C. A. Swensson, C. A. Bäckman, and C. W. Foss. Assistants at various times were C. M. Esbjörn, C. J. Petri, E. Nelander, S. M. Hill, J. S. Carlson, and G. B. Anderson. *Sources:* Erickson 64; WorldCat.

Center for Research Libraries: Vol. 1, no. 1–vol. 3, no. 1; January 1887–January 1889

Evangelical Lutheran Church in America Archives: Vols. 1–2; 1887–1888
Gustavus Adolphus College Archives: Vols. 1–3; January 1887–January 1889
Lutheran Theological Seminary at Gettysburg: Vols. 1–3, no. 1; 1887–1889
Minnesota Historical Society: Vol. 1, no. 1–vol. 3, no. 1; January 1887–January 1889
Wisconsin Historical Society: BX8001 .L155 Vols. 1–2; 1887–1888
WorldCat: Augustana College: Vols. 1–2, nos. 1–4; vol. 3, no. 1; 1887–1889

Luth. Kyrkotidning

[*Lutheran Church Paper*]
[Vasa, MN: s.n.] (January 1, 1872–February 1872)
Red Wing, MN: L. E. Svendjens boktryckeri (February 15, 1872–December 1872)
Årg. 1, nos. 1–24
January 1, 1872–December 15, 1872
Continues: *Luthersk Kyrko-tidning* (Vasa, MN)
Continued by: *Luthersk Kyrkotidning* (Red Wing, MN)
Sometimes referred to as: *Luthersk Kyrko-tidning* or *Luth. Kyrkotidning* (Vasa, MN)

In December 1871, Eric Norelius established a Swedish-language paper *Luthersk Kyrko-tidning* with the plan that it be published in the interest of the Minnesota Conference of the Augustana Lutheran Synod. A month later in January 1872 the title was adjusted to *Luth. Kyrkotidning*.

Another change occurred in February 1872 when the paper was printed in Red Wing, Minnesota, at L. E. Svendjens Boktrycheri. Even though the December 1871 issue was numbered as year 1, number 1, the first issue in 1872 was also numbered year 1, number 1.

Intended to be a semimonthly issued on the first and fifteenth of each month, it held to this plan throughout 1872 with twenty-four issues produced. Usually it included sixteen pages, 15 cm. × 23 cm. The annual subscription price was one dollar. Articles and news items were of particular interest to the Augustana Lutheran clergy in Minnesota.

As of January 1873 it returned to its earlier title *Luthersk Kyrkotidning*. It continued to be printed in Red Wing, Minnesota. *Sources:* Erickson 66; http://jkm.ipac.dynixasp.com/; http://lms01.harvard.edu/F/; LIBRIS; WorldCat.

Center for Research Libraries: Vol. 1, nos. 2–24; January 15–December 15, 1872

Gustavus Adolphus College Archives: Vol. 1, nos. 1–24; January 1–
    December 15, 1872
Harvard University Divinity School: Årg. 1, nos. 2–24; 1872, Microfilm
Luther College (Iowa): BX8001 .L985 Vol. 1; 1872
Lutheran School of Theology at Chicago: BX8001 .L95 1872
Lutheran Theological Seminary at Gettysburg: Vol. [1]; [1872]
Minnesota Historical Society: BX8001 .L986 Vol. 1, nos. 1–24; January
    1–December 15, 1872, Paper and Microfilm
University of Minnesota–Minneapolis: BX8049 .L88x Vol. 1, no. 23; De-
    cember 1, 1872
Erickson: Augustana College
    Royal Library of Sweden
LIBRIS: Swedish Emigrant Institute: Vol. 1, nos. 1–24; 1872

Luther Academy Catalog

Wahoo, NE: Luther Academy
1884–1908
Continued by: *Luther College Catalog*

Luther Academy was founded on November 10, 1883. The academic
program expanded in 1909 when Luther College was established. High
school instruction was offered continuously. *Source:* Midland Lutheran
College Archives.

Midland Lutheran College: 1884–1908

Luther Academy Visitor

Wahoo, NE: Faculty of Luther Academy
Vol. 1, no. 1–vol. 5?
December 15, 1904–1909
Continued by: *Luther College Visitor*
Sometimes referred to as: *Luther Visitor*

Issued monthly chiefly in English with some Swedish text, this was the
voice of Luther Academy. "Christian Culture True Enlightenment" was
included as its subtitle. The title was changed in 1909 to *Luther College Visitor* to recognize the expanded academic program of the school. *Sources:*
Midland Lutheran College Archives; WorldCat.

Midland Lutheran College: 1904–1909, Paper and Microfilm
Nebraska State Historical Society: Film 378.782 L97Jv 1904–1909, Mi-
    crofilm

Luther Bladet: Tidning för Central Distriktet av California Konferensen av den Evangeliskt Lutherska Augustana–Synoden

[*Luther Newsletter: Newspaper for the Central District of the California Conference of the Evangelical Lutheran Augustana Synod*]
Escalon, CA: [s.n.]
No. 1–?
1922–19??

Written in both Swedish and English text, this newsletter was issued specifically for the Central District of the California Conference. *Source:* LIBRIS.

LIBRIS: Swedish Emigrant Institute: 1922
No United States holdings reported.

Luther College Advocate

Wahoo, NE: Luther College
1918–1935; 1941–1962

This publication was issued quarterly during 1918–1931 with the subtitle "Quarterly Record of Work & Purpose of Luther College." It was issued bimonthly during 1932–1935. Resuming publication again in 1941, it continued to 1962. *Source:* Midland Lutheran College Archives.

Midland Lutheran College: 1918–1935; 1941–1947; 1949–1962

Luther College and Academy Yearbook

Wahoo, NE: Faculty and Students of Luther College and Academy
1914–1962

During the early years at Luther College and Luther Academy, a yearbook was issued irregularly, due to financial constraints. As of 1949 it was issued at the end of each academic year.

The 1914 volume had the title *Viking*. The 1923 volume is the fortieth anniversary album. It was published by a staff chosen by the board of directors, the faculty, and the senior class of Luther College. It was published with the title *Luther College 1923* by the Augustana Book Concern.

The 1928 volume had the title *Luther College.*
The 1933 volume *Luther* is the fiftieth anniversary album.
The 1943 volume is the sixtieth anniversary album. It had the title *Anchor*.
The 1947 volume had the title *The Key.*

Beginning with volumes issued annually as of 1949 the title was *The Triangle*. Publication continued through 1962 when Luther College closed its campus and merged with Midland College. The title derives from the popular campus walk in front of and south of the Old Main building. *Sources:* http://library.ilcso.illinois.edu; Midland Lutheran College Archives.

Augustana College: LD7501 .W22 L86 1923
Midland Lutheran College: 1914, 1923, 1928, 1933, 1943, 1947, 1949, 1951, 1953–1962

Luther College Catalog

Wahoo, NE: Luther College
1909–1962
Continues: *Luther Academy Catalog*

Luther College was established in 1909 as an expanded program of Luther Academy. It closed at the end of the 1962 academic term and then merged with Midland Lutheran College.

The Archives at Midland Lutheran College has custody of all materials transferred from Luther College and Academy. Holdings include publications, committee reports, administrative papers, file folders, catalogs, newspapers, bulletins, and other miscellaneous papers. *Source:* Midland Lutheran College Archives.

Augustana College Swenson Center: incomplete file
Midland Lutheran College: 1909–1962

Luther College Visitor

Wahoo, NE: Faculty and Students of Luther College
Vol. 5, no. 7–vol. 55?
June 1909–April 1959
Continues: *Luther Academy Visitor*
Sometimes referred to as: *Luther Visitor*

In 1909, when the academic program at Luther Academy was expanded, the newspaper title was changed to *Luther College Visitor*. Some Swedish text was used in the early years. The paper was issued monthly from June 1909 through May 1918, and then monthly during the school year from August 1918 through March/April 1959. *Sources:* Midland Lutheran College Archives; WorldCat.

Midland Lutheran College: 1909–1925, [1926], 1927–1947, [1949–1950, 1955], Paper; 1909–1959, Microfilm
Nebraska State Historical Society: 1909–1910, 1912–1959, Microfilm

Luther Visitor

See *Luther Academy Vistor* and *Luther College Visitor*.

Lutheran Beacon

[s.l.: s.n.]
1931–1933

This paper was issued for the Pittsburgh District of the New York Conference of the Augustana Lutheran Synod. *Source:* Lundeen, group 6.

Lundeen: Evangelical Lutheran Church in America Archives: 1931–1933

Lutheran Bible Institute Bulletin

See *L. B. I. Bulletin*.

The Lutheran Brotherhood Bond

Minneapolis, MN: The Brotherhood
Vol. 29, no. 3–vol. 46, no. 3
July 1952–July 1969
Continues: *The Bond* (1924)
Continued by: *The Bond* (Minneapolis, MN: 1969)

Issued monthly, except for August, from 1952 to 1959, *The Lutheran Brotherhood Bond* periodical was published in the interest of friends and policy holders of insurance with the Lutheran Brotherhood fraternal insurance firm. From 1959 to 1969 it was issued each month. Then it assumed its earlier title *The Bond*. As the organ of the Lutheran Brotherhood insurance firm, it has continued publishing to 2002. *Sources:* LIBRIS; WorldCat.

California Lutheran University: 1960+
Lutheran Theological Seminary at Gettysburg: Vols. 29–[36], 37– ; 1952–[1960], 1961–
Minnesota Historical Society: BX8001 .B6 Vols. 29:3–46:3; 1952–1969
Pacific Lutheran Theological Seminary: Vols. [28–30], 31–32, [33–34], 35–39, [40–46]; 1952–1969

Trinity Lutheran Seminary: 1953–1969
Wartburg Theological Seminary: Vols. 29–46; 1952/53–1969
LIBRIS: Royal Library of Sweden: Vols. 29–31; 1952/1953–1954/1955

Lutheran Brotherhood of America Bulletin

See *L. B. A. Bulletin.*

The Lutheran Companion (1911)

Rock Island, IL: Augustana Book Concern
Vol. 19, no. 1–vol. 57, no. 52
January 7, 1911–December 28, 1949
Merged with: *Augustana* (1889) to form *Augustana Lutheran*
Continues: *Young Lutheran's Companion*
Sometimes referred to as: *Lutheran Companion* (Rock Island, IL: 1911) or
  Companion

Beginning in 1911, *The Lutheran Companion* was designated the official English organ of the Augustana Lutheran Synod. Continuing its predecessor, the *Young Lutheran's Companion*, and with an enlarged program and scope, it served through 1949 as the major English-language weekly publication of the Augustana Synod during those years.

The 1935 Augustana anniversary album states that "what *Augustana* has been to the fathers *The Lutheran Companion* will be to their children and it will continue to reflect the religious and cultural life of the Synod" (*After Seventy-Five Years* 115). The same publication continues: "*The Lutheran Companion* supplies the younger families and our English speaking membership with inspiration for their spiritual life and information about the work of our Synod and the Church at large" (145).

The gradual genealogy of the *Lutheran Companion* can be seen from *The Alumnus*, the *Augustana Journal*, and the *Young Lutheran's Companion*. Continuing that serial numbering, it adopted the title *The Lutheran Companion* in 1911 with volume 19. Its size was increased from eight to twelve pages. In its early years to 1915, C. J. Södergren assumed editorial duties assisted by C. A. Wendell and E. W. Olson. C. J. Bengston who had been on the editorial staff of *Augustana* became the full-time editor in January 1915. The paper was then increased to sixteen pages and later to twenty-four pages in 1926. During the Bengston tenure, *The Lutheran Companion* did indeed become the official English organ of the Augustana Church during this language transition period from Swedish to English.

In February 1934, E. E. Ryden became editor, where he served the Augustana Synod publishing activity for twenty-seven years until 1961. At the end of 1949, *The Lutheran Companion* merged with *Augustana* (1889) to form the *Augustana Lutheran*.

During these thirty-eight years, the subscriber list of *The Lutheran Companion* increased to where it was sent to a majority of Augustana homes and was widely read by Augustana Synod members. Every Augustana congregation received a copy. Weekly copies were sent to every state and every continent. In 1917 there were 6,741 weekly copies sent; in 1926 the mailing list had increased to 11,398; in 1929 there were in excess of 19,000 copies sent out; in 1942 the circulation was 25,217; and in the late 1940s there were 41,000 subscribers. By the 1930s it exceeded *Augustana* in readership.

Capps comments that the reputation of *The Lutheran Companion* "had gained under Bengston as the principal spokesman for the most conservative opinions in the Swedish-American community continued and grew under the editorship of Ryden, who exemplified in the extreme the suspicion of change of many second-generation Swedish-Americans" (128). Indeed, it was the major Augustana Synod serial publication of the twentieth century.

Note: The ELCA Archives in Chicago has an index to *The Lutheran Companion* in a card file. This was prepared by Gilbert Adolphson. Articles are indexed by subject and title, but not by author. Volume and page numbers only are given. *Sources: After Seventy-Five Years* 115, 145; Augustana ELC, Century, 146; Capps 128; Hultgren 2001; Olson 1933, 61; Stephenson 350; WorldCat.

Augustana College: Vols. 19–57; 1911–1949
Bethany College: Vols. 19–57; 1911–1949
Evangelical Lutheran Church in America Archives: AUG/14/6 Vols. 28–57; 1920–1949, Paper and Microfilm
Gustavus Adolphus College: Vols. 21–57; 1913–1949
Luther Seminary: BX8001 .L93 Vols. 30, 32–37, 39–57; 1922, 1924–1929; 1931–1949, Paper; BX8001 .L93 Vols. 19–57; 1911–1949, Microfilm
Lutheran Theological Seminary at Gettysburg: Vols. [19–23, 26], 31–35, [36], 37, [38], 39–49, [50–51], 53–57; 1911–1949
Lutheran Theological Seminary at Philadelphia: Vols. [19], 20–24, [25], 26–28, [29], 30, [31–33], 34–35, [36–37], 38–39, [40], 41, [42], 43–45, [46–48], 49–57; 1911–1949
Midland Lutheran College: Vols. 50–57; 1942–1949
North Park University: BX8001 .L45 Vols. 44–57; 1936–1949
Pacific Lutheran Theological Seminary: 1911–1949, Microfilm
Pacific Lutheran University: Vols. 19–57; 1911–1949

Texas Lutheran University: Vols. 42–57; 1934–1949
Trinity Lutheran Seminary: 1918–1949
Wartburg Theological Seminary: Vols. 19–57; 1911–1949

The Lutheran Companion (1952)

Rock Island, IL: Augustana Book Concern
Vol. 97, no. 1–vol. 108, no. 52
January 2, 1952–December 26, 1962
ISSN 0024–743X
Merged with: *Lutheran* (Philadelphia, PA: 1919) and *Lutheran Counselor* and *Lutheran Tidings* (Cedar Falls, IA) to form *Lutheran* (Philadelphia, PA: 1963)
Continues: *Augustana Lutheran*
Sometimes referred to as: *Lutheran Companion*

With the first weekly issue in January 1952, the official organ of the Augustana Evangelical Lutheran Church returned to its former name *The Lutheran Companion*. This continued the *Augustana Lutheran* periodical. E. E. Ryden continued as editor until early 1961 when in March P. E. Gustafson became the new editor. Circulation increased from 61,164 subscribers in 1953 to 93,443 in 1958. During this time many local congregations placed the cost of subscriptions in their annual budget, which then made it possible to send a copy to the home of each member. Some of the volumes include an index at the end of the year, particularly volumes 99 through 108.

After its first year under this renewed title, *The Lutheran Companion* was the subject of the following report which emphasized its importance:

> *The Lutheran Companion* which reaches more readers than ever before in the history of this publication, is essential reading for every alert and informed Augustana Church man and woman. In these days of rapid change, the Church faces urgent and compelling opportunities in all departments of her activity. Week by week these opportunities and the outline of what the Church is doing to meet them are reflected in the pages of *The Lutheran Companion*.
>
> The intriguing story of our expanding American missions program, the compelling urgency of foreign missions, the importance of Christian education, the ministry of mercy, significant developments in our relationships with other Lutherans or other Christians all find their way into the pages of *The Lutheran Companion*, thus making our official Church press the basic medium of information in our Church's life.
>
> The Augustana Lutheran Church has established a record in American Lutheranism in circulation. It gives evidence that its readers are interested in

the Church press from the stimulating editorials to the most interesting paragraphs found under the heading, "Among the Churches." (*Augustana Annual* 1953, 87)

In a later summary report the mission of the paper was outlined:

Through the pages of this official church paper, the membership of the Church keeps receiving a steady stream of information pertaining to the entire program of the Church in education, missions, and social work. They keep abreast of the developments within the whole Christian Church at home and abroad, and thereby develop into stronger churchmen.

   An informed Church is an effective church, and the Board of Directors of the Augustana Book Concern, through the Editorial Staff of *The Lutheran Companion*, is making every effort to keep the Augustana Lutheran Church one of the best informed churches in the nation through the pages of *The Lutheran Companion*. (*Augustana Annual* 1954, 74)

With its final issue of December 26, 1962, the *Lutheran Companion* merged with three other Lutheran periodicals to form *Lutheran* published in Philadelphia, Pennsylvania, as of 1963. *Sources: Augustana Annual* 1953, 87; 1954, 74; Nystrom 65; WorldCat.

   Augustana College: Vols. 97–108; 1952–1962
   California Lutheran University: 1956–1962
   Evangelical Lutheran Church in America Archives: AUG 14/6 Vols. 97–108; 1952–1962, Paper and Microfilm
   Gustavus Adolphus College: Vols. 97–108; 1952–1962
   Luther Seminary: BX8001.L93 Vols. 97–108; 1952–1962 Paper and Microfilm
   Lutheran Theological Seminary at Gettysburg: Vols. 97–108; 1952–1962
   Lutheran Theological Seminary at Philadelphia: Vols. 97–108; 1952–1962
   Midland Lutheran College: Vols. 97–107; 1952–1961
   North Park University: BX8001 Vols. 97–108; 1952–1962
   Pacific Lutheran Theological Seminary: Vols. 97–108; 1952–1962 Microfilm
   Pacific Lutheran University: BX8001 .L46 Vols. 97–108; 1952–1962
   Texas Lutheran University: Vols. 97–98, 102–107; 1952–1953; 1956–1961
   Trinity Lutheran Seminary: 1952–1962
   Wartburg Theological Seminary: Vols. 97–108; 1952–1962

Lutheran Libraries

   Minneapolis, MN: Lutheran Church Library Association
   Vols. 1–44

Fall 1958–2002
ISSN 0024–7472
Continued by: *Libraries Alive*

The official journal of the Lutheran Church Library Association began publication in 1958 in Minneapolis. The local parish library movement among Augustana Lutherans was spearheaded by Erwin John, a lay member of Mount Olivet Lutheran Church, an Augustana Synod congregation in Minneapolis. There he organized a well-stocked collection of materials to meet the reading interests of lay members. It was his enthusiasm and dedication that led to the formation of the Lutheran Church Library Association.

The journal, *Lutheran Libraries*, was published quarterly. It included articles assisting laypersons in organizing a parish library, suggestions for purchases, and other helpful subjects related to library service in local congregations. An index exists for the years 1962–1972. *Source:* WorldCat.

California Lutheran University: 1958–2002
Gustavus Adolphus College: Vols. 1–28; 1958–1986
Luther Seminary: Z675 .C5L8 Vols. 1–44; 1958/1959–2002
Lutheran School of Theology at Chicago: Z675 .L8 L80 Vols. 1–44; 1958–2002
Lutheran Theological Seminary at Gettysburg: Vols. 1–44; 1958–2002
Lutheran Theological Seminary at Philadelphia: Vols. [1–3], 4–21, 24–33, 36–40; 1958–1979, 1982–1991, 1994–1997
Pacific Lutheran Theological Seminary: Vols. [1–3], 4– [1959–1961], 1961/62–
Pacific Lutheran University: Z671 .L8 Vols. 21–43; 1978–2001
Texas Lutheran University: Vols. 1– ; 1959–
Trinity Lutheran Seminary: 1958–2002
Wartburg Theological Seminary: Vols. 1–44; 1958–2002
WorldCat: Bethany College: Vols. 25– ; 1983–
    Evangelical Lutheran Church in America

Lutheran Messenger

[s.l.; s.n.]
1920–1925?

Lundeen records this as a Columbia Conference publication. *Source:* Lundeen, group 6.

Lundeen: Evangelical Lutheran Church in America Archives: 1920, no.1; 1921–1924; 1925, no. 2–3.

*Lutheran Publications: A Complete Listing of Books in
Print Published by the Lutheran Publishing Houses of America*

Rock Island, IL: Augustana Book Concern
Minneapolis, MN: Augsburg Publishing House
1924?–1974–1975?

This consolidated publisher's catalog lists publications from the Augustana Book Concern, Augsburg Publishing House, Concordia Publishing House, Fortress Press, and the Northwestern Publishing House. Indexes are also included. *Sources:* http://ruth.luthersem.edu; Lundeen, group 9.

Luther Seminary: Z7845 .L9L9 1924, 1952–1953, 1959–1960, 1964–1975
Lundeen: Evangelical Lutheran Church in America Archives: 1951–1960,
    1962–1963

Lutheran Q.

See *Lutheran Quarterly*.

Lutheran Quarterly

Gettysburg, PA: Editorial Council of Lutheran Theological Seminaries
Vol. 1, no. 1–vol. 29, no. 2
February 1949–May 1977
ISSN 0024–7499
Formed by the union of: *Lutheran Church Quarterly* and *Augustana Quarterly*
Continued by: *Lutheran Quarterly* (Milwaukee, WI)
Sometimes referred to as:
    Lutheran Quarterly (Gettysburg, PA: 1949)
    Lutheran Quarterly (Gettysburg, PA: 1949)
    Lutheran q.
    LQ
Indexed in:
    America, History and Life. 1963–1977 0002–7065
    Historical Abstracts. Part A. Modern History Abstracts. 1963–1977
    0363–2717
    Historical Abstracts. Part B. Twentieth Century Abstracts. 1963–1977
    0363–2725

In 1949, the *Augustana Quarterly* joined the *Lutheran Church Quarterly* to form a new theological journal, the *Lutheran Quarterly*. Conrad Bergendoff, the esteemed Augustana theologian, was its first editor.

This scholarly journal, held in high regard for its contents and editorial policies, is indexed in several major abstract services, as indicated above. According to the OCLC WorldCat database, at least 192 libraries worldwide own files of *Lutheran Quarterly*. *Sources:* LIBRIS; WisCat; WorldCat.

Augustana College: Vols. 1–29; 1949–1977
Bethany College: Vols. 1–28; 1949–1976
California Lutheran University: 1949–1977
Evangelical Lutheran Church in America Archives: AUG 14/11 1949–1977
Gustavus Adolphus College: Vols. 1–28; 1949–1976
Luther Seminary: BX8001 .L953 Vols. 1–29:2; 1949–1977
Lutheran School of Theology at Chicago: BX8001 .L617 Vols. 1–29; 1949–1977
Lutheran Theological Seminary at Gettysburg: Vols. 1–29:2; 1949–1977
Lutheran Theological Seminary at Philadelphia: Vols. 1–29:2; 1949–1977
Midland Lutheran College: Vols. 1–29; 1949–1977
North Park University: BX8001 .L617 Vols. 1–29; 1949–1977
Pacific Lutheran Theological Seminary: Vols. 1–29; 1949–1977
Texas Lutheran University: Vols. 1–29; 1949–1977
Trinity Lutheran Seminary: 1949–1977
Wartburg Theological Seminary: Vols. 1–23, 25–29; 1949–1977
LIBRIS: Lund University: Vols. 1–29:2; 1949–1977

Lutheran Quarterly Review

See *Lutersk Kvartalskrift*.

Lutheran Review

Modesto, CA: [s.n.]
1931–1943

This publication was the official monthly organ of the California Conference of the Augustana Lutheran Synod. *Sources:* Ander 1956, 164; Lundeen, group 6.

Lundeen: Evangelical Lutheran Church in America Archives: 1931–1943

Lutheran Social Service News

[s.l. : s.n.]
1956–1962

Lundeen states that this was a quarterly publication issued by the New York Conference of the Augustana Lutheran Synod. *Source:* Lundeen, group 6.

Lundeen: Evangelical Lutheran Church in America Archives: 1956–1962

Lutheran Teacher

See *Church School Teacher*.

Lutheran Voice

See *Views*.

Lutheran Women

Rock Island, IL: Augustana Book Concern
Vols. 1–3
March 1960–December 1962
ISSN 0458-5089
Formed by the union of: *Lutheran Woman's Work* and *Lutheran Women's World*
Continued by: *Lutheran Women* (Philadelphia: 1963) (ISSN 0024-7596)
Sometimes referred to as: *Lutheran Women* (Rock Island, IL)

Published for the United Lutheran Church Women, the Augustana Lutheran Church Women, the Lutheran Guild of the Suomi Synod, and the Women's Mission Society, AELC, this periodical was issued monthly, except for August.

At the end of 1962, and with the merger of these several Lutheran synods, the *Lutheran Women* magazine was consolidated with *Lutheran Woman's Work* magazine to form a new periodical *Lutheran Women* (Philadelphia: 1963). This was published in Philadelphia, Pennsylvania, as of early 1963. *Sources:* http://jkm.ipac; Matthews 156; WorldCat.

Augustana College: BX8001 .L85 Vols. 1–3; 1960–1962
Bethany College: Vols. 1–3; 1960–1962
California Lutheran University: 1960–1962
Evangelical Lutheran Church in America Archives: ULCA 29/8/1 Vols. 1–3; 1960–1962
Gustavus Adolphus College: Vols. 1–3:11; 1960–1962
Luther Seminary: BV4415 .L85 Vols. 1–3; 1960–1962

Lutheran School of Theology at Chicago: BV2540 .A1 .L910 Vols. 1–3; 1960–1962
Lutheran Theological Seminary at Gettysburg: Vols. 1–3; 1960–1962
Lutheran Theological Seminary at Philadelphia: Vols. 1–3; 1960–1962
Midland Lutheran College: Vols. 1–3; 1960–1962
Pacific Lutheran Theological Seminary: Vols. 1–3; 1960–1962
Pacific Lutheran University: BX8001 .L78 Vols. 1–3; 1960–1962
Wartburg Theological Seminary: Vol. 3, nos. 1–2, 4–11; 1962

Lutheran Women's World

Rock Island, IL: Augustana Lutheran Church Women
Vol. 54, no. 1–vol. 55, no. 2
January 1959–February 1960
Continues: *Mission Tidings*
Continued by: *Lutheran Women*

In 1958, the Women's Missionary Society, and in its early years known as the Woman's Home and Foreign Mission Society of the Augustana Synod, changed its name to Augustana Lutheran Church Women. A summary report of this action read:

> The synod gave ready approval in principle to a plan submitted by a special committee to change the name and scope of the work of the Women's Missionary Society. Henceforth it will be known as the Augustana Lutheran Church-women, and its new constitution, which was finally adopted by the organization at its biennial convention in Minneapolis in September [1958], calls for a program which is intended to embrace all the women of the Church. (*Augustana Annual* 1959, 44)

Its official monthly periodical in January 1959 then took the name *Lutheran Women's World*. That name was used through its February 1960 issue at which time it merged with *Lutheran Woman's Work* to become *Lutheran Women*. Mabel Olson and Carol L. Widen were editors of *Lutheran Women's World*.

In an advertisement the description read: "Each issue contains a colorful and interesting coverage of the operation of the Church-at-large near and far away . . . especially for women!" (*Augustana Annual* 1959, 214). Sources: *Augustana Annual* 1959, 44, 214; WorldCat.

Augustana College: BX8001 .L849 Vols. 54–55; 1959–1960
Bethany College: Vols. 54–55; 1959–1960
California Lutheran University: 1959

Evangelical Lutheran Church in America Archives: AUG 40/8/3/2
  Vols. 54–55; 1959–1960
Gustavus Adolphus College: Vols. 54:1–55:2; 1959–1960
Lutheran School of Theology at Chicago: BV2350 .M5 Vols. 54–55;
  1959–1960

Luthersk Kvartalskrift

See *Lutersk Kvartalskrift.*

Luthersk Kyrkotidning

[*Lutheran Church Paper*]
Rock Island, IL: [Augustana Book Concern]
Vol. 1, no. 1–vol. 2, no. 11
June 1908–June 1910

This little periodical was planned as a missionary news sheet to be read
by Swedish-speaking people in Brooklyn, New York. It was especially designed for readers who were not affiliated with a Lutheran congregation,
urging readers to provide Christian education and baptism for their children
and encouraging adults to "open their homes and hearts to the Lord's light
and truth." *Sources: Luthersk Kyrkotidning,* June 1908; WorldCat.

  Harvard University Divinity School: Vol. 1, nos. 1–4, 6–12; vol. 2, nos.
    1–11; 1908–1910, Microfilm
  Minnesota Historical Society: BX8001 .L9858 Vol. 1, no. 1–vol. 2, no. 11;
    June 1908–June 1910

Luthersk Kyrkotidning (Red Wing, MN)

[*Lutheran Church Paper*]
Red Wing, MN: L.E. Svendjens Boktryckeri (January 1873)
Red Wing, MN: Å. C. F. de Remee, "Argus" office (February–December
  1873)
Årg. 2, nos. 1–17
January 1873–December 1873
Merged with: *Det Rätta Hemlandet och Augustana* and *Missionären*
  (Chicago, IL) and *Nytt och Gammalt* to form *Augustana* (1874)
Continues: *Luth. Kyrkotidning*
Sometimes referred to as: *Luthersk Kyrkotidning*

Originally established by Eric Norelius in December 1871 at Vasa, Minnesota, *Luthersk Kyrkotidning* was issued in Red Wing, Minnesota, for all

of 1873. It continued to be published in the interest of the Minnesota Conference of the Augustana Lutheran Synod.

Earlier in 1872 it had been issued semimonthly. However, during 1873 it was sometimes issued only monthly for a total of seventeen issues. Usually it included sixteen pages of 15 cm. × 23 cm. size. The annual subscription price was one dollar. Articles and news items were of particular interest to the Augustana Lutheran clergy in Minnesota.

The editors of four separate papers, which in 1873 were currently being published at various places within the Augustana Synod, met to discuss their concern about the possibility that so many publications could work against Synod unity. They decided to combine *Luthersk Kyrkotidning* (Red Wing, MN) with *Det Rätta Hemlandet och Augustana*, and *Missionären* (Chicago, IL) and *Nytt och Gammalt* to form a new *Augustana* (1874). This new paper issued its first number in January 1874 with E. Norelius, T. N. Hasselquist and O. Olsson continuing as editors. *Sources:* Erickson 66; http://jkm.ipac.dynixasp.com/; http://lms01.harvard.edu/F/; LIBRIS; WorldCat.

Center for Research Libraries: Vol. 2, nos. 1–8, 10–17 (January–June 1873, September–December 1873

Gustavus Adolphus College Archives: Vol. 2, no. 1–vol. 2, no. 17; January–December 1873, Paper and Microfilm

Harvard University Divinity School: Årg. 2; 1873 Microfilm

Luther College (Iowa): BX8001 .L985 Vol. 2; 1873

Lutheran School of Theology at Chicago: BX8001 .L95 Vol. 2; 1873

Minnesota Historical Society: BX8001 .L986 Vol. 2, nos. 4–6, 8, 11–15; April–November 1873, Paper and Microfilm

University of Minnesota–Minneapolis: BX8049 .L88x Vol. 2, no. 6; May 1873

Erickson: Augustana College

Royal Library of Sweden

LIBRIS: Swedish Emigrant Institute: Vol. 2, no.1–vol. 2, no.17; 1873

Luthersk Kyrko-tidning (Vasa, MN)

[*Lutheran Church Paper*]
[Vasa, Goodhue Co., MN: s.n.]
Årg. 1, no. 1
December 1, 1871
Continued by: *Luth. Kyrkotidning*
Sometimes referred to as: *Luthersk Kyrko-tidning*

Established by Eric Norelius in late 1871, *Luthersk Kyrko–tidning* was published in the interest of the Minnesota Conference of the Augustana Lutheran Synod. This was an eight-page paper. The plan was that it would be issued semimonthly on the first and fifteenth of each month.

In January 1872 this paper was succeeded by *Luth. Kyrkotidning*, a paper that continued the intention of Norelius to present items of interest to Augustana Lutherans, especially the clergy, in Minnesota. *Sources:* Erickson 66; http://jkm.ipac.dynixasp.com/; http://lms01.harvard.edu/F/; LIBRIS; WorldCat.

Gustavus Adolphus College Archives: Vol. 1, no. 1; December 1, 1871, Paper and Microfilm
Harvard University Divinity School: Årg. 1, no. 1; 1871, Microfilm
Luther College (Iowa): BX8001 .L985 Vol. 1; 1871
Lutheran School of Theology at Chicago: BX8001 .L95 1871
Minnesota Historical Society: BX8001 .L986 Vol. 1, no. 1; December 1, 1871, Paper and Microfilm

Luthersk Qvartalsskrift

See *Lutersk Kvartalskrift*.

Luthersk Tidskrift för Hednamission och Diakoni

[*Lutheran Periodical for Foreign Missions and Diaconate*]
St. Paul, MN: Foreign Mission Society
Vol. 1, no. 1–vol. 6, no. 2
January 1903–February 1908
Continued by: *Kina Missionären*
Sometimes referred to as: *Luthersk Tidskrift*

A growing concern among Minnesota Conference clergy about foreign missions led to the beginning of a Swedish language periodical named *Luthersk Tidskrift för Hednamission och Diakoni* in 1903. This followed some serious discussions in 1901 among several clergy about the spiritual needs of the Chinese. The Minnesota Conference further studied the matter to the point where they voted to encourage the Augustana Synod to begin a mission in China. This paper further discussed the subject of supporting an interest especially for a mission in Honan Province. It included devotional articles about missions programs, letters from Augustana missionaries in China, and general promotional articles. Combined with this content were deaconess news and information, especially from the Bethesda Motherhouse in St. Paul, Minnesota.

A. F. Almer and C. A. Hultkrans were the editors of this sixteen-page monthly. In 1905 A. W. Edwins also served as editor, as did J. N. Brandelle as of 1907. Joining all of these men as an editorial committee in 1907 were J. E. Linner and J. E. Kjellgren. After the final issue in February 1908 it became *Kina Missionären*. *Sources:* Andreen 1905, 176; Erickson 51; Lundeen, group 8; Tiedge 9.

> Augustana College Swenson Center: Vol. 3, no. 2
> Evangelical Lutheran Church in America Archives: AUG 24/4/2 Vols. 1–5; 1903–1907; also Vol. 6, no. 2; February 1908
> Gustavus Adolphus College Archives: Vol. 4, nos. 2–8, 11, 12; vol. 5, nos. 1–3, 5–8, 10–12 [1906–1907]
> Erickson: Lutheran School of Theology at Chicago: Vols. 1–6; 1903–1908
> Minnesota Historical Society: Vol. 5; 1907
> Royal Library of Sweden

Lyceum Annual

> Rock Island, IL: Augustana College and Theological Seminary
> Vols. 3–5
> 1892–1894
> Continues: *Balder*

The literary annual, *Balder*, which had been published by the Lyceum student organization at Augustana College in 1890 and 1891, changed its name with the 1892 edition to the *Lyceum Annual*. It continued to publish stories, poems, and essays in both Swedish and English text. For further information about the Lyceum organization see paragraph at *Balder*.

The final issue was published in 1894. In 1902, the Lyceum organization took on the responsibility for a monthly periodical, *Augustana Observer*, the student paper. *Sources:* Ander 1956, 164; Bergendoff 96–97, 205; LIBRIS; ULS.

> Augustana College Swenson Center
> Library of Congress: LD271 .A6655 L9 1892–1894
> LIBRIS: Swedish Emigrant Institute: Vols. 3–5; 1892–1894

– M –

Manhem: Gustavus Adolphus Annual

> St. Peter, MN: Published by the senior class
> 1904
> Continued by: *Runes* (1906)

The first student annual at Gustavus Adolphus College was called *Manhem*. It was published by the senior class of 1904. An interesting feature in this yearbook was a cartoon "'To Stay, Or Not To Stay' depicting contending factors in the matter of whether the College should stay in St. Peter or move to Minneapolis" (Lund 1987, 39). *Sources:* Lund 1987, 39; Peterson 58.

Gustavus Adolphus College: LD 2091.G62G65 1904

Messenger

Minneapolis, MN: Minnesota College
1922–1931
Continues: *The Picayune*

The administration of Minnesota College (see narrative at *Picayune*) published this monthly paper for the churches and laypersons of the Minnesota Conference, as of 1922. It replaced the student newspaper *The Picayune*.

In 1925 it became a semimonthly paper when it was returned to student editors. When the school closed in 1931, publication ended. According to Peterson, assets were turned over to Gustavus Adolphus College. *Source:* Peterson 160.

No holdings reported.

Messenger

See *Bethany Messenger* (1902).

Minnesota Conference Advance

Minneapolis, MN: Executive Committee of the Minnesota Conference
Vol. 1, no. 1–vol. 6, no. 7
June 1943–December 1948
Continued by: *Advance*
Other title: *Advance* (Minneapolis, MN)

The *Minnesota Conference Advance* was designated as the official organ of the Lutheran Minnesota Conference of the Augustana Lutheran Synod. For the first year, it was issued quarterly, becoming a bimonthly with the July 1944 issue. Effective in 1949, the title was shortened to *Advance*. *Source:* WorldCat.

Augustana College Swenson Center: Vol. 5, no. 1–vol. 6, no. 7; 1947–
   1948
Evangelical Lutheran Church in America Archives: 1943–1948
Gustavus Adolphus College Archives: Vols. 1–6; 1943–1948
Harvard University Divinity School: Vols. 1–6; 1943–1948
Minnesota Historical Society: BX8049.1 .A34 Vols. 1–6; 1943–1948

Minnesota Conference Charities

Minneapolis, MN: Minnesota Conference Board of Christian Charities
   1941–1946?

This was a quarterly publication of the Minnesota Conference of the
Augustana Synod. *Sources:* Ander 1956, 165; Lundeen, group 6.

Lundeen: Evangelical Lutheran Church in America Archives: 1942, 1946

Minnesota Lutheran

St. Paul, MN: Minnesota Stats Tidning, Inc.
Clear Lake, WI: [s.n.]
Vol. 62, no. 9–vol. 63, no. 26
March 1, 1939–June 26, 1940
Continues: *Minnesota Stats Tidning* (St. Paul, MN: 1895)

Following the end of the *Minnesota Stats Tidning* and *Skaffaren* saga in
1939, which had begun many years earlier in 1877, there appeared a new
weekly newspaper with an English title, *Minnesota Lutheran*. This was the
continuation of *Minnesota Stats Tidning* (St. Paul, MN: 1895). Primarily in
English, there were still some articles published using the Swedish language.
   For the first several months it continued publication in St. Paul, Minnesota. Beginning with the August 16, 1939, issue it was published at
Clear Lake, Wisconsin, a small town in Polk County. Carl K. Towley was
the editor. The issue dated June 26, 1940, was the last. *Sources:* Capps 178;
LIBRIS; WorldCat.

Center for Research Libraries: Vol. 62, no. 9–vol. 63, no. 26; 1939–1940
Gustavus Adolphus College Archives: March 1, 1939–June 26, 1940, Mi-
   crofilm
Minnesota Historical Society: Vol. 62, no. 9–vol. 62, no. 32; March 1,
   1939–August 9, 1939, Microfilm
LIBRIS: Royal Library of Sweden: March 1939–June 1940

Minnesota Posten

[*The Minnesota Post*]
Red Wing, MN: [s.n.]
Vol. 1, nos. 1–24
November 7, 1857–October 13, 1858
Absorbed by: *Hemlandet, det Gamla och det Nya*

In 1857, the young Augustana clergyman, Eric Norelius, established the first Swedish-language newspaper in Minnesota. He gave it the title *Minnesota Posten*. Its purpose was to serve the Swedish people living in the Minnesota territory.

However, there seemed to be an air of competition with the Swedish paper, *Hemlandet, det Gamla och det Nya* which had been established in 1855 by T. N. Hasselquist in Galesburg, Illinois. In spite of the fact that both men were Swedish Lutherans and their respective publications were devoted to that cause, there were strained relations. Norelius wrote in his history of the Augustana Synod regarding this situation:

> I freely confess that it was largely my youthful lack of wisdom which led me to start a paper in Minnesota—a paper with the same program as Hemlandet. But underlying also was the old conflict between the center and the periphery, and I need hardly mention that Minnesota lay in the periphery. I also confess that I have taken the initiative in many undertakings that have been at variance with the views entertained by Dr. Hasselquist and many others, not because I disapproved of the fundamental idea of centralization, but because they made it too narrow. In Illinois, in those days, there was opposition to a Minnesota Conference; there was opposition to a high school in Minnesota; and of course there was opposition to the very thought of a paper in Minnesota. To some degree Hasselquist shared that narrow view, though his clear thinking often made him take exception to it.
>
> However, I may state, in justification of my action, that at the time preceding the Civil War, everybody in every state was on the lookout, nervously asking what the future might have in store for him. At that time Minnesota had no railroads to connect it with the outside world, and for months each year the Mississippi River was covered with ice. But we had the telegraph, and through the newspapers it was possible for the people to learn the news of the day. To us in Minnesota a paper was a prime necessity. (Backlund 19–20)

Minnesota Posten was issued twice each month in Red Wing, Minnesota, from November 7, 1857, to October 13, 1858. It contained four pages, each with six columns. Annual subscription price was one dollar.

Apparently, there was considerable difficulty with payment for the paper by its subscribers. Already, in its sixth number Norelius told his

subscribers that "owing to scarcity of cash these days, the editor will receive for subscription on the paper agricultural and other products, for
which the prevailing market price will be paid" (Linder 1931, 337).
However, this suggestion was not successful, for in October 1858 a notice indicated that the paper would not be issued for the time being due
to the fact that payments were not forthcoming.

Efforts to continue the paper finally led to its merger with Hasselquist's
Hemlandet, the older more firmly established paper. Perhaps the venture
was premature, obviously lacking financial support. Perhaps the challenge from Hasselquist led Norelius to agree to a merger. In order to make
the consolidation a harmonious one, Hasselquist arranged that Norelius
be the editor of *Hemlandet* in 1859. With the press of other responsibilities,
Norelius limited his work as editor to only that year. *Sources:* Backlund
18–20; LIBRIS; Linder 1931, 337; Stephenson 189; WorldCat.

Augustana College Swenson Center
Gustavus Adolphus College Archives: November 7, 1857–October 13,
    1858, Microfilm
Harvard University Divinity School: 1857–1858, Microfilm
Minnesota Historical Society: Vol. 1, nos. 1–24; November 7, 1857–
    October 13, 1858, Microfilm
LIBRIS: Royal Library of Sweden: 1857–1858

Minnesota Stats Tidning (1877)

[*Minnesota State Newspaper*]
Minneapolis, MN: H. Mattson
Vol. 1, no. 1–vol. 6, no. 10
January 4, 1877–March/April 1882
Merged with: *Skaffaren* (Red Wing, MN: 1878) to form *Skaffaren och Min-
    nesota Stats Tidning*
Sometimes referred to as: *Minnesota Stats Tidning* or *Minnesota Stats Tid-
    ning* (Minneapolis, MN: 1877)

The *Minnesota Stats Tidning* began publication with its January 4, 1877,
issue in Minneapolis, Minnesota. The paper was primarily the publishing
venture of Colonel Hans Mattson, who was assisted by Alfred Söderström
and Axel Dahlstrand. Magnus Lunnow joined the venture upon the death
of Dahlstrand. A Swedish-born immigrant, Mattson had served as an of-
ficer for the Union in the Civil War and was also a land agent for the St.
Paul and Pacific Railroad.

This weekly Swedish-language newspaper was devoted to general
news and exhibited liberal political and social policies. Politically it was

Republican. Apparently it left the reporting of church news to the religious paper *Skaffaren*. However, there seemed to be a journalistic battle between the two papers for a time, especially regarding secret Swedish societies. There were accusations from *Skaffaren* that the *Minnesota Stats Tidning* paper was hostile to the Christian religion by supporting dance and saloons.

In 1881, the warfare between the two papers subsided when Mattson sold his paper to *Skaffaren* because he was sent to Calcutta as the United States consul. In early 1882, the two papers consolidated under the name *Skaffaren och Minnesota Stats Tidning. Sources:* Backlund 60; Blegen 248, 304; LIBRIS; Stephenson 421; WorldCat.

Minnesota Historical Society: Vol. 1, no. 1–vol. 6, no. 10; January 4, 1877–March 7, 1882, Microfilm
LIBRIS: Royal Library of Sweden: 1877–1881

Minnesota Stats Tidning (1895)

[*Minnesota State Newspaper*]
St. Paul, MN; Minneapolis, MN: Skaffaren Publishing Co.
Vol. 19, no. 44–vol. 62, no. 8
October 30, 1895–February 22, 1939
Continues: *Skaffaren* (St. Paul, MN: 1885)
Continued by: *Minnesota Lutheran* (St. Paul, MN)
Sometimes referred to as: *Minnesota Statstidning* or *Minnesota Stats Tidning* (St. Paul, MN: 1895)

The Swedish-language newspaper published weekly in St. Paul, Minnesota, survived several name changes involving its relationship with *Skaffaren* when in 1895 it established a more firm position among foreign language papers. Finally with the October 30, 1895, issue it became *Minnesota Stats Tidning*, which name continued through February 22, 1939. By this time, some of the material included in the newspaper was published in the English language alongside Swedish articles.

Apparently, as a general newspaper its editorial policy regularly promoted the work of the Minnesota Conference of the Augustana Lutheran Synod. It exhibited a special conservative Christian attitude in its policies. Although not the property of the Minnesota Conference, it was considered its official organ.

P. A. Mattson, former president of Gustavus Adolphus College and president of the Minnesota Conference, was editor. By 1931 the paper encountered increasing financial difficulties so it was taken over by a group of Lutheran Church leaders in the twin cities. Circulation had steadily fallen from 12,513 in 1915 to 8,173 in 1925 and then to 4,520 in 1935. *Minnesota Stats Tidning* was continued in 1939 by the *Minnesota Lutheran,* an English-language publication. *Sources:* Backlund 61; Bengston 459; Capps 118, 233; LIBRIS; WorldCat.

> Augustana College Swenson Center
> Center for Research Libraries: December 19, 1917–February 22, 1939
> Gustavus Adolphus College Archives: October 30, 1895–February 22, 1939, Paper and Microfilm
> Minnesota Historical Society: Vol. 19, no. 44–vol 62, no. 8; October 30, 1895–February 22, 1939, Microfilm
> University of North Dakota: Vol. 19, no. 44–vol. 62, no. 8; October 30, 1895–February 22, 1939, Microfilm AN49 .M55x
> LIBRIS: Royal Library of Sweden: 1901–1939

Mission-Tidings: The Official Organ of the Women's Missionary Society, Lutheran Augustana Synod

> Rock Island, IL: Augustana Book Concern for the Woman's Missionary Society, Lutheran Augustana Synod
> Vol. 20, no. 5–vol. 53, no. 7
> October 1925–December 1958
> Continues: *Missions-Tidning*
> Continued by: *Lutheran Women's World*
> Sometimes referred to as: *Mission Tidings*

The official magazine in English of the Women's [sometimes Woman's] Missionary Society was issued in its first number dated October 1925. It was published as a monthly from 1925 through June 1953 with the exception of any July issues. After that, from July 1953 through 1958, it was issued every month.

Historical information about this magazine is included herein with the *Missions-Tidning* entry. Separate Swedish and English sections had been bound together in issues from January 1922, when it was acknowledged that in order to maintain the support of the younger generation of women it would be necessary to print English-language material. However, the older generation still wished to read their Swedish. The separately titled Swedish section *Missions-tidning* became increasingly smaller until it disappeared completely after the March 1938 issue.

With the January 1927 issue its name was *Mission Tidings*. Beginning with the September 1949 issue its masthead indicated it to be the official organ of the Woman's Missionary Society of the Augustana Lutheran Church. In 1927 there were 24,516 subscribers and in 1948 more than

29,000. By 1956 the number was 29,800 or one out of three women in the Church. Subscription was then one dollar a year in advance.

As the official magazine of the Woman's Missionary Society, *Mission-Tidings* continued the contents policy established by *Missions-Tidning*. Reports from the various mission fields along with feature articles and general mission news filled its pages with interesting text. Resources for local programs were regularly featured. It was promoted as "the link between your missions and you" (*Augustana Annual* 1956, 178). Until 1944 the July or August issue contained the minutes of the proceedings of the annual convention of the Women's Missionary Society. The following served as editors: May Mellander through 1927, (having begun her work in 1918 with *Missions-Tidning*) Augusta Highland (1927–1950), Burnice Fjellman (1950–1951), Ethel D. Palmquist (1951–1952), and Mabel Olson (1954–1958).

With the change of the organization's name in 1958 to the Augustana Lutheran Church Women, *Mission Tidings* published its last issue in December 1958. The next month it took the new name *Lutheran Women's World. Sources: After Seventy-Five Years* 230–41; *Augustana Annual* 1956, 178; Augustana ELC Century, 130; Erickson 69–70; http://mnhs.mnpals .net/F/; LIBRIS; Olson 1957; WorldCat.

Augustana College: BX8001 .L848 Vols. 22–53; 1928–1958

Evangelical Lutheran Church in America Archives: AUG 40/8/3/2 Vols. 19–53; 1925–1958

Fuller Theological Seminary: Vols. [37–51]; [1942–1956]

Gustavus Adolphus College Archives: Vol. 20, no. 5–vol. 32, no. 7; vol. 33, nos. 1,3,4,7–11; vols. 34–35; vol. 36, nos. 2–11; vol. 37, nos. 1–2, 4–11; vol. 42, nos. 1–7, 9–11; vols. 43–53; 1925–[1938], 1939–1940, [1941–1942, 1947], 1948–1958

Gustavus Adolphus College: Periodicals: Vol. 20, no. 5–vol. 53, no. 7; 1925–1958

Lutheran School of Theology at Chicago: BV2350 .M5 Vol. 20, no. 5–vol. 53, no. 7; 1925–1958

Minnesota Historical Society: BV2540 .A1 M6 1925–1958

University of Illinois: 266.05 MISS Vols. 20–40; 1925–1948

LIBRIS: Royal Library of Sweden: Vols. 20–44; 1925/26–December 1949 Swedish Emigrant Institute: Vols. [20, 22], 23–27; [1925, 1927] 1928–1932

Missionären: Månadsblad för Worcester Distriktet af Evangeliskt Lutherska New York Konferensen

[*The Missionary: Monthly Paper for the Worcester District of the Evangelical Lutheran New York Conference*]

Rock Island, IL: Augustana Book Concern
Worcester, MA: [s.n.]
Vols. 1–10
1906–1914

This monthly publication was issued for the congregations in the
Worcester District of the New York Conference of the Augustana
Lutheran Synod. It included district and local church news. *Source:* Ander
1956, 166.

Augustana College Swenson Center: Vols. 1–10; 1906–1914

Missionären: Tidskrift för Inre och Yttre Mission (Chicago, IL)

[*The Missionary: Journal for Home and Foreign Mission*]
Chicago, IL: Hemlandets Office
Vol. 1, no. 1–vol. 4, no. 12
January 1870–December 1873
Merged with: *Det Rätta Hemlandet och Augustana* and *Luth. Kyrkotidning*
   (Vasa, MN) and *Nytt och Gammalt* to form *Augustana* (Rock Island, IL:
   1874)

A missionary paper, separate from other Augustana papers, issued its
first number in January 1870 under the editorship of Eric Norelius. *Missionären* was published in Chicago by the Svenska Lutherska Tryckföreningen (Swedish Lutheran Publication Society).
   The primary focus was to present news and articles about mission work
in the young Augustana Synod. Issued monthly, it contained sixteen
pages with two columns in a format varying from 15 cm. × 22 cm. to 16
cm. × 25 cm. Annual subscription price was fifty cents. Norelius relin-
quished the editor position in June 1871, after which J. P. Nyquist took the
post until December 1873.
   Lund offers some interesting observations about the paper and its editors, Norelius and Nyquist:

[Nyquist's] immediate predecessor as editor had been Norelius and the com-
parison of the paper under the two editors lends the following observations.
Nyquist used more religious poems and verses from hymns. Nyquist began
each issue—quite often the whole first page—with a prayer. He introduced
some stories which were substantially lighter than the usual run of doctrinal
discussion and sermons. Both Nyquist and Norelius, like many other editors
of the time, copied or lifted pieces verbatim from other magazines. As
Nyquist observed, "We would rather have a good borrowed piece than a bad
one of our own." His "borrowed pieces" included not only the usual collec-

tion of sermons, but also items from an American Lutheran paper and selections from the works of a medieval author, Thomas a Kempis. Prior to its merger with another publication in January of 1874 it had had its greatest circulation. Nyquist explained its demise in terms of the will of God "for those troublous times," of economics and of the necessity of unity within the church. His fluent style of writing in *Missionären* as well as in other publications shows him to be a well-educated man. (Lund 1963, 42–43)

Late in 1873 (October 28), the editors of four papers that were currently being published at various places met to discuss their concern about the possibility that so many publications could work against synod unity. They decided then to combine *Det Rätta Hemlandet och Augustana,* and *Luth. Kyrkotidning* (Vasa, MN) and *Nytt och Gammalt* to form *Augustana* (Rock Island, IL: 1874). This new paper issued its first number in January 1874 with E. Norelius, T. N. Hasselquist, and O.Olsson continuing to serve as editors. *Sources:* Erickson 71; Lund 1963, 42–43; Matthews 169; Nystrom 55; WorldCat.

Augustana College Swenson Center
Evangelical Lutheran Church in America Archives: AUG 14/9 Vols. 1–4; 1870–1873
Gustavus Adolphus College Archives: Vol. 1, no. 1–vol. 2, no. 9; vol. 3–vol. 4, no. 12; January 1870–December 1873
Lutheran School of Theology at Chicago: BX8001 .M530 Vols. 1–4; 1870–1873
Lutheran Theological Seminary at Gettysburg: Vols.[1–2], 3–4; 1870–1873
Erickson: Minnesota Historical Society: Vol. 1; 1870
  Royal Library of Sweden: Vols. 1–3, [4]; 1870–1873
WorldCat: United Libraries (Illinois): Vols. 1–3; 1870–1873

Missionären: Svensk Luthersk Missionstidning **(Moline, IL)**

[*The Missionary: Swedish Lutheran Missions Paper*]
[Moline, IL: s.n.]
Vol. 1, no. 1–vol. 3, no. 12
January 1876–December 1878
Merged with: *Augustana* (1874) to form *Augustana och Missionären*
Sometimes referred to as: *Missionären* (Moline, IL: 1876)

A further effort to inform Augustana Synod members about mission activity took form in a new paper *Missionären*. This publication, taking the same title as a paper issued from 1870 to 1873 in Chicago, was printed in Moline, Illinois. Its first number was dated January 1876. Erickson states, however, that actually the first number appeared in December 1875 as volume 2, number 24 of *Augustana*. The Lutheran School of Theology at Chicago library online catalog confirms this statement, indicating that this issue of *Augustana* "was the first issue of a separate monthly periodical published as a companion to *Augustana*." The Gustavus Adolphus College Archives also owns this December 1875 issue.

Editors were Erl. Carlsson and A. G. Setterdahl from January 1876 through June 1878. A. R. Cervin and C. P. Rydholm followed as editors from July through December 1878.

Strictly focused on mission news and promoting an interest in missions, this new *Missionären* was issued monthly in a twenty-four page, two-column format (16 cm. × 24 cm.) for an annual subscription price of one dollar.

The general official Swedish organ of the Synod, *Augustana*, was being published at the same time also. In the interest of unity and in consideration of financial realities, *Missionären* (Moline) and *Augustana* (1874) were consolidated to form *Augustana och Missionären* with its first issue in January 1879. *Sources:* Erickson 72; http://jkm.ipac; LIBRIS; Matthews 169; Thorstensson; WisCat; WorldCat.

> Augustana College Swenson Center: BX8001 .A83 V21 Vols. 1–3; 1876–1878
> Evangelical Lutheran Church in America Archives: AUG 14/10 1876–1878
> Gustavus Adolphus College Archives: Vol. 1, no. 1–vol. 3, no. 12; 1876–1878
> Lutheran School of Theology at Chicago: Vols. 1–3
> Lutheran Theological Seminary at Gettysburg: Vols. 1–3; 1876–1878
> New York Public Library Research Library: Vol. 1, no. 2–vol. 2, no. 11; February 1876–November 1877
> University of Minnesota–Minneapolis: BX8049 .M57 Vols. 1–3; 1876–1878
> Wisconsin Historical Society: Pamphlets 61-4139 Vol. 1, nos. 2–4, 6–7, 10–11; vol. 2, nos. 1, 4–5, 7–12; vol. 3; February–April, June–July, October–November, 1876; January, April–May, July–December, 1877; 1878
> Erickson: Minnesota Historical Society: Vols. 1–3; 1876–1878
> LIBRIS: Lund University: Årg. 1–3; 1876–1878
> Royal Library of Sweden
> Swedish Emigrant Institute: Årg. 1–3; 1876–1878

Missionary Calendar

> Rock Island, IL: Augustana Book Concern for Board of World Missions, Augustana Evangelical Lutheran Church

Vols. 1–10
1921–1930
Sometimes referred to as: *The Missionary Calendar*

Edited by the Educational Committee of the Augustana Foreign Missionary Society, *The Missionary Calendar* was published as an annual from 1921 to 1930. It was considered the yearbook of the Society. The organization had various names, including the Augustana Hednamissions Förening, the Women's Home and Foreign Missionary Society and the Augustana Association for Christian Missions.

According to GRACE, the later editions had individual titles: volume 7, *In His Name*; volume 8, *Forward Evangelism*; volume 9, *Jesus, the Light of the World*; volume 10, *More than Conquerors*. *Sources:* http://grace.gtu.edu/search; WorldCat.

Augustana College: BV2050 .A9 Vols. 5, 7, 8, 10
Evangelical Lutheran Church in America Archives: AUG 24/2/1 Vols. 1–8; 1921–1928
Midland Lutheran College: 284.1 Au45m Nos. 2, 4, 6, 8–10
Pacific Lutheran Theological Seminary: BV2540.A1 A8 Vols. 1–10; 1921–1930
Yale University: NE6 Au45 Vols. 1–10; 1921–1930

Missions-Tidning: Organ för Kvinnornas Hem- och Hedna-missions-förening inom Augustana-Synoden

[*Missions Paper: organ for Woman's Home and Foreign Missions Society in Augustana Synod*]
Rock Island, IL: Augustana Book Concern for the Woman's Home and Foreign Mission Society of the Augustana Synod
Vol. 1, no. 1–vol. 20, no. 4
June 1906–September 1925
Continued by: *Mission-Tidings*
Sometimes referred to as: *Missions-tidning* (Rock Island, IL) or *Missions tidning* or *Mission-tidings*

The official magazine of the Woman's Home and Foreign Mission Society of the Augustana Synod began publication in 1906 as the Swedish-language paper named *Missions-Tidning*. It was produced in time to be distributed with a warm reception at the organization's annual convention that year in Denver, Colorado. At its convention the previous year in 1905, the society resolved to establish its own paper.

Alma Swensson, wife of the president of Bethany College in Lindsborg, Kansas, ably edited this small quarterly, which soon became a monthly with the June 1908 issue. She continued as editor of this title until 1918, when her main responsibility thereafter was writing for and editing the Swedish section until her death in 1939. For the first several years until 1912 the magazine was written using the Swedish language exclusively. Beginning in 1912, every other issue was in English. In 1912 the organization name was printed as the Women's Home and Missionary Society. Also serving as editor, in addition to Alma Swensson, was May Mellander from 1918 through 1925, and as assistants Mathilda Peterson, and Betty Nilsson.

Beginning as a twelve-page magazine, *Missions-Tidning* grew to sixteen pages in 1910, to twenty-four pages in 1918, and thirty-two pages even later. In order to encourage a wide reading audience the subscription price was kept low. At first it was twenty-five cents per year, then increased to fifty cents in mid-1920.

Readers increased from 3,111 subscribers in 1910 to 8,650 in 1915. A large spurt of interest then occurred bringing the subscribers to 14,000 in 1917. However, in 1919 that number had fallen to 10,710.

In 1918, two separate sections, one Swedish and the other English, were published in each issue. Emmy Evald, the dynamic president of the Society for forty-three years, wrote for a special page called "Among Ourselves" in both the Swedish and English languages. Beginning with the January 1922 edition there was a separately titled English section in each issue with the heading "Mission-tidings." In September 1925, the final issue with the name *Missions-Tidning* was published, thereafter followed by the English name *Mission-Tidings*.

Significant emphasis was placed on education about missions. Women who were missionaries wrote articles about their work and sent letters and pictures from the mission field in order to communicate accurate, firsthand information with the women in the synod who were supporting their efforts. As early as 1909 there was a page for children. Reports of Conference meetings and routine reports of the national organization were printed. Regularly included program materials and mission studies designed for meetings of local groups proved to be educational. *Sources:* Erickson 69–70; LIBRIS; Olson 1957; Spong 1998, 4; Spong 1999, 254; WorldCat.

Augustana College Swenson Center: incomplete file
Evangelical Lutheran Church in America Archives: AUG 40/8/3/2
    Vols. 1–19; 1906–1924
Gustavus Adolphus College: Vol. 15–vol. 20, no. 4; 1921–1925
Gustavus Adolphus College Archives: Vol. 10, no. 9–vol. 20, no. 4;
    1915–1925
Lutheran School of Theology at Chicago: BV2350 .M5 Vols. 5–20;
    1910–1925
Minnesota Historical Society: 1906–1925

University of Illinois: 266.05 MISS Vols. 5, 7–20; 1913, 1915–1925
LIBRIS: Swedish Emigrant Institute [14–18, 20]; [1919, 1921–1925]

The Moccasin: An Annual of Minnesota College:
Published by the Academic Class of . . .

Minneapolis, MN: Minnesota College
1912–1920?
Continued by: *Picayune* (Annual)

This was the student yearbook published at Minnesota College. *Sources:*
http://mnhs.mnpals.net; WorldCat.

Minnesota Historical Society: LD7514.M55M6; 1912; 1920

Mosaic: Opening Doors to Extraordinary Lives

See *Bethphage Messenger*

My Church: An illustrated Lutheran Manual Pertaining
to the History, Work, and Spirit of the Augustana Synod

My Church: A Yearbook of the Lutheran Augustana Synod of North America
Rock Island, IL: Augustana Book Concern
Vols. 1–32
1915–1946
Volume 14 includes index for volumes 1–14
Volumes 15–32 are indexed individually
Merged with: *Almanac, Evangelical Lutheran Augustana Synod of North*
America to form *Augustana Annual*

The English annual *My Church* was started by the Augustana Book
Concern in 1915 as "a serial record of events in the [Augustana] Synod
and in the Lutheran Church in general" (Olson 1933, 63). The early subtitle, "an illustrated Lutheran manual pertaining to the history, work and
spirit of the Augustana synod," is descriptive of its contents and purpose.
Later in the 1940s the subtitle was changed to "a yearbook of the Lutheran
Augustana Synod of North America."
    Contents are similar to that of *Korsbaneret*, the Swedish-language an-
nual for the Augustana Synod, including general articles about the synod,
information about congregations, and especially new churches, obituaries, and biographies. It also included maps showing in detail the territory
of each Conference and giving statistics.

Editors were Ira O. Nothstein (1915–1928), S. J. Sebelius (1929–1931), D. Nystrom (1932–1937), and C. H. Sandgren (1938–1946).

My Church was merged with the *Almanac* to become the *Augustana Annual* in 1948.

Nystrom summarizes the importance of *My Church* by stating that it "performed a similar mission to that of *Korsbaneret* and, in a measure, to that of *Prärieblomman*. Those who have access to a complete file of this publication will find it a source book of historical information about the Augustana Church and a varied portrayal of its life" (Nystrom 80–81). *Sources:* Hultgren 2001; Nystrom 80–81; Olson 1933, 63; Stephenson 309; WisCat; WorldCat.

Augustana College Swenson Center: BX8049 .M9 Vols. 1–32; 1915–1946
Bethany College: 1915–1944
Evangelical Lutheran Church in America Archives: AUG 14/5 Vols. 1–32; 1915–1946
Evangelical Lutheran Church in America Archives Region 5—IA: Vols. 1–12, 14, 26; 1915–1926, 1928, 1940
Evangelical Lutheran Church in America Archives Region 8—PA (Greenville): Vol. 1; 1915
Gustavus Adolphus College: BX8049. M8 Vols. 1–32; 1915–1946
Harvard University Divinity School: 906 Luth.6 A923 my 1915–1946
Lutheran School of Theology at Chicago: BX8009 .M9 Vols. 1–32; 1915–1946
Luther Seminary: BX8049 .M8 1915–1916; 1920; 1924–1925; 1927–1931; 1933–1936; 1938–1942; 1944–1945
Midland Lutheran College: Vols. 1–12; 1915–1926
Minnesota Historical Society: BX8049 .M8 Vols. 1–32; 1915–1946
New York Public Library Research Library: Vols. 5–6, 8, 10
Pacific Lutheran Theological Seminary: BX8041.M9 Vols. 1, 3–14, 16–18, 20–21, 24–29
Trinity Lutheran Seminary: BX8049 .N68 1915–1928; 1940
Wartburg Theological Seminary: Vols. 1–16, 18, 20–23, 26–30

– N –

Nåd och Sanning: Ev. Luth. Tidning

[*Grace and Truth: Evangelical Lutheran Paper*]
Chicago, IL: Engberg-Holmberg Pub. Co.
Vols. 1–6
April 11, 1877–December 1882
Vol. 7–vol. 9, no. 4

October 1, 1884–October 20, 1886
Became: *Vårt Land och Folk* (or *Wårt Land och Folk*)

Published by Augustana pastors, this religious periodical was designed for devotional purposes. It included poetry, hymns, all religious in tone, and also mission news from the Augustana Synod.

Individuals associated with *Nåd och Sanning* include C. A. Evald and C. O. Lindell of Chicago, F. A. G. Skeppstedt (1878), and C. E. Lindberg (1881–1882). In 1882, it was the venture of the Sv. Ev. Lutherska Pastorssällskapet (Swedish Evangelical Lutheran Pastors Society) in Chicago. Others associated with the publication included C. B. L. Boman, M. C. Ranseen, F. Nibelius, J. Vibelois, and C. Granath.

Issued semimonthly in the Swedish language, *Nåd och Sanning* numbered sixteen pages with a single column (16 cm. × 25 cm.) until January 1881 when a larger format (29 cm. × 40 cm.) permitted three columns and a weekly issue. Subscription price was $1.00 annual in 1877, $1.25 for 1878–1880, and 50 cents per year thereafter.

A break in publishing occurred from January 1883 to October 1884. Late in 1886, it became *Vårt Land och Folk*, which was later absorbed by *Hemvännen* in December 1888 and published in Rock Island, Illinois. *Sources:* Ander 1956, 167; Erickson 78; LIBRIS; *Minnesskrift* 458–59; Setterdahl 10; WorldCat.

Augustana College Swenson Center: BX8001 .N3 1877–October 20, 1886, Microfilm; also: BX8001 .N3 Vol. 2; 1878
Chicago Historical Society: PN4885 .S8N2 [1886: vol. 9, no. 29–vol. 10, no. 20] Microfilm
Evangelical Lutheran Church in America Archives: Vols. [1], 2–4; [1877], 1878–1880
Erickson: Gustavus Adolphus College: [1877] 1878–1880, [1881–1882]
Lutheran School of Theology at Chicago: Vols. 1–4
LIBRIS: Royal Library of Sweden: 1884–1886

New England Conference News

West Haven, CT: New England Conference of the Lutheran Augustana Synod
Vol. 1, no. 1–vol. 3
September 1, 1945–August 1947
Continued by: *New England Lutheran* (1948)

The New England Conference of the Evangelical Lutheran Augustana Synod issued this paper as its official publication from September 1945 through August 1947. It was continued by the *New England Lutheran* in 1948. *Source:* WorldCat.

Harvard University Divinity School: Vols. 1–3; 1945–1947, Microfilm

New England Luther Leaguer

Worcester, MA: [s.n.]
Vol. 1–vol.?
September 1926–1955?

This publication was the official organ of the New England Conference Luther League of the Augustana Lutheran Synod. *Sources:* Ander 1956, 167; Lundeen, group 6; ULS.

Lundeen: Evangelical Lutheran Church in America Archives: 1927–1955
ULS: Augustana College: Vol. [1]+

New England Lutheran (1948)

West Haven, CT: New England Conference of the Evangelical Lutheran Augustana Synod
Vol. 1, no. 1–vol. 11
March 1948–February 1962
Continues: *New England Conference News*
Continued by: *New England Lutheran* (West Haven, CT: 1963)
Other titles:
  New England Lutheran (West Haven, CT: 1948)
  The New England Lutheran

The New England Conference of the Evangelical Lutheran Augustana Synod issued this paper as its official publication from March 1948 to March 1959. Beginning with the June 1959 issue, it was copublished with the New England Conference of the United Lutheran Synod of New York and New England. For its final issues from December 1961 to February 1962, it was published also cooperatively with District 1 of the Eastern Conference of the American Evangelical Lutheran Church and by the Eastern Conference of the Finnish Lutheran Church.

Frequency of publication varied. In 1963 it continued the same title with the merger of sponsoring church bodies. *Sources:* Lundeen, group 6; WorldCat.

Harvard University Divinity School: Vols. 1–11; 1948–1962, Microfilm
Lutheran Theological Seminary at Gettysburg: 1948–1962
Lundeen: Evangelical Lutheran Church in America Archives:
   1948–1959

News Bulletin

Minneapolis, MN: Lutheran Brotherhood of America
1926–1936
Sometimes referred to as: *Brotherhood News Bulletin*
Source: Lundeen, group 6.

Lundeen: Evangelical Lutheran Church in America Archives:
   1926–1936

Newsletter/Augustana Historical Society

Rock Island, IL: The Society
Vol. 1, no. 1–vol. 9
Fall 1983–Winter 1994
New series: Vol. 1–
2002–
ISSN 0897-9758
Other title: *Augustana Historical Society Newsletter*

Issued semiannually, the *Newsletter* provides information to members
of the Augustana Historical Society about activities and general news.
Sources: LIBRIS; WorldCat.

Augustana College Swenson Center: F536.A96 N4 Vols. 1–7; Fall
   1983–Summer 1992; New series: Vol. 1– ; 2002–
Evangelical Lutheran Church in America Archives
Yale University: F536 A95 Vol. 5, no. 2–vol. 7, no. 1/2; vols. 8–9;
   1990–1994
LIBRIS: Royal Library of Sweden

Newsletter/Board of World Missions

Minneapolis, MN: Board of World Missions, Augustana Evangelical
   Lutheran Church
1956–1962
Sometimes referred to as: *World Missions Newsletter*

Issued by the Board of World Missions of the Augustana Synod, this news sheet included topics concerned with missions outside of the United States. *Sources:* http://lrc.elca.org?8080/webcat/; Lundeen, group 8.

Evangelical Lutheran Church in America Archives: AUG 24/1/7 1956–1962

Newsletter of Augustana Brotherhood

Rock Island, IL: Augustana Brotherhood
1958–1961
Source: Lundeen, group 6.

Lundeen: Evangelical Lutheran Church in America Archives: 1958–1961

Nios Årsbok

See *Årsbok/Svenska Litterära Sällskapet de Nio.*

None of the Above

St. Peter, MN: Gustavus Adolphus College
Vol. 84, nos. 1–15
September 15, 1972–May 18, 1973
Continues: *Junction*
Continued by: *Gustavian Weekly* (1973)

At the beginning of the 1972–1973 academic year, the student newspaper at Gustavus Adolphus College took this new title. It continued as a biweekly with the title *None of the Above* for only that year. *Source:* http://www.mnpals.net/F/.

Gustavus Adolphus College Archives: Vol. 84; 1972–1973

North Star Signal: utgifven af North Star College för Kyrkan, Skolan och Hemmet

[*North Star Signal: published by North Star College for Church, School and Home*]
Warren, MN: North Star College
Vol. 1–vol. 5, no. 53
August 15, 1910–October 1916

Other title: *Skölvännen: North Star Signal: Tidning för Kyrkan, Skolan och Hemmet*

Published monthly, but at times irregularly, the *North Star Signal* was issued from North Star College for those of the general reading audience who were friends of the school. The paper was written in both the Swedish and English languages. No issues were published for August through October 1914. Ander uses 1918 for the closing date rather than 1916. *Sources:* Ander 1956, 169; http://mnhs.mnpals.net; LIBRIS; WorldCat.

Minnesota Historical Society: 871 Vol. 1–vol. 5, no. 53; August 15, 1910–October 1916, Microfilm
LIBRIS: Swedish Emigrant Institute: Årg 4:41; July 1914

Nytt Bibliotek för Barn och Ungdom

[*New Library for Children and Youth*]
Rock Island, IL: Augustana Book Concern
Vols. 1–14?
1900?–1915?
Other title: *Nytt Bibliotek*

This series was planned for young readers with a good basic knowledge of the Swedish language. It included both short stories and poetry of an "edifying and religious nature" (Blanck 158). Contributions were written by authors who were active in Sweden in the publishing of religious material for children and youth. At least 47,000 copies were issued during the lifetime of the series. *Sources:* Blanck 1997, 158; LIBRIS; WorldCat.

Augustana College Swenson Center: BV4515 .N9 Vols. 1–2, 4–6, 8–14
New York Public Library Research Library: No. 7
North Park University: 839.73 N993n
University of Minnesota – Minneapolis: BV4575 N9x Vol. 3
LIBRIS: Royal Library of Sweden: Vols. 1–9, 13–14
    Swedish Emigrant Institute: Vols. 11–12
    Uppsala University: Vols. 1–5

Nytt och Gammalt: Kristlig Tidskrift

[*New and Old: Christian Publication*]
Lindsburg, [*sic*] KS: O.Olsson
Årg. 1, nos. 1–6

April, 1873–November 1873

Merged with: *Det Rätta Hemlandet och Augustana* and *Luthersk Kyrkotid-ning* (Red Wing, MN) and *Missionären* (Chicago, IL) to form *Augus-tana* (1874)

The first Swedish newspaper published in Kansas, *Nytt och Gammalt*, was the effort of Olof Olsson in 1873 at Lindsborg (spelled Lindsburg in the paper). Only six monthly numbers from April through November were issued. It joined with three other papers later that year to become *Augustana*.

The paper contained thirty pages (15 cm. × 23 cm.) with the subscription price of fifty cents for six issues. Lindquist (1953) writes of *Nytt och Gammalt*:

It was written in Olsson's pioneer home and published in Salina [Kansas]. In the greeting to his readers, he compared their new experience to launching out on the wide ocean in a small boat. . . . There were clearly written sermons and devotional items, chapters from church history, doctrinal treatises . . ., re-ports on church meetings in the [Smoky] valley, questions and answers on Luther's Small Catechism, and reports on the work of the Augustana Synod, which Olsson supported wholeheartedly in his publication.

The issues of *Nytt och Gammalt* point to the democratic spirit of Olsson. He printed criticism that had come to him about the publication. . . . Letters and suggestions from readers were solicited in order that the publication might be improved. . . . One is impressed with the high quality of the material, even while realizing that the writer had a multitude of other responsibilities as pi-oneer pastor and leader.

When Olsson announced in the November issue that *Nytt och Gammalt* would cease publication, he made it clear that economic difficulties did not cause this action. He explained that the decision was based upon his desire to join in consolidating Swedish religious periodicals for the sake of unity and strength. (59)

Sources: Erickson 83; LIBRIS; Lindquist 1953, 59; WorldCat.

Augustana College Swenson Center: BX8001 .N9 Vol. 1, nos. 1–6; 1873

Bethany College: 050 N999 E Lindq. 232

Center for Research Libraries: Vol. 1, nos. 1–5; April–October 1873

Evangelical Lutheran Church in America Archives: AUG 14/8 Vol. 1; April–Nov 1873

Gustavus Adolphus College Archives: Vol. 1, nos. 1–6; April–November 1873

Harvard University Divinity School: Vol. 1; 1873

Library of Congress: BX8001 .N9 Vol. 1, nos. 1–6; 1873

Lutheran School of Theology at Chicago: Rare BX8009 .N9 Vols. 1–6; 1873

Erickson: Royal Library of Sweden: Vols. 1–6; 1873
    University of Illinois: Vols. 1–5; 1873
LIBRIS: Swedish Emigrant Institute: Vol. 1, nos. 1–6; 1873

– O –

The Observer

Rock Island, IL: Augustana College
Vol. 17, no. 1–
September 13, 1972–
Continues: *Augustana Observer* (1902)

The newspaper published by students at Augustana College modified its
title in 1972 to *The Observer*. It is published weekly during the academic year
as a means of communicating news and articles of interest for students,
staff, faculty, and friends. *Source:* http://library.ilcso.illinois.edu/aug.

Augustana College: Special Collections LH1.A9 A91

Observer

See *Augustana Observer* (1902) and *The Young Observer*.

Occasional Paper/Augustana College Library

Rock Island, IL: Augustana College Library
1959–1978
Nos. 5–14
ISSN 0571-8929
Continues: *Augustana Library Publications. Occasional Paper*
Continued by: *Augustana College Library Occasional Paper*
Other titles:
    Occasional Paper (Augustana College Library, Rock Island, IL)
    Augustana College, Rock Island, IL. *Occasional papers*
    Augustana College (Rock Island, IL) Denkmann Memorial Library
        Occasional paper

The following ten titles were issued with this series name from 1959
through 1978:

1. *Science and Liberal Education in the Space Age*, by Glenn T. Seaborg,
   1959.

2. *Humanity's Great Adventure*, by Reuben G. Gustavson, 1960.
3. *Perspective in American Education*, by Conrad Bergendoff and Mark VanDoren, 1961.
4. *The Quest for Community*, by Orval Hobart Mowrer, 1962.
5. *Categories and Variables in Special Education*, by Maynard C. Reynolds, 1968.
6. *Expatriates and Repatriates: A Neglected Chapter in United States History*, by Theodore Saloutos, 1972.
7. *Meteorites: The Poor Man's Space Probe*, by Edward John Olsen, 1973.
8. *Jenny Lind Chapel: Pioneer Church at Andover: "An Historic Shrine of Swedish-American Lutheranism,"* by Erwin Weber, 1975.
9. *The Interdisciplinary Dilemma: A Case for Flexibility in Academic Thought*, by Roald Fryxell, 1977.
10. *Race and Sex Effects in the Conformity Behavior of Children*, by Gordon N. Cantor, 1978.

Sources: Augustana College Library Occasional Papers Inventory as of 11/03; LIBRIS; WorldCat.

Augustana College: 5–14
WorldCat: Bethany College: 12, 14
  California Lutheran University: 5, 7, 10–14
  Gustavus Adolphus College: 5, 7, 10–14
  Lutheran Theological Seminary at Philadelphia: 8, 12
  North Park University: 12–13
LIBRIS: Lund University: 5–14
  Royal Library of Sweden: 12
  Uppsala University: 9–14

The Olive Leaf

Rock Island, IL: Ungdomens Vänner; Augustana Tract Society; Augustana Book Concern
Vol. 1, no. 1–vol. 72, no. 39
January 1883–1954
Continued by: *Junior Life*
Sometimes referred to as: *Olive Leaf*

The first English language paper for Augustana Sunday church school children was *The Olive Leaf*. It was initially published monthly by the Ungdomens Vänner Society in Rock Island, Illinois, beginning in 1883. This group was also known later as the Augustana Tract Society. They controlled publication through the second number of volume 6 in 1888. In 1886, O. Olsson was the editor.

Beginning with volume 7 in 1889, *The Olive Leaf* was published by the Lutheran Augustana Book Concern. For a number of years, C. W. Foss edited the paper, which was designed to be of interest to youth in the intermediate grades. In its later years, Lauree Nelson Rystrom served as editor.

Gradually it advanced from being a monthly to a semimonthly and by 1917 it was issued weekly. Circulation in 1917 was 20,500 weekly copies, in 1926 it was 42,372 copies, reaching its highest point at 44,500 in December 1922.

Indeed, this was the first periodical in English for children published by the Augustana Synod. Stephenson makes the observation that "strangely enough, the English publication [for youth] antedated the Swedish" (461), which was *Barnens Tidning* born in 1886.

With volume 72 in 1954, *The Olive Leaf* name was changed to *Junior Life* in order to appeal more readily to the intended readership among children. *Sources: Augustana Annual* 1954, 72; Lundeen, group 7; Nystrom 86; Olson 1933, 78; Stephenson 350, 461; ULS.

Augustana College Swenson Center: 1886, 1892, 1922–1924, 1942
Evangelical Lutheran Church in America Archives: AUG 25/5/5 Vols. [1–7], 8, [9–10], 11–18, [19–23], 24, [25], 26, [27], 28–29, [30], 31–35, [40], 43–72; [1883–1889], 1890, [1891–1892], 1893–1900, [1901–1905], 1906, [1907], 1908, [1909], 1910–1911, [1912], 1913–1917, [1922], 1925–1954
Gustavus Adolphus College Archives: Vols. 7:1–9:11; 10:2–12; 18:1–5, 7–9; 36:5, 7–8, 10–11, 14, 17–21, 23; 37:1–3, 5–6; 39, no. 2; 60–71; 1889–1899, [1900, 1918–1919, 1921], 1942–1953
Lutheran Theological Seminary at Gettysburg: Vols. [1–2, 5, 7–11], 12–16, [17–18], 19–20, [21], 22–23, [24–25], 26–28, [29–33], 34, [35], 36–40; 1883–1922

One: The Magazine for Christian Youth

[Columbus, OH: Joint Youth Publications Council]
Vol. 1, no. 1–vol. 16, no. 11
September 1951–December 1966
Merged with: *Arena* (St. Louis, MO) to form *Arena One*
Other titles:
  One for Christian Youth (September 1956–June 1960)
  One for Lutheran Youth (July/August 1960–1966)

This was published for the Departments of Youth Activity and Parish Education of the American Lutheran Church in cooperation with the Luther Leagues of the Augustana Lutheran Church and the Lutheran Free

Church. Young people in the Augustana Luther League organization were familiar with this magazine for Lutheran youth. *Sources:* http://library.uts .columbia.edu; Lundeen, group 6; Matthews 1985, 214; Wartburg.

Lutheran Theological Seminary at Gettysburg: Vols. 1–14, 16; 1951–1966
Trinity Lutheran Seminary: 1951–1966
Union Theological Seminary: 1955–1966
Wartburg Theological Seminary: Vol. 1–vol. 16, nos. 3, 8–11; 1951–[1966]
Lundeen: Evangelical Lutheran Church in America Archives: 1955–1962

Österns Härold

[*The Eastern Herald*]
Brooklyn, NY: Österns Härold Pub. Co.
New Britain, CT: [s.n.]; October 12, 1898–
Vol. 4, no. 34–vol.?
May 28, 1896–January 30, 1913
Continues: *Framåt* (Brooklyn, NY: 1894)
Absorbed: *Svenska Connecticut Posten* and *Hartford-Posten* and *Bridgeport-Posten* (all in 1899)
Merged with: *Svea*

When *Framåt* changed its name to *Österns Härold* in 1896, some organizational and editorial changes occurred in addition to the title change. A Swedish-language weekly, it served as an organ of the New England Conference of the Augustana Synod, at the same time continuing its coverage of political events.

In 1898 (October 12), it relocated and began publication in New Britain, Connecticut. In 1899, it absorbed three regional Swedish language papers namely: *Svenska Connecticut Posten*, *Hartford-Posten*, and *Bridgeport-Posten*. By 1913 it was absorbed by *Svea* in Worcester, Massachusetts. *Sources:* Ander 1956, 170; Backlund 48; LIBRIS; Söderström 50; WorldCat.

Augustana College Swenson Center
Connecticut State Library: Microfilm
WorldCat: Chicago Historical Society: 1901–1903, 1905–1908, 1911
    Connecticut Historical Society: 1907
LIBRIS: Royal Library of Sweden: 1901–1913, Paper; May 28, 1896–
    January 30, 1913, Microfilm
    Swedish Emigrant Institute: May 28, 1896–January 30, 1913 Microfilm

Österns Väktare

[*Eastern Watchmen*]
Jamestown, NY: [s.n.]
Vol. 1, no. 1–vol. 3, no. 1
November 1888–November 27, 1890
Continued by: *Vårt Land*

By a special decision of the New York Conference of the Augustana Lutheran Synod, the new newspaper *Österns Väktare* was established in 1888. This was an attempt to publish a weekly Christian political newspaper that would serve the interests of and promote the cause of the Conference.

For the first year, Ludvig Holmes served as the editor. The following year M. N. Englund was editor. A. A. Magnuson, F. N. Andren, A. J. Lindblad, and C. A. Swanson were also directors of the limited publishing company.

The final issue appeared on November 27, 1890. The next number dated December 4, 1890, was the first issue of *Vårt Land*, which succeeded the earlier newspaper. *Sources:* Bengston 469; LIBRIS; Setterdahl 27.

Augustana College Swenson Center: November 28, 1889–November 1890, Microfilm
LIBRIS: Royal Library of Sweden: 1888–1890
Swedish Emigrant Institute: November 28, 1889–November, 1890, Microfilm

Our Church

[s.l.]: Minnesota Conference, Augustana Lutheran Synod
1921–1928

This was a news publication issued by the Red River District of the Minnesota Conference of the Augustana Lutheran Synod. *Sources:* Ander 1956, 171; Lundeen, group 6.

Lundeen: Evangelical Lutheran Church in America Archives: 1921–1928

Our Church Messenger

[s.l.]: Minnesota Conference, Augustana Lutheran Synod
1903?–1908?

Source: Lundeen, group 6

Lundeen: Evangelical Lutheran Church in America Archives: 1903–
1908

– P –

Pastor's Paragraphs

Minneapolis, MN: Board of Home Missions, Lutheran Augustana
Synod
February 1944–Autumn 1947?
Merged with: *Augustana Overseas* (Minneapolis, MN: 1947) to form *Augustana Missions* (Minneapolis, MN: 1948)

Introducing the first issue in February 1944, the editor S. E. Engstrom,
Executive Director of Home Missions, wrote that

> Pastor's Paragraphs . . . is to be a monthly informal news message to the Augustana Synod Pastors. We believe that it will encourage and increase the very fine "Esprit de Corps" which now exists in our Synod; that it will serve as a clearing house for ideas, suggestions and information; that it will number among its contributing editors all the pastors of our Synod, sharing with others plans, programs and activities which they have found successful in their own parishes.

Continuing he wrote: "The introduction of 'Pastor's Paragraphs' at this
time ties in with the 1944 program for congregational life and growth."
Designed as a "Pastor's 'Sounding Board' only," it was sent monthly
only to pastors and theological students. Publication ceased in 1947/1948
when it merged with *Augustana Overseas* to form *Augustana Missions*.
Source: Pastor's Paragraphs Feb. 1944, Autumn 1947.

Gustavus Adolphus College Archives: February, March, April 1944;
February, March, May 1945; Autumn 1947

Pedagogen: Kristlig Skoltidning

[*The Teacher: Christian School Paper*]
Lindsborg, KS: Bethany Academy
Rock Island, IL: Augustana Book Concern
Vol. 1, no. 1–vol. 3
February 1885–February 2, 1887
Continues: *Academica*
Continued by: *Framåt*

Issued on an irregular time schedule with the intent of it being a monthly, *Pedagogen* was devoted to news of Bethany Academy and College in order to promote the new institution. The masthead subtitle read: *Tidskrift för främjande af sann uppfostran* (Periodical for the promotion of true upbringing). Carl A. Swensson was the editor and moving force in assuring publication. Edward Nelander also contributed articles. The paper included news about other Augustana Synod institutions also. Total production was twelve Swedish and three English issues. *Pedagogen* was succeeded by *Framåt* in 1887. *Sources:* Bengston 462; Dowie 248; http://tomos.oit.umn.edu/F; LIBRIS; Lindquist 168, 257; Setterdahl 16.

Augustana College Swenson Center: Microfilm
Bethany College: Microfilm
University of Minnesota–Minneapolis: BX8049 .P43x Vol. 1, no. 1; vol. 2, no. 7/8; vol. 3, no. 13 [1885–1887]
Setterdahl: Kansas Historical Society: Microfilm
LIBRIS: Royal Library of Sweden: 1885–1887

People's Friend

See *Folkvännen*.

The Picayune

Minneapolis, MN: Minnesota College
January 1909?–1922
Continued by: *Messenger*

Belonging to the Minnesota Conference of the Augustana Lutheran Church, Minnesota College opened in October 1904 in Minneapolis. Located near the University of Minnesota campus, it had its own buildings and land. The high school academy, and music and commerce departments comprised the substantial divisions responsible for the major course offerings of the school, with some evening classes.

According to Peterson, in 1909 the student monthly periodical, *The Picayune*, began publication in English. However, the Minnesota Historical Society owns a microfilm of *The Picayune* beginning with volume 1, number 1 in December of 1921. At this time it was published weekly during the school year. The following year it was replaced by the *Messenger*, edited by the college administration. Faculty also contributed to the contents of the paper. *Sources:* http://mnhs.mnpals.net; Peterson 160; WorldCat.

Minnesota Historical Society: December 9, 1921–May 25, 1922, Microfilm

The Picayune (Annual)

Minneapolis, MN: Students of Minnesota College
1921?–?
Continues: *The Moccasin*

Students of Minnesota College prepared their annual yearbook as a special edition of their newspaper, *The Picayune*, giving it the same title. *Source:* WorldCat.

Minnesota Historical Society: 1922

Prärieblomman: Kalender för . . .

[*The Prairie Flower: Calendar for (the year. . .)*]
Title is followed by year of issue
Rock Island, IL: Lutheran Augustana Book Concern
Vols. 1–13
1900, 1902–1913 (1901 never published)

An annual devoted to Swedish and Swedish-American culture, literature, history, biography and art entitled *Prärieblomman*, issued by the Lutheran Augustana Book Concern, has been lauded as "one of the leading literary periodicals and exponents of the Augustana Synod's cultural work" (Blanck 1997, 93). Another writer claims that "among the annuals in Swedish, the best undoubtedly was *Prärieblomman*. . . . It contained articles and biographies of great historical value for Swedish-Americans" (Benson, Magazines, 207). Svensson asserts that *Prärieblomman* "was addressed to the larger Swedish-American community, and in particular to those with aesthetic and cultural aspirations" (157).

Prärieblomman: Kalender för . . . was published in December each year, making it a perfect Christmas gift. The first issue dated 1900 appeared in December 1899, published by a Chicago group named Vitterhetens Vänner (Friends of Belles-Lettres). The objective "was to establish a Swedish-American counterpart to the national Swedish literary annuals" (Svensson 157). Anders Schön and Johan Enander, both journalists active in Augustana circles, were associated with this group. Enander was the editor of this first volume.

In April 1900, the group offered to the Lutheran Augustana Book Concern the opportunity to continue the publication of *Prärieblomman*.

A. Schön was appointed editor and continued those responsibilities for the entire life of the periodical. A. G. Anderson was the business manager. The second issue appeared in December 1901 for the year 1902, thus missing publication for the year 1901. As an annual calendar, it was issued shortly before the year for which it was intended. *Prärieblomman* ceased with the December 1913 issue, succumbing to financial difficulties and a declining reader audience.

This literary calendar was profusely illustrated with reproductions of Swedish-American paintings and photographs of famous Swedish Americans.

> It included biographical sketches of notable Swedes and Swedish Americans, articles about Swedish immigrants in various states, Swedish-American art, music, and literature and the histories of different Swedish-American educational institutions. The annual also contained an abundance of original Swedish-American stories and poems. There were few articles that dealt with non-Swedish-American subjects. . . . Several Swedish poems were published in English translation to introduce prominent Swedish authors to the immigrant community and to America at large. . . . *Prärieblomman* emphasized an early Swedish presence on the North American continent and underscored significant achievements by notable Swedish immigrants. . . . The annual included many contributions about the cultural activities of the Augustana Synod, but surprisingly few about its theology or churches. (Svensson 157–59, 164)

Prärieblomman was issued in book form, consisting of two hundred fifty to three hundred pages each year. Its circulation varied between two thousand and twenty-five hundred copies each year. During its existence, it included contributions from around one hundred Swedish-American writers and artists, many of them associated with the Augustana Synod.

In her observations regarding the design of the publication, Svensson suggests "that a floral name implied that a literary work would contain a selection of texts from many different authors" (158). The farm girl, with blond hair and dressed in her best clothes, is sitting in the middle of a wild prairie landscape, where she is holding a prairie flower. "This contemplative picture idealizes both the Swedish pioneers and the moral sentiments found in the annual. Moreover, it suggests that a 'Swedishness' has taken root in the American environment, reflected in the stories and poems in *Prärieblomman*, which shaped the ethnic consciousness that the annual promoted" (Svensson 158).

Further commendation of *Prärieblomman* is written as follows: "*Prärieblomman* became perhaps the best example of the significance that the Synod attached to the preservation and dissemination of a Swedish-American cultural heritage in America. In this way . . . [it] became [a] leading exponent of the ethnic dimension of the Synod's life" (Blanck 1999, 44).

In concluding her study of *Prärieblomman*, Svensson shares her evaluation of the significance of the literary annual:

> *Prärieblomman* sought to become a showcase for Swedish-American culture. It sought recognition from two directions, the Swedish mother and the American bride. The contents of the annual point to a resistance among Swedish immigrants to accept completely the dominant culture that American society offered its newcomers. Instead, *Prärieblomman* embarked on a mission of creating a Swedish America and a Swedish-American culture. With its dual cultural perspective, *Prärieblomman* was able to portray the Swedish immigrants as bearers of a national heritage to the New World, painting in almost utopian terms a vision of how what were considered typically Swedish values would constitute a vital building stone in the American nation that was taking shape. In this way Swedish Americans, like many other American ethnic groups, could justify their emigration while maintaining a distinctive Swedish-American character in the multiethnic American environment. (Svensson 165)

Sources: Andreen 1905, 177; Benson, Magazines 207; Blanck 1997, 93; Blanck 1999, 44; Svensson 157–65; ULS.

Augustana College Swenson Center: AY19 .S8 P73x 1900–1913 (1901 missing)
Evangelical Lutheran Church in America Archives: AUG 14/1 1900, 1902–1913
Gustavus Adolphus College: AY19.P7 1900, 1902–1913
Luther Seminary: PT9990.A1P8 1900, 1902–1904
Lutheran School of Theology at Chicago: E184 .S2 P7 1900, 1902–1913
Lutheran Theological Seminary at Gettysburg: AY19 .P7 1900
Minnesota Historical Society: AY75 .P9 1900, 1902–1913
New York Public Library Research Library: Vols. 2–13; 1902–1913
Pacific Lutheran Theological Seminary: AY19.S8P7 1900–1913
Trinity Lutheran Seminary: 1900, 1902–1903, 1905–1907, 1909–1913
University of Chicago: AY19 .P7 1902–1903, 1905, 1907–1910
University of Illinois: 839.7 P88 Vols. 1–13; 1900, 1902–1912
University of Minnesota–Minneapolis: AY19 .S8 P73x 1900, 1902–1912; also 839.5 P883 1900, 1902–1913
Yale University: Ay19 P7 1900, 1903–1909, 1911–1913
LIBRIS: Royal Library of Sweden
    Swedish Emigrant Institute

Publication/Augustana Historical Society

Rock Island, IL: Augustana Historical Society
no. 20–
1963–

ISSN 0067–0588
Published irregularly; each number has a distinctive title
Continues: *Augustana Historical Society Publications*
Other titles:
  Publication (Augustana Historical Society)
  Augustana Historical Society Publication

The *Augustana Historical Society Publications* series continued in 1963 with this adjusted title. Issued on an irregular basis, each number has a distinctive title and individual author. Each is listed herewith.

20. *The Swedish Immigrant Community in Transition: Essays in Honor of Dr. Conrad Bergendoff*, edited by J. Iverne Dowie and Ernest M. Espelie. Contents: "Town and Gown by the Mississippi," by J. Iverne Dowie; "The Background of Swedish Immigration, 1840–1850," by Gunnar Westin; "The Best Americanizers," by C. Emanuel Carlson; "The Sacred Music of the Swedish Immigrants," by Carl L. Nelson; "Prärieblomman, an Immigrant Community in Central Kansas," by Emory Lindquist; "Augustana and Gustavus, Partners or Competitors," by Doniver A. Lund; "The Academies of the Augustana Lutheran Church," by Paul M. Lindberg; "Paul Peter Waldenström and Augustana," by Karl A. Olsson; "Language in Exile," by Nils Hasselmo; "An Immigrant Community During the Progressive Era," by O. Fritiof Ander; "The Swedish-American Press and Isolationism," by F. Herbert Capps; "Primary Sources in Denominational Historiography," by G. Everett Arden; "Augustana, a People in Transition," by Conrad Bergendoff; "Dr. Bergendoff, Christian Scholar and Educator," by Edgar M. Carlson; "Bibliography of the Published Writings of Dr. Conrad Bergendoff, 1918–1963," compiled by Ernest M. Espelie. 1963.
21. *The Immigration of Ideas: Studies in the North Atlantic Community. Essays Presented to O. Fritiof Ander*, edited by J. Iverne Dowie and J. Thomas Tredway. 1968.
22. *Vision for a Valley: Olof Olsson and the Early History of Lindsborg*, by Emory Lindquist. 1970.
23. *An Immigrant's Two Worlds: a Biography of Hjalmar Edgren*, by Emory Lindquist. 1972.
24. *An Immigrant's American Odyssey: a Biography of Ernst Skarstedt*, by Emory Lindquist. 1974.
25. *The Americanization of Carl Aaron Swensson*, by Daniel Merle Pearson. 1977.
26. *Shepherd of an Immigrant People: the Story of Erland Carlsson*, by Emory Lindquist. 1978.

27. *My Story: Immigrant, Executive, Traveler,* by Birger Swenson. 1979.
28. *The Augustana Ministerium: a Study of the Careers of the 2,504 Pastors of the Augustana Evangelical Lutheran Synod/Church, 1850–1962,* by Conrad Bergendoff. 1980.
29. *One Hundred Years of Oratorio at Augustana: A History of the Handel Oratorio Society, 1881–1980,* by Conrad Bergendoff. 1981.
30. *Peter Fjellstedt: Missionary Mentor to Three Continents,* by Emmet E. Eklund. 1983.
31. *The Pioneer Swedish Settlements and Swedish Lutheran Churches in America, 1845–1860: Selected Chapters from Volume 1 of Eric Norelius' De Svenska Luterska Församlingarnas och Svenkarnes Historia i Amerika (1890),* translated by Conrad Bergendoff. 1984.
32. *The Missionary Spirit in the Augustana Church,* by George F. Hall. 1984.
33. *An Historical Survey of the Augustana College Campus,* by Glen E. Brolander. 1985.
34. *Seven Sermons from the 125th Anniversary Year of Augustana College, Rock Island, IL,* edited by Phil Schroeder. Contents: "A Covenant to the People," by Peter Beckman; "For the Sake of the Gospel," by W. Robert Sorensen; "Taking the Form of a Servant," by Richard Swanson; "The Ascension of our Lord and Ascension Chapel," by Dorothy Parkander; "Living on an Inheritance," by Conrad Bergendoff; "Every Head Bowed, Every Mind Open," by Roald Tweet; "Two Kingdoms—One College," by Thomas Tredway. 1986.
35. *Prophetic Voice for the Kingdom: the Impact of Alvin Daniel Mattson upon the Social Consciousness of the Augustana Synod,* by Gregory Lee Jackson. 1986.
36. *His Name was Jonas: a Biography of Jonas Swensson,* by Emmet E. Eklund. 1988.
37. *The Church of Sweden on the Delaware, 1638–1831,* by Conrad Bergendoff. 1988.
38. *The Story of John Fryxell,* edited by Fritiof M. Fryxell. 1990.
39. *A History of the Augustana Library, 1860–1990: An International Treasure,* by Conrad Bergendoff. 1990.
40. *In the Astronomy Tradition at Augustana,* by Harry E. Nelson. 1992.
41. *An Historical Survey of the Augustana College Campus,* by Glen E. Brolander. Rev. ed. 1992.
42. *Looking West: Three Essays on Swedish American Life by Jules Mauritzson,* edited by Ann Boaden, Dag Blanck; translated by Conrad Bergendoff. 1994.
43. *A Century of Art at Augustana College, 1894–1995: A Catalog Published in Conjunction with the Exhibition of the Same Title, October 14–November 11, 1995, Held at the Augustana College Art Gallery, Rock Island, Illinois,* compiled by Sherry C. Maurer. 1995.

44. *Aspects of Augustana and Swedish America: Essays in Honor of Dr. Conrad Bergendoff on His 100th Year,* edited by Raymond Jarvi. Contents: "The Mosaic of Augustana's Swedish Lutheran Origins," by Emmet E. Eklund; "Molding Ministers to Fit Congregations: Religious Leadership among New England's Swedes," by Maria Erling; "Conrad Bergendoff and the Swedish-American Church Language Controversy of the 1920s," by H. Arnold Barton; "The Troublesome Language Question," by Elder M. Lindahl; "Weighing the Stars and Hearing the Word: Conrad Bergendoff's Idea of Christian Higher Education at Augustana College and Theological Seminary," by Ann Boaden; "Conrad Bergendoff and the LCA Merger of 1962," by Mark A. Granquist; "North Stars and Vasa Orders: On the Relationship between Sweden and Swedish America," by Dag Blanck; "The Fourth R—Religious Education in Sweden and the USA," by Bernhard Erling; "Bibliography of the Published Writings of Dr. Conrad Bergendoff, 1963–1995," by Judith Belan. 1995.

45. *America, Reality & Dream: The Freeman Letters from America & Sweden, 1841–1862,* edited by Axel Friman, George M. Stephenson, and H. Arnold Barton. 1996.

46. *On and beyond the Mississippi: Essays Honoring Thomas Tredway,* edited by Dag Blanck and Michael Nolan. 2004.

Sources: LIBRIS; WorldCat.

Augustana College: 20–46
Gustavus Adolphus College: 21–25, 34, 40, 45
Lutheran School of Theology at Chicago: 25–26, 28–39, 44
Lutheran Theological Seminary at Gettysburg: F536. A96 20–46
Trinity Lutheran Seminary: 20, 22–23, 26, 44
Wartburg Theological Seminary: 20–23, 28, 35
WorldCat: Bethany College: 20–33, 35–36
   California Lutheran University: 20–33, 35–36
   Evangelical Lutheran Church in America Archives: 20–40, 44–45
   Luther Seminary: 20, 25–32, 35–37, 44
   Lutheran Theological Seminary at Philadelphia: 20–23, 26, 28, 32, 35, 44
   Lutheran Theological Southern Seminary: 20, 24, 28, 31, 35
   Midland Lutheran College: 20–21
   North Park University: 20–28, 30–32, 36, 41–42, 44–45
   Pacific Lutheran Theological Seminary: 20–21, 23–32, 34–38, 44
   Pacific Lutheran University: 20–28, 30–31, 36–37, 44–45
LIBRIS: Lund University: 20–45
   Royal Library of Sweden: 20–40, 45
   Swedish Emigrant Institute: 20–45
   Uppsala University: 20–39, 42, 45

– Q –

The Quarterly Release

[s.l.]: Augustana Lutheran Church Women
Vols. 1–5
September 1957–November 1962

According to the historical note provided by the ELCA Archives, this publication was "designed for use by local Women's Missionary Society/
Augustana Lutheran Church Women officers, and division and department
workers." It contained "important directives and needed information" for
women working at the local level. Dolores Runbeck, WMS Director of Promotion, was in charge of the publication. As an eight-page pamphlet, it was
issued quarterly with two issues each year containing "information and directives for Department chairpersons." Included in each issue "was a message to local presidents, information on new resources available, suggestions
for division leaders and department chairpersons, sections on membership,
service, and education, news about the mission periodicals *Mission Tidings*
and *Lutheran Women's World*, and a page for leaders of Children's and
Teen–Age divisions." *Sources:* http://lrc.elca.org; WorldCat.

Evangelical Lutheran Church in America Archives: AUG 40/8/3/3:
Vols. [1–2], 3–5; 1957–1962

– R–

Rätta Hemlandet

[*The True Homeland*]
Galesburg, IL: [Swenska Boktryckeriet]
Chicago, IL: Svenska Lutherska Tryckföreningen
Vol. 1, no. 1–vol. 7, no. 12
July 11, 1856–December 1862
Continued by: *Rätta Hemlandet och Missionsbladet*
Sometimes referred to as: *Det Rätta Hemlandet*

As *Hemlandet, det Gamla och det Nya* gained popularity among the
Swedish-American reading audience, it became more evident to T. N.
Hasselquist, its editor and publisher, that at that time it was not practical
to combine secular news and religious matter in the same paper.
Consequently, in spite of all of his responsibilities as a pioneer pastor
and Augustana Synod leader, Hasselquist decided to start a second paper

with the name *Det Rätta Hemlandet*. The first issue of this new paper was dated July 11, 1856. From 1856 through 1857 it was issued biweekly, in coordination with *Hemlandet*, also issued biweekly. One title was issued one week and the other the following week, so subscribers had a current Swedish language newspaper each week with this alternating publication schedule. Beginning in January 1858 it was issued monthly.

Det Rätta Hemlandet was almost exclusively a devotional and theological journal. It became a source of personal comfort and religious inspiration for its readers. Hasselquist edited and published the paper from his modest printing shop, Swenska Boktryckeriet, in Galesburg, Illinois, from its beginning in 1856 through 1858.

In January 1859, the operation was moved to Chicago where the Svenska Lutherska Tryckföreningen took it over. This Swedish Lutheran Publication Society was a stock company owned and controlled by a group of clergy and laymen in the Mississippi Conference of the Synod of Northern Illinois. From 1859 through 1862 the paper was issued monthly.

Det Rätta Hemlandet was devoted wholly to religious articles. Hasselquist gave considerable space in each issue to the subject of missions. In 1856, no less than 10 percent of the space was taken with foreign missions matters. Within a year, by 1857, at least 25 percent was concerned with foreign missions. Some of his sermons and those of colleagues were also included. At times, the verses of hymns were printed on the front page.

Hasselquist, as the founder and editor, continued alone until 1858 when Erland Carlsson joined him as coeditor. Later that year Carlsson handled editorial duties alone. A. R. Cervin offered some assistance until 1857. Later Eric Norelius wrote about this paper: "It was edited with eminent tact and ability, used a dignified and Christian language which everybody could understand and in a spirit in which the Christian people recognized themselves" (Augustana ELC. Century, 143).

The final issue of *Det Rätta Hemlandet* was dated December 1862. In January 1863, it was followed by *Det Rätta Hemlandet och Missionsbladet*.

Index for *Rätta Hemlandet* (Vols. 1–7; 1856–1862) is included in the index also for *Rätta Hemlandet och Missionsbladet* (Vols. 8–14; 1863–1869), for *Rätta Hemlandet och Augustana* (Vols. 14–18; 1869–1873), and also for *Augustana* (1874) (Vols. 19–23; 1874–1878). This index is printed in volume 22 (1877) of *Augustana* (1874), it being a cumulative index for volumes 1–22 (1856–1877). *Sources:* Augustana ELC, Century, 143; LIBRIS: Matthews 213; WorldCat.

Augustana College Swenson Center: BX8001 .H3 July 1856–December 1861

Evangelical Lutheran Church in America Archives: AUG 14/7 Vols. 1–7; 1856–1862, Paper and Microfilm

Gustavus Adolphus College Archives: Vol. 1, no. 1–vol. 7, no. 12; July 11, 1856–December 1862

Harvard University Divinity School: Vols. 1–7; 1856–1862, Microfilm

Illinois State Historical Library: F8967L R237

Luther Seminary: BX8001 .A9 Vols. 1–7; July 1856–December 1862, Microfilm

Lutheran School of Theology at Chicago: BX8001 .A810 Vols. 1–7; 1856–1862, Microfilm

Lutheran Theological Seminary at Gettysburg: Vols. [4–5], April–May 1859–May, August 1860

Minnesota Historical Society: BX8049.1 .R23 Vols. 1–7; 1856–1862

Wartburg Theological Seminary: Vols. [4–6], 7; [1859–1861], 1862

WorldCat: American Theological Library Association: Microfilm

LIBRIS: Swedish Emigrant Institute: Årg. 1, [2], 3–5; 1856–1860

Rätta Hemlandet och Augustana:
Tidskrift för Swenska Lutherska Kyrkan i Amerika

[*The True Homeland and Augustana: Publication for Swedish Lutheran Church in America*]

Chicago, IL: Swenska Lutherska Tryckföreningen

Vol. 14, no. 12–vol. 18, no. 12

First issue also called "1. Årg., n:o 12" in continuation of numbering of *Augustana* (1868)

December 1869–December 1873

Formed by the union of: *Rätta Hemlandet och Missionsbladet* and *Augustana* (1868)

Merged with: *Luthersk Kyrkotidning* (Red Wing, MN) and *Nytt och Gammalt* and *Missionären* (Chicago, IL) to form *Augustana* (1874).

Sometimes referred to as: *Det Rätta Hemlandet och Augustana*

Another change for *Det Rätta Hemlandet* arrived at the end of 1869 when in December, *Det Rätta Hemlandet och Missionsbladet* merged with the monthly *Augustana* (1868) to form *Det Rätta Hemlandet och Augustana*, a new monthly.

This paper was published in Chicago by the Swenska Lutherska Tryckföreningen (Swedish Lutheran Publication Society). Volume numbering continued that established by *Augustana* (1868). It also continued the numbering of *Det Rätta Hemlandet*. The issues for September through December of 1871 (being volume 16, numbers 1 through 8) were not published because the Great Chicago Fire destroyed the printing facilities and storehouse. T. N. Hasselquist and A. R. Cervin were editors. In general, the paper reported Augustana Synod news and reports of mission activity both in the United States and abroad.

Late in 1873, the editors of several different papers that were issued at various locations and designed to appeal to Augustana members and associates met to discuss their concern about this situation possibly becoming a divisive factor in the young Synod. Consequently, these papers—*Luthersk Kyrkotidning* (Red Wing, MN), *Nytt och Gammalt*, and *Missionären* (Chicago, IL) merged into one, taking the name *Augustana* as of 1874.

Index for *Rätta Hemlandet och Augustana* (Vols. 14–18; 1869–1873) is included in the index also for *Rätta Hemlandet* (Vols. 1–7; 1856–1862) and also for *Rätta Hemlandet och Missionsbladet* (Vols. 8–14; 1863–1869) and also for *Augustana* (1874) (Vols. 19–23; 1874–1878). This index is printed in volume 22 (1877) of *Augustana* (1874) it being a cumulative index for volumes 1–22 (1856–1877). *Sources:* Erickson 3; LIBRIS; Matthews 213; ULS; WorldCat.

Augustana College Swenson Center: BX8001 .H3 A9
Bethany College: December 1869–February 1871
Evangelical Lutheran Church in America Archives: AUG 14/7 Vols. 15, [16], 17–18; 1870, [1871], 1872–1873, Paper; AUG 14/7 Vols. 15–18; 1870–1873, Microfilm
Gustavus Adolphus College Archives: Vol. 15, no. 1–vol. 17, no. 12; vol. 18, nos. 2/3–8, 10–12; January 1870–December 1872; February/March 1873–August, October–December 1873
Harvard University Divinity School: Vol. 14, no. 12; vol. 15–vol. 16, nos. 1–7/8; vols. 17–18; December 1869–1870; January–July/August 1871; 1872–1873, Microfilm
Luther Seminary: BX8001.A9 Vol. 14, no. 12–vol. 18. no. 12; December 1869–1873, Microfilm
Lutheran School of Theology at Chicago: BX8001 .A810 Vols. 14–17; 1869–1873, Microfilm
Lutheran Theological Seminary at Gettysburg: Vol. 14, no. 12, vols. [15–16], 17, [18]; 1869–1873
Minnesota Historical Society: BX8049.1 .R23 Vol. 14, no. 12–vol. 18, no. 12; 1869–1873
University of Minnesota–Minneapolis: BX8049 .R34x Vol. 16, nos. 1, 3, 7/8; vols. 17–18, nos. 9,12; [1871], 1872–[1873]
WorldCat: American Theological Library Association: Microfilm
LIBRIS: Swedish Emigrant Institute: Årg. 14:12, Årg. 15; December 1869, 1870

Rätta Hemlandet och Missionären

Reference to this title is made in at least three different sources. One mentions 1867. Another mentions 1869 and a merger with *Augustana*. It is considered that the use of "Missionären" is a misprint in the text of these sources where "Missionsbladet" was intended.

Rätta Hemlandet och Missionsbladet

[*The True Homeland and Missions Paper*]
Chicago, IL: [Swenska Lutherska tryckföreningen]
Vol. 8, no. 1–vol. 14, no. 11
January 1863–November 1869
Merged with: *Augustana* (1868) to form *Rätta Hemlandet och Augustana*
Continues: *Rätta Hemlandet*
Sometimes referred to as: *Det Rätta Hemlandet och Missionsbladet*

Recognizing the growing interest in missions, both home and foreign, within the newly organized Scandinavian Evangelical Lutheran Augustana Synod and the continuing interest in religious and devotional material in *Det Rätta Hemlandet*, it was decided to adjust the title and expand the paper.

As of January 1863, the new title was *Det Rätta Hemlandet och Missionsbladet*. A separate missionary department was added to *Det Rätta Hemlandet* in 1863, thus leading to the new title. The following announcement was printed in the first issue of this renamed paper: "With the new year it will be the aim of *Rätta Hemlandet* to devote itself more seriously than ever to the cause of missions. Doubtless many of its friends will appreciate this because they love to hear about the struggles, difficulties, victories, and general progress of the Kingdom of God throughout the world" (Arden 1963, 119). Editor was T. N. Hasselquist. He was assisted by A. R. Cervin in 1868 and 1869.

The paper continued under this title as a monthly publication through its November 1869 issue. At that time it merged with *Augustana* (1868) to form *Det Rätta Hemlandet och Augustana*.

Index for *Rätta Hemlandet och Missionsbladet* (Vols. 8–14; 1863–1869) is included in index for *Rätta Hemlandet* (Vols. 1–7; 1856–1862), for *Rätta Hemlandet och Augustana* (Vols. 14–18; 1869–1873) and also for *Augustana* (1874) (Vols. 19–23; 1874–1878). This index is printed in volume 22 (1877) of *Augustana* (1874) it being a cumulative index for volumes 1–22 (1856–1877). *Sources:* Arden 1963, 119; Matthews 213; ULS; WorldCat.

Augustana College Swenson Center: BX8001 .H3 M5
Bethany College: October–November 1869
Evangelical Lutheran Church in America Archives: AUG 14/7 Vols. 12–14; 1867–1869, Paper; Vols. 8–14; 1863–1869, Microfilm
Gustavus Adolphus College Archives: Vol. 8, no. 1–vol. 14, no. 11; January 1863–November 1869

Harvard University Divinity School: Vols. 8–14, no. 11; 1863–1869, Microfilm

Illinois State Historical Library: F8967L R237

Luther Seminary: BX8001 .A9 Vols. 8–14, no. 11; 1863–November 1869, Microfilm

Lutheran School of Theology at Chicago: BX8001 .A810 Vols. 8–14; 1863–1869, Microfilm

Lutheran Theological Seminary at Gettysburg: Vols. [12–14, no. 11]; [1867–1869]

Minnesota Historical Society: BX8049.1 .R23 Vols. 8–14; 1863–1869

University of Texas at Austin: 054.85 R189 June 1867–May 1868

Wartburg Theological Seminary: Vols. [8], 9, [10]; [1863], 1864 [1865]

WorldCat: American Theological Library Association: Microfilm

Reflector

Minneapolis, MN: Lutheran Bible Institute
1950–?

According to Peterson, this was the annual student publication of the Lutheran Bible Institute. It was first issued in 1950. *Source:* Peterson 168.

No holdings reported.

Resource

Philadelphia, PA: Lutheran Church Press
Vols. 1–14, no. 3
October 1959–December 1972
ISSN 0034–5652
Merged with: *Lutheran Teacher* to form four age-level editions: *Learning with Young Children in the Parish* and *Learning with Children in the Parish* and *Learning with Youth in the Parish* and *Learning with Adults in the Parish*
Continues: *Church School Teacher* and *Parish School*

As an important aid for individuals involved with the educational ministry in local congregations, *Resource*, a "magazine of parish education," was issued as a cooperative project by four different Lutheran synods. It was published monthly with a combined issue for August and September.

The volumes for 1959–1962 were sponsored by the boards of parish education of the American Evangelical Lutheran Church, the Augustana Lutheran Church, the Finnish Lutheran Church of America, and the

United Lutheran Church in America. Following the 1962 merger, the Board of Parish Education of the Lutheran Church in America sponsored the volumes from 1963–1972. *Source:* WorldCat.

Augustana College: BV1460 .R48 Vols. 1–3; 1959–1962
Harvard University: Vols. 1–14, no. 3; 1959–1972
Luther Seminary: Vols. 1–13, no. 7; 1959–1972
Lutheran School of Theology in Chicago: BX8012 .R40 Vols. 1–14; 1959/60–1972
Lutheran Theological Seminary at Gettysburg: Vols. 1–14; 1959–1972
Lutheran Theological Seminary at Philadelphia: Vols. 1–14; 1959–1972
Pacific Lutheran Theological Seminary: Vols. 1–9; vol. 10, nos. 1–7, 9, 11; vol. 11, no. 1; vols. 12–14; 1959–September 1968; [1969–1970]; 1970–1972
Texas Lutheran University: Vols. 1–14, no. 3; October 1959–December 1972

The Rockety-I

Rock Island, IL: Augustana College
1912–
Continues: *The Jubilee* 1910

Published by the senior class of Augustana College as their annual, *The Rockety-I* title first appeared in 1912. In 1919, this policy changed when the junior class published the annual.

Through the years, *The Rockety* has presented a comprehensive view in words and photographs of activity at the Augustana College campus.

The *Rockety-I* was preceded by the first Senior *Class Annual* in 1900, *The Garnet and Silver-Gray* in 1905, and *The Jubilee* in 1910. From 1906 through 1909, the June issue of the *Augustana Observer* was the senior class annual. *Sources:* Bergendoff 149, 172, 206; LIBRIS; WorldCat.

Augustana College LD271.A6655 R6 1911/12-Special Collections (incomplete file)
Minnesota Historical Society: LD271 .A6655 1913
University of Minnesota–Minneapolis: L9271 .A665 R63x 1917
LIBRIS: Royal Library of Sweden: 1913

Runan

[*The Rune*]
Rock Island, IL: Augustana College Svenska Vitterhetssällskapet
1900?–1915?

Members of this literary society, the Svenska Vitterhetssällskapet, at Augustana College prepared a handwritten publication titled *Runan* which was read aloud regularly at the group's meetings. Limited to eighteen members, the group focused on topics dealing with Swedish literature, especially those authors studied in the Swedish curriculum at the college. The group felt it important to preserve the Swedish language, literature, and history for Swedish immigrants and for their children. Poems by Swedish-American authors were frequently read.

Blanck cites specific issues in 1902, 1903, 1905, 1906, and 1909. *Source:* Blanck 1997, 103–6.

Augustana College

Runes

St. Peter, MN: Published by the senior class of Gustavus Adolphus College
1906
Continues: *Manhem* (1904)
Continued by: *Valkyria* (1909)

This is the next Gustavus Adolphus College annual to follow the 1904 *Manhem* publication. *Source:* Peterson 74.

Gustavus Adolphus College: LD 2091.G62G65 1906

– S –

Saga

Rock Island, IL: Augustana College
No. 1–
Spring 1938–

Published by students at Augustana College, the literary annual *Saga* first appeared in 1938. It continued with a yearly schedule through 1984, after which it was issued twice annually.

Sponsored by the student Writer's Club, *Saga* included works of prose, poetry, and art. Its size has varied. Closely associated with the annual for the first thirty years (1938–1968), was the faculty advisor Henriette C. K. Naeseth. *Source:* WorldCat.

Augustana College LH1.A937 S2 1938–

Schibboleth

Chicago, IL: [s.n.] (1878)
Moline, IL: [s.n.] (1879)
January 1878–December 1879
Sometimes referred to as: *Shibboleth* or *Schibbolet*

S. P. A. Lindahl and A. G. Setterdahl collaborated on a paper known as *Schibboleth*, which had as its purpose to speak out against lodges and all secret societies and orders. Ander writes that this periodical was "dedicated to a war against secret societies" (Ander 1956, 173). Olson writes that Lindahl, through this paper, "carried on a crusade against lodges and all manner of secret orders" (Olson 1933, 58). Lindahl also expressed his opposition to alcohol and drunkenness.

The paper was issued monthly from January 1878 through December 1879, at which time it ceased publication. *Sources:* Ander 1956, 173; LIBRIS; Olson 1933, 58; Setterdahl 11.

Augustana College: Microfilm
LIBRIS: Royal Library of Sweden: 1878–1879

The Seminary Review

Rock Island, IL: Lutheran School of Theology at Chicago, Rock Island campus
Vol. 14, no. 4–vol. 19, no. 2
1962–1967
Merged with: *Record* (Lutheran School of Theology, Maywood Campus) to form *Context*
Continues: *Augustana Seminary Review*
Sometimes referred to as: *Seminary Review*

Continuing the *Augustana Seminary Review*, following the Lutheran Church in America merger in 1962, this was issued three times each year by the Rock Island campus of the Lutheran School of Theology at Chicago through 1967. The first issue of each volume was the seminary catalog, which now is not included in some library files.

Scholarly articles on theological subjects were prepared by members of the seminary faculty. Some articles were written by contemporary theologians and other church leaders. *Source:* WorldCat.

Augustana College: Vols. 14–19; 1962–1967
Gustavus Adolphus College: Vol. 14, no. 4–vol. 18; 1962–1966
Harvard University Divinity School: Period. 134.38 Vol. 14, no. 4–vol. 19, no. 2; 1962–1967

Luther Seminary: BV4070 .L963 Vols. [14]–19; 1963–1967
Lutheran School of Theology at Chicago: Vols. 14–19; 1962–1967
Lutheran Theological Seminary at Gettysburg: Vols. 14–17, [18–19]; 1962–1967
Pacific Lutheran Theological Seminary: Vol. 14, no. 4; vols. 15–16; vol. 17, nos. 2–4; vol. 18, nos. 2–3; [1962], 1963–1964, [1965–1966]
Princeton Theological Seminary: Vols. 14–19; 1962–1967
Wartburg Theological Seminary: Vols. 14–18; 1963–1966

Shibboleth

See *Schibboleth*.

Silfver Jubileums Minneskrift: Kalendar

See *Calendar*.

Sions-Bladet: Evangeliskt-Lutherskt Traktat och Nyhetsblad

[*Zions Paper: Evangelical Lutheran Tract and Newspaper*]
Tacoma, WA: A. M. Green
Vol. 1, no. 1–vol. 18, no. 12
1907–December 1926
Continued by: *Columbia Lutheran*

A paper for the Augustana Lutheran Church in the Pacific Northwest with the title *Sions-Bladet* was published and edited by A. M. Green, a pastor in Tacoma, Washington. It was issued as an eight-page monthly for a subscription price of twenty-five cents per year. Ander says that it was originally a parish paper begun in 1901 (Ander 1956, 174). Other sources indicate that it began in 1907. Text was primarily in Swedish with some English used. *Sions-Bladet* was continued by *Columbia Lutheran* in 1927. *Sources:* Ander 1956, 174; Erickson 92; WorldCat.

University of Washington: Vol. [5, no.1–vol. 18, no. 11]; [January 15, 1912–November 1926], Microfilm
Erickson: Royal Library of Sweden: Vol. 13, no. 1–vol. 18, no. 12; January 20, 1920–December 1926

Sions Väktare

[*Zions Watchmen*]
Winnipeg, Manitoba, Canada: [s.n.]
Vol. 1, no. 1–?

December 1892–August 1893
Continued by: *Väktaren*
Sometimes referred to as: *Sions Väktaren*

The monthly *Sions Väktare* began publication in Winnipeg, Manitoba, Canada late in 1892 under the leadership of Svante Udden, the first Swedish Lutheran minister to reside and work in Canada. It was a modest paper of only four pages. Under that title it existed for only a few months until August 1893, when the name was changed to *Väktaren*. *Sources:* Baglo 1962, 35; Setterdahl 34.

Augustana College: Microfilm

Sjukvännen

[*Friend of the Sick*]
Omaha, NE: Immanuel Deaconess Hospital
March 1894–March 1901

According to Ander (174), this publication was issued by the Immanuel Deaconess Hospital from 1896 to 1901. According to Söderström (40), this item was first issued in March 1894 and ended with the March 1901 issue. A quarterly at first, it changed to an irregular schedule with at least one issue each year. *Sources:* Ander 1956, 174; Söderström 40.

Augustana College Swenson Center: March 1901

Skaffaren

Red Wing, MN: E. Norelius
St. Paul, MN: [s.n.]
Vol. 1, no. 1–vol. 4, no. 17
December 1878–April 26, 1882
Merged with: *Minnesota Stats Tidning* (Minneapolis, MN: 1877) to form *Skaffaren och Minnesota Stats Tidning*
Continues: *Ev. Luthersk Tidskrift*
Sometimes referred to as: *Skaffaren* (Red Wing, MN: 1878)

A further publishing effort of Eric Norelius in Minnesota was issued as *Skaffaren* from December 1878 through April 26, 1882. This was a large format Swedish newspaper that was the successor to *Ev. Luthersk Tidskrift*, sometimes referred to as *Evangelisk Luthersk Tidskrift*.

Skaffaren was published in Red Wing, Minnesota, until September 1879. It was published at St. Paul, Minnesota, for the remainder of its existence under this title from September 19, 1879, through April 26, 1882.

For the first two months *Skaffaren* appeared monthly. With the February 1, 1879, through December 18, 1879, issues it was published semimonthly. With the first issue in 1880 (January 7) to the April 26, 1882, issue it appeared weekly.

Skaffaren as a denominational paper has been characterized as "militant," as containing "controversial and polemical materials, some of it personal and acrimonius," and as "rabidly opposed" to secret societies such as the Masons and the Grange. E. Norelius and P. Sjöblom were editors, assisted by H. von Stockenström as associate editor.

In May 1882, *Skaffaren* merged with *Minnesota Stats Tidning* (Minneapolis, MN: 1877) to form *Skaffaren och Minnesota Stats Tidning*. *Sources:* Ander 1956, 186; Backlund 120; LIBRIS; Stephenson 274, 318; WorldCat.

Augustana College Swenson Center
Gustavus Adolphus College Archives: December 1878–April 26, 1882, Microfilm
Minnesota Historical Society: December 1878–April 26, 1882, Microfilm
LIBRIS: Royal Library of Sweden: 1878–1882

Skaffaren (St. Paul, MN: 1885)

St. Paul, MN; Minneapolis, MN: Lutheran Publication Society of the Northwest
Vol. 9, no. 11–vol. 19, no. 43
March 18, 1885–October 23, 1895
Continues: *Skaffaren och Minnesota Stats Tidning*
Continued by: *Minnesota Stats Tidning* (St. Paul, MN: 1895)

Yet another change of newspaper title in Minnesota took effect in 1885 when *Skaffaren* emerged as the new title of the former *Skaffaren och Minnesota Stats Tidning*. It continued publication in St. Paul and Minneapolis, Minnesota, at the Lutheran Publication Society of the Northwest each week.

This title existed for ten years from the March 18, 1885, issue through October 23, 1895. At that time it became the *Minnesota Stats Tidning* again. *Sources:* LIBRIS; WorldCat.

Augustana College Swenson Center: incomplete file
Gustavus Adolphus College Archives: March 18, 1885–October 23, 1895, Microfilm

Minnesota Historical Society: Vol. 9, no. 11–vol. 19, no. 43; March 18,
1885–October 23, 1895, Microfilm
LIBRIS: Royal Library of Sweden: 1885–1893: Paper; 1885–1895: Microfilm

Skaffaren och Minnesota Stats Tidning

St. Paul, MN; Minneapolis, MN: Lutheran Publication Society of the
Northwest
Vol. 6, no. 18–vol. 9, no. 10
May 3, 1882–March 11, 1885
Formed by the union of: *Skaffaren* (Red Wing, MN: 1878) and *Minnesota
Stats Tidning* (Minneapolis, MN: 1877)
Continued by: *Skaffaren* (St. Paul, MN: 1885)

This new Swedish-language newspaper title appeared with the merger
of *Skaffaren* (Red Wing, MN: 1878) and *Minnesota Stats Tidning* (Minneapolis, MN: 1877).

For nearly three years, from May 3, 1882, through March 11, 1885, *Skaffaren och Minnesota Stats Tidning* was published weekly in St. Paul and
Minneapolis, Minnesota, by the Lutheran Publication Society of the
Northwest. Officers in this group were Otto Wallmark, Berndt Anderson,
and A. P. Croonquist.

This paper was considered to be the mouthpiece of the Minnesota Conference of the Augustana Lutheran Synod as it reported regularly church
news from the region.

In March 1885, it resumed the title *Skaffaren*, thus dropping the *Minnesota Stats Tidning* portion. *Sources:* Backlund 81; Bengston 459; LIBRIS;
WorldCat.

Augustana College Swenson Center
Gustavus Adolphus College Archives: May 3, 1882–March 11, 1885, Mi-
crofilm
Minnesota Historical Society: Vol. 6, no. 18–vol. 9, no. 10; May 3, 1882–
March 11, 1885, Microfilm
LIBRIS: Royal Library of Sweden: 1882–1885: Paper and Microfilm

Skolvännen

[*The School Friend*]
Rock Island, IL: Augustana College and Theological Seminary
Issued intermittently between 1878 and 1894

May 1, 1878–May 1880 (first series) 15 numbers
August 15, 1883–December 19, 1883 : Nos. 16–19
April 1887–October 31, 1887: Nos. 20–22
1894: Nos. 23–24
Sometimes referred to as: *Skolwännen* or *Skol-Vännen*

Published intermittently for a number of years, *Skolvännen* was issued to publicize the financial needs of Augustana College and Theological Seminary. Olof Olsson, a professor in the seminary, was the editor and at most times the sole contributor to what may be termed a series of tracts, rather than a newspaper.

Because of the purchase of property in Rock Island and the construction of a new building, the school faced a debt of $27,000 in 1878. A resolution adopted by the Board of Directors on April 17, 1878 read:

> That a committee consisting of Professor O. Olsson and Messrs. C.A. Swensson and J.H. Randall be appointed to . . . issue a paper to be called *Skolvännen* for a period of six weeks, to advocate this cause, said paper to be distributed free throughout the Synod or wherever it will be met with favor. The paper is to be issued in fifteen thousand copies. Besides this paper a requisite number of envelopes is to be printed and sent to the congregations of the Synod, said envelopes to be distributed to members of the congregation by their respective pastors and church councils. (Arden 1960, 181–82)

Olsson was appointed solicitor to gather funds. Swensson and Randall were students. This special paper for free distribution to the congregations was received with enthusiasm and support. Arden continues his narrative of the situation:

> This apparently all-too-modest action by an institution facing financial ruin was a far wiser decision, however, than even the editor himself could possibly have realized at the time. Dr. Olsson had been connected with the school only two years, but he had a facile pen, a resourceful mind, and what was most needed, a courageous enthusiasm for the cause of education. Olsson referred to himself as "The Beggar Boy," a title he humorously claimed had been officially conferred upon him by an academic institution. His style of writing was highly original, light, cheerful and chatty—"childlike and good-humored," is the way Hasselquist put it. Though his appeal was urgent and insistent, he always emphasized the motive of love in all Christian giving. He often asked for large and substantial gifts from those who were blessed with an abundance of worldly goods, but he pleaded especially for many small gifts, as being an even greater blessing. And most of the contributions which were received were small, sometimes given at some sacrifice. (182)

Bergendoff comments about the paper: "For a year in a homely, whimsical style he [Olsson] pictured the importance and plight of the institution, and the responsibilities of the people it served" (Bergendoff 58–59). Within a few years, a major portion of the debt was eliminated.

In 1882, in relation to planning for Jubilee Hall, *Skolvännen* was to be revived and issued twice each month. The paper reappeared in 1883, with specific issues dated from August 15 to December 19. Again, the message was solicitation of funds for this building and a new college building, Memorial Hall or Old Main.

In 1887, at the request of the synod, Olsson revived *Skolvännen* again. In it he asked each member of the synod to contribute fifty cents to the college to help fund the finishing of construction of Memorial Hall. An example of his straightforward style follows:

Writing in the April issue, 1887, of his little paper, Olsson declared, "Is it necessary? What? This very question: Is it necessary to make an ingathering for the new college building in Rock Island once again? Judge for yourselves, dear friends. Here that building has been standing now a long, long time without windows, without doors, and entirely unfinished inside. Railway trains and street cars pass it daily with masses of strangers and of our local citizens. All are looking and pointing their fingers at this new but old structure which the Augustana Synod has reared but, as it seems, never intends to complete. What kind of a church body can it be that takes care of its oldest and foremost educational institution in that fashion? If that is love, surely its affection is of a very peculiar kind. Should a congregation build a church and then let it stand for years with nothing but walls and a roof, what would you say of such a congregation?" (Arden 1960, 198–99)

People responded by giving more than $13,000 by this means of solicitation. In the October 31, 1887, issue, Olsson said farewell to his readers, due to his ill health.

Both Bergendoff and Ander as well as Söderström use 1894 as the final year of any numbers of *Skolvännen*. Apparently, its mission had been fulfilled. *Sources:* Ander 1956, 175; Arden 1960, 181–83, 197–99; Bergendoff 58–59, 64; Söderström 25; Stephenson 335, 347.

Augustana College Swenson Center: 1878–1880, 1883, 1887

Skolvännen: North Star Signal

See *North Star Signal.*

The Social Missions Review

Minneapolis, MN?: Commission on Social Missions, Augustana Evangelical Lutheran Church
1952?–195?

The Commission on Social Missions began to issue it's publication *The Social Missions Review* as "a source of information and guidance in the field of social missions" in 1952 (Augustana Annual 1953, 82). This publication helped to emphasize the welfare work of the Church. In 1954 a Board of Social Missions was created to replace the commission, thus giving further support to the ministry of mercy. *Source: Augustana Annual* 1953, 82; 1954, 93; 1955, 93.

No holdings reported.

Solglimten: Textblad för de Minsta Barnen i Söndagsskolan

[*Glimpses of the Sun: Text Paper for the Smallest Children in Sunday Schools*]
Rock Island, IL: Augustana Book Concern
Vol. 1, no. 1–vol. 18?
January 1906–1924?

This Swedish lesson paper was designed for the smallest children in the Sunday School, or the second class. Along with a lesson for each Sunday, there were Bible verses, illustrations, and a brief story. Contents were much like *Solstrålen*.
The paper was issued quarterly in December, March, June and September. It contained thirty-two pages in large print. With the scarcity of files, the ending date was not determined. *Sources:* Erickson 98; Lundeen, Parish education.

Erickson: Royal Library of Sweden [1908–1914]
Lundeen: Evangelical Lutheran Church in America Archives: [1906–1924]

Solstrålen: Textblad för de Minsta Barnen i Söndagsskolan

[*The Sunbeam: Text Paper for the Smallest Children in Sunday Schools*]
Rock Island, IL: Augustana Book Concern
Vol. 1, no. 1–vol. 21?
1904/1905–1924?

This Swedish lesson paper was designed for the very smallest children in the Sunday School, or the first class. Along with a lesson for each Sunday, there were Bible verses, illustrations, and a brief story. Contents were much like *Solglimten*.

The paper was issued semimonthly through November, 1908. It became a quarterly with volume 5 in December, 1908. Pages were in large print. Subscription price was twenty-five cents per year. *Sources:* Erickson 98; LIBRIS; Lundeen, Parish education.

University of Minnesota–Minneapolis: BS556 .S65x Vol. 16, no. 4; August–November 1920
Erickson: Augustana College: Vol. 10, no. 2; 1914
    Royal Library of Sweden: Vols. [2, 4–6]; [1905/1906–1909/1910]
Lundeen: Evangelical Lutheran Church in America Archives: [1904–1924]
LIBRIS: Swedish Emigrant Institute: [Årg. 9; 12–16, 18]; [1913, 1916–1921]

Söndagsskolans Textblad

[*Sunday School Text Paper*]
Rock Island, IL: Augustana Book Concern
Vol. 1, no. 1–vol.?
January 5, 1890–?

This Swedish lesson leaflet for Sunday Schools was issued weekly. Price was fifteen cents per year, with a further reduction for multiple copies. Lundholm mentions this series as being a thriving Augustana Book Concern publication in 1893. *Sources:* Erickson 100; Lundholm 144.

Erickson: Royal Library of Sweden: Vols. [1, 4]; [1890, 1893]
No United States holdings reported.

Stadsmissionären

[*The City Missionary*]
Chicago, IL: [s.n.]
January 1909–1924
Continued by: *City Missionary*
Sometimes referred to as: *Stads Missionären*

Ander states that this publication was the "official organ of the Chicago Lutheran Inner Missionary Society" and the "official organ of the Augustana Inner Mission." Lundeen identifies the organization as the Chicago Lutheran Inner Mission Society. The paper was issued monthly in Swedish text. In 1925, it took the English title *City Missionary. Sources:* Ander 1956, 176; Lundeen, group 6; Söderström 22.

Augustana College Swenson Center: October 1914
Lundeen: Evangelical Lutheran Church in America Archives: [1909–1924]

Student-Katalog: eller Förteckning på de Studerande vid Augustana College and Seminary

[*Student Catalog: or List of the Students at Augustana College and Seminary*]
Paxton, IL: Augustana College and Seminary
1871/1872–1875/1876
Continued by: *Catalogue*/Augustana College and Seminary

This catalog was issued during the time of the location at Paxton, Illinois, of Augustana College and Seminary. Prior to this time there was a prospectus, or *Katalog*, issued in 1868. All issues were in Swedish text.

Subjects taught and lists of faculty were printed in the catalog. Names and biographical information about students such as birth place, date of arrival in America, father's occupation, date of matriculation, and date entered were included.

Following the move of the academic institution to Rock Island, Illinois, the annual catalogs were issued in English. *Sources:* Bergendoff 47, 203; LIBRIS.

Augustana College
LIBRIS: Royal Library of Sweden: 1872–1876

Superior Light

[s.l.]: Superior Conference, Augustana Lutheran Synod
1947–1962

This was a news publication issued by the Superior Conference of the Augustana Lutheran Synod. *Source:* Lundeen, group 6.

Lundeen: Evangelical Lutheran Church in America Archives: 1947–1962

Sven. Can.-Tidn.

See *Svenska Canada-Tidningen*.

Svenska Amerikanaren Hemlandet

[*The Swedish American and the Homeland*]
Chicago, IL: Swedish American Printing Co.
Vol. 38, no. 40–vol. 39, no. 52
October 1, 1914–December 30, 1915
Formed by the union of: *Svenska Amerikanaren* (Chicago, IL: 1885) and
  Gamla och Nya Hemlandet
Continued by: *Svenska Amerikanaren* (Chicago, IL: 1916)
Sometimes referred to as: *Svenska Amerikanaren och Hemlandet*

With the last issue of *Gamla och Nya Hemlandet* (or more generally referred to as *Hemlandet*) dated September 24, 1914, its owner C. S. Peterson
sold the paper to *Svenska Amerikanaren*. Financial diversions and intense
competition for subscribers led Peterson to this inevitable decision. Oliver
A. Linder was editor at this time. Weekly circulation in early 1914 was es-
timated at forty-seven thousand. However, after this merger with *Hemlandet* eighty thousand subscribers were claimed. The importance of *Svenska Amerikanaren* was greatly augmented by this merger.

Ironically, over the years *Svenska Amerikanaren* had been the foremost
liberal opponent of *Hemlandet*. During those same years *Hemlandet* had
been very friendly toward the Augustana Synod with which it had close
contacts. In 1916, the word *Hemlandet* was dropped from the title. *Sources:*
Capps 234; WisCat; WorldCat.

Augustana College Swenson Center
Center for Research Libraries: October 1914–1915
Wisconsin Historical Society: October 1, 1914–December 30, 1915, Mi-
  crofilm
WorldCat: Illinois State Historical Library: 1914–1915
  Kansas State Historical Library: 1914–1915

Svenska Canada-Tidningen

[Swedish Canada News]
Winnipeg, Manitoba, Canada: Canada Weekly Printing Co.
Vol. 15, no. 25–vol. 40, no. 52
June 19, 1907–December 29, 1932
ISSN 0839-5624
Continues: *Canada*
Continued by: *Canada-tidningen* ISSN 0839-5632
Sometimes referred to as: *Svenska Canadatidningen* or *Sven. Can.–tidn.* or
  Swedish Canada news

Following a precarious existence of its predecessors for fifteen years under several different titles, the *Svenska Canada-Tidningen* became the prop-

erty of the Canada Weekly Printing Company in 1906, still under the title *Canada*. With the leadership of P. M. Dahl, it published the first issue under this new title on June 19, 1907. Its predecessors had persevered under difficult circumstances considering the pioneering conditions under which the Swedish Canadians were living.

By 1907, the paper was considered entirely political. It made no effort to speak primarily to the Swedish Lutheran churches or population but was a general paper for all Swedish people in Canada. *Sources:* Backlund 74; Baglo 1962, 35; LIBRIS; Setterdahl 35; WorldCat.

Augustana College Swenson Center: Microfilm
Evangelical Lutheran Church in Canada Archives: 1914, 1919
National Library of Canada: NJ .FM 1719 June 19, 1907–December 29, 1932, Microfilm
Setterdahl: Legislative Library, Winnipeg, Manitoba, Canada: Microfilm
LIBRIS: Royal Library of Sweden: July 1907–July 1919, Paper; June 19, 1907–December 29, 1932, Microfilm

Svenska Litterära Sällskapet de Nios Årsbok

See *Årsbok/Svenska Litterära Sällskapet de Nio.*

Svenska Posten

Svenska Posten was the name proposed as early as 1853 by T. N. Hasselquist for a newspaper that appeared on January 3, 1855, as *Hemlandet, det Gamla och det Nya.*

Some sources indicate that discussion about publishing activities had begun in 1854 among several early Augustana leaders, including L. P. Esbjörn, T. N. Hasselquist, and Erland Carlsson. Originally, Carlsson was to be the editor. Being overwhelmed with other duties, he was not able to begin the proposed paper. However, several extant letters with the 1853 date speak of concern about establishing a Swedish-language newspaper that would address the interests of the Swedish immigrants. As the dynamic Augustana Synod leader in its early decades, Hasselquist was intent upon providing a Swedish-language newspaper, as no such paper existed in the Midwest where many of the immigrants had settled.

On November 15, 1853, Hasselquist wrote from Galesburg, Illinois, to his colleague Erland Carlsson, the pastor from Sweden stationed at Chicago to befriend many Swedish immigrants arriving in mid-century, of his concerns about a Swedish-language newspaper:

> Have you given any thought to the proposed Swedish newspaper? I hear many express a longing for such a one, especially for complete news from the home country. You must not put the matter out of mind, for we must seek to

free our people from immoral and unchurchly papers. The Lord lend you courage! For His sake we will do all; He deserves that we do what we can for Him. May our faith be greatly increased and may we be consumed by love to the brethren! God bless us! (Olson "Early Letters" 111)

Some five weeks later on December 22, 1853, Hasselquist wrote from Galesburg to Carlsson again on the subject: "Have you given further thought to the publication of a newspaper? We must risk a sample issue; but I am sure it will carry itself. I still maintain that if you do not take the journalistic field, some one of the proselyting powers will do so, to the detriment of our congregations" (Olson "Early Letters" 111).

And again, about five weeks later on January 30, 1854, Hasselquist pleads with Carlsson that they must start a paper: "Have you got a paper ("Svenska Posten" it might be named) started? There is such a constant inquiry for it, that you would hardly believe it; especially now that the news from Sweden begins to have an ominous sound. . . . But I must now close with a loud call for the paper!" (Olson "Early Letters" 112).

Svenska Posten never materialized. Instead, the first issue of *Hemlandet, det Gamla och det Nya* was published on January 3, 1855, in Galesburg, Illinois, by Hasselquist. *Source:* Olson "Early Letters" 111–12.

Swedish American Genealogist

Winter Park, FL; Rock Island, IL: Swedish American Genealogist
Vol. 1, no. 1–
March 1981–
ISSN 0275–9314

According to the journal website, the *"Swedish American Genealogist* is a quarterly journal devoted to Swedish American biography, genealogy, and personal history." It is published by the Swenson Swedish Immigration Research Center at Augustana College. Nils William Olsson established the journal in 1981. Readers doing Swedish-American genealogical research locate substantial information in this journal.

Each December issue includes an index of personal names and place names for that year. Subscribers may forward genealogical queries, asking for assistance from readers. Currently, the editor is Elisabeth Thorsell in Sweden. *Sources:* http://www.augustana.edu/administration/Swenson/ SAG; LIBRIS; WorldCat.

Augustana College Swenson Center: E184 .S23 S88 Vols. 1–22; 1981–2002
Gustavus Adolphus College: Vols. 1–24+; 1981–2004 + current

Iowa State Historical Society: E184 .S23 S88 Vols. 1–22; 1981–2002
Kansas State Historical Society
Minnesota Historical Society: CS42 .S877 Vols. 1–; 1981–
New York Public Library Research Library: Vols. 1–22+; 1981–2004
North Park University: Vols. 16–21; 1996–2001
Pacific Lutheran University: SIE CT1310 .S84 Vols. 1–; 1981–
Texas State Library: 1981–2004
University of Minnesota – Minneapolis: Vols. 1–24, nos. 1–3; 1981–2004
+ current
Wisconsin Historical Society: E184 .S23 S88 Vols. 1–22; 1981–2002 + current
WorldCat: Bethany College
LIBRIS: Royal Library of Sweden

Swedish Canada News

See *Svenska Canada-Tidningen.*

Swenson Center News: Publication of the Swenson Swedish Immigration Research Center

Rock Island, IL: The Center
No. 1–
1986–
ISSN 0895–7126

The Swenson Swedish Immigration Research Center at Augustana College publishes this annual newsletter, which is available in January each year. The newsletter includes information about activity at the center, as well as general interest articles on a variety of Swedish-American topics. It is available without charge. Past issues have been scanned on to the center website at http://www.augustana.edu/administration/swenson/SAG.html. *Sources:* http://www.augustana.edu/administration/swenson/SAG.html; LIBRIS; WorldCat.

Augustana College Swenson Center: E184.S23 S84 No. 1–; 1986–
Harvard University: E184 .S23 S97x Nos. 1–15; 1986–2001 + current
Iowa State Historical Society: E184 .S23 S97 Nos. 1–17; 1986–2003
Minnesota Historical Society: Nos. 1–6; 1986–1991
Pacific Lutheran University: SIE E184 .S23 S94x 1986–1999
University of Illinois: 929.37305 SW Vols. 1–5; 1986–1990
Wisconsin Historical Society: 01–8217 Nos. 13–16; 1999–2002

LIBRIS: Lund University: 1986–
Royal Library of Sweden: 1986–
Uppsala University: 1986–1997

– T –

Tabitha: Kvartalsskrift från Bethesda Diakonisshem

[*Tabitha: Quarterly Writing from Bethesda Deaconess Home*]
St. Paul, MN: Tabitha Society
Vol. 1, no. 1–vol. 6, nos. 3/4
October 1909–December 1914

Including news from Bethesda Hospital and Bethesda Deaconess Home in St. Paul, Minnesota, *Tabitha* was a quarterly consisting of eight pages. That publication schedule was followed regularly until 1914 when issues appeared only in June and December.

The paper also included information about the work and mission of the Minnesota Conference. *Source:* Erickson 102.

Erickson: Augustana College: Vols. 1–2
    Minnesota Historical Society: Vols. [1–2, 5–6]; [1909–1910, 1913–1914]
    Royal Library of Sweden: Vols. [1]; 2–6

Teen Talk

Rock Island, IL: Augustana Book Concern
Vol. 32, no. 40–vol. 41, no. 34
October 3, 1954–August 25, 1963
Continues: *Young People*
Continued by: *Viewpoint*

The weekly Sunday church school paper for the upper age, intermediate, and senior classes, *The Young People*, was replaced in 1954 by *Teen Talk*. It was considered that this new title would be more appealing to its intended readership.

An advertisement for *Teen Talk* read: "A sparkling new eight-page weekly designed for young people. Featuring character building fiction and science stories as well as devotional materials on a young person's level. Containing also an interesting news column, fun page, letters to the editor and a weekly feature on solving teen-age problems, adding to the popularity and effectiveness of this outstanding young people's paper" (*Augustana Annual* 1957, 205). A single subscription was $1.15 or 90 cents for five or more.

Another advertisement read: "edited so as to have not only an interesting design or 'eye appeal' but to contain materials that the children will enjoy reading and, more important, that will aid in Christian development" (*Augustana Annual* 1956, 182).

Designed to aid teachers in the parish education program, it was correlated with the Christian Growth series widely used in local congregations. As an Augustana publication of the Parish Education Department, its final issue was published in August 1963. *Sources: Augustana Annual* 1956, 182; 1957, 205; Lundeen, group 7; WorldCat.

Evangelical Lutheran Church in America Archives: AUG 25/5/6 Vols. 32–37, [40], 41; 1954–1959, [1962], 1963
Gustavus Adolphus College Archives: Vols. 32–41; 1954–1963

Teologisk Tidskrift

See *Augustana Theological Quarterly*.

Textblad för Söndagsskolan

[*Text Paper for Sunday Schools*]
Rock Island, IL: Augustana Book Concern
Vol. 1, no. 1–vol. 21?
December 1904–1925?

This Swedish lesson leaflet for older children and for Bible classes in Sunday schools was issued quarterly in March, June, September, and December beginning in 1906. Prior to that it was issued semimonthly. Of substantial size with thirty-two pages, its subscription price was twenty-five cents per year. Editors included J. A. Sandell through 1906, O. J. Siljeström to 1909, when O. V. Holmgrain became editor. *Sources:* Bengston 465; Erickson 105; LIBRIS.

Augustana College Swenson Center: Summer 1910–Spring 1911
Erickson: Royal Library of Sweden: Vols. [2, 4–6, 8–14]: [1905, 1907–1910, 1912–1918]
LIBRIS: Swedish Emigrant Institute: Årg. [12–17, 21]; [1916–1918, 1920, 1925]

Theological Studies and Issues

Rock Island, IL: Augustana College and Theological Seminary
Nos. 1–2
1940–1941

This short-lived serial has only two numbers:

1. *The Theology of History*, by Adolf Hult. 1940.
2. *Taught of God*, by Adolf Hult. 1941.

Source: WorldCat.

Harvard University: C 1750.231 Nos. 1–2
Luther Seminary: BR115.H5H9 No. 1
Lutheran School of Theology at Chicago: BR115 .H5 H9 No. 1
Lutheran Theological Seminary at Philadelphia: D16.9.H856 No. 1
Ohio State University: BX8065.A9 Nos. 1–2
Trinity Lutheran Seminary: BR115 .H5 H8 Vol. 1; 1940
University of Illinois: 230 AU42T No. 1
University of Michigan: BX8065.H92 No. 2
University of Texas at Austin: 284.106 T342 Nos. 1–2
Wartburg Theological Seminary: BR115 .H5 H8 1940
Wheaton College: 901 H879T; No. 1
Yale University: Mpk51 T343 1; Nos. 1–2

Thru 8 Stories

Rock Island, IL: Augustana Book Concern
Vol. 33, no. 1–vol. 36, no. 34
January 1960–August 25, 1963
Continues: *'til 8 Stories*

This weekly leaflet for the youngest Sunday church school children was
a continuation of *'til 8 Stories*. It took the new name *Thru 8 Stories* beginning in January 1960. The leaflet was published until the last issue in August 1963. *Source:* Lundeen, group 7.

Augustana College Swenson Center: 1960–1963
Evangelical Lutheran Church in America Archives: AUG 25/5/7 Vol.
   [36: no. 2, January 13–no. 34, August 25]; 1963
Gustavus Adolphus College Archives: Vol. 33, no. 1–vol. 36, no. 34; January 1960–August 25, 1963

Tidskrift

See *Ev. Luthersk Tidskrift* and *Tidskrift för Svensk Ev. Luth. Kyrkohistoria i
N. Amerika och för Teologiska och Kyrkliga Frågor.*

**Tidskrift för Svensk Ev. Luth. Kyrkohistoria
i N. Amerika och för Teologiska och Kyrkliga Frågor**

[*Journal for Swedish Evangelical Lutheran Church History in North America
and for Theological and Ecclesiastical Questions*]
Rock Island, IL: Lutheran Augustana Book Concern
Vol. 1, nos. 1–2 (1898); nos. 3–4 (1899)
1898–1899
Became: *Tidskrift för Teologi och Krykliga Frågor*
Continued by: *Augustana Theological Quarterly*
Sometimes referred to as: *Tidskrift för Svensk Evangelisk Luthersk Kyrko-
historia i No. Amerika* or *Tidskrift*

In 1898–1899, this extensive volume was published as the first volume
of what became *Tidskrift för Teologi och Kyrkliga Frågor* the following year.
It was an ambitious venture with the purpose of providing historical material especially prior to the founding of the Augustana Synod. Respected
Augustana writers including E. Norelius, C. L. E. Esbjörn, T. N. Hasselquist, and E. Carlsson contributed sections. As an early historical account, it has special value for the history of the early years of the Swedish
Lutheran Church in America.
The following year (1900), the title was shortened to *Tidskrift för Teologi
och Krykliga Frågor* or *Augustana Theological Quarterly*. Editors, publisher,
and general content continued as originally planned. *Sources:* Ander 1956,
182; Erickson 7; LIBRIS; Olson 1933, 52; WorldCat.

Augustana College Swenson Center: BX8049 .6 .N83 1899
Bethany College: 1899
Evangelical Lutheran Church in America Archives: AUG 14/15
    1898–1899, Paper and Microfilm
Gustavus Adolphus College Archives: Vol. 1; 1899
Luther Seminary: Vol. 1; 1898
Minnesota Historical Society: BX8049.1 .T5 1899; BX8049.6 .N83 1899
University of Minnesota–Minneapolis: Vol. 1, nos. 1, 4; 1898–1899
LIBRIS: Royal Library of Sweden
    Swedish Emigrant Institute: 1898–1899

Tidskrift för Svensk Evangelisk Luthersk Kyrkohistoria i N. Amerika

See *Tidskrift för Svensk Ev. Luth. Kyrkohistoria i No. Amerika och för Teologiska och Kyrkliga Frågor.*

Tidskrift för Teologi och Kyrkliga Frågor

See *Augustana Theological Quarterly*.

Til 8 Stories

Rock Island, IL: Augustana Book Concern
Vol. 27, no. 40–vol. 32, no. 52
October 1954–December 1959
Continues: *The Little Folks*
Continued by: *Thru 8 Stories*
Sometimes referred to as: *'Til 8 Stories*

This weekly leaflet designed for the youngest Sunday church school children was a replacement for *The Little Folks*. It took the new name *'Til 8 Stories* with the first issue in October 1954. The Board of Parish Education of the Augustana Lutheran Synod was the issuing agency.

An advertisement for *'Til 8 Stories* read: "Introducing an up-to-date four-page story paper for Kindergarten and Primary children. Large size, gay appealing two-color printing, using the best in stories, poems and puzzles and containing fun projects all designed to meet today's need for this important age group" (*Augustana Annual* 1957, 205). A single subscription was eighty cents or sixty-five cents for five or more.

Another advertisement read: "edited so as to have not only an interesting design or 'eye appeal' but to contain materials that the children will enjoy reading and, more important, that will aid in Christian development" (*Augustana Annual* 1956, 182).

Designed to aid teachers in the parish education program, it was correlated with the Christian Growth series widely used in local congregations. Beginning in January 1960, the name was changed to *Thru 8 Stories*. *Sources: Augustana Annual* 1956, 182; 1957, 205; Lundeen, group 7.

Augustana College Swenson Center: 1956–1959
Evangelical Lutheran Church in America Archives: AUG 25/5/7 Vols. 27–31, [32]; 1954–1958, [1959]
Gustavus Adolphus College Archives: Vol. 27, no. 40–vol. 32, no. 52; October 1954–December 1959

Till Verksamhet: Tidskrift för Luther Academy samt för Prästsällskapet i Saunders Co.

[*To the Work: Newspaper for Luther Academy and also for the Ministerial Association in Saunders County*]

Wahoo, NE: Luther Academy
Rock Island, IL: Augustana Book Concern
August 1, 1885–December 1886
Continued by: *Wahoo-Bladet*
Sometimes spelled: *Till Werksamhet*

A Swedish-language paper published on behalf of Luther Academy at Wahoo, Nebraska, *Till Verksamhet* was issued on an irregular monthly basis from 1885 through 1886. Copy was prepared by S. M. Hill and Martin Noyd, both teachers at Luther Academy. The goal of the small paper was to provide information that would promote the Swedish Lutheran mission activity in Nebraska and awaken interest in collecting financial support for Luther Academy. It was distributed free. Its subtitle indicates that it was for the clergy in the immediate area of Saunders County also. Contents may be compared to *Skolvännen*, the promotional paper issued by Augustana College under the editorship of Olof Olsson.

Dowie states that it "not only supported the program of the school but also provided Swedish Lutherans in Nebraska with their own church paper" (217). He also states that "it is a valuable source for the period when the Nebraska Conference was founded and Luther [Academy] was fighting to establish itself as an educational institution of the Conference" (Dowie 248). *Sources:* Dowie 217, 248; Erickson 136; LIBRIS; *Minnesskrift* 463.

Midland Lutheran College: August, September, October 1885; January,
    February, April, June, September, December 1886
NB: Not at Nebraska State Historical Society
Erickson: Royal Library of Sweden: Vol. 1, no. 1; August 1885
LIBRIS: Royal Library of Sweden: April–December 1886

The Triangle

See *Luther College & Academy Yearbook*.

– U –

Ungdomens Tidning

[*Youth's Paper*]
Chicago, IL: Printer at 35 S. Clark St.
Nos. 1–3
October 15, 1892; December 1, 1892; December 15, 1892

Publication of an illustrated paper for Swedish-American Lutheran youth was the dream of three prominent Augustana Synod men. C. A. Swensson, L. G. Abrahamson, and C. O. Lindell planned to issue on about the first and fifteenth of each month such a paper for the annual subscription price of one dollar.

This new paper had the name *Ungdomens Tidning*. In each issue Swensson wrote under his column title "For Ourselves" "about everything imaginable in his intimate, chatty manner" (Swan 58). Abrahamson wrote an article about Columbus, in anticipation of the 1893 Exposition in Chicago, and also some travel letters. Lindell wrote about "Nature in Winter Attire." G. W. Swan wrote a regular column "Leisure Hours in the Library . . . by a Book-Lover."

After only three issue numbers the project ended. Swensson, who was the originator of the venture, realized that the demands on his time to fulfill his responsibilities as professor and pastor left no time for the children's paper. Regretfully, he suggested that it be turned over to *Fosterlandet*, which was a weekly political paper published in Chicago then. However, that plan never materialized and the *Ungdomens Tidning* venture ended three issues after it began. *Source:* Swan 42, 57–58.

Augustana College Swenson Center

Ungdoms-Vännen: Illustrerad Tidskrift för Ungdom

[*The Friend of Youth: An Illustrated Magazine for Young People*]
St. Paul, MN: [s.n.] (November 1895–December 1897); Minneapolis, MN: Olson & Sjöstrand (January 1898–November 1899)
Rock Island, IL: Lutheran Augustana Book Concern (December 1899–November/December 1918)
Vol. 1, no. 1–vol. 23, no. 11/12
November 1895–November/December 1918
Absorbed: *Valkyrian*
Sometimes referred to as: *Ungdomsvännen* or *Ungdoms-Vännen* (1895) or *Ungdoms-vännen* (St. Paul, MN)

In 1895, a group of four young Augustana Synod pastors in Minnesota started a new magazine *Ungdoms-Vännen*, using the name of an earlier publication that ended in 1887. Good friends from their student days at Augustana Theological Seminary, they were J. L. Haff, C. A. Hultkrans, J. T. Kjellgren, and J. F. Seedoff.

In its initial announcement, the group stated that its purpose for starting their new magazine was:

through Christian, instructive, and cultural reading to forward true godliness among your Swedish youth. We have ventured to publish a Swedish magazine for young people, because we believe that there is room for such a publication, without encroaching upon the territory of others. It must be deplored that within our large denomination we do not have a periodical designed especially for young people. *Ungdoms-Vännen* does not want to encroach upon any other magazine, but desires within its own field to labor for the good of the church. The contents of the periodical will consist of: "The Story of a Journey in Bible Lands," by Rev. J. L. Haff. Biographies of Famous Men in both Church and State, stories, literature, choice selections from the works of distinguished writers, meditations and articles on various questions of general interest, reviews of good and valuable books, etc. (Swan 1936, 63)

The first issue was dated November 1895, had sixteen pages and the same format (22 cm. × 30 cm.) and makeup as its predecessor of the same title. Issued as a monthly, its annual subscription price was one dollar. It was published through December 1897 in St. Paul and through November 1899 in Minneapolis at the Olson and Sjöstrand establishment. G. W. Olson was the business manager. In December 1899 (volume 4, no. 12) its ownership was transferred to the Lutheran Augustana Book Concern and therefore moved to Rock Island, Illinois. S. G. Youngert was selected as the chief editor.

During these four years in Minnesota a variety of quality articles were printed. History of the Augustana Synod, sometimes written by Eric Norelius, serial stories, poetry, biographies of famous people, literary pieces, book reviews, travel narratives, and other articles of general interest were featured. Illustrations were numerous.

With the move to Rock Island there were changes. The subtitle then became "Illustrerad Tidskrift för Hemmet" [Illustrated Magazine for the Home]. It consisted of thirty-two pages. It now had the support of the Lutheran Augustana Book Concern and the Augustana Lutheran Synod. Quality content was assured with writers including Ludvig Holmes, L. A. Johnston, C. A. Evald, S. M. Hill, C. A. Swensson, A. Schön, and E. A. Zetterstrand. Later contributors included G. N. Swan, J. A. Krantz, A. Bergin, P. M. Lindberg, F. M. Eckman, J. Mauritzson, A. A. Stomberg, K. G. W. Dahl, and P. Thelander.

In January 1910, the literary magazine published in New York, *Valkyrian*, merged with *Ungdoms–Vännen*. After 1911, editorial policy seemed to change. In 1912 Youngert was the sole editor, in 1913–1914 the editors were Ernst W. Olson and O. V. Holmgrain, in 1915–1918 (March) Ernst W. Olson served alone and to the end of 1918 C. J. Bengston held the position.

Change became more obvious in 1913, when it was recommended that *Ungdoms-Vännen* "become a purely literary magazine and that a new journal be started for reports from religious youth groups that had previously been included in *Ungdomsvännen*" (Blanck 1997, 175). The concern was that it remain "a positively Christian literary magazine" with more articles of a Christian nature written by Augustana Synod authors (Blanck 1997, 175, from Augustana Book Concern Minutes, July 1, 1913).

Augustana Book Concern published the periodical on the fifteenth of each month with thirty-two pages (8" × 11"), for $1.50 per year. Swan writes that "the make-up was quite elegant, with splendid, well-chosen illustrations, and a full-page reproduction on the front page of each number" (Swan 66).

During its lifetime, *Ungdoms-Vännen* experienced high acclaim and moderate success. When the Lutheran Augustana Book Concern took it over in 1900, there were about 3,500 subscribers, meaning that it was then being published at a financial loss. In 1905, the circulation was about 7,000, reaching its highest at 9,753 in 1912. Readership dropped during the war from 6,591 in 1914 to 4,650 in 1917, and finally to 3,337 in October 1918. Thus the decision was made to end publication in 1918. The final issue was dated December 1918.

Mention has been made that support fell back due to perceived German sympathies. Also, the Americanization of immigrants made English the language in use so foreign-language periodicals were no longer popular among the younger generation. Some may have felt that it was not appropriate for its intended reading audience.

Readers of *Ungdoms-Vännen* enjoyed fiction and poetry by such notable Swedish authors as J. L. Runeberg and E. Tegner. Swedish-American authors including C. W. Andeer and L. Holmes were regular contributors. While the focus was on Swedish and Swedish-American topics there were many quality articles related to history, literature, art, religion, biographies, and cultural topics. *Ungdoms-Vännen* was one of only two literary magazines supported by the Augustana Synod, the other being *Prärieblomman*.

About this fine magazine, Swan (1936) further reminisces:

> Now and then, as I turn over the leaves of the old bound volumes of the magazine, I sometimes recall these words from an old song, "Here lies a world of riches" because they constitute a literary gold mine, containing much of the best and much of lasting value, of what has been written in Swedish-America, especially during the two decades when the Swedish language was held in high esteem. The value of the magazine can hardly be overestimated; it gives us an insight into our intellectual and cultural life, and the literary historian of the future will no doubt, figuratively speaking, explore its riches when we have been long since forgotten. (68)

Sources: Blanck 1997, 174–76; Capps 235; Erickson 112–13; Larsson & Tedenmyr T129; LIBRIS; Swan 62–68; ULS; WorldCat.

Augustana College Swenson Center: BX8001 .U5 Vols. 1–23; 1895–1918
Evangelical Lutheran Church in America Archives: Vols. [1–2], 3–23; [1895–1897], 1898–1918

Gustavus Adolphus College: Vols. 1–23; 1895–1918

Harvard University Divinity School: Vols. 1–2, [3], 4–23; 1895–1896, [1898], 1899–1918

Lutheran Theological Seminary at Philadelphia: 1902–1912

Minnesota Historical Society: AP49 .U57 Vols. [1–23]; [1895–1918]

University of Chicago: fAP209 .U55 Vols. 1–11, [12–14]; 1895–1906, [1907–1909]

University of Illinois–Urbana–Champaign: Vols. 7–16, 22–23; 1902–1911, 1917–1918

University of Iowa: Vols. 1–12, [13–14], 20–23; 1895–1907, [1908–1909], 1915–1918

University of Minnesota–Minneapolis: BX8049 .U545x Vol. 2, nos. 1–2, 11–12, 18; vol. 5, nos. 2–3, 5–6, 10–11, 13–17, 19–20, 23; vol. 6, nos. 1–12; vol. 7, nos. 1–12; vol 8, nos. 8, 11; [1897, 1900], 1901–1902, August, November 1903

Erickson: Lutheran School of Theology at Chicago: Vols. 1–23

WorldCat: American Theological Library Association: Microfilm

LIBRIS: Royal Library of Sweden

Swedish Emigrant Institute: Årg. [1–2], 4–10, [11–13, 16, 21–23]; 1896–1918

Ungdomsvännen: Illustrerad Tidskrift för Främjande af Sann Gudsfruktan och Allmänt Nyttiga Kunskapers Spridning

[*The Friend of Youth: Illustrated Magazine for the Promotion of True Godliness and the Spreading of Useful General Information*]

Chicago, IL: Enander & Bohman (1879–October 1881)

Moline, IL: Wistrand & Thulin; Thulin & Anderson (November 1881–March 1883)

Rock Island, IL: Augustana Tract Society (April 1883–July 1884)

Rock Island, IL: Augustana Book Concern (August 1884–June 1887)

Vol. 1, no. 1–vol. 9

January 1, 1879–June 1887

Absorbed by: *Hem-Vännen*

Sometimes referred to as: *Ungdoms-vännen* or *Ungdoms-vännen* (Chicago, IL)

A society that took the name Ungdomens Vänner (The Friends of Youth) was organized in 1877 by a group of students and several members of the faculty at Augustana College and Theological Seminary. This group included T. N. Hasselquist, O. Olsson, C. J. Petri, C. A. Swensson, M. Wahlström, and C. M. Esbjörn. They adopted as their purpose "to promote and encourage the publication and dissemination of Christian literature for children and youth and especially to publish a Swedish paper for children" (Arden 1963, 205).

In January 1879, the society took on the responsibility of publishing a bimonthly for young people named *Ungdomsvännen*. The editors were J. A. Enander and O. Olsson. In an announcement on the cover of the first issue, signed "O. O.," the following aim was set forth:

> A new magazine in these hard times, what folly! Indeed, if the times were not hard, it would not have occurred to us at all to launch something new in the field of publications. It is just because of the hard times that we have felt ourselves obliged and compelled to undertake the publishing of a new paper. Many surmise that it is the love of money, the desire for profit, that has prompted us. Oh, no! The times certainly are hard, but that is due to more than a scarcity of money. If the lack of money were the greatest suffering among our people in general, then the harm would have its limits. But the most severe and dangerous hardship consists in the seduction of the minds of the youth through reading the harmful books and magazines found in every nook and corner. . . . This country is well supplied with this kind of literature, which seeks by all the enticements of a filthy art to stimulate to the very uttermost man's evil desire, unbelief, scorn, selfishness, and impudence, because there is profit in that type of publication. Our paper proposes, in the light of righteousness, to devote itself to the history of the world and of the church, God's wonders in nature, famous men who have labored in church and state, and such subjects as are necessary for true and general education. Attention will be paid especially to subjects which are of importance in giving our youth a genuine culture. (Swan 1936, 41)

This first issue was dated January 1, 1879. The magazine was printed in Chicago by the Enander & Bohman firm from 1879 through October 1881. From November 1881 it was printed in Moline, Illinois, by Wistrand and Thulin, and from December 15, 1882, until March 1883 by Thulin and Anderson.

The Ungdomens Vänner society reorganized in 1883 to become the Augustana Tract Society, soliciting memberships and donating net income to the support of Augustana College and Seminary. They continued responsibility for issuing *Ungdomsvännen* until July 1884. With the August 1884 issue it was published by the Augustana Book Concern (the private stock company). In May 1887, the Augustana Book Concern Board resolved to publish their monthly *Ungdomsvännen* with the new name *Hemvännen*. The final issue of *Ungdomsvännen* was printed in June 1887. As Swan suggests, a fault may have been "that it was altogether too religious for some people and not religious enough for others" (Swan 42).

Individuals associated with the publication as editors at various times included J. A. Enander and O. Olsson (1879), C. A. Swensson (1879–March 1887), J. Lindahl, E. Norelius, C. M. Esbjörn, E. A. Fogelström, J. A. Udden, and C. A. Bäckman.

For an annual subscription price of $1.00 ($1.50 in 1879), readers received a substantial publication (20 cm. × 27 cm.) from twelve to thirty-two pages. It was published as a bimonthly during 1879–1885, then as a monthly during 1886–June 1887.

Well-written articles and essays on a wide variety of subjects from art, history, science, world affairs, and religion, as well as biographies, poetry, and religious meditations were included. Many significant literary serial stories were published over the years. The distinct emphasis was on Christian religion and character building. *Sources:* Arden 1963, 205; Erickson 111; LIBRIS; Stephenson 355; Swan 40–43.

> Augustana College Swenson Center: BX8001 .U49 Vols. 1–9; 1879–1887
> Evangelical Lutheran Church in America Archives: AUG 25/5/8 Vols. 1–4, [5], 6–7, [8–9]; 1879–1882, [1883], 1884–1885, [1886–1887], Paper; Vols. 1–8, [9]; 1879–1886, [1887], Microfilm
> Gustavus Adolphus College Archives: 1879–1881; 1882 (Nos. 1–22); 1883–1886; 1887 (Nos. 1–6)
> Harvard University Divinity School: Vol. 1, nos. 1–17, 21–24; vol. 2, nos. 1–6, 8–24; vols. 3–6; vol. 7, nos. 1, 5, 17–24; vol. 8; [1879–1880], 1881–1884, [1885], 1886
> Lutheran School of Theology at Chicago: AP49 .U450 Vols. 1–9; 1879–1887
> University of Chicago: AP49 .U57 Vols. 2–3; 1880–1881
> University of Minnesota–Minneapolis: BX8049 .U54x Vol. 2, nos. 1–2, 11–12; vol. 5, nos. 2–3, 5–6, 10/11, 13–17, 19–20, 23; [1880, 1883]
> Erickson: Royal Library of Sweden: Vols. 1–9
> LIBRIS: Swedish Emigrant Institute: Årg. 1–2, [3–5]; 1879–1883

Uniting Word

> [s.l.]: Augustana Luther League
> 1950?–?
> Sometimes referred to as: *The Uniting Word*

Bergstrand writes that "thousands of our Leaguers were members of the Pocket Testament League with its promise to carry a Testament and read a portion daily. We supplied many Bible study helps; and each year a supplementary guide, *The Uniting Word*, to each of our 40,000 Leaguers" (Bergstrand 7). This was a daily devotional and Bible reading study guide for young people.

One Leaguer wrote of it: "The 'Uniting Word,' the daily Bible reading guide, helps us in our private, family, and League devotions. It gives us a feeling of unity with Christ and with one another when we know that our fellow Leaguers everywhere are reading the same passages and praying the same thoughts. Many Leagues send these little booklets to their boys in the service" (*Augustana Annual* 1952, 83). *Sources: Augustana Annual* 1952, 83; Bergstrand 7.

No holdings reported.

The *Upsala Alumni Gazette*

East Orange, NJ: Upsala College Alumni Association
Vol, 1, no. 1–
Fall 1969–1977?
Continues: *Upsala Alumni Magazine*
Continued by: *Upsala Reports*

The publication of the Upsala College Alumni Association with the title *The Upsala Alumni Gazette* began with the Fall 1969 issue. The numbering of volumes appears to be inconsistent as volume numbers restart in December 1973 and are absent in 1977. This was issued on a quarterly schedule, every 3 months. *Source:* WorldCat.

Augustana College Swenson Center: LH1.U67 U67 A4 [Vol. 1:1 (Fall 1969)–1977]

Upsala Alumni Magazine

East Orange, NJ: Upsala College Alumni Association
Fall 1953–Spring 1969?
Continues: *Upsala Alumni News*
Continued by: *The Upsala Alumni Gazette*

The publication of the Upsala College Alumni Association was issued on a quarterly schedule, every 3 months, from the Fall of 1953 to the middle of 1969. *Source:* WorldCat.

Augustana College Swenson Center: LH1.U67 U67 A48 [1953–1969]

Upsala Alumni News

East Orange, NJ: Upsala College Alumni Association
May 1945?–Spring 1953
Continued by: *Upsala Alumni Magazine*
Other title: *Upsala College Alumni News*

The publication of the Upsala College Alumni Association was issued three times per year. The final issue with this title was dated Spring of 1953. *Source:* WorldCat.

Augustana College Swenson Center: LH1.U67 U67 [1945–1953]

Upsala College Catalog

Kenilworth, NJ; East Orange, NJ; Upsala College
1893–1994/1995
Other titles:
  Catalog of Upsala College
  Catalog of Upsala Institute of Learning

The New York Conference started a college in the basement schoolroom of Bethlehem Lutheran Church in downtown Brooklyn in October of 1893. It soon was given the name Upsala College. The school's first catalog was issued in 1893. Initially the faculty of five had sixteen students. By the end of the academic year there were 75 students.

Typically each catalog contained announcements for the following academic year. The final catalog was dated 1994/1995. The school closed in May 1995. *Sources:* Bergendoff 93; http://catnyp.nypl.org/; LIBRIS; WorldCat.

Augustana College Swenson Center: 1893–1962, 1967–1968, 1974–1994/
  1995
New York Public Library Research Library: 1899/1900–1935/1936 incomplete file
Princeton University: 6693.3179.92 1904/1905–1908/09, 1918/1919–
  1919/1920
WorldCat: East Orange, New Jersey Library
LIBRIS: Royal Library of Sweden: 1907–1908

Upsala Gazette

Kenilworth, NJ: Upsala College
Vol. 1, no. 1–vol. 20
September 1905–Commencement 1924
Continued by: *Upsala Gazette*

This newspaper, prepared by students at Upsala College during its location in Kenilworth, New Jersey, was issued on a monthly schedule during the academic year from 1905 to 1924. In the summer of 1924 the college moved to East Orange, New Jersey. *Source:* WorldCat.

Augustana College Swenson Center: LH1.U67 U67; 1905–1911, [1912],
  1913–1924

Upsala Gazette

East Orange, NJ: Upsala College
Vol. 21, no. 1–vol. 84?

October 3, 1924–April 1990
Continues: *Upsala Gazette*
Continued by: *The Gazette*

Having moved from Kenilworth, New Jersey, to East Orange, New Jersey, during the summer of 1924, Upsala College students continued their newspaper with the same title, *Upsala Gazette*. It was issued on a biweekly schedule during the academic year. No newspapers were published during the 1990–1991 academic year. *Source:* WorldCat.

Augustana College Swenson Center: LH1.U67 U67 1924–1990

Upsala Reports

East Orange, NJ: Upsala College
Vol, 1, no. 1–vol. 16, no. 2
May 1974–Fall/Winter 1992
Continues: *The Upsala Alumni Gazette* (as of 1977)

Originally published as issues of the *Upsala Bulletin*, it continued in 1977 as the periodical published by the Upsala College Alumni Association. It appeared on a quarterly schedule, every 3 months, through the Fall/Winter 1992 issue. *Source:* WorldCat.

Augustana College Swenson Center: LH1.U67 R46 Vol. 1–16; 1974–1992

The Upsalite

East Orange, NJ: Upsala College
1929–1992

Published by the Student Publications Board of Upsala College, this was the student annual. *Sources:* LIBRIS; WorldCat.

Augustana College Swenson Center: LA331.U67 1929–1992
WorldCat: East Orange, New Jersey Library
    Free Public Library of Newark, New Jersey
    New Jersey Historical Society Library
LIBRIS: Royal Library of Sweden: 1954

Utah Missionären: Organ för Sv. Ev. Luth. Zion-församlingen i Salt Lake City

[*Utah Missionary: Organ for Swedish Evangelical Lutheran Congregations in Salt Lake City*]

Salt Lake City, UT: Utah Missionären
Vol. 1, no. 1–vol. 3, no. 6
January 1889–June 1891

The *Utah Missionären* was a monthly publication of the Utah Missions
Distrikten (District) of the Augustana Synod. J. A. Krantz served as the editor and contributor. The viewpoint of the paper was anti–Mormonism. It
was published from January 1889 to June 1891. *Sources:* Ander 1956, 183;
http://tomos.oit.umn.edu/F; Larsson & Tedenmyr T131.

University of Minnesota–Minneapolis: BV2803 .U8 U83x Vol. 1, no. 7;
    July 1889
NB: No holdings located in Utah

– V –

Väktaren: Månadstidning för Kyrkans Ungdom och Hemmet
[*Watchmen: Monthly paper for Christian youth and home*]
Winnipeg, Manitoba, Canada: [S. Udden]
Vol. 1, no. 9–vol. 3?
September 1893–October 31, 1895
Continues: *Sions Väktare*
Continued by: *Canada*
Merged with: *Den Skandinaviske Canadiensaren* to form *Canada* (Win-
    nipeg, Manitoba)

The first Swedish Lutheran minister to reside and work in Canada, Svante
Udden, soon recognized the need for a paper that would speak for the
Lutheran church and also help unite the Swedish immigrants who were
scattered in a number of distant locations in Canada. His monthly *Sions Väktare* soon became *Väktaren*, a monthly for Christian youth and homes.

Udden found time to write extensively even though his missionary
work required ministering to many isolated small communities. With
amazing zeal and courage, he established the Augustana Church in
Canada during his six-year ministry there.

In 1894, Udden became a partner in the paper, *Väktaren*, with K. Fleming, a typesetter. In August of 1895, Fleming purchased the publication
and changed its name to *Canada Väktaren*. In November of 1895 it became
simply *Canada* after merging with *Den Skandinaviske Canadiensaren*.

Baglo (1962) writes:

When Udden was editing the paper it was a typical church paper offering
news of the congregations, but also featuring secular news from Sweden and

Canada. Inspirational articles were mingled with government land advertisements, news of the Swedish royal family and Canadian Prime Minister Laurier and birth and death notices. It filled a definite need. (35)

Sources: Baglo 1962, 35; http://tomos.oit.umn.edu/F; Larsson & Tedenmyr T138; Setterdahl 35.

Augustana College Swenson Center: Microfilm
University of Minnesota–Minneapolis: BX8049 .V44x Vol. 2, no 4; April 1894
Setterdahl: Legislative Library, Winnipeg, Man., Canada: Microfilm

Väktaren: Evangelisk Luthersk Missions och Traktattidning

[*Watchmen: Evangelical Lutheran Missions and Tract Paper*]
Chicago, IL: [s.n.]
January 1904–December 1905

A group of Augustana Lutheran pastors in Chicago began this publication in 1904. Editors and founders included M. Noyd, A. Hult, H. O. Lindeblad, J. W. Swanbeck, A. P. Fors, and G. K. Stark.

A monthly in quarto size, *Väktaren* included eight pages. Its purpose was to report on missions. Lundeen states that it was associated with the Lutheran Inner Mission Society. In December 1905 it ceased publication. *Sources:* Ander 1956, 183; Andreen 1905, 176; Lundeen, group 6.

Augustana College Swenson Center
Lundeen: Evangelical Lutheran Church in America Archives: 1904–1905

Valkyria: Gustavus Adolphus Annual

St. Peter, MN: Published by the junior class at Gustavus Adolphus College
1909
Continues: *Runes* (1906)
Continued by: *Breidablick* (1912)

This is the next Gustavus Adolphus College annual to follow the 1906 *Runes* publication. It was published by the junior class rather than the senior class. The cartoonist Eben Lawson made his debut then and continued to produce cartoons through the 1930 annual *Gustavian*. *Source:* Peterson 74.

Gustavus Adolphus College: LD 2091.G62 G65 1909
Minnesota Historical Society: LD2091 .G6 G8798 1909

Valkyrian: Illustrerad Månadsskrift

[*The Valkyrie: Illustrated Monthly Writing*]
New York, NY: Charles K. Johansen
Vol. 1–vol. 13, no. 12
January 1897–December 1909
Merged with: *Ungdomsvännen* (1895)

In January 1897, Charles K. Johansen of New York (and originally from Kalmar, Sweden) began a publishing venture with the first issue of *Valkyrian*. He had assisted his father Håkan Johansen with publication of *Nordstjernan*, at that time the oldest, largest and most widely circulated Swedish paper in the East. Even though it was dated January 1897, this first issue appeared as a Christmas gift to the public in December 1896.

Johansen's plan for *Valkyrian* is shown in the early announcement:

Simultaneously with *Valkyrian's* entrance upon the arena of world events, a lance in one hand and a shield in the other, its publisher desire[s] to explain its origin and purpose. During many years my thoughts have busied themselves incessantly with the idea that a beautifully illustrated Swedish-American magazine, solid and popular in its content, low in price, must have a field and be generally appreciated by the public. The Swedish-American public supports at the present time half a hundred weeklies. It seems to me that it ought also be possible for it to support one magazine. It is of course true that many magazines have been published heretofore and, after a longer or shorter period, have discontinued, but the reasons for this were in part that they have not had the backing of sufficient capital and in part that the price per copy or per year has been too high.

This is not the situation of *Valkyrian*. It is mailed to all parts of the U.S.A. at ten cents a copy or $1.00 a year. The reason the magazine has been named *Valkyrian* is this: The editors as well as the publishers revel in everything Scandinavian, whether they find it on this or on the other side of the Atlantic. As time passes the readers of *Valkyrian* will find it to be an original as well as a valuable library, where all the memorable exploits and great deeds which have been performed on American soil by men and women from the North, or their descendants, will be described in detail, not only in words but also in pictures. Swedish-Americans, who have distinguished themselves in church, literature, science, or art; those who have secured fame on the battlefield or in the realms of invention or industry; those who have in our active fraternal and society life proved themselves deserving of mention—in a word, all the men and women who have labored for the development and progress of our adopted country, will be represented in *Valkyrian* in a fair and worthy manner. Many Swedish authors have promised contributions on Swedish subjects, and our best writers will month by month provide *Valkyrian* with original articles.

The literary department will contain an abundance of well-chosen novels, short stories, sketches, and poems. The editing of *Valkyrian* has been entrusted to Mr. Edward Sundell, who, during many years of service to the press, has become known for his faithful and conscientious work. In the hope that this Swedish-American Valkyrie will occupy an honored and respected place in the arena of publications, I now turn to the Swedish-American public confident of their favor and support. (Swan 1936, 81–82)

Valkyrian was an ambitious venture, being issued as an eighty-four page monthly in a large octavo format, at a price of ten cents each copy or one dollar annually. Each volume had continuous paging beyond 650 pages per volume. "The contents were timely, chosen with care, and generally illustrated, including biographies, with portraits of famous men and women, historical sketches, stories, travelogues, poetry, and light fiction" (Swan 1936, 81). It was well illustrated, with very few advertisements. Serialized novels, plays, and occasional pieces of music were also printed.

Editors were Edward Sundell until the end of 1906, followed by Charles Johansen until 1909 when Vilhelm Berger served as editor.

In spite of its quality contents and ambitious program, *Valkyrian* faltered financially. At the end of 1909 it merged with *Ungdomsvännen*, the literary magazine being published by the Augustana Book Concern. Readers interested in literature in Swedish-America were saddened to see the end of an independent *Valkyrian*. Swan comments: "in its bound volumes one finds much of the best that has been printed in Swedish in America" (Swan 1936, 83).

Many of the best Swedish authors as well as many of the Swedish-American authors contributed items to *Valkyrian*. Several prominent Augustana authors—Ludvig Holmes, C. W. Andeer, A. A. Sward, J. A. Enander, and others—contributed to *Valkyrian*.

As the editorial philosophy evolved, Blanck states: "although the journal sought to establish a cultural distance from the Augustana Synod, this proved difficult. The synod affected *Valkyrian's* attempt at creating its separate Swedish-American culture and, . . . instead [it] became willing promotor [*sic*] of Augustana's view of Swedish-American culture" (Blanck 1997, 183). With its purchase by the Augustana Book Concern in January 1910, *Valkyrian* was brought into the Augustana fold and then merged with *Ungdomsvännen*.

A comprehensive study of *Valkyrian* was prepared by Gunnar Thander as a PhD thesis in 1996 at the University of Minnesota. Included in his "*Valkyrian* 1897–1909: A Study in Swedish-American ethnicity" is an index and also an author index to *Valkyrian*. Sources: Blanck 1997, 183; Erickson 115; http://tomos.oit.umn.edu; LIBRIS; Swan 81–86; WorldCat.

Augustana College Swenson Center
Harvard University: PS can 403.2 Vol. 12; 1908

New York Public Library Research Library: Vols. [2–13]
University of Minnesota–Minneapolis: PN9 .V35x Vols. 1–13; 1897–1909
University of Washington: 058 VA Vols. [1–5]; [1897–July 1901]
Yale University: A87 V23 Vols. [3], 4–5, [6–8], 9; [1899], 1900–1901, [1902–1904], 1905
Erickson: Gustavus Adolphus College: October 1897, 1898–1907, [1908]
LIBRIS: Royal Library of Sweden: Årg. 1–13
    Swedish Emigrant Institute: Årg. 1–5, [6–8], 9–11, [12], 13; 1897–1909

*Vår Nya Kyrkotidning: Traktat och Nyhetsblad för
Providence-distriktet af Svenska Lutherska New York-Konferensen*

[*Our New Church Paper: Tract and Newspaper for the Providence District of
the Swedish Lutheran New York Conference*]
Pontiac, RI: [s.n.] (November 1903–October 1904)
Auburn, RI: [s.n.] (November 1904–December 1907)
Rock Island, IL: Augustana Book Concern (1908–1915)
November 1903–1915

This publication was issued for the congregations in the Providence
District of the New York Conference of the Augustana Lutheran Synod. It
included district and local church news. *Sources:* Ander 1956, 184; Söderström 52.

No holdings reported

Vårt Hem: Evangelisk Luthersk Illustrerad Tidning

[*Our Home: Evangelical Lutheran Illustrated Paper*]
Rock Island, IL: Augustana Book Concern
Oakland, CA: [s.n.]
Vols. 1–5
1909–1913

Sources: Ander 1956, 184; LIBRIS; ULS.

Augustana College Swenson Center: 1912
ULS: Minnesota Historical Society: Vols. 1–[4–5]
LIBRIS: Swedish Emigrant Institute: Vol. 4, nos. 4, 5; 1912

Vårt Land

[*Our Country*]
Jamestown, NY: Vårt Land Publishing Co.

Vol. 3, no. 2–vol.27?
December 4, 1890–September 10, 1920
Continues: *Österns Väktare*
Absorbed by: *Wårt Nya Hem*

With the December 4, 1890, issue of *Österns Väktare* the paper changed
its name to *Vårt Land*. It continued as a weekly, becoming an exclusively
political newspaper ("Svensk politisk veckotidning"). It was noted that
"Vartland [*sic*] is a Swedish political weekly newspaper devoted to American citizenship and the upbuilding of republican institutions" (WisCat).
Primarily in Swedish text, there were some columns in English. S. A.
Carlson, mayor of Jamestown, New York, was the editor. Backlund writes
that "for many years *Vårt Land* was recognized as one of the foremost
Swedish newspapers in the United States" (71). It was absorbed by *Wårt
Nya Hem* in 1920. *Sources:* Ander 1956, 184; Backlund 71; LIBRIS; Setter-
dahl 28; http://www.wiscat.net/; WorldCat.

Augustana College Swenson Center: December 4, 1890–September 10,
   1920, Microfilm
University of Minnesota–Minneapolis: F129 .J36 V33x Vol. 3, no. 27; vol.
   21, no. 6; May 28, 1891; February 2, 1893
Wisconsin Historical Society: 1890–September 10, 1920, Microfilm
LIBRIS: Royal Library of Sweden: 1890–1898; [1900–1920]

Vårt Land och Folk

[*Our Land and People*]
Chicago, IL: Engberg–Holmberg Publishing Co.
Vol. 9, no. 5–vol. 11?
October 27, 1886–November 9, 1888
Continues: *Nåd och Sanning*
Absorbed by: *Hemvännen* in 1888
Sometimes referred to as: *Wårt Land och Folk*

Issued weekly in Swedish text, this paper was the successor to *Nåd och
Sanning*. Both were issued in Chicago by the same publisher,
Engberg–Holmberg. At the end of 1888, it was absorbed by *Hemvännen*.
Sources: LIBRIS; Olson 1933, 26; Swan 1936, 44; WorldCat.

Augustana College Swenson Center
Chicago Historical Society: PN4885 .S8 N2 October 27–December 29,
   1886; January 5, 1887–October 10, October 24–31, November 9, 1888,
   Microfilm
LIBRIS: Royal Library of Sweden: 1886–1888

Vestkusten

[*West Coast*]
San Francisco, CA: Swedish Pub. Co. of San Francisco; West Coast Publishing Co. (1945–)
Vol. 2, no. 1–vol. 107, no. 6
January 1887–April 1, 1993
Continues: *Ebenezer*
Sometimes referred to as: *Vestkusten* (San Francisco, CA) or *The West Coast*

Beginning as an Augustana Lutheran parish paper with the title *Ebenezer* in 1886, the long-lived *Vestkusten* enjoyed a substantial record of publication. Rather than continuing as a religious paper, it adopted a secular program and became a political newspaper ("Liberal politisk veckotidning för svenskarne i Amerika"). At first a monthly, it became a weekly in May 1887. In June 1968, it became a semimonthly, adding English text articles to what had previously been a Swedish paper. Beginning in 1945, issues also have the English title *The West Coast*.

In 1894, *Vestkusten* was purchased by Ernst Skarstedt and Alexander Olsson, who had been a typesetter since 1890. Olsson became the sole owner in 1896, working in every capacity from editor to typesetter. The paper was published continuously in San Francisco except for April through August of 1906 when, because of the earthquake and fire, it was printed in Oakland. The *Vestkusten* establishment was gutted, but before militia arrived, Olsson gathered the subscription list and his typewriter. Securing type and equipment was difficult and costly, but Olsson received help from other newspaper publishers, both local and distant. After the establishment was rebuilt, the paper prospered.

Over the years *Vestkusten* was an influential paper with a good circulation. Because of its long existence, it is an important historical source for Swedes in California and the Lutheran church on the West Coast. After 1968, it was published for varying periods of time in Oakland, San Jose, and Mill Valley, California. *Sources:* Ander 1956, 185; Backlund 57–58; LIBRIS; Linder 1931, 339; Setterdahl 6; WorldCat.

Augustana College Swenson Center: Microfilm
Center for Research Libraries: December 13, 1917–April 1, 1993
University of Minnesota–Minneapolis: F869 .S3 V47x Vols. [6, 9–10, 21, 30, 40, 42, 71, 75, 79]; [1891, 1894–1895, 1906, 1915, 1925, 1927, 1956, 1960, 1964]
LIBRIS: Royal Library of Sweden: 1887–1967, Microfilm

Vid Juletid: Vinterblommor samlade för de små

[*At Yuletide: Winter Blossoms Gathered for the Little Ones*]
Rock Island, IL: Lutheran Augustana Book Concern
Vols. 1–13
1898–1910 (Blanck uses 1896 as beginning date)

As a Christmas magazine for children, *Vid Juletid* was an ambitious annual publishing effort by those involved. Professors of Swedish at Augustana College were editors. E. A. Zetterstrand served with the assistance of A. O. Bersell until 1904 when Jules Mauritzson took the editorial position. In total, at least 72,000 copies were printed in Swedish text.
Blanck (1997) writes that

> it was a Christmas magazine similar to those published in Sweden at the turn of the century. In fact, *Vid Juletid* drew heavily on texts from the Swedish magazines, and many of its contributions were . . . by such well-known contemporary literary fairy tale authors in Sweden as Elisabeth Beskow, Hugo Gyllander, Hedvig Indebetou, Amanda Kerfstedt, and Harald Ostenson. Most of these fairy tales had already been published in Sweden and, although there was a basic tone of Christian morality to many of the stories, they are much less explicitly religious than the contributions in the other magazines. . . . *Vid Juletid* thus shows a high cultural profile . . . and was the Christmas magazine that was most like its Swedish counterparts. (159)

The language used required a good basic knowledge of Swedish. Blanck concludes:

> Among all the periodical publications for youth, *Vid Juletid* was clearly the most ambitious and included contributions that went beyond the basic Christian morality in many other works. Several contemporary national Swedish authors were represented in the journal, who thus also became a part of the Swedish-American cultural tradition. (160)

Sources: Blanck 1997, 158–60; Larsson & Tedenmyr 1157; LIBRIS; WorldCat.

Augustana College Swenson Center: AY75 .V94 Vols. 1–13
Brown University: Vols. 6, 12; 1903, 1909
Gustavus Adolphus College: PN6071.C6M3 1910
Minnesota Historical Society: PZ57 .V43 Nos. 12–13
Pacific Lutheran University: SIE PZ57 .V5 1903, 1907, 1910
University of Minnesota–Minneapolis: AY19 .S8 V53x Nos. 1, 4, 10 (1907)
LIBRIS: Royal Library of Sweden: Vols. 1–13
   Swedish Emigrant Institute: Vols. 4, 6–13

Views

Haney, B.C., Canada: [s.n.]
1955–1962

The demise of *Canada News* in 1920 left a void in providing Canada Conference news to congregations there. In 1933, the Conference joined the American Lutheran Conference in support of the *Lutheran Voice*, as an inter-Lutheran news magazine. Canada Conference news was published therein.

In 1954, the Canada Conference began serious consideration of providing a publication for the Augustana churches in Canada. In 1955, *Views* appeared, edited by Ralph Wallin. Beginning as a modest quarterly magazine, it became a monthly distributed at Canada Conference expense to all Canada Conference congregations and members. In the magazine's later years, Duane Emberg served as editor. It continued until 1962, the year of the merger of Augustana and other Lutheran church bodies. *Source:* Baglo 1962, 37.

Evangelical Lutheran Church in Canada Archives: 1955–1962

Viking

See *Luther College & Academy Yearbook.*

Vox Collegi

St. Peter, MN: Gustavus Adolphus College
Vol. 1, no. 1
September 1891
Continues: *Annual Messenger*
Continued by: *Heimdall*
Frequently spelled: *Vox Collegii*

Following publication of the *Annual Messenger* earlier in 1891, the same student editors issued a printed paper in September. Only one issue appeared. In November 1891, it was followed by *Heimdall*. *Sources:* Lund 1987, 30; Peterson 58.

Gustavus Adolphus College: Paper and Microfilm

– W –

Wahoo-Bladet

Wahoo, NE: Swedish Ministerial Association of Saunders County, Nebraska

1888–December 1890
Absorbed: *Till Verksamhet*
Absorbed by: *Nykterhetsbasunen*
Sometimes spelled: *Wahoobladet* or *Wahoo Bladet*

Till Verksamhet was absorbed by the *Wahoo-Bladet* in 1888. This was a short-lived temperance publication supported by the Augustana clergy of the Saunders County, Nebraska area. *Sources:* Ander 1956, 185; Erickson 136; LIBRIS.

Augustana College Swenson Center: December 1889; August 1890; October 1890
Midland Lutheran College: December 1889; June 15, 1890; July 1890; August 1890; October 1890
LIBRIS: Royal Library of Sweden: December 1888–October 1890

Wårt Land och Folk

See *Vårt Land och Folk.*

West Central Lutheran

Rock Island, IL: Augustana Book Concern
July 1958–November 1962
Continues: *Kansas Conference Lutheran*

At this time (June–July 1958), the Kansas Conference of the Augustana Lutheran Synod changed its name to the West Central Conference. Consequently, the name of the official organ was changed to the *West Central Lutheran*. It continued until the merger to form the Lutheran Church in America. *Sources:* LIBRIS; Lundeen, group 6.

Lundeen: Evangelical Lutheran Church in America Archives
LIBRIS: Royal Library of Sweden: July 1958–November 1962

The West Coast

See *Vestkusten.*

Western Lutheran

Olympia, WA: Western Lutheran Publishing Committee
Vol. 1, no. 1–vol. 24, no. 5

September 15, 1937–November 14, 1960
Formed by the union of: *Columbia Lutheran* and *Pacific Lutheran Herald*

The *Western Lutheran* began publication with its September 15, 1937, issue. Its two predecessors were the *Columbia Lutheran* and the *Pacific
Lutheran Herald*, which had been the official organ of the Pacific District of
the Norwegian Lutheran Church of America. At times it was noted as "a
news medium for the West Coast churches of the American Lutheran
Conference" in California, Oregon, and Washington.

Issued as a semimonthly paper, the *Western Lutheran* appears to have
moved about from publishing place to publishing place on the West
Coast:

Sacramento, CA: September 29, 1944–July 11, 1952
Portland, OR: September 8, 1952–July 15, 1957
Gresham, OR: August 19, 1957–November 18, 1957
Stockton, CA: December 23, 1957–November 14, 1960, at which time it
    ceased publication.

Sources: ULS; WorldCat.

Center for Research Libraries: Vols. 1–9, [10], 11–13, [14], 15, [16], 17–21,
    [22], 23–24:5; 1937–1945, [1946], 1947–1949, [1950], 1951, [1952–1953],
    1954–1957, [1958–1959], 1960
Fuller Theological Seminary: Vols. [10, 14–15], 16, [17], 18–20, [21],
    22–23, [24]; [1947, 1950–1952], 1953, [1953–1954], 1955–1957,
    [1957–1958], 1959–1960, [1960]
Luther Seminary: BX8001 .W4 Vols. [1–2, 22, 24]
Trinity Lutheran Seminary: 1939–1960
University of Washington: Vol. [1, no. 4–vol. 22, no. 21]; [October 20,
    1937–July 27, 1959], Microfilm A7085
ULS: University of Illinois

What's New in Books

Rock Island, IL: Augustana Book Concern
1946–1962

Lundeen reports that this was the "publication announcement and review
medium" for the Augustana Book Concern. *Source:* Lundeen, group 9.

Augustana College: 1955–1962
Lundeen: Evangelical Lutheran Church in America Archives:
    1946–1958, [1959–1960]

World Missions Newsletter

See *Newsletter/Board of World Missions.*

– Y –

Young Lutheran's Companion

Rock Island, IL: Augustana Book Concern
Vol. 15, no. 1–vol. 18, no. 53
January 5, 1907–December 31, 1910
Continues: *Augustana Journal*
Continued by: *Lutheran Companion* (1911)
Sometimes referred to as: *The Young Lutheran's Companion* or *Companion*

In January 1907, the name of the *Augustana Journal* was changed to the *Young Lutheran's Companion*. It continued as an eight-page weekly issued by the Augustana Book Concern. Some wanted it to be purely a young people's paper rather than an English organ for the Evangelical Lutheran Augustana Synod of North America. However, because of the growing concern about the language question with English being consistently more in demand, it seemed critical that an English-language publication be available to the entire synod readership. O. V. Holmgrain served as the editor in 1907 and 1908. C. J. Södergren took over that position in 1909.

Again, the name was changed in 1911, when it became the *Lutheran Companion*. Over the few years of its existence it evolved from being a young people's paper to becoming the English official organ of the Augustana Lutheran Synod. *Sources:* Nystrom 62–63; WorldCat.

Augustana College: BX8001 .L25 Vols. 15–18; 1907–1910
Bethany College: Vols. 15–18; 1907–1910
Duke University: fL973c Vols. 15–18; 1907–1910
Evangelical Lutheran Church in America Archives: AUG 14/6 Vols. 15–18; 1907–1910, Microfilm
Gustavus Adolphus College: Vols. 15–17; 1907–1909
Luther Seminary: BX8001.L93 Vols. 15–18; 1907–1910, Microfilm
Lutheran School of Theology at Chicago: BX8001 .L4510 Vols. 15–18; 1907–1910, Microfilm
Lutheran Theological Seminary at Gettysburg: Vols. [15–18]; [1907–1910]
Lutheran Theological Seminary at Philadelphia: Vols. [15–18]; [1907–1910]
Pacific Lutheran Theological Seminary: 1907–1910, Microfilm

Pacific Lutheran University: BX8001 .L45 Vols. 16–18; 1908–1910
Wartburg Theological Seminary: Vols. 15–18; 1907–1910

The Young Observer

Rock Island, IL: Augustana University Association
June 1892–March/April 1894
Merged with: *The Alumnus* to form *The Augustana Journal*
Sometimes referred to as: *Observer* or *Young Observer*

This literary monthly was founded by several Augustana students, led by C. A. Rosander in 1892. It appeared every month, at the beginning as an eight-page paper with an 11" × 15" format. Subscription price for the first year was seventy-five cents. Beginning with the fifth number, the editor was Ernst Wilhelm Olson.

When number 13 in January 1893 was issued, the format was reduced to one-half and the price reduced to twenty-five cents a year. By early 1894, there was a delay in production with the double number in March/April being the last one. Assuming that circulation was almost exclusively with present and former students and that income was limited, the editors felt that future prospects for the publication were cloudy. Consequently, they ceased issuing any more numbers.

The Young Observer had served nobly as a publication for young people interested in literature, but also for older readers. Especially significant were the translations of Swedish poetry done by Olson.

During its short life, *The Young Observer* coexisted with a competitor, the monthly *The Alumnus*, which was published by the Alumni Association of Augustana College. Finally, after heated exchanges in print, the two merged to form *The Augustana Journal* in July 1894. *Source:* Swan 68–70.

Augustana College

The Young People

Rock Island, IL: Augustana Book Concern
Vol. 1, no. 1–vol. 32, no. 39
January 7, 1923–September 26, 1954
Continued by: *Teen Talk*
Sometimes referred to as: *Young People*

Planned as a weekly paper of special interest to Sunday church school readers in the upper-age classes, *The Young People* began publication in January 1923. Some readers of *The Olive Leaf*, the paper for intermediate grades, may have been interested in *The Young People* also. In its later years, Emeroy Johnson served as editor.

Later in 1954, its name was changed to *Teen Talk*, that title being considered more appealing to the potential reader. *Sources: Augustana Annual* 1954, 72; WorldCat.

Augustana College Swenson Center

Evangelical Lutheran Church in America Archives: AUG 25/5/6 Vols. 1, 3–32; 1923, 1925–1954

Gustavus Adolphus College Archives: Vol. 10, nos. 1–20, 26, 28, 35, 39–40; vol. 11, nos. 1–2, 4–7, 10, 13–17, 19–27, 32–35, 37–38; vols. 19–29; vol. 32, nos. 1–26; [1932–1933], 1941–1951, [1954]

Chapter 2

Augustana Evangelical Lutheran Church Convention Minutes/Reports

INTRODUCTION

Regularly published annually, the official proceedings of each annual convention of the Augustana Evangelical Lutheran Church (and its preceding names) include minutes from these important meetings.

Minutes are entirely in the Swedish language from 1860 through 1923 and the English language thereafter from 1924 through 1962. However, occasional reports are in the alternate language. Beginning in 1923 an English summary was separately issued. As shown in the 1924 minutes and continuing until 1930, a resolution was passed each year authorizing the publication of a free pamphlet in both English and Swedish that would include the Synod president's annual message as well as resolutions and decisions of special interest. This practice ended with the 1930 editions.

According to the ELCA Archives, the volumes of minutes also include a

> church directory, listing of officers, boards, committees, commissions, pastors, and necrology; rules of procedure for Synod, reports of officers, executive council, boards, commissions, and committees; reports of American, social and foreign missions; reports from educational institutions and youth work; reports of auxiliaries; reports of ecumenical organizations; and elections, ordinands and Augustana statistics

Some of these publications also include minutes of the Augustana Churchmen, Augustana Brotherhood, Augustana Lutheran Church Women, and Women's Missionary Society.

All are available for research at the ELCA Archives in both print and microform. The original manuscript minutes from 1860 through 1945

(1916–1922 are lacking) are also owned by the ELCA Archives. Those for 1860–1915 are handwritten in the Swedish language. The minutes for 1923–1945 are typed in the English language. Dowie cautions that "while this record of the yearly meetings of the synod preserves reports and decisions of the church body, it does not cover the debates which proceeded [*sic*] the adoption of reports and the formulation of church policy" (252).

An index to the annual convention minutes, 1860–1962, was compiled by D. Verner Swanson and Ruth L. Swanson Farley in 1962. It provides a listing of significant actions and events. An earlier comprehensive index for the years 1860–1909 is included in the 1910 minutes. *Sources*: Dowie 252; http://lrc.elca.org/WebOPAC; Thoreson.

INDEX: MINUTES OF THE
AUGUSTANA LUTHERAN CHURCH, 1860–1962

Compiled by D. Verner Swanson and Ruth L. Swanson Farley
Rock Island, IL: Augustana Book Concern
1962

This index provides a register of significant actions and events of the Augustana Evangelical Lutheran Church as recorded in the official published minutes. *Sources*: http://lrc.elca.org/WebOPAC/; WorldCat.

Augustana College Swenson Center: BX8049 .A2
Evangelical Lutheran Church in America Archives: BX8049 .A32 Index 1860–1962
Fuller Theological Seminary: BX8049 .A33
Lutheran Theological Seminary at Gettysburg: BX8049 .A33 H 1962
Lutheran Theological Seminary at Philadelphia: BX8049 .A35
Pacific Lutheran Theological Seminary: BX8049 .M668
Pacific Lutheran University: BX8049 .A32
University of Minnesota–Minneapolis: BX8049 .E952x 1962

PROTOKOLL HÅLLET VID SKANDINAVISKA
EV. LUTHERSKA AUGUSTANA SYNODENS

Rock Island, IL: Augustana Book Concern
1917
Sometimes referred to as: *Augustana-Synodens Protokoll, 1860–1878*

The minutes of the Augustana Synod annual meetings from 1860 through 1878 were reprinted in this single volume of 1,104 pages. The Swedish language is used throughout. *Source*: WorldCat.

Augustana College Swenson Center
Bethany College: 284.10973 E93p E
Evangelical Lutheran Church in America Archives
Harvard University Divinity School
Lutheran School of Theology at Chicago: BX8051 .A2
Lutheran Theological Seminary at Philadelphia: BX8049 .A3
Yale University: MiL60 Au4 A10b

PROTOKOLL HÅLLET WID SKANDINAVISKA EV. LUTHERSKA AUGUSTANA SYNODENS . . . ÅRSMÖTE

Chicago, IL: Svenska Luth. Tryckföreningen
1860–1883
Continued by: *Officielt Referat öfwer förhandlingarna wid Skandinaviska Ev. Luth. Augustana-Synodens . . . årsmöte*
Sometimes referred to as: *Scandinavian Evangelical Lutheran Augustana Synod of North America Protokoll*

Proceedings of the annual meetings of the Scandinavian Evangelical Lutheran Augustana Synod of North America from the first meeting in 1860 (June 5–11) through the twenty-fourth meeting in 1883 (June 14–22) were published with this title. The Swedish language is used throughout. A reprint of the 1860–1878 synod reports was issued in 1917 by the Augustana Book Concern. *Source*: WorldCat.

American Theological Library Association: Microfilm S0093A
Augustana College Swenson Center: BX8049 .A2 1860–1883
Bethany College: 1880–1883
Evangelical Lutheran Church in America Archives: 1860–1883
Evangelical Lutheran Church in America Archives Region 5 (Iowa): 1860–1879, 1882–1883
Harvard University Divinity School: 906 Luth.6 A923 A 1860–1883
Lutheran School of Theology at Chicago: BX8051 .A2 1860–1883
Lutheran Theological Seminary at Gettysburg: BX8049 .A33 1860–1861, 1863–1864, 1866–1867, 1869, 1871–1883
Lutheran Theological Seminary at Philadelphia: BX8049 .A35 1860–1878
Midland Lutheran College: 1870–1883
Pacific Lutheran University: BX8049 .A33 1860–1883

Trinity Lutheran Seminary: MF-353 1860–1883
University of Minnesota–Minneapolis: 284.1 Au45m 1860–1883
Wisconsin Historical Society: BX8049 .S57 1860–1883
Yale University: MGL9 AE A 1860–1883; MiL60 Au4 A10 1875–1877,
1879, 1881–1883

OFFICIELT REFERAT ÖFWER
FÖRHANDLINGARNA WID SKANDINAVISKA
EV. LUTH. AUGUSTANA-SYNODENS . . . ÅRSMÖTE

Rock Island, IL: Augustana Book Concern
1884–1890
Continues: *Protokoll hållet wid Skandinaviska Ev. Lutherska Augustana-Synodens . . . årsmöte*
Continued by: *Referat öfwer förhandlingarna wid Skand. Evangelisk-Lutherska Augustana-Synodens . . . årsmöte*
Sometimes referred to as: *Scandinavian Evangelical Lutheran Augustana Synod of North America. Officielt Referat*

Proceedings of the annual meetings of the Scandinavian Evangelical Lutheran Augustana Synod of North America from the twenty-fifth meeting in 1884 (June 19–26) through the thirty-first meeting in 1890 (June 16–24) were published with this title. The Swedish language is used throughout. *Source*: WorldCat.

American Theological Library Association: Microfilm S0093B
Augustana College Swenson Center: BX8049 .A2 1884–1890
Evangelical Lutheran Church in America Archives: 1884–1890
Evangelical Lutheran Church in America Archives Region 5 (Iowa):
1884–1890
Harvard University Divinity School: 906 Luth.6 A923 A 1884–1890
Lutheran School of Theology at Chicago: BX8051 .A2 1884–1890
Lutheran Theological Seminary at Gettysburg: BX8049 .A33 1884–1890
Lutheran Theological Seminary at Philadelphia: BX8049 .A35
1888–1890
Midland Lutheran College: 1884–1890
Pacific Lutheran University: BX8049 .A33 1884–1890
Trinity Lutheran Seminary: MF-353 1884–1890
University of Minnesota–Minneapolis: 284.1 Au45m 1884–1890
Wisconsin Historical Society: 1884–1890
Yale University: MGL9 AE A 1884–1890; MiL60 Au4 A10 1887–1888,
1890

REFERAT ÖFWER FÖRHANDLINGARNA WID SKAND. EVANGELISK-LUTHERSKA AUGUSTANA SYNODENS ... ÅRSMÖTE

Rock Island, IL: Lutheran Augustana Book Concern
1891–1894
Continues: *Officielt referat öfwer förhandlingarna wid Skandinaviska Ev. Luth. Augustana-Synodens ... årsmöte*
Continued by: *Referat öfwer förhandlingarna wid Evangelisk-Lutherska Augustana Synodens ... årsmöte*
Sometimes referred to as: *Scandinavian Evangelical Lutheran Augustana Synod of North America Referat* or *Referat/Scandinavian Evangelical Lutheran Augustana Synod of North America*

Proceedings of the annual meetings of the Scandinavian Evangelical Lutheran Augustana Synod of North America from the thirty-second meeting in 1891 (June 16–23) through the thirty-fifth meeting in 1894 (June 5–11) were published with this title. The Swedish language is used throughout. *Source*: WorldCat.

American Theological Library Association: Microfilm S0093C
Augustana College Swenson Center: BX8049 .A2 1891–1894
Evangelical Lutheran Church in America Archives: 1891–1894
Evangelical Lutheran Church in America Archives Region 5 (Iowa): 1891–1894
Harvard University Divinity School: 906 Luth.6 A923 A 1891–1894
Lutheran School of Theology at Chicago: BX8051 .A2 1891–1894
Lutheran Theological Seminary at Gettysburg: BX8049 .A33 1891–1894
Lutheran Theological Seminary at Philadelphia: BX8049 .A35 1891–1894
Midland Lutheran College: 1891–1894
Pacific Lutheran University: BX8049 .A33 1891–1894
Trinity Lutheran Seminary: MF-353 1891–1894
University of Minnesota–Minneapolis: 284.1 Au45m 1891–1894
Wisconsin Historical Society: 1891–1894
Yale University: MGL9 AE A 1891–1894; MiL60 Au4 A10 1892

REFERAT ÖFWER FÖRHANDLINGARNA WID EVANGELISK-LUTHERSKA AUGUSTANA SYNODENS ... ÅRSMÖTE

Rock Island, IL: Lutheran Augustana Book Concern, Augustana Book Concern
1895–1923

Continues: *Referat öfwer förhandlingarna wid Skand. Evangelisk-Lutherska Augustana-Synodens . . . årsmöte*
Continued by: *Minutes of the . . . annual convention/Evangelical Lutheran Augustana Synod of North America*
Sometimes referred to as: *Evangelical Lutheran Augustana Synod of North America. Referat*, or *Referat/Evangelical Lutheran Augustana Synod of North America.*
Other titles:
  1901–1905: *Referat öfwer förhandlingarna wid Augustana Synodens . . . årsmöte*
  1906–1921: *Referat af förhandlingarna wid Augustana Synodens . . årsmöte*
  1922: *Referat av förhandlingarna wid Augustana Synodens . . . årsmöte*
  1923: *Referat over förhandlingarna wid Augustana Synodens . . . årsmöte*

Proceedings of the annual meetings of the Evangelical Lutheran Augustana Synod of North America from the thirty-sixth meeting in 1895 (June 6–15) through the sixty-fourth meeting in 1923 (June 8–14) were published with this title, with variations as noted herein. The Swedish language is used throughout. However, in 1923 the Synod authorized the publication of an English summary of the Swedish minutes. *Source:* WorldCat.

American Theological Library Association: Microfilm S0093D
Augustana College Swenson Center: BX8049 .A2 1895–1923
Bethany College: 1906, 1908
Evangelical Lutheran Church in America Archives: 1895–1923
Evangelical Lutheran Church in America Archives Region 5 (Iowa): 1895–1905, 1907–1908, 1910, 1913–1914, 1916–1920, 1922
Fuller Theological Seminary: BX8049 .A33 1920
Harvard University Divinity School: 906 Luth.6 A923 A 1895–1923
Lutheran School of Theology at Chicago: BX8051 .A2 1895–1923
Lutheran Theological Seminary at Gettysburg: BX8049 .A33 1895–1899, 1901–1923
Lutheran Theological Seminary at Philadelphia: BX8049 .A35 1895–1923
Midland Lutheran College: 1895–1897, 1918
New York Public Library: ZSX 1901, 1904, 1915, 1917–1920, 1922
Pacific Lutheran University: BX8049 .A33 1895–1923
Trinity Lutheran Seminary: MF-353 1895–1923; BX8049 .A2 1920–1923
University of Minnesota–Minneapolis: 284.1 Au45m 1895–1919
Wisconsin Historical Society: 1895

Yale University: MGL9 AE A 1895–1908, 1910–1911, 1913–1915, 1917–1923; MiL60 Au4 A10 1895, 1899, 1901–1908, 1910, 1912–1913, 1915–1923

MINUTES OF THE . . . ANNUAL CONVENTION/EVANGELICAL LUTHERAN AUGUSTANA SYNOD OF NORTH AMERICA

Rock Island, IL: Augustana Book Concern
1924–1936
Continues: *Referat öfwer förhandlingarna wid Evangelisk-Lutherska Augustana-Synodens . . . årsmöte*
Continued by: *Report of the . . . annual convention/Evangelical Lutheran Augustana Synod of North America*
Sometimes referred to as: *Evangelical Lutheran Augustana Synod of North America: Minutes of the . . . annual convention*

Proceedings of the annual conventions of the Evangelical Lutheran Augustana Synod of North America from the sixty-fifth meeting in 1925 through the seventy-seventh meeting in 1936 were published with this title. Some years included the number of the convention and the place where it was held in the title. In 1930 the synod resolved that from that year onward the annual minutes would be printed in the English language only. The publication also includes Minutes of the Augustana Brotherhood convention and Minutes of the Woman's Missionary Society convention for that year. *Source:* WorldCat.

American Theological Library Association: Microfilm S0093E
Augustana College Swenson Center: BX8049 .A2 1924–1936
Evangelical Lutheran Church in America Archives: 1924–1936
Evangelical Lutheran Church in America Archives Region 5 (Iowa): 1924–1936
Evangelical Lutheran Church in America Archives Region 9 (SC): 1934
Fuller Theological Seminary: BX8049 .A33 1925, 1931–1936
Harvard University Divinity School: 906 Luth.6 A923 A 1924–1936
Lutheran School of Theology at Chicago: BX8051 .A2 1924–1936
Lutheran Theological Seminary at Gettysburg: BX8049 .A33 1924–1936
Lutheran Theological Seminary at Philadelphia: BX8049 .A3 1924–1936
Midland Lutheran College: 1925, 1928–1936
New York Public Library: ZSX 1931–1936
Pacific Lutheran University: BX8049 .A33 1924–1936
Trinity Lutheran Seminary: MF-353 1924–1936; BX8049 .A2 1924–1936

University of Minnesota–Minneapolis: 284.1 Au45m 1924–1936
Yale University: MGL9 AE A 1925–1936; MiL60 Au4 A10 1924–1936

REPORT OF THE . . . ANNUAL CONVENTION/EVANGELICAL LUTHERAN AUGUSTANA SYNOD OF NORTH AMERICA

Rock Island, IL: Augustana Book Concern
1937–1947
Continues: *Minutes of the . . . Annual Convention/Evangelical Lutheran Augustana Synod of North America*
Continued by: *Report of the . . . Synod/Augustana Evangelical Lutheran Church*
Sometimes referred to as: *Evangelical Lutheran Augustana Synod of North America. Report of the . . . annual convention*
Other titles:
Augustana Synod Minutes [1938–]
Through Opening Doors, 1946
Church That Serves in Love, 1947

Proceedings of the annual conventions of the Evangelical Lutheran Augustana Synod of North America from the seventy-eighth meeting in 1937 through the eighty-eighth meeting in 1947 were published with this title. Most years included the number of the convention and the place where it was held in the title. The publication also includes Minutes of the Augustana Brotherhood convention and Minutes of the Woman's Missionary Society convention for that year. *Source*: WorldCat.

American Theological Library Association: Microfilm S0093F
Augustana College Swenson Center: BX8049 .A2 1937–1947
Evangelical Lutheran Church in America Archives: 1937–1947
Evangelical Lutheran Church in America Archives Region 5 (Iowa): 1937–1947
Evangelical Lutheran Church in America Archives Region 9 (SC): 1937–1947
Fuller Theological Seminary: BX8049 .A33 1938–1939, 1941–1947
Harvard University Divinity School: 906 Luth.6 A923 A 1937–1947
Lutheran School of Theology at Chicago: BX8051 .A2 1937–1947
Lutheran Theological Seminary at Gettysburg: BX8049 .A33 1937–1947
Lutheran Theological Seminary at Philadelphia: BX8049 .A3 1937–1947
Midland Lutheran College: 1937–1947

New York Public Library: ZSX 1937–1947
Pacific Lutheran University: BX8049 .A33 1937–1947
Seattle Public Library: R284.1 EV14Ra 1943–1947
Trinity Lutheran Seminary: MF-353 1937–1947
University of Minnesota–Minneapolis: 284.1 Au45m 1937–1947
Yale University: MGL9AE A 1937–1947; MiL60 Au4 A10 1937–1947

REPORT OF THE ... SYNOD/AUGUSTANA
EVANGELICAL LUTHERAN CHURCH

Rock Island, IL: Augustana Book Concern
1948–1962
Continues: *Report of the ... Annual Convention/Evangelical Lutheran Augustana Synod of North America.*
Continued by: *Minutes of the Constituting Convention/Lutheran Church in America*
Sometimes referred to as: *Augustana Evangelical Lutheran Church: Report of the ... Synod* or *Report of the annual convention: Augustana Evangelical Lutheran Church*
Other titles:
They Came with the Bread of Life, 1948
His Witnesses, 1949
Serving the Living God, 1950
Responsible Church, 1951
Living Word Humanity's Hope, 1952
Church—a Courageous Witness in a Discouraged World, 1953
Life, Light, and Labor, 1954
Accountable to God, 1955
Unity of the Spirit, 1956
You Have Been Called, 1958
Knit Together in Love, 1959
His Kingdom Is Forever, 1960
God's Grace and Man's Responsibility, 1961
Abiding Verities, 1962

Proceedings of the annual conventions of the Augustana Evangelical Lutheran Church (name change as of 1948) from the 89th convention in 1948 (June 7–13) through the 103rd convention in 1962 (June 25–27) were published with this title. Also included were the Minutes of the Augustana Brotherhood convention and the Minutes of the Woman's Missionary Society convention for that year. *Sources*: http://ecco.easterncluster.com; WorldCat.

American Theological Library Association: Microfilm S0093G

Augustana College Swenson Center: BX8049 .A33 1948–1962

Evangelical Lutheran Church in America Archives: 1948–1962

Evangelical Lutheran Church in America Archives Region 5 (Iowa): 1948–1962

Evangelical Lutheran Church in America Archives Region 9 (SC): 1948–1962

Fuller Theological Seminary: BX8049 .A33 1948–1962

Harvard University Divinity School: 906 Luth.6 A923 A 1948–1962

Lutheran School of Theology at Chicago: BX8051 .A2 1948–1962

Lutheran Theological Seminary at Gettysburg: BX8049 .A33 1948–1962

Lutheran Theological Seminary at Philadelphia: 1948–1962

Midland Lutheran College: 1948–1962

Pacific Lutheran University: BX8049 .A33 1948–1962

Seattle Public Library: R284.1 Ev14Ra 1949–1962

Trinity Lutheran Seminary: MF-353 1948–1962

University of Illinois at Urbana–Champaign: 284.1 AU452 1952–1962

University of Iowa: BX8049 .A33 1951–1962

University of Minnesota–Minneapolis: 284.1 Au45m 1948–1962

Yale University: MGL9 AE A 1948–1962; MiL60 Au4 A10 1948–1949, 1951–1962

Chapter 3

Augustana Evangelical Lutheran Church Conference Convention Minutes/Reports

INTRODUCTION

Reports, minutes, proceedings, and statistics from each of the regional Conferences of the Augustana Evangelical Lutheran Church were published regularly (usually annually) following the annual convention of the Conference. In the early years of the Augustana Evangelical Lutheran Church (under former names) these publications were in the Swedish language. Not all Conferences held the first convention in the year of organization.

Typically, these publications contain reports from Conference officers, departments, committees, Conference academic and social welfare institutions and auxiliary organizations such as missionary societies. Statistics regarding membership, finances, property, congregations, and other relevant numbers were also included.

Most publications were printed at the Augustana Book Concern (Lutheran Augustana Book Concern in early years) in Rock Island, Illinois. Some of the very early reports were printed at the Thulin & Anderson and the Wistrand & Thulin establishments in Moline, Illinois. Other early reports were printed at the Star Printing Company in Chicago, Illinois, or at the Skaffarens printing establishment in St. Paul, Minnesota.

Individuals wishing to research these items may be able to locate files at the appropriate regional Evangelical Lutheran Church in America Archives. Access and assistance are available by appointment. Most of the Conference reports are available at the Evangelical Lutheran Church in America Archives in Chicago. Contact the reference archivist there for specific information.

CALIFORNIA CONFERENCE

Minutes of the . . . annual convention . . .
1st–70th
1893–1962
Other titles (title varies slightly for some years):
Officielt Referat öfver förhandlingarna vid California-Konferensens
California-Konferensens af Augustana-Synoden Protokoll
Protokoll California-Konferensens af Augustana-Synoden
Referat öfver California-Konferensens af Augustana-Synoden
*Referat öfver förhandlingarna vid California-Konferensens av den Evange-
liskt Lutherska Augustana-Synoden*
*Referat öfver förhandlingarna vid California-Konferensens av den Ev.
Lutherska Augustana-Synoden*
*Referat av förhandlingarna vid California-Konferensens av den Ev. Luth.
Augustana-Synoden*
*Referat, California-Konferensens av den Ev. Luth. Augustana-
Synoden*
*Annual Convention of the California Conference Augustana Synod and the
California Conference Woman's Missionary Society*

Minutes and reports were in Swedish until 1922. Some annual reports include minutes of the conventions of the Conference Lutheran Brotherhood and the Conference Woman's Missionary Society.

The California Conference was formed in 1893 by dividing the Pacific Conference into two separate Conferences, the other being the Columbia Conference. A history of the California Conference for the years 1893–1953 was published in 1953 by the Church Press in Glendale, California, in observance of the sixtieth anniversary of the California Conference. *Sources:* Thoreson; WorldCat.

Augustana College Swenson Center: 1893–1962
Evangelical Lutheran Church in America Archives: 1893–1962
Fuller Theological Seminary: 1895, 1900–1902, 1904–1911, 1913–1920, 1922–1932, 1935–1936, 1939–1949, 1951–1962
Lutheran Theological Seminary at Gettysburg: BX8049.1 .C2 A3 H 1895–1898, 1900–1930, 1932
New York Public Library Research Library: 1901
Pacific Lutheran University: BX8049.1 .C3 A3 1946
Trinity Lutheran Seminary: 1922–1945
University of Minnesota–Minneapolis: BX8049.1 .C2 E93x 1895

CANADA CONFERENCE

Minutes of the . . . annual convention . . .
1st–50th
1913–1962
Other titles (title varies slightly for some years):
Referat över . . . årsmötets förhandlingar
Referat af förhandlingarna vid Canada-konferensens af Evangeliskt Luther-
ska Augustana-synoden
Förhandlingar vid Canada-konferensens

Minutes and reports were in Swedish until 1923. The Canada Conference was formed in 1913 from the Minnesota Conference. A history of the Canada Conference with the title *The Story of Augustana Lutherans in Canada* was prepared by Ferdinand Baglo and published in 1962. *Sources:* Thoreson; WorldCat.

Augustana College Swenson Center: 1913–1962
Evangelical Lutheran Church in America Archives: 1913–1962
Evangelical Lutheran Church in America Archives Region 5 (Iowa): 1931; 1962
Evangelical Lutheran Church in Canada Archives: 1913–1962
Lutheran Theological Seminary at Gettysburg: BX8049.1 .C3 A3 H 1922–1932
Minnesota Historical Society: 1913
Trinity Lutheran Seminary: 1931–1932
University of Minnesota, Minneapolis: BX8063.C2 E93x 1938

CENTRAL CONFERENCE

Report of the annual convention
106th–109th
1959–1962

In 1958 the Illinois Conference was renamed the Central Conference. *Sources:* Thoreson; WorldCat.

Augustana College Swenson Center: 1959–1962
Evangelical Lutheran Church in America Archives: 1959–1962
Evangelical Lutheran Church in America Archives Region 5 (Iowa): 1959–1962

Lutheran Theological Seminary at Gettysburg: BX8049.1 .C4 A3 H 1959,
1961–1962
Pacific Lutheran University: BX8049.1 .C4 A3 1961
Trinity Lutheran Seminary: 1959–1962

COLUMBIA CONFERENCE

Minutes of the . . . annual convention . . .
1st–70th
1893–1962
Other title: *Referat öfver förhandlingarna vid Columbia-konferensens*

The Columbia Conference was formed in 1893 by dividing the Pacific
Conference into two separate Conferences, the other being the California
Conference.
   It included Swedish Lutheran churches in the area of Washington, Ore-
gon, Idaho, Utah, and Montana.
   Some minutes include convention reports of the Women's Missionary
Society of the Columbia Conference.
   A fifty-year history of the Columbia Conference from 1893 to 1943 was
prepared by Carl J. Renhard and Carl H. Sandgren in 1943 featuring historical glimpses of Lutheran mission work in the Pacific Northwest. A
memory album with the title *Columbia konferensen i ord och bild* recognizing the first ten years of the Columbia Conference was published in 1903
in Swedish text. *Sources:* Thoreson; WorldCat.

Augustana College Swenson Center: 1893–1962
Evangelical Lutheran Church in America Archives: 1893–1896, 1902,
1904–1962
Lutheran Theological Seminary at Gettysburg: BX8049.1 .C7 A3 H 1894,
1896, 1904–1905, 1908–1937
Pacific Lutheran University: BX8049.1 .C6 A3 1894–1896, 1902,
1904–1962
Trinity Lutheran Seminary: 1895–1961
University of Washington: 979.5Au45m 1894–1896, 1902, 1906–1907; 1956

ILLINOIS CONFERENCE

Minutes of the . . . annual convention . . .
1st–105th

1854–1958

Other titles (title varies slightly for some years):

Protokoll hållet wid Illinois-konferensens möte . . .

Officielt referat öfwer förhandlingarna wid Illinois-konferensens . . . årsmöte . . .

Förhandlingar vid Illinois-konferensens . . . årsmöte

Referat av förhandlingarna vid Illinois-konferensens af den Ev. Luth. Augustana-synoden . . . årsmöte

Referat öfver förhandlingarna vid Illinois-konferensens af Ev. Luth. Augustana-Synoden

Illinois Conference minutes

Minutes and reports were in Swedish until 1923. There exists at the Evangelical Lutheran Church in America Archives an English translation of the 1861–1878 minutes.

The Illinois Conference is considered to be the later name for the Mississippi Conference of the Synod of Northern Illinois. Consequently, its organization date is often listed as 1853. In 1870 when some conferences were reorganized, the Illinois Conference was officially created. In 1959 it was renamed the Central Conference.

A centennial history of the Illinois Conference with the title *History of the Illinois Conference, Augustana Evangelical Lutheran Church* was prepared by G. Everett Arden and published in 1953 by the Illinois Conference. A seventy-fifth anniversary jubilee album with the title *The Illinois Conference, 1853–1928: Jubilee Album* was issued in 1928. A fifty-year anniversary album with the title *Illinois-konferensen, 1853–1903* was issued in 1904. *Sources:* http://lrc.elca.org/WebOPAC; Thoreson; WorldCat.

Augustana College Swenson Center: 1854–1958

Evangelical Lutheran Church in America Archives: 1854–1958

Evangelical Lutheran Church in America Archives Region 5 (Iowa): 1931–1958

Lutheran School of Theology at Chicago: BX8052.I4 A1 1881–1908

Lutheran Theological Seminary at Gettysburg: BX8049.1 .I3 A3 H 1879–1880, 1886,1893, 1895, 1899, 1901–1904, 1906–1917, 1919–1932, 1934

Lutheran Theological Seminary at Philadelphia: BX8049.1 .I3 A2 1925–1929, 1935–1949

Trinity Lutheran Seminary: 1930–1932, 1957

University of Illinois at Urbana–Champaign: 284.1 Ev152r 1904–1905

University of Minnesota: BX8049.1 .I4 E933x 1912, 1922, 1925

Wisconsin Historical Society: 1880, 1886, 1893, 1895

IOWA CONFERENCE

Minutes of the . . . annual convention . . .
1st–94th
1869–1962
Other titles (title varies slightly for some years):
  Referat öfwer förhandlingarna wid Iowa-konferensens af Evangelisktlutherska
    Augustana-synoden . . . årsmöte
  Protokoll hållet wid Iowa-konferensens, årsmöte . . .
  Officielt referat öfver förhandlingarna vid Iowa-konferensens . . .
    årsmöte . . .
  Officielt referat av förhandlingarna
  Official minutes of the annual convention

The Iowa Conference was organized in 1868, following the division of the Mississippi Conference of the Synod of Northern Illinois into eastern and western sections. The western area then became the Iowa Conference.

The Iowa Conference minutes for 1869–1880 were reissued in a single volume in 1907. A comprehensive history of the Iowa Conference was prepared by Emil Lund with the title *Iowa-Konferensens af Augustana-Synoden: Historia* in Swedish text and published in 1916. A history of the first seventy-five years of the Iowa Conference with the title *75th Anniversary of the Iowa Conference of the Evangelical Lutheran Augustana Synod* was prepared by Reuben C. Anderson and published in 1943. *Sources:* Larsson & Tedenmyr 543; Thoreson; WorldCat.

Augustana College Swenson Center: 1869–1962
Evangelical Lutheran Church in America Archives: 1869–1962
Evangelical Lutheran Church in America Archives Region 5 (Iowa):
    1869–1912, 1914–1962
Iowa State Historical Society: BX8049.1.I6 M55 1922
Lutheran Theological Seminary at Gettysburg: BX8049.1 .I8 A3 H
    1869–1880, 1887, 1889–1890, 1892–1934
Pacific Lutheran University: BX8049.1 .I8 A3 1961
Trinity Lutheran Seminary: 1887–1961
University of Illinois at Urbana-Champaign: 284.1 EV15I 1919–1920
University of Minnesota–Minneapolis: 1897–1898
Wisconsin Historical Society: 1882, 1887, 1889, 1892, 1894–1895

KANSAS CONFERENCE

Minutes of the . . . annual convention . . .
1st–88th
1870–1958

Other titles (title varies slightly for some years):
Protokoll hållna vid Kansas-konferensens möten åren . . .
Referat öfver förhandlingarna vid Kansas-Konferensens . . .
Protokoll öfver förhandlingarna vid Kansas-konferensens af Skand. Ev. Luth. Augustana-synoden . . . årsmöte . . .
Referat öfwer föhandlingarna wid Kansas-konferensens af Ev. luth. Augustana-synoden . . . årsmöte . . .
Minutes of the Kansas Conference . . .

Minutes and reports were in Swedish until 1924. The Kansas Conference was created in 1870 upon the reorganization of several Augustana Synod Conferences. It was renamed the West Central Conference in 1959. *Sources:* Thoreson; WorldCat.

Augustana College Swenson Center: 1870–1958
Bethany College: 284.10978 A923 kr E 1882; 1948; 1953
Evangelical Lutheran Church in America Archives: 1870–1958
Fuller Theological Seminary: BX8049.1 .K38 1892
Kansas State Historical Society: 1870–1882, 1885–1958
Lutheran Theological Seminary at Gettysburg: BX8049.1 K2 A3 H 1870–1879, 1881–1883, 1885–1886, 1893–1934
Trinity Lutheran Seminary: 1901–1932
University of Illinois at Urbana-Champaign: 284.1EV15K 1920
University of Minnesota–Minneapolis: 1903, 1905
University of Texas at Austin: BX8049.1K3 A948 1915
Wisconsin Historical Society: 1870–1879, 1881–1883, 1885, 1892

MINNESOTA CONFERENCE

Minutes of the . . . annual convention . . .
1st–104th
1858–1962
Other titles (title varies slightly for some years):
Minnesota konferensens protokoll
Protokoll hållet wid Minnesota-konferensens . . . årsmöte . . .
Protokoll wid Swenska Evangel. Lutherska Minnesota-konferensens årsmöte . . .
Protokoll vid Sv. Ev. Luth. Minnesota-konferensens årsmöte . . .
Referat öfwer förhandlingarna wid Minnesota-konferensens . . . årsmöte . . .
Referat öfver förhandlingarna vid Minnesota-konferensens af Skand. Ev. Luth. Augustana-synoden . . . årsmöte . . .

*Referat öfver förhandlingarna vid Minnesota-konferensens af Ev. Luth.
Augustana-synoden . . . årsmöte . . .*
*Officielt referat öfver förhandlingarna vid Minnesota-konferensens af Ev.
Luth. Augustana-synoden . . . årsmöte . . .*
*Referat öfver förhandlingarna vid Minnesota-konferensens af Ev. Luth.
Augustana-synoden . . . årsmöte . . .*
*Referat öfver förhandlingarna vid Minnesota-konferensens af Sv. Ev. Luth.
Augustana-synoden årsmöte . . .*
*Referat öfver förhandlingarna vid den Luth. Minnesota konferensens af
Augustana-synoden . . . årsmöte . . .*
*Referat af förhandlingarna vid Luth. Minnesota-konferensens af Augustana-
synoden . . . årsmöte . . .*
*Referat öfver förhandlingarna vid Lutherska Minnesota-konferensens af
Augustana-synoden . . . årsmöte . . .*
Referat över . . . årsmötets förhandlingar
Report from the . . . Annual Convention of the Evangelical Lutheran Min-
nesota Conference . . .
Minutes of the . . . Annual Convention of the Lutheran Minnesota Confer-
ence of the Augustana Synod . . .

Minutes and reports were in Swedish through 1928, also in English
from 1920 through 1928, and only in English beginning in 1929. At times
the reports include minutes of other meetings of the Conference in addition to the annual meeting.

"Minnesota-konferensens af Augustana-Synoden Protokoll från 1858 till
1868" or the reports of the meetings from July 1, 1858, through May 21, 1868,
are printed in *Tidskrift för Svensk. ev. luth. kyrkohistoria i N. Amerika och för teologiska och kyrkliga frågor* (no. 1, 1899). A transcription of the handwritten minutes of proceedings of the Minnesota Conference meetings held between October 8, 1868, and May 25, 1879, was prepared by Conrad Peterson and
issued in mimeographed format by Gustavus Adolphus College in 1951
with the title *Minnesota konferensens protokoll, 1869–1878* [i.e., 1868–1879].
Copies are at the Swenson Swedish Immigration Research Center at Augustana College, Gustavus Adolphus College, Lutheran Theological Seminary
at Gettysburg, Minnesota Historical Society, University of Minnesota at Minneapolis, and Wisconsin Historical Society.

An index to the minutes of the annual convention reports for 1858 to
1962 was issued in 1972 by the Minnesota Synod of the Lutheran Church
in America. A copy is at the Minnesota Historical Society.

The Minnesota Conference was organized in 1858 in the Evangelical
Lutheran Synod of Northern Illinois. In 1860 it became the Minnesota
Conference of the Scandinavian Evangelical Lutheran Augustana Synod
of North America.

Several histories of the Minnesota Conference include:

1. A two-volume history with the title *Minnesota-Konferensens av Augustana-Synoden och dess församlingars historia*, prepared by Emil F. S. Lund and published in 1926.
2. *A Church is Planted: The story of the Lutheran Minnesota Conference, 1851–1876*, prepared by Emeroy Johnson and published in 1948.
3. *God Gave the Growth: The story of the Lutheran Minnesota Conference, 1876–1958*, prepared by Emeroy Johnson and published in 1958.
4. *The Beginnings and Progress of Minnesota Conference of the Lutheran Augustana Synod of America*, issued in 1929 in commemoration of the seventieth anniversary.
5. *Minnesskrift 1858–1908 tillegnad Minnesota-Konferensens af Ev. luterska Augustana-synoden 50-års jubileum* issued in 1908 in commemoration of the fiftieth anniversary.

Sources: http://www.mnpals.net/F/; Thoreson; WorldCat.

Augustana College Swenson Center: 1858–1962
Evangelical Lutheran Church in America Archives: 1858–1962
Evangelical Lutheran Church in America Archives Region 5 (Iowa): 1930
Lutheran Theological Seminary at Gettysburg: BX8049.1.M6 A3 H 1863–1881, 1883, 1889, 1892–1901, 1903–1933
Minnesota Historical Society: 1880–1962
Trinity Lutheran Seminary: 1868–1931
Union Theological Seminary: MGL9 ARR A 1928
University of Minnesota at Minneapolis: BX8049.1 .M6 A94x 1880–1899; 284.1 Au453mi 1902–1906, 1908–1910, 1912–1913, 1915–1916, 1921–1923, 1925, 1927–1935, 1937–1944, 1946–1962
Wisconsin Historical Society: 1881, 1883
WorldCat: American Theological Library Association: 1883–1962, Microfilm

NEBRASKA CONFERENCE

Minutes of the . . . annual convention . . .
1st–76th
1887–1962
Other titles (title varies slightly for some years):
   Officielt referat öfver Nebraska-Konferensens af Ev. Lutherska Augustana-Synoden . . .
   Nebraska Conference Minutes

Minutes and reports were in Swedish until 1923. The Nebraska Conference was organized out of the Kansas Conference in 1886. It included congregations in South Dakota and Wyoming, as well as in Nebraska.

A history of the Nebraska Conference with the title *The Nebraska Conference of the Augustana Synod: Survey of Its Work with Sketches of Its Congregations, Institutions, Organizations, and Pioneers* was prepared by Charles F. Sandahl and published in 1931. A later history recognizing the seventieth anniversary with the title *Through the Years: Glimpses from the Seven Decades of History of the Nebraska Conference at 70th Anniversary* was prepared by J. Edor Larson and published in 1956. A twenty-fifth anniversary jubilee album with the title *Nebraska-konferensens tjugufem-års minne den 11 Augusti 1886–1911* was issued in 1911. *Sources:* http://lrc.elca .org/WebOPAC; Thoreson; WorldCat.

Augustana College Swenson Center: 1887–1962
Evangelical Lutheran Church in America Archives: 1887–1962
Lutheran Theological Seminary at Gettysburg: BX8049.1 .N2 A3 H 1888–1889, 1892–1894, 1896–1904, 1906–1931, 1933–1934, 1938–1939, 1941, 1949–1951
Lutheran Theological Seminary at Philadelphia: BX8049.1 .N2 A2 1923–1938, 1947–1959
Midland Lutheran College: 1887–1908, 1926, 1939, 1950–1962
Nebraska State Historical Society: 284.7Sw32 1905
Trinity Lutheran Seminary: 1896–1930, 1948, 1958, 1960

NEW ENGLAND CONFERENCE

Minutes of the . . . annual convention . . .
1st–50th
1913–1962
Title varies slightly for some years.

Minutes and reports were in Swedish until 1929. Some annual reports include minutes of the conventions of the Augustana Brotherhood and of the Woman's Missionary Society.

The New England Conference was formed from the New York Conference in 1912.

A fifty-year history of the New England Conference with the title *50 Years in New England: A History of the New England Conference, 1912–1962* was prepared by Luther E. Lindberg and published by the New England Conference in 1962. *Sources:* Thoreson; WorldCat.

Augustana College Swenson Center: 1913–1962
Evangelical Lutheran Church in America Archives: 1913–1962
Lutheran Theological Seminary at Gettysburg: BX8049.1 .N4 A3 H
 1922–1931, 1939, 1942–1949
University of Minnesota–Minneapolis: BX8049.1 .N6 A36x 1913

NEW YORK CONFERENCE

Minutes of the . . . annual convention . . .
1st–93rd
1870–1962
Other titles (title varies slightly for some years):
 Protokoll hållet wid New York-konferensens . . . årsmöte . . .
 *Referat öfver förhandlingarna vid New York-konferensen af Ev. Luth.
 Augustana-synoden . . . årsmöte . . .*
 Referat öfver förhandlingarna vid årsmötet
 *Referat öfver förhandlingarna vid New York conferensens af Evangelisk-
 Lutherska Augustana-Synoden*
 *Förhandlingar vid New York-konferensens av Augustana-Synod . . .
 årsmöte*
 New York konferensens referat

Minutes and reports were in Swedish until 1925 and issued in both
English and Swedish through 1930. The New York Conference was cre-
ated in 1870 when the Augustana Synod Conferences were reorganized.
In 1912 the New England Conference was formed from a portion of the
New York Conference.

A fifty-year jubilee album was issued in Swedish in 1921. In celebration
of thirty years, a booklet was issued in Swedish in 1900 at the festival in
New Britain, Connecticut. A short history of the New York Conference
with the title *The New York Conference of the Augustana Lutheran Church; Its
Place of Founding* was issued in 1952 by the Conference. *Sources:* Thoreson;
WorldCat.

Augustana College Swenson Center: 1870–1962
Evangelical Lutheran Church in America Archives: 1870–1962
Lutheran Theological Seminary at Gettysburg: BX8049.1 .N7 A3 H
 1870–1881, 1884–1885, 1887–1888, 1890–1932, 1934–1936, 1940–1942,
 1946, 1949–1958, 1961
Lutheran Theological Seminary at Philadelphia: BX8049.1 .N46 1899,
 1926–1931, 1946–1949, 1951–1955, 1957–1958, 1960, 1962

New York Public Library Research Library: 1901
Trinity Lutheran Seminary: [1888–1907], 1928, 1948–1951, 1962
University of Minnesota–Minneapolis: BX8049.1 .N7 E94x 1924–1927,
   1930, 1934–1935
Wisconsin Historical Society: 1885

PACIFIC CONFERENCE

Referat öfver förhandlingarna vid Pacific-Konferensens . . .
1st–6th
1888–1893

Minutes and reports were in Swedish. The Pacific Conference was organized in 1888 from the Pacific (West Coast) Mission of 1882. In1893 the
Pacific Conference was divided, thus forming the California Conference
and the Columbia Conference. *Sources:* Thoreson; WorldCat.

Augustana College Swenson Center: 1889–1893
Evangelical Lutheran Church in America Archives: 1889 (handwritten),
   1892 (handwritten), 1893
Wisconsin Historical Society: 1892

RED RIVER VALLEY CONFERENCE

Minutes of the . . . annual convention . . .
1st–50th
1913–1962
Title varies slightly for some years.

Minutes and reports were in Swedish until 1928. The Red River Valley
Conference was organized in 1912 out of the Minnesota Conference. A
history of the Red River Valley Conference with the title *History of the Red
River Valley Conference of the Augustana Lutheran Church* was prepared by
J. Edor Larson and published in 1953. *Sources:* Thoreson; WorldCat.

Augustana College Swenson Center: 1913–1962
Evangelical Lutheran Church in America Archives: 1913–1962
Lutheran Theological Seminary at Gettysburg: BX8049.1 .R4 A3 H
   1913–1914, 1916–1920, 1922–1933, 1948–1960
Lutheran Theological Seminary at Philadelphia: BX8049.1 .R4 A2
   1930–1939, 1951–1962

Minnesota Historical Society: BX8049.1 .R4 A22 1933, 1939, 1941, 1948, 1952, 1960

Trinity Lutheran Seminary: 1922–1931, 1933, 1940–1942, 1945, 1947, 1950–1953, 1955–1956, 1958–1960

SUPERIOR CONFERENCE

Minutes of the . . . annual convention . . .
1st–53rd
1910–1962
Other titles (title varies slightly for some years): *Superior Conference Minutes*

Minutes and reports were in Swedish until 1923. The Superior Conference was organized in 1910 out of the Illinois Conference. Michigan was the main portion, with some Wisconsin congregations. *Sources:* Thoreson; WorldCat.

Augustana College Swenson Center: 1910–1962
Evangelical Lutheran Church in America Archives: 1910–1962
Lutheran Theological Seminary at Gettysburg: BX8049.1 .S9 A4 H 1910–1914, 1916–1929
Lutheran Theological Seminary at Philadelphia: BX8049.1 .S8 A2 1921–1928, 1931–1962
Trinity Lutheran Seminary: 1922–1927
University of Illinois–Urbana-Champaign: 284.1 EV15S 1921

TEXAS CONFERENCE

Minutes of the . . . annual convention . . .
1st–40th
1923–1962
Other titles (title varies slightly for some years):
   Referat Texas-konferensens av Augustana-synoden . . . årsmöte . . .
   Texas conference of the Lutheran Augustana synod

Minutes and reports were in Swedish through 1929. The Texas Conference was organized in 1923 from that geographical portion of the Kansas Conference. A brief history of the Texas Conference with the title *One Family of God, a Brief History of the Texas Conference of the Augustana Lutheran Church* was prepared by M. L. Lundquist and published in 1962. *Sources:* Thoreson; WorldCat.

Augustana College Swenson Center: 1923–1962

Evangelical Lutheran Church in America Archives: 1923–1962

Evangelical Lutheran Church in America Archives Region 5 (Iowa): 1944

Lutheran Theological Seminary at Gettysburg: BX8049.1 .T4 A3 H 1923–1932

Pacific Lutheran University: BX8049.1 .T4 A3 1948–1951, 1962

Trinity Lutheran Seminary: 1923–1956

University of Texas at Austin: T284.1 EV14AT 1927–1932, 1935 BX8049.1 .T4 A38 1923

WEST CENTRAL CONFERENCE

Minutes of the . . . annual convention . . .
89th–92nd
1959–1962

In 1959 the Kansas Conference was renamed the West Central Conference to recognize the geographical areas of Colorado and Missouri in the conference. A history recognizing the ninetieth anniversary of the West Central Conference (formerly the Kansas Conference) with the title *90th Anniversary, West Central Conference, Augustana Lutheran Church, 1870–1960* was published in 1960. *Sources:* Thoreson; WorldCat.

Augustana College Swenson Center: 1959–1962

Bethany College: 284.10978 A923wm 1962

Evangelical Lutheran Church in America Archives: 1959–1962

Kansas State Historical Society: 1959–1962

Appendix A

Augustana Evangelical Lutheran Church Names

OFFICIAL NAMES FOR THE AUGUSTANA EVANGELICAL LUTHERAN CHURCH

1. Scandinavian Evangelical Lutheran Augustana Synod of North America, June 5, 1860–1894
2. Evangelical Lutheran Augustana Synod in North America, 1895–1947
3. Augustana Evangelical Lutheran Church, 1948–1962

Literature and bibliographic records about the Augustana Evangelical Lutheran Church and its publications use a number of variants of the official names. Following are those most frequently used in a variety of source materials:

1. Augustana Evangelical Lutheran Church of North America
2. Augustana Lutheran Church
3. Augustana Synodens
4. Evangelical Lutheran Augustana Synod of North America
5. Lutheran Augustana Synod
6. Scandinavian Evangelical Lutheran Augustana Synod in North America

Appendix B

Contact Information for Project Participants

ELCA SEMINARIES

Luther Seminary Library
Gullixson Hall
2375 Como Avenue
St. Paul, MN 55108
651/641-3447
Online catalog: http://ruth.luthersem.edu

Lutheran School of Theology at Chicago
Jesuit-Krauss-McCormick Library
1100 E. 55th Street
Chicago, IL 60615-5199
773/256-0739 or 773/256-0703
Online catalog: http://www.jkmlibrary.org/ie/resources/catalog/

Lutheran Theological Seminary at Gettysburg
Abdel Ross Wentz Library
66 Seminary Ridge
Gettysburg, PA 17325-1795
717/338-3014
Online catalog: http://ecco.easterncluster.com

Lutheran Theological Seminary at Philadelphia
Krauth Memorial Library
7301 Germantown Avenue

Philadelphia, PA 19119-1794
215/248-6329
Online catalog: http://www.ltsp.edu/krauth/ecco.html

Lutheran Theological Southern Seminary
Lineberger Memorial Library
4201 N. Main Street
Columbia, SC 29203-5898
803/786-5150
Online catalog: http://ecco.easterncluster.com

Pacific Lutheran Theological Seminary—affiliated with the Graduate
   Theological Union: Flora Lamson Hewlett Library
2400 Ridge Road
Berkeley, CA 94709
510/649-2500
Online catalog: http://grace.gtu.edu/search

Trinity Lutheran Seminary
Hamma Library
2199 E. Main Street
Columbus, OH 43209-2334
614/235-4136
Online catalog: http://www.tcgcohio.org/

Wartburg Theological Seminary
Reu Memorial Library
333 Wartburg Place
P.O. Box 5004
Dubuque, IA 52004-5004
563/589-0267
Online catalog: http://www.dbq.edu:8675/

COLLEGES AND UNIVERSITIES

Augustana College
Thomas Tredway Library
639 38th Street
Rock Island, IL 61201-2296
309/794-7206
Online catalog: http://library.ilcso.illinois.edu/aug

Bethany College
Wallerstedt Library
235 E. Swensson St.
Lindsborg, KS 67456-1897
785/227-3380 Ext. 8165
Online catalog: http://www.bethanylb.edu/search/

California Lutheran University
Pearson Library
60 W. Olsen Road
Thousand Oaks, CA 91360-2787
805/493-3255
Online catalog: http://puma.clunet.edu/

Gustavus Adolphus College
Folke Bernadotte Memorial Library
800 West College Ave.
St. Peter, MN 56082
507/933-7556
Online catalog: http://mnpals.gustavus.edu

Midland Lutheran College
Luther Library
900 N. Clarkson
Fremont, NE 68025
402/941-6259
Online catalog: http://www.niclc.org/

North Park University
Brandel Library
3225 W. Foster Avenue
Chicago, IL 60625-4895
773/244-5580
Online catalog: http://library.ilcso.illinois.edu/npu

Pacific Lutheran University
Robert A. L. Mortvedt Library
12180 Park Avenue S.
Tacoma, WA 98447-0013
253/535-7500
Online catalog: http://library.plu.edu/

Swenson Swedish Immigration Research Center
Augustana College
639 38th Street
Rock Island, IL 61201-2296
309/794-7204
E-mail: sag@augustana.edu
Website: http://www.augustana.edu/swenson

Texas Lutheran University
Blumberg Memorial Library
1000 W. Court St.
Seguin, TX 78155-5978
830/372-8100
Online catalog: http://bulldogs.tlu.edu/

ARCHIVES

Evangelical Lutheran Church in America Library
8765 West Higgins Road
Chicago, IL 60631-4109
800/638-3522
Online catalog: http://lrc.elca.org/WebOPAC/index.asp

Evangelical Lutheran Church in America Archives
321 Bonnie Lane
Elk Grove Village, IL 60007
847/690-9410
E-mail: archives@elca.org
Online catalog: http://lrc.elca.org:8080/webcat/

The churchwide archives also works in partnership with ELCA synodical and regional archives where records of more local interest for synods and congregations may be found. For information about these archives, refer to "Regional/Synodical Archives" link at: http://www.elca.org/archives/regsyn.html. Several of these regional archives own Augustana materials identified in this union list.

Archives of Evangelical Lutheran Church in Canada
Lutheran Theological Seminary
114 Seminary Crescent
Saskatoon, Saskatchewan S7N OX3
Canada

Tel: 306-966-7850
Online catalog: http://library.usask.ca/dbs/stu.html

LIBRARIES IN SWEDEN

Lund University Library
P.O. Box 134
SE-221 00 Lund
Sweden
Tel: +46 46 222 00 00
Online catalog: http://www.lub.lu.se/

The Royal Library
Box 5039
SE-102 41 Stockholm
Sweden
Tel: 08 463 40 00
E-mail: kungl.biblioteket@kb.se
Online catalog: http://www.kb.se/

Swedish Emigrant Institute
Vilhelm Mobergs gata 4
P.O. Box 201
SE-351 04 Växjö
Sweden
Tel: +46 470 201 20
E-mail: info@swemi.nu
Online catalog: http://www.swemi.nu/eng/

Uppsala University Library
P.O. Box 510
SE-751 20 Uppsala
Sweden
Tel: +46 018 471 39 00
Online catalog: http://aluco.its.uu.se/

Contact information for additional libraries included in the title holdings lists may be located in the current edition of the *American Library Directory* or by accessing the library or institution website.

Appendix C

Lending Libraries

Research for this annotated union list required study and review of a variety of bibliographies, histories, and other resources. That research was completely dependent upon the generosity of several libraries that were willing to loan specific printed materials. Those libraries are as follows:

Beaver Dam Community Library, Beaver Dam, Wisconsin
Carthage College, Kenosha, Wisconsin
Concordia University, Rincker Memorial Library, Mequon, Wisconsin
Hedberg Public Library, Janesville, Wisconsin
Irvin L. Young Memorial Library, Whitewater, Wisconsin
Lutheran Theological Seminary, A. R. Wentz Library, Gettysburg, Pennsylvania
Mankato State University, Mankato, Minnesota
Midland Lutheran College, Luther Library, Fremont, Nebraska
Milwaukee Public Library, Milwaukee, Wisconsin
Milwaukee School of Engineering Library, Milwaukee, Wisconsin
Reference and Loan Library, Wisconsin Department of Public Instruction, Madison, Wisconsin
Superior Public Library, Superior, Wisconsin
Swenson Swedish Immigration Research Center, Augustana College, Rock Island, Illinois
University of Minnesota–Minneapolis, Minneapolis, Minnesota
University of Wisconsin–Madison, Madison, Wisconsin
University of Wisconsin–Superior, Superior, Wisconsin
University of Wisconsin–Whitewater, Harold Andersen Library, Whitewater, Wisconsin

Watertown Public Library, Watertown, Wisconsin
Wisconsin Library Services, Madison, Wisconsin
Wisconsin State Historical Society, Madison, Wisconsin

The generosity and professional assistance of staff at each library are hereby gratefully acknowledged.

Works Consulted

CONTENTS

PRINT SOURCES

After Seventy–Five Years, 1860–1935: A Jubilee Publication: Seventy–Fifth Anniversary of the Augustana Synod and Augustana College and Theological Seminary. Rock Island, IL: Augustana Book Concern, 1935.

American Library Directory, 2003–2004. Medford, NJ: Information Today, 2003.

Ander, O. Fritiof. *The Cultural Heritage of the Swedish Immigrant: Selected References.* Augustana Library Publications 27. Rock Island, IL: Augustana College Library, 1956.

———. "Swedish–American Newspapers and the Republican Party, 1855–1875." *Augustana Historical Society Publications* 2, 1932: 64–78.

Ander, O. Fritiof, and Oscar L. Nordstrom, eds. *The American Origin of the Augustana Synod from Contemporary Lutheran Periodicals, 1851–1860: A Collection of Source Material.* Augustana Historical Society Publications 9. Rock Island, IL: Augustana Historical Society, 1942.

Andreen, Gustav. "The Augustana Synod: Its History and Development." In *The Swedish Element in America.* Vol. 2. Ed. Erik G. Westman. Chicago: Swedish–American Biographical Society, 1931, 71–99.

——. "Den Nuvarande Svensk–Amerikanska Pressen." *Prärieblomman* (1905): 165–84.

Arden, G. Everett. *Augustana Heritage: A History of the Augustana Lutheran Church.* Rock Island, IL: Augustana Book Concern, 1963.

——. *The School of the Prophets: The Background and History of Augustana Theological Seminary, 1860–1960.* Rock Island, IL: Augustana Theological Seminary, 1960.

Augustana Annual, 1952–1959. Rock Island, IL: Augustana Book Concern, 1952–1959.

Augustana Evangelical Lutheran Church Centennial Committee. *A Century of Life and Growth: Augustana 1848–1948.* Rock Island, IL: Augustana Book Concern, 1948.

Augustana Lutheran Church General Anniversary Committee. *Centennial Essays: Augustana Lutheran Church, 1860–1960.* Rock Island, IL: Augustana, 1960.

The Augustana Synod: A Brief Review of its History, 1860–1910. Rock Island, IL: Augustana Book Concern, 1910.

Backlund, J. Oscar. *A Century of the Swedish American Press.* Chicago: Swedish American Newspaper, 1952.

Baglo, Ferdy E. "Augustana Lutherans in Canada." *Augustana Heritage Newsletter* ns. 1.3 (May 2000): 4–11.

——. *Augustana Lutherans in Canada.* Augustana Lutheran Church, Canada Conference, 1962.

Bates, Barbara Snedeker. "Denominational Periodicals: the Invisible Literature." *Phaedrus* 7 (Spring/Summer 1980): 13–18.

Bengston, C. J. "Tidningpressen inom Augustana–Synoden." In *Minnesskrift: Med Anledning af Augustana–Synodens Femtioåriga Tillvaro; Historisk Öfversikt af hvad som Uträttats under Åren 1860–1910.* Rock Island, IL: Augustana Book Concern, 1910. 437–74.

Benson, Adolph B. "Magazines." In *Swedes in America, 1638–1938.* Ed. Adolph B. Benson and Naboth Hedin. New Haven: Yale University Press, 1938. 206–8.

Benson, Adolph B., and Naboth Hedin, eds. *Swedes in America, 1638–1938.* New Haven: Yale University Press, 1938.

Bergendoff, Conrad. *Augustana . . . a Profession of Faith: A History of Augustana College 1860–1935.* Augustana Library Publications 33. Rock Island, IL: Augustana College Library, 1969.

Bergstrand, Wilton E. "Augustana Heritage Festival: Remarks." *Augustana Heritage Newsletter* vol. 2, no. 3 (November 1997): 6–7.

Blanck, Dag. "The Augustana Synod and the Swedish–American Community." *The Augustana Heritage: Recollections, Perspectives, and Prospects.* Ed. Arland J. Hultgren and Vance L. Eckstrom. Chicago: Augustana Heritage Association, 1999. 39–52.

——. *Becoming Swedish–American: The Construction of an Ethnic Identity in the Augustana Synod, 1860–1917.* Dissertation Uppsala University, 1997. Studia Historica Upsaliensia 182. Uppsala, Sweden: Uppsala University, 1997.

Blegen, Theodore C. *Minnesota: A History of the State.* Minneapolis: University of Minnesota, 1963.

Burke, Maurice. "Bethphage: 90 Years of God's Love for People with Disabilities." *Augustana Heritage Newsletter* ns. 3.2 (Spring 2003): 10–15.

Capps, Finis Herbert. *From Isolationism to Involvement: The Swedish Immigrant Press in America, 1914–1945*. Chicago: Swedish Pioneer Historical Society, 1966.

The Chicago Manual of Style. 15th ed. Chicago: University of Chicago Press, 2003.

"Constitution of the Augustana Historical Society." *Augustana Historical Society Publications* 2, 1932: 86–87.

Dowie, James Iverne. *Prairie Grass Dividing*. Rock Island, IL: Augustana Historical Society, 1959.

Engelsk–Svensk Ordbok: Swedish–English Dictionary. 2nd rev. ed. Oxford, England: Berlitz, 1996.

Erickson, E. Walfred. *Swedish American Periodicals: a Selective and Descriptive Bibliography*. New York: Arno, 1979.

Gibaldi, Joseph. *MLA Handbook for Writers of Research Papers*. 6th ed. New York: Mod. Lang. Assn. of America, 2003.

———. *MLA Style Manual and Guide to Scholarly Publishing*. 2nd ed. New York: Mod. Lang. Assn. of America, 1998.

Gregory, Winifred, ed. *American Newspapers, 1821–1936: A Union List of Files Available in the United States and Canada*. New York: Kraus Reprint, 1967.

Griswold, Ada Tyng, comp. *Annotated Catalogue of Newspaper Files in the Library of the State Historical Society of Wisconsin*. 2nd ed. Madison, WI: The Society, 1911.

Hamrin, Margareta. "A Study of Swedish Immigrant Children's Literature Published in the United States, 1850–1920." *Phaedrus* (Spring 1979): 71–78.

Hendrickson, Charles. "The Music of the Augustana Synod." *Augustana Heritage Newsletter* ns. 2.3 (Fall 2001): 4–10.

Hultgren, Arland J., and Vance L. Eckstrom, eds. *The Augustana Heritage: Recollections, Perspectives, and Prospects*. Chicago: Augustana Heritage Association, 1999.

Johnson, F. A. "The Publishing Interests of the Augustana Synod." *The Augustana Synod: A Brief Review of Its History, 1860–1910*. Rock Island, IL: Augustana Book Concern, 1910. 173–97.

Kastrup, Allan. *The Swedish Heritage in America: the Swedish Element in America and American-Swedish Relations in Their Historical Perspective*. St. Paul, MN: Swedish Council of America, 1975.

Larsson, Gunilla, and Eva Tedenmyr. "The Royal Library and Swedish-American Imprints." *Swedish-American Historical Quarterly* 43:3 (July 1992): 179–93.

———. *Svenskt tryck i Nordamerika: katalog över Tell G. Dahllöfs samling = Swedish-American Imprints: a Catalogue of the Tell G. Dahllöf Collection*. Acta Bibliothecae Regiae Stockholmiensis 47. Stockholm: Kungl. Biblioteket; Chicago: Distributed in the U.S. through The Swedish-American Historical Society, 1988.

Linder, Oliver A. "Newspapers." *Swedes in America, 1638–1938*. Ed. Adolph B. Benson and Naboth Hedin. New Haven: Yale University Press, 1938, 181–90.

———. "The Swedish-American Press." *The Swedish Element in America*. Ed. Erik G. Westman. Vol. 2. Chicago: Swedish–American Biographical Society, 1931. 324–43.

Lindquist, Emory. *Bethany in Kansas: the History of a College*. Lindsborg, KS: Bethany College, 1975.

———. *Smoky Valley People: a History of Lindsborg, Kansas*. Lindsborg, KS: Bethany College, 1953.

Lund, Doniver A. *Gustavus Adolphus College: A Centennial History 1862–1962*. St. Peter, MN: Gustavus Adolphus College Press, 1963.

———. *Gustavus Adolphus College: Celebrating 125 Years.* St. Peter, MN: Gustavus Adolphus College, 1987.

Lundeen, Joel W., ed. *Preserving Yesterday for Tomorrow: A Guide to the Archives of the Lutheran Church in America.* Chicago: Archives of the Lutheran Church in America, 1977.

Lundholm, A. T. "The Printed Word." *After Seventy-Five Years: 1860–1935; a Jubilee Publication.* Rock Island, IL: Augustana Book Concern, 1935. 137–46.

Matthews, Donald N., and Sara Mummert, eds. *Union List of Periodicals of the Members of the Washington Theological Consortium and Contributing Institutions.* 4th ed. Gettysburg, PA: Washington Theological Consortium, 1985.

———. *Union List of Periodicals of the Southeastern Pennsylvania Theological Library Association.* 3rd key ed. Gettysburg, PA: SEPTLA, 1986.

Minnesskrift: Med Anledning af Augustana–Synodens Femtioåriga Tillvaro; Historisk Öfversikt af hvad som Uträttats under Åren 1860–1910. Rock Island, IL: Augustana Book Concern, 1910.

Mott, Frank Luther. *American Journalism: a History: 1690–1960.* 3rd ed. New York: Macmillan, 1962.

———. *American Journalism: A History of Newspapers in the United States through 250 Years, 1690 to 1940.* New York: Macmillan, 1942.

———. *A History of American Magazines.* Vols. 2–4. Cambridge, MA: Belknap-Harvard University Press, 1957–1967.

Nelson, Helge. *The Swedes and the Swedish Settlements in North America.* New York: Arno, 1979.

New Serial Titles: A Union List of Serials Commencing Publication after December 31, 1949; 1950–1970 Cumulative. 4 vols. Washington, DC: Library of Congress; New York: Bowker, 1973.

Newspapers in the State Historical Society of Wisconsin: a Bibliography with Holdings. 2 vols. New York: Norman Ross, 1994.

Nothstein, Ira O. "The Swedish–American Newspaper Collection at Augustana College, Rock Island, Illinois." *Swedish Pioneer Historical Quarterly* 3.2 (April, 1952): 45–55.

Nystrom, Daniel. *A Ministry of Printing: History of the Publication House of Augustana Lutheran Church, 1889–1962.* Augustana, 1962.

Olson, Ernst W. "Augustana Book Concern: Publishers to the Augustana Synod; History of its Activities Since 1889, with an Introductory Account of Earlier Publishing Enterprises." *Augustana Historical Society Publications* 3, 1933: 3–80.

———, trans. "Early Letters to Erland Carlsson: Introduction and Translation by E. W. Olson: from a File for the Years 1853 to 1857." *Augustana Historical Society Publications* 5, 1935: 107–33.

Olson, Mabel F. "It's 50 Years Old . . .'Mission Tidings' 1906–1956." In *Augustana Annual 1957.* Rock Island, IL: Augustana Book Concern, 1957. 57–58.

Peterson, Conrad. "The Other Schools." *Remember Thy Past: a History of Gustavus Adolphus College, 1862–1952.* St. Peter, MN: Gustavus Adolphus College Press, 1953. 136–76.

———. *Remember Thy Past: A History of Gustavus Adolphus College, 1862–1952.* St. Peter, MN: Gustavus Adolphus College Press, 1953.

Petti, Vincent, and Kerstin Petti. *English–Swedish, Swedish–English Dictionary*. New York: Hippocrene, 1993.

Prisma's Modern Swedish–English Dictionary. 1st American ed. Minneapolis: University of Minnesota; Stockholm, Bokförlaget Prisma, 1984.

"Reports to the Home Missionary Society, 1849–1856." Augustana Historical Society Publications 5, 1935: 35–84.

Schersten, Albert F. "The Historical and Cultural Background of Swedish Immigrants of Importance to their Assimilation in America." Augustana Historical Society Publications 2, 1932: 47–63.

Setterdahl, Lilly, comp. *Swedish–American Newspapers: a Guide to the Microfilms Held by Swenson Swedish Immigration Research Center, Augustana College, Rock Island, Illinois*. Augustana Library Publications 35. Rock Island, IL: Augustana College Library, 1981.

Söderström, Alfred. *Blixtar på Tidnings–Horisonten samlade och magasinerade*. Warroad, MN: s.n., 1910.

Spong, Doris Hedeen. "Led by the Spirit." *Augustana Heritage Newsletter* vol. 3, no. 3 (March 1998): 1–5.

———. "Led by the Spirit: The Women's Missionary Society and the Augustana Lutheran Church Women." *The Augustana Heritage: Recollections, Perspectives, and Prospects*. Ed. Arland J. Hultgren and Vance L. Eckstrom. Chicago: Augustana Heritage Association, 1999. 251–58.

Stephenson, George M. *The Religious Aspects of Swedish Immigration*. New York: Arno, 1969.

Svensk–Amerikanska Pressen och Svenska Journalistförbundet i Amerika. Rock Island, IL: Augustana Book Concerns Tryckeri och Binderi, 1923.

Svensson, Birgitta. "*Prärieblomman* (1900–1913): A Swedish–American Cultural Manifestation." *Swedish-American Historical Quarterly* 43 (July 1992): 156–69.

Swan, G. N. *Swedish-American Literary Periodicals*. Augustana Historical Society Publications 6. Rock Island, IL: Augustana Historical Society, 1936.

Tiedge, Jane. "40 Years in China: Augustana's Sr. Ingeborg Nystul." *Augustana Heritage Newsletter* ns. 3.1 (Fall 2002): 9, 12–17.

Titus, Edna Brown, ed. *Union List of Serials in Libraries of the United States and Canada*. 3rd ed. 5 vols. New York: Wilson, 1965.

Voigt, Louis, ed. *Lutheran Serials Checklist*. Springfield, OH: Wittenberg Univ. Library, 1971.

Westman, Erik G., ed. *The Swedish Element in America*. 2 vols. Chicago: Swedish-American Biographical Society, 1931.

ELECTRONIC DATABASE SOURCES
FOR UNION LIST OF TITLES A–Z

Note: Access to WorldCat was extended by the Harold Andersen Library, University of Wisconsin–Whitewater, Whitewater, Wisconsin. Therefore, that access location applies to all sources herein listed as being from WorldCat. The following URL applies to all sources herein listed as being from WorldCat: http://FirstSearch.oclc.org/WebZ/

The national database of Sweden is LIBRIS, which can be accessed from a personal computer. The following URL applies to all sources herein listed as being from LIBRIS: http://websök.libris.kb.se/websearch.

Each entry on the following list indicates a website or online catalog that provided information subsequently included in the relevant title entry in the union list. An online catalog of an institution accessed only for holdings information is not included in the following list. All websites cited can be accessed from a personal computer.

Academic catalog/Gustavus Adolphus College. 11 May 2004 http://mnpals.gustavus
    .edu.

Academica. 16 Feb. 2004 http://library.bethanylb.edu/search/.

The Advance. OCLC: 7664460 Update: 20001201. 16 July 2003 http://FirstSearch
    .oclc.org/WebZ/.

All Yours. OCLC: 1777633 Update: 20030416. 15 July 2003 http://FirstSearch.oclc
    .org/WebZ/.

Almanac. OCLC: 14277259 Update: 20011102. 16 July 2003 http://FirstSearch.oclc
    .org/WebZ/.

Almanack. 5 January 2005 http://tomos.oit.umn.edu/F/.

Almanack, för året efter Jesu Kristi födelse . . . OCLC: 1479183 Update: 20030111. 14
    July 2003 http://FirstSearch.oclc.org/WebZ/.

Almanack för året efter Jesu Kristi födelse . . . 28 Sept. 2003 http://websök.libris.kb
    .se/websearch.

The Alumnus. OCLC: 1639097 Update: 20001101. 16 July 2003 http://FirstSearch
    .oclc.org/WebZ/.

The Alumnus. OCLC: 43945779 Update: 20000719. 16 July 2003 http://FirstSearch
    .oclc.org/WebZ/.

Annual Messenger. 11 May 2004 http://mnpals.gustavus.edu.

Arkivfynd. OCLC: 7722052 Update: 20040528. 9 October 2004 http://FirstSearch
    .oclc.org/WebZ/.

Arkivfynd. 2 May 2004 http://websök.libris.kb.se/websearch.

Årsbok. 10 Oct. 2003 http://websök.libris.kb.se/websearch.

Årsbok. OCLC: 36640593 Update: 20020822. 16 July 2003 http://FirstSearch.oclc
    .org/WebZ/.

Augustana. OCLC: 5105241 Update: 20011020. 15 July 2003 http://FirstSearch.oclc
    .org/WebZ/.

Augustana. OCLC: 13294691 Update: 20000720. 15 July 2003 http://FirstSearch
    .oclc.org/WebZ/.

Augustana. OCLC: 7632568 Update: 20020404. 14 July 2003 http://FirstSearch.oclc
    .org/WebZ/.

Augustana. OCLC: 12700555 Update: 20020313. 14 July 2003 http://FirstSearch
    .oclc.org/WebZ/.

Augustana (1874). 17 November 2004 http://jkm.ipac/.

Augustana: kyrklig tidskrift för Swenska Lutherska Kyrkan i N. Amerika. OCLC:
    12675511 Update: 20020424. 12 July 2003 http://FirstSearch.oclc.org/WebZ/.

Augustana: kyrklig tidskrift för Swenska Lutherska Kyrkan i N. Amerika. OCLC:
    12691282 Update: 20020506. 12 July 2003 http://FirstSearch.oclc.org/WebZ/.

Augustana: kyrklig tidskrift för svenska lutherska kyrkan i N. Amerika. 29 Sept. 2003 http://websök.libris.kb.se/websearch.

Augustana: tidning för den svenska luterska kyrkan i Amerika. 28 Sept. 2003 http:// websök.libris.kb.se/websearch.

Augustana: tidskrift för Swenska Lutherska Kyrkan i Amerika. OCLC: 12675596 Update: 20020322. 12 July 2003 http://FirstSearch.oclc.org/WebZ/.

Augustana: tidskrift för Swenska Lutherska Kyrkan i Amerika. OCLC: 12690842 Update: 20020502. 12 July 2003 http://FirstSearch.oclc.org/WebZ/.

Augustana: tidskrift för svenska lutherska kyrkan i Amerika. 28 Sept. 2003 http:// websök.libris.kb.se/websearch.

Augustana Annual: Yearbook for the Evangelical Lutheran Augustana Synod. OCLC: 1695115 Update: 20020311. 15 July 2003 http://FirstSearch.oclc.org/WebZ/.

Augustana Annual: Yearbook of the Augustana Evangelical Lutheran Church. 28 Sept/ 2003 http://websök.libris.kb.se/websearch.

Augustana Annual. 8 February 2005 http://207.56.64.20/.

Augustana Bulletin. 11 February 2005 http://lms01.harvard.edu/F/.

Augustana Churchmen. OCLC: 52418901 Update: 20030612. 14 July 2003 http:// FirstSearch.oclc.org/WebZ/.

Augustana College Bulletin. 7 Oct. 2003 http://websök.libris.kb.se/websearch.

Augustana College Catalog. OCLC: 25452681 Update: 19990820. 16 July 2003 http:// FirstSearch.oclc.org/WebZ/.

Augustana College Library Occasional Paper. [keyword search] 14 July 2003 http:// FirstSearch.oclc.org/WebZ/.

Augustana College Library Occasional Paper. 1 March 2004 http://websök.libris.kb .se/websearch.

Augustana College Library Publications. [keyword search] 14 July 2003 http:// FirstSearch.oclc.org/WebZ/.

Augustana College Library Publications. 1 March 2004 http://websök.libris.kb.se/ websearch.

Augustana College Magazine. 28 September 2003 http://websök.libris.kb.se/ websearch.

The Augustana Foreign Missionary. OCLC: 26181413 Update: 20001214. 14 July 2003 http://FirstSearch.oclc.org/WebZ/.

The Augustana Heritage Newsletter. 7 March 2004 < http://jkmlibrary.org/ie/ resources/catalog.

Augustana Historical Society [keyword search]. 19 July 2003 http://FirstSearch .oclc.org/WebZ/.

Augustana Historical Society Publications. OCLC: 1518627 Update: 20001117. 14 July 2003 http://FirstSearch.oclc.org/WebZ/.

Augustana Historical Society Publications. 12 March 2004 http://websök.libris.kb .se/websearch.

Augustana Historical Society Publications. 21 June 2003 http://grace.gtu.edu/search.

Augustana Historical Society Publications. 21 April 2002 http://www.wiscat.net.

The Augustana Home Altar. OCLC: 51808189 Update: 20030306. 12 July 2003 http://FirstSearch.oclc.org/WebZ/.

Augustana Journal. OCLC: 1639087 Update: 20001101. 12 July 2003 http:// FirstSearch.oclc.org/WebZ/.

Augustana Journal. OCLC: 43946005 Update: 20000501. 12 July 2003 http://FirstSearch.oclc.org/WebZ/.

Augustana Library Publications. OCLC: 1518625 Update: 20011017. 14 July 2003 http://FirstSearch.oclc.org/WebZ/.

Augustana Library Publications. [keyword search]. 19 July 2003 http://FirstSearch.oclc.org/WebZ/.

Augustana Library Publications. 1 March 2004 http://websök.libris.kb.se/websearch.

Augustana Library Publications. 29 Sept. 2003 http://www.wiscat.net.

Augustana Library Publications. Occasional Paper. 1 March 2004 http://websök.libris.kb/se/websearch.

The Augustana Lutheran. OCLC: 1779538 Update: 20011018. 12 July 2003 http://FirstSearch.oclc.org/WebZ/.

Augustana Lutheranen. OCLC: 12700412 Update: 20020501. 16 July 2003 http://FirstSearch.oclc.org/WebZ/.

Augustana Lutheranen. OCLC: 7632531 Update: 20020425. 14 July 2003 http://FirstSearch.oclc.org/WebZ/.

Augustana-Men. OCLC: 52418900 Update: 20030612. 14 July 2003 http://FirstSearch.oclc.org/WebZ/.

Augustana Missions. OCLC: 7642577 Update: 20010102. 14 July 2003 http://FirstSearch.oclc.org/WebZ/.

Augustana Missions. OCLC: 52418896 Update: 20030612. 14 July 2003 http://FirstSearch.oclc.org/WebZ/.

Augustana Missions. OCLC: 7642621 Update: 20020425. 14 July 2003 http://FirstSearch.oclc.org/WebZ/.

Augustana Missions. 29 March 2005 http://lrc.elca.org:8080/webcat/.

Augustana Missions. 14 June 2003 http://grace.gtu.edu/search.

Augustana Observer. OCLC: 52063100 Update: 20030415. 12 July 2003 http://FirstSearch.oclc.org/WebZ/.

Augustana Observer. OCLC: 17276004 Update: 20020517. 12 July 2003 http://FirstSearch.oclc.org/WebZ/.

Augustana Observer (1881). 30 November 2004 http://tomos.oit.umn.edu/.

The Augustana Observer. OCLC: 12047101 Update: 20001205. 12 July 2003 http://FirstSearch.oclc.org/WebZ/.

The Augustana Observer. 28 Sept. 2003 http://websök.libris.kb.se/websearch> (NB Two different records).

The Augustana Observer. 22 June 2003 http://www.wiscat.net.

Augustana och Missionären. OCLC: 1779539 Update: 20001108. 14 July 2003 http://FirstSearch.oclc.org/WebZ/.

Augustana och Missionären. OCLC: 12700093 Update: 20000720. 14 July 2003 http://FirstSearch.oclc.org/WebZ/.

Augustana och Missionären. 29 March 2005 http://mnhs.mnpals.net/.

Augustana och Missionären: Weckotidning för Kyrka och Mission. 29 Sept. 2003 http://websök.libris.kb.se/websearch.

Augustana Overseas. OCLC: 7642548 Update: 20010103. 14 July 2003 http://FirstSearch.oclc.org/WebZ/.

Augustana Overseas. OCLC: 7642600 Update: 20001130. 14 July 2003 http:// FirstSearch.oclc.org/WebZ/.

Augustana Overseas. 21 Oct. 2003 http://lrc.elca.org/WebOPAC.

The Augustana Quarterly. OCLC: 1518628 Update: 20011017. 14 July 2003 http:// FirstSearch.oclc.org/WebZ/.

The Augustana Quarterly. OCLC: 25416811 Update: 20000218. 14 July 2003 http:// FirstSearch.oclc.org/WebZ/.

Augustana Quarterly. 22 June 2003 http://www.wiscat.net.

Augustana Seminary Review. OCLC: 1518629 Update: 20011017 14 July 2003 http:// FirstSearch.oclc.org/WebZ/.

The Augustana Theological Quarterly. OCLC: 6343131 Update: 20000601. 14 July 2003 http://FirstSearch.oclc.org/WebZ/.

The Augustana Theological Quarterly. OCLC:.7637922 Update: 20000727. 14 July 2003 http://FirstSearch.oclc.org/WebZ/.

Augustana Theological Quarterly. Tidksrift för teologi och kyrkliga frågor. OCLC: 1518632 Update: 20011017. 12 July 2003 http://FirstSearch.oclc.org/WebZ/.

The Augustana Theological Quarterly: Tidskrift för teologi och kyrkliga frågor. 29 Sept. 2003 http://websök.libris.kb.se/websearch.

Barnens Tidning. 22 Sept. 2003 http://websök.libris.kb.se/websearch.

Barnvännen. OCLC: 8691127 Update: 19950308. 12 July 2003 http://FirstSearch .oclc.org/WebZ/.

Barnvännen. 2 Feb. 2004 http://websök.libris.kb.se/websearch.

Betania: luthersk månadstidning. 7 Oct. 2003 http://websök.libris.kb.se/websearch.

Bethanian (Bethany College Yearbook). 16 Feb. 2004 http://library.bethanylb .edu/search/.

Bethany Annual ("The Story of Bethany"). 24 Feb. 2004 http://library.bethanylb .edu/search/.

Bethany College Bulletin. 16 Feb. 2004 http://library.bethanylb.edu/search/.

Bethany College Bulletin/Alumni News. 16 Feb. 2004 http://library.bethanylb .edu/search/.

Bethany College Bulletin/Bethany Magazine. 26 Feb. 2004 http://library.bethanylb .edu/search/.

Bethany College Catalog. 23 Feb. 2004 http://library.bethanylb.edu/search/.

Bethany College Messenger. 16 Feb. 2004 http://library.bethanylb.edu/search/.

Bethany Magazine. 16 Feb. 2004 http://library.bethanylb.edu/search/.

Bethany Messenger. 16 Feb. 2004 http://library.bethanylb.edu/search/.

Bethany Messenger. 7 Oct. 2003 http://websök.libris.kb.se/websearch.

Bethanys Budbärare. 16 Feb. 2004 http://library.bethanylb.edu/search/.

Bethany's Messenger. 16 Feb. 2004 http://library.bethanylb.edu/search/.

Bethphage Biblioteket. 18 November 2004 http://jkm.ipac/.

Bethphage Messenger. OCLC: 16963491 Update: 20020115. 15 July 2003 http:// FirstSearch.oclc.org/WebZ/.

Bethphage Messenger. 8 February 2005 http://www.niclc.org/.

Bethphagebiblioteket. 7 Oct. 2003 http://websök.libris.kb.se/websearch.

Bible Banner. OCLC: 1519704 Update: 20011017. 12 July 2003 http://FirstSearch .oclc.org/WebZ/.

Bible Banner. 18 November 2004 http://jkm.ipac/.

The Bible Study Quarterly. OCLC: 23868007 Update: 20001228. 12 July 2003 http://FirstSearch.oclc.org/WebZ/.

The Bible Study Quarterly. OCLC: 23868043 Update: 20001215. 12 July 2003 http://FirstSearch.oclc.org/WebZ/.

The Bible Study Quarterly. OCLC: 23868031 Update: 20001205. 12 July 2003 http://FirstSearch.oclc.org/WebZ/.

Blommor vid vägen. OCLC: 12622076 Update: 19980825. 15 July 2003 http://FirstSearch.oclc.org/WebZ/.

Blommor vid vägen. 7 Oct. 2003 http://websök.libris.kb.se/websearch.

Bond/Lutheran Brotherhood. OCLC: 7349401 Update: 20011021. 16 July 2003 http://FirstSearch.oclc.org/WebZ/.

Bond. 9 Oct. 2003 http://websök.libris.kb.se/websearch.

The Bond. 29 November 2004 http://mnhs.mnpals.net/F/.

Breidablick: Jubilee Annual. OCLC: 17625792 Update: 20001214. 15 July 2003 http://FirstSearch.oclc.org/WebZ/.

Breidablick: Jubilee Annual. 11 May 2004 http://mnpals.gustavus.edu.

Bulletin/Lutheran Bible Institute. 6 October 2004 http://mnhs.mnpals.net/F/.

Calendar, [1910–1924]. OCLC: 49884507 Update: 20030402. 19 July 2003 http://FirstSearch.oclc.org/WebZ/.

Calendar/Minnesota College. OCLC: 41215856 Update: 20040516 2 October 2004 http://FirstSearch.oclc.org/WebZ/.

Canada. 7 Oct. 2003 http://websök.libris.kb.se/websearch.

Canadian Crusader. OCLC: 1607407 Update: 20011017 2 October 2004 http://FirstSearch.oclc.org/WebZ/.

Canadian Crusader. 7 October 2004 http://ruth.luthersem.edu/.

Catalog of Upsala College. OCLC: 44086470 Update: 20000519. 16 July 2003 http://FirstSearch.oclc.org/WebZ/.

Catalog of Upsala College. 9 February 2005 http://catnyp.nypl.org/.

Catalogue. OCLC: 42383995 Update: 20040420. 2 October 2004 http://FirstSearch.oclc.org/WebZ/.

Catalogue of Bethany Academy at Lindsborg, Kansas. OCLC: 37969381 Update: 19971119. 16 July 2003 http://FirstSearch.oclc.org/WebZ/.

Catalogue of Bethany Academy at Lindsborg, Kansas. 16 Feb. 2004 http://library.bethanylb.edu/search/.

Catalogue of Gustavus Adolphus College. 5 Feb. 2004 http://websök.libris.kb.se/websearch.

Catalogue of Gustavus Adolphus College. 11 May 2004 http://mnpals.gustavus.edu.

Catalogue of Hope Academy, Moorhead, Minnesota. OCLC: 22571226 Update: 20040515. 9 October 2004 http://FirstSearch.oclc.org/WebZ/.

Catalogue of Hope Academy, Moorhead, Minnesota. 6 April 2005 http://www.mnpals.net/F/.

Catalogue of Upsala College. 5 February 2004 http://websök.libris.kb.se/websearch.

Church School Teacher. OCLC: 12701840 Update: 20001201. 14 July 2003 http://FirstSearch.oclc.org/WebZ/.

Church School Teacher. OCLC: 1770715 Update: 19920515. 14 July 2003 http://FirstSearch.oclc.org/WebZ/.

The Church School Teacher. 29 Sept. 2003 http://websök.libris.kb.se/websearch.

Class Annual. 20 January 2005 http://library.ilcso.illinois.edu/aug/.

College Breezes. OCLC: 7360203 Update: 19950221. 15 July 2003 http://FirstSearch .oclc.org/WebZ/.

College Breezes. 11 May 2004 http://mnpals.gustavus.edu.

College Calendar/Minnesota College. OCLC: 41215854 Update: 20020516. 2 October 2004 http://FirstSearch.oclc.org/WebZ/.

Columbia Lutheran. OCLC: 9722081 Update: 20011213. 15 July 2003 http:// FirstSearch.oclc.org/WebZ/.

Columbia Lutheran. 24 October 2004 http://catalog.lib.washington.edu/.

The Conference Messenger: Spokesman for Illinois Conference Missions and Welfare Work. 8 Oct. 2003 http://websök.libris.kb.se/websearch.

Daisy (Bethany College Yearbook). 16 Feb. 2004 http://library.bethanylb.edu/ search/.

The Deaconess Banner. OCLC: 1776585 Update: 20030416. 15 July 2003 http:// FirstSearch.oclc.org/WebZ/.

The Deaconess Banner: (Diakoniss baneret). 5 Feb. 2004 http://websök.libris.kb .se/websearch.

The Deaconess Banner = (Diakoniss baneret). 21 June 2003 http://grace.gtu.edu/ search.

Dorkas. 5 January 2005 http://tomos.oit.umn.edu/.

Dorkas: en halsning fran Diakonissanstalten i Omaha. OCLC: 35729845 Update: 20010508. 12 July 2003 http://FirstSearch.oclc.org/WebZ/.

Dorkas: en julhalsning fran Diakonissanstalten i Omaha. OCLC: 43579818 Update: 20010514. 12 July 2003 http://FirstSearch.oclc.org/WebZ/.

Dorkas: en julhälsning från Diakonissanstalten i Omaha. 29 Sept. 2003 http://websök .libris.kb.se/websearch.

Ev. Luthersk tidskrift. OCLC: 8043483 Update: 20020513. 15 July 2003 http:// FirstSearch.oclc.org/WebZ/.

Ev. Luthersk Tidskrift. 17 November 2004 http://jkm.ipac/.

Ev. Luthersk Tidskrift. 29 March 2004 http://library.ilcso.illinois.edu/aug/.

Evang. luth. barntidning. 29 Sept. 2003 http://websök.libris.kb.se/websearch.

Evangelisk luthersk tid–skrift för kyrkan skolan och hemmet. 13 Oct. 2003 http://websök .libris.kb.se/websearch.

Folkvännen. OCLC: 22914520 Update: 20030607. 15 July 2003 http://FirstSearch .oclc.org/WebZ/.

För–gät–mig–ej: årskalender. 8 Oct. 2003 http://websök.libris.kb.se/websearch.

För–gät–mig–ej: fosterländsk och luthersk ungdomskalender för jubelåret 1893. 8 Oct. 2003 http://websök.libris.kb.se/websearch.

Förgat mig ej; kristlig, osekterisk tidskrift. OCLC: 27767453 Update: 19930319. 15 July 2003 http://FirstSearch.oclc.org/WebZ/.

Förgät–Mig–Ej (1902). 5 January 2005 http://tomos.oit.umn.edu/.

"Forget–Me–Not": The Annual of Bethany College, Lindsborg, Kansas, 1902. 24 Feb. 2004 http://library.bethanylb.edu/search/.

Fortieth Anniversary Album. 26 October 2004 http://library.ilcso.illinois.edu/aug/.

Församlingsvännen: evangelisk–luthersk illustrerad tidning för Pittsburg–distriktet. 13 Oct. 2003 http://websök.libris.kb.se/websearch.

Fosterlandet. OCLC: 9382209 Update: 20001117. 12 July 2003 http://FirstSearch .oclc.org/WebZ/.

Fosterlandet. 29 Sept. 2003 http://websök.libris.kb.se/websearch.

Framåt. OCLC: 25118859 Update: 20001206. 12 July 2003 http://FirstSearch.oclc .org/WebZ/.

Framåt. 2 Feb. 2004 http://websök.libris.kb.se/websearch> (NB Two separate records).

Framåt = Forward. OCLC: 26385379 Update: 19990526. 12 July 2003 http:// FirstSearch.oclc.org/WebZ/.

Fridens härold. 8 Oct. 2003 http://websök.libris.kb.se/websearch.

Fylgia. OCLC: 45383496 Update: 20001117. 15 July 2003 http://FirstSearch .oclc.org/WebZ/.

Fylgia. 4 Oct. 2003 http://websök.libris.kb.se/websearch.

Gamla och nya hemlandet. OCLC: 1606833 Update: 20001117. 12 July 2003 http:// FirstSearch.oclc.org/WebZ/.

Gamla och nya hemlandet. 29 Sept. 2003 http://websök.libris.kb.se/websearch.

The Garnet and Silver-Gray. 20 January 2005 http://library.ilcso.illinois.edu/aug/.

The Gazette. OCLC: 62332561 Update: 20051123. 21 Oct. 2006 http://FirstSearch .oclc.org/WebZ/

God jul. OCLC: 8631363 Update: 19950306. 12 July 2003 http://FirstSearch.oclc .org/WebZ/.

God jul: illustrerad jultidning för svenskarna i Amerika. 4 Oct. 2003 http://websök .libris.kb.se/websearch.

Greater Gustavus Quarterly. OCLC: 15348049 Update: 19980831. 15 July 2003 http:// FirstSearch.oclc.org/WebZ/.

Greater Gustavus Quarterly. 11 May 2004 http://mnpals.gustavus.edu.

Greater Gustavus Quarterly. 30 November 2004 http://tomos.oit.umn.edu/F/.

Greater Gustavus Quarterly. 30 November 2004 http://mnhs.mnpals.net/.

Guldax. 7 Oct. 2003 http://websök.libris.kb.se/websearch.

Guldax. 29 October 2004 http://tomos.oit.umn.edu/F/.

The Gustavian. 11 May 2004 http://mnpals.gustavus.edu.

The Gustavian. 30 November 2004 http://mnhs.mnpals.net/.

Gustavian Weekly. OCLC: 7359987 Update: 20001215. 15 July 2003 http://FirstSearch .oclc.org/WebZ/.

Gustavian Weekly. 2 Feb. 2004 http://websök.libris.kb.se/websearch.

Gustavian Weekly. 11 May 2004 http://mnpals.gustavus.edu.

The Gustavian Weekly (1973). 6 April 2005 http://www.mnpals.net/F/.

Gustaviana. 5 Feb. 2004 http://websök.libris.kb.se/websearch.

Gustaviana. 11 May 2004 http://mnpals.gustavus.edu.

Gustavus Adolphus Journal. OCLC: 7942201 Update: 20020702. 15 July 2003 http:// FirstSearch.oclc.org.WebZ/.

Gustavus Adolphus Journal. OCLC: 7942151 Update: 20001206. 15 July 2003 http:// FirstSearch.oclc.org/WebZ/.

Gustavus Journal. 11 May 2004 http://mnpals.gustavus.edu.

The Gustavus Quarterly. 11 May 2004 http://mnpals.gustavus.edu.

Heimdall. 11 May 2004 http://mnpals.gustavus.edu.

Hemlandet, det gamla och det nya. OCLC: 15998121 Update: 20001117. 12 July 2003 http://FirstSearch.oclc.org/WebZ/.

Hem-vännen. 13 Oct. 2003 http://websök.libris.kb.se/websearch.

Hemvännen. OCLC: 45495621 Update: 20001207. 12 July 2003 http://FirstSearch .oclc.org/WebZ/.

Honan Glimpses. OCLC: 48017529 Update: 20030111. 15 July 2003 http://FirstSearch .oclc.org/WebZ/.

The Jubilee 1910. 2 Feb. 2004 http://websök.libris.kb.se/websearch.

The Jubilee 1910. 24 Feb. 2004 http://library.bethanylb.edu/search/.

Julklockorna: en julbok för de unga. OCLC: 28759086 Update: 20020321. 15 July 2003 http://FirstSearch.oclc.org/WebZ/.

Julklockorna: en julbok för de unga. OCLC: 28759087 Update: 20020328. 15 July 2003 http://FirstSearch.oclc.org/WebZ/.

Julklockorna: en julbok för de unga. 9 Oct. 2003 http://websök.libris.kb.se/ websearch.

Junction. 6 April 2005 http://www.mnpals.net/F/.

Junior Life. OCLC: 52062820 Update: 20030415. 14 July 2003 http://FirstSearch .oclc.org/WebZ/.

Juvelskrinet. 31 March 2005 http://mnhs.mnpals.net/F/.

Kansas Conference Lutheran. 9 Oct. 2003 http://websök.libris.kb.se/websearch.

Kansas-posten. OCLC: 11898096 Update: 20001208. 14 July 2003 http://FirstSearch .oclc.org/WebZ/.

Kansas posten. 30 Sept. 2003 http://websök.libris.kb.se/websearch.

Kansas–posten. 8 February 2005 http://ksuc–agent.auto–graphics.com/.

Kansas Stats Tidning. OCLC: 11900451 Update: 20001221. 15 July 2003 http:// FirstSearch.oclc.org/WebZ/.

Kansas stats tidning. 9 Oct. 2003 http://websök.libris.kb.se/websearch.

Kina missionären. OCLC: 26181386 Update: 20001228. 12 July 2003 http:// FirstSearch.oclc.org/WebZ/.

Kina missionären. 2 Feb. 2004 http://websök.libris.kb.se/websearch.

Korsbaneret; Kristlig Kalendar. OCLC: 1755260 Update: 20030111. 12 July 2003 http:// FirstSearch.oclc.org/WebZ/.

Korsbaneret: kristlig kalendar. 30 Sept. 2003 http://websök.libris.kb.se/websearch.

Korsbaneret . . . Kristlig Kalendar för 1880–. OCLC: 39941475 Update: 19980927. 12 July 2003 http://FirstSearch.oclc.org/WebZ/.

Korsbaneret . . . Kristlig Kalendar för 1880–. OCLC: 40958112 Update: 19990314. 12 July 2003 http://FirstSearch.oclc.org/WebZ/.

Korsbaneret: kristlig kalendar för . . . 6 January 2005 http://tomos.oit.umn.edu/F/.

Kyrkosangen: musiktidning for forsamlingskoren inom den evang. lutherska Augustana-Synoden. OCLC: 50544164 Update: 20030111. 14 July 2003 http://FirstSearch .oclc.org/WebZ/.

L.B.A. Bulletin. OCLC: 13000700 Update: 19980825. 15 July 2003 http://FirstSearch .oclc.org/WebZ/.

L.B.A. Bulletin. 2 April 2005 http://lrc.elca.org:8080/webcat/.

L.B.I. Bulletin. 29 March 2005 http://mnhs.mnpals.net/.

Lek–kamraten: bilder för de små. 14 Oct. 2003 http://websök.libris.kb.se/websearch.

Lindsborgs-posten. OCLC: 14403339 Update: 19890731. 15 July 2003 http://FirstSearch.oclc.org/WebZ/.

Lindsborgs-posten. 3 Oct. 2003 http://websök.libris.kb.se/websearch.

The Little Folks. OCLC: 52062821 Update: 20030415. 14 July 2003 http://FirstSearch.oclc.org/WebZ/.

Lutersk Kvartalskrift=Lutheran Quarterly Review. OCLC: 10240271 Update: 20001212. 14 July 2003 http://FirstSearch.oclc.org/WebZ/.

Luth. Kyrkotidning. OCLC: 7632639 Update: 20001218. 12 July 2003 http://FirstSearch.oclc.org/WebZ/.

Luth. Kyrkotidning. 2 October 2003 http://websök.libris.kb.se/websearch.

Luth. Kyrkotidning. 29 March 2005 http://jkm.ipac.dynixasp.com/.

Luth. Kyrkotidning. 28 March 2005 http://lms01.harvard.edu/F/.

Luther Academy Visitor. OCLC: 34502314 Update: 20001228. 15 July 2003 http://FirstSearch.oclc.org/WebZ/.

Luther Bladet. 9 October 2003 http://websök.libris.kb.se/websearch.

Luther College Visitor. OCLC: 34502325 Update: 20001228. 16 July 2003 http://FirstSearch.oclc.org/WebZ/.

Lutheran Brotherhood Bond. OCLC: 1756288 Update: 20011018. 16 July 2003 http://FirstSearch.oclc.org/WebZ/.

The Lutheran Brotherhood Bond. 9 October 2003 http://websök.libris.kb.se/websearch.

The Lutheran Companion. OCLC: 1779503 Update: 20001108. 14 July 2003 http://FirstSearch.oclc.org/WebZ/.

The Lutheran Companion. OCLC: 43947453 Update: 20000501. 14 July 2003 http://FirstSearch.oclc.org/WebZ/.

The Lutheran Companion. OCLC: 1779502 Update: 20011018. 14 July 2003 http://FirstSearch.oclc.org/WebZ/.

The Lutheran Companion. OCLC: 43948148 Update: 20001005. 14 July 2003 http://FirstSearch.oclc.org/WebZ/.

Lutheran Libraries. OCLC: 1756299 Update: 20011018. 16 July 2003 http://FirstSearch.oclc.org/WebZ/.

Lutheran Publications. 7 October 2004 http://ruth.luthersem.edu/.

Lutheran Quarterly. OCLC: 1589952 Update: 20030301. 14 July 2003 http://FirstSearch.oclc.org/WebZ/.

The Lutheran Quarterly. 30 Sept. 2003 http://websök.libris.kb.se/websearch.

Lutheran Quarterly. 28 Dec. 2001 http://www.wiscat.net.

Lutheran Women. OCLC: 1589135 Update: 20011017. 15 July 2003 http://FirstSearch.oclc.org/WebZ/.

Lutheran Women. 18 November 2004 http://jkm.ipac/.

Lutheran Women's World. OCLC: 1756313 Update: 20011018. 15 July 2003 http://FirstSearch.oclc.org/WebZ/.

Lutheran Women's World. OCLC: 16818995 Update: 20030416. 15 July 2003 http://FirstSearch.oclc.org/WebZ/.

Luthersk kyrko–tidning. 2 Oct. 2003 http://websök.libris.kb.se/websearch.

Luthersk kyrkotidning. OCLC: 7632665 Update: 20001226. 12 July 2003 http://FirstSearch.oclc.org/WebZ/.

Luthersk Kyrkotidning. OCLC: 5912597 Update: 19801016. 19 July 2003 http:// FirstSearch.oclc.org/WebZ/.

Luthersk Kyrkotidning (Red Wing, MN). 29 March 2005 http://jkm.ipac.dynixasp .com/.

Luthersk Kyrkotidning (Red Wing, MN). 28 March 2005 http://lms01.harvard .edu/F/.

Luthersk Kyrkotidning (Vasa, MN). 29 March 2005 http://jkm.ipac.dynixasp.com/.

Luthersk Kyrkotidning (Vasa, MN). 28 March 2005 http://lms01.harvard.edu/F/.

Luthersk tidskrift för hedramission [sic] och diakoni. OCLC: 10378677 Update: 19960310. 16 July 2003 http://FirstSearch.oclc.org/WebZ/.

The Lyceum Annual. 30 Sept. 2003 http://websök.libris.kb.se/websearch.

Manhem: Gustavus Adolphus Annual. 11 May 2004 http://mnpals.gustavus.edu.

Minnesota Conference Advance. OCLC: 1758122 Update: 20011018. 16 July 2003 http://FirstSearch.oclc.org/WebZ/.

Minnesota Lutheran. OCLC: 1714442 Update: 20030517. 16 July 2003 http:// FirstSearch.oclc.org/WebZ/.

Minnesota Lutheran. 10 Oct. 2003 http://websök.libris.kb.se/websearch.

Minnesota posten. OCLC: 6060305 Update: 20001214. 12 July 2003 http:// FirstSearch.oclc.org/WebZ/.

Minnesota posten. 30 Sept. 2003 http://websök.libris.kb.se/websearch.

Minnesota stats tidning. OCLC: 21922139 Update: 20030607. 16 July 2003 http:// FirstSearch.oclc.org/WebZ/.

Minnesota stats tidning. OCLC: 1644784 Update: 20030517. 16 July 2003 http:// FirstSearch.oclc.org/WebZ/.

Minnesota stats tidning. OCLC: 49708195 Update: 20030328. 16 July 2003 http:// FirstSearch.oclc.org/WebZ/.

Minnesota stats tidning. OCLC: 1588754 Update: 20030416. 16 July 2003 http:// FirstSearch.oclc.org/WebZ/.

Minnesota stats tidning. 10 Oct. 2003 http://websök.libris.kb.se/websearch> (NB Two different records).

Missionären (Moline, IL). 18 November 2004 http://jkm.ipac/.

Missionären: tidskrift för inre och uttre mission. OCLC: 13220589 Update: 20000501. 12 July 2003 http://FirstSearch.oclc.org/WebZ/.

Missionären/Svensk Luthersk Missionstidning. OCLC: 28143139 Update: 20000501. 14 July 2003 http://FirstSearch.oclc.org/WebZ/.

Missionären: Svensk luthersk missionstidning. 2 Oct. 2003 http://websök.libris.kb .se/websearch.

Missionären: Svensk luthersk missionstidning/redigerad af Erl. Carlsson och A.G.Setter-dahl. 2 Oct. 2003 http://websök.libris.kb.se/websearch.

Missionären/Svensk Luthersk Missionstidning. 31 Jan. 2004 http://www.wiscat.net.

The Missionary Calendar. OCLC: 39270617 Update: 20010424. 16 July 2003 http:// FirstSearch.oclc.org/WebZ/.

The Missionary Calendar of the Augustana Foreign Missionary Society. 14 June 2003 http://grace.gtu.edu/search.

Mission-Tidings. 28 September 2003 http://websök.kb.se/websearch.

Mission-Tidings. 24 January 2005 http://mnhs.mnpals.net/F/.

Mission–Tidings: The Official Organ of the Woman's Missionary Society, Lutheran Augustana Synod. OCLC: 11367753 Update: 20001215. 12 July 2003 http://FirstSearch.oclc.org/WebZ/.

Mission Tidings: Official Organ of the Woman's Missionary Society, Lutheran Augustana Synod. OCLC: 23865284 Update: 20001221. 12 July 2003 http://FirstSearch.oclc.org/WebZ/.

Missions–tidning: Organ för Kvinnornas Hem–och Hedna–missions–förening inom Augustana-Synoden. OCLC: 11367802 Update: 20001213. 12 July 2003 http://FirstSearch.oclc.org/WebZ/.

Missions–tidning: Organ för Kvinnornas missionsförening inom Augustana–synoden. 28 Sept. 2003 http://websök.libris.kb.se/websearch.

The Moccasin. OCLC: 21589806 Update: 20040518. 2 October 2004 http://FirstSearch.oclc.org/WebZ/.

The Moccasin. 6 October 2004 http://mnhs.mnpals.net/.

My Church. 22 June 2003 http://www.wiscat.net.

My Church: An Illustrated Lutheran Manual. OCLC: 1604823 Update: 20030416. 19 July 2003 http://FirstSearch.oclc.org/WebZ/.

My Church: A Yearbook of the Lutheran Augustana Synod of North America. OCLC: 44924697 Update: 20000901. 14 July 2003 http://FirstSearch.oclc.org/WebZ/.

Nåd och sanning. OCLC: 26459953 Update: 19990526. 12 July 2003 http://FirstSearch.oclc.org/WebZ/.

Nåd och sanning. 2 Oct. 2003 http://websök.libris.kb.se/websearch.

New England Conference News. OCLC: 6527355 Update: 20001222. 19 July 2003 http://FirstSearch.oclc.org/WebZ/.

The New England Lutheran. OCLC: 6527414 Update: 20001219. 16 July 2003 http://FirstSearch.oclc.org/WebZ/.

The New England Lutheran. OCLC: 10311993 Update: 20020705. 16 July 2003 http://FirstSearch.oclc.org/WebZ/.

Newsletter/Augustana Historical Society. OCLC: 10346074 Update: 19970214. 2 October 2004 http://FirstSearch.oclc.org/WebZ/.

None of the Above. 6 April 2005 http://www.mnpals.net/F/.

North Star Signal. OCLC: 18137910 Update: 20001130. 15 July 2003 http://FirstSearch.oclc.org/WebZ/.

North Star Signal. OCLC: 19757968 Update: 20010724. 15 July 2003 http://FirstSearch.oclc.org/WebZ/.

North Star Signal microform. 29 November 2004 http://mnhs.mnpals.net/.

Nytt bibliotek för barn och ungdom. OCLC: 21878805 Update: 19900618. 16 July 2003 http://FirstSearch.oclc.org/WebZ/.

Nytt bibliotek för barn och ungdom. 10 Oct. 2003 http://websök.libris.kb.se/websearch.

Nytt och gammalt. OCLC: 7632593 Update: 20020513. 12 July 2003 http://FirstSearch.oclc.org/WebZ/.

Nytt och gammalt: kristlig tidskrift/utgifven af O. Olsson. 2 Oct. 2003 http://websök.libris.kb.se/websearch.

The Observer. 23 May 2004 http://library.ilcso.illinois.edu/aug/.

Occasional Paper. OCLC: 14061208 Update: 20011019. 14 July 2003 http://FirstSearch.oclc.org/WebZ/.

Occasional Paper/Augustana College Library. 1 March 2004 http://websök.libris.kb
.se/websearch.

Olive Leaf. OCLC: 1761221 Update: 20030416. 12 July 2003 http://FirstSearch
.oclc.org/WebZ/.

One: The magazine for Christian Youth. 26 October 2004 http://library.uts.columbia
.edu/.

Österns härold = *The Eastern Herald.* OCLC: 27757057 Update: 20030530. 16 July
2003 http://FirstSearch.oclc.org/WebZ/.

Österns Härold. 25 April 2004 http://websök.libris.kb.se/websearch.

Österns Väktare. 25 April 2004 http://websök.libris.kb.se/websearch.

Pedagogen. 2 Oct. 2003 http://websök.libris.kb.se/websearch.

Pedagogen. 16 Feb. 2004 http://library.bethanylb.edu/search/.

Pedagogen. 6 January 2005 http://tomos.oit.umn.edu/F/.

The Picayune. OCLC: 22718865 Update: 20031010. 2 October 2004 http://FirstSearch
.oclc.org/WebZ/.

The Picayune. 6 October 2004 http://mnhs.mnpals.net/.

The Picayune. OCLC: 44387010 Update: 20040516. 2 October 2004 http://FirstSearch
.oclc.org/WebZ/.

Prärieblomman calendar för . . . OCLC: 1776210 Update: 20030416. 12 July 2003
http://FirstSearch.oclc.org/WebZ/.

Prärieblomman: kalendar. 29 Sept. 2003 http://websök.libris.kb.se/websearch.

Publication/Augustana Historical Society. OCLC: 5730065 Update: 20000216. 14 July
2003 http://FirstSearch.oclc.org/WebZ/.

Publication/Augustana Historical Society. 28 September 2003 http://websök.libris
.kb.se/websearch.

The Quarterly Release. OCLC: 49884502 Update: 20040511. 2 October 2004 http://
FirstSearch.oclc.org/WebZ/.

The Quarterly Release. 4 March 2004 http://lrc.elca.org/.

Det Rätta hemlandet. OCLC: 12675067 Update: 20000501. 12 July 2003 http://
FirstSearch.oclc.org/WebZ/.

Det Rätta hemlandet. OCLC: 12690556 Update: 20020320. 12 July 2003 http://
FirstSearch.oclc.org/WebZ/.

Det Rätta hemlandet. 2 Oct. 2003 http://websök.libris.kb.se/websearch.

Rätta hemlandet och Augustana. OCLC: 7632612 Update: 20020501. 12 July 2003
http://FirstSearch.oclc.org/WebZ/.

Rätta hemlandet och Augustana. OCLC: 12691053 Update: 20030311. 12 July 2003
http://FirstSearch.oclc.org/WebZ/.

*Det Rätta hemlandet och Augustana: månadtlig tidskrift för swenska lutherska kyrkan i
Amerika.* 26 Sept. 2003 http://websök.libris.kb.se/websearch.

Det Rätta hemlandet och missionsbladet. OCLC: 12675167 Update: 20000501. 12 July
2003 http://FirstSearch.oclc.org/WebZ/.

Det Rätta hemlandet och missionsbladet. OCLC: 12690728 Update: 20020402. 12 July
2003 http://FirstSearch.oclc.org/WebZ/.

Resource. OCLC: 1763791 Update: 20040411. 26 February 2005 http://FirstSearch
.oclc.org/WebZ/.

The Rockety-1. OCLC: 16172268 Update: 19950331. 16 July 2003 http://FirstSearch
.oclc.org/WebZ/.

The "Rockety-1 . . ." 10 Oct. 2003 http://websök.libris.kb.se/websearch.

Runes. 11 May 2004 http://mnpals.gustavus.edu.

Saga. OCLC: 15615907 Update: 20010427. 16 July 2003 http://FirstSearch.oclc .org/WebZ/.

Schibboleth. 3 Oct. 2003 http://websök.libris.kb.se/websearch.

The Seminary Review. OCLC: 1716770 Update: 20011017. 26 February 2005 http:// FirstSearch.oclc.org/WebZ/.

Silfver jubileums minneskrift: kalendar. OCLC: 44190011 Update: 20000606. 19 July 2003 http://FirstSearch.oclc.org/WebZ/.

Sions-Bladet. OCLC: 9706614 Update: 20020704. 16 July 2003 http://FirstSearch .oclc.org/WebZ/.

Skaffaren. OCLC: 1764913 Update: 20030517. 15 July 2003 http://FirstSearch.oclc .org/WebZ/.

Skaffaren. OCLC: 21922162 Update: 20030607. 15 July 2003 http://FirstSearch.oclc .org/WebZ/.

Skaffaren. 3 Oct. 2003 http://websök.libris.kb.se/websearch> (NB Two different records).

Skaffaren och Minnesota stats tidning. OCLC: 21922143 Update: 20030607. 15 July 2003 http://FirstSearch.oclc.org/WebZ/.

Skaffaren och Minnesota stats tidning. 3 Oct. 2003 http://websök.libris.kb.se/ websearch.

Skolvännen: North Star Signal: tidning för kyrkan, skolan och hemmet. 10 Oct. 2003 http://websök.libris.kb.se/websearch.

Solstrålen: textblad för de minsta barnen i söndagsskolan. 13 Oct. 2003 http://websök .libris.kb.se/websearch.

Student–Katalog . . . Augustana College and Seminary. 1 March 2004 http://websök .libris.kb.se/websearch.

Svenska amerikanaren hemlandet. OCLC: 9611386 Update: 20030530. 12 July 2003 http://FirstSearch.oclc.org/WebZ/.

Svenska amerikanaren hemlandet. 22 June 2003 http://www.wiscat.net.

Svenska Canada–tidningen. OCLC: 21102782 Update: 20030606. 16 July 2003 http:// FirstSearch.oclc.org/WebZ/.

Svenska Canada–tidningen. 7 Oct. 2003 http://websök.libris.kb.se/websearch.

Swedish American Genealogist. OCLC: 7250412 Update: 20040213. 2 October 2004 http://FirstSearch.oclc.org/WebZ/.

Swedish American Genealogist. 7 October 2004 http://websök.libris.kb.se/ websearch.

Swedish American Genealogist. 18 June 2004 http://www.augustana.edu/ administration/swenson/SAG.html/.

Swenson Center News. OCLC: 15146665 Update: 20040210. 2 October 2004 http:// FirstSearch.oclc.org/WebZ/.

Swenson Center News. 28 September 2004 http://websök.libris.kb.se/websearch.

Swenson Center News. 18 June 2004 http://www.augustana.edu/administration/ swenson/SAG.html/.

Teen Talk. OCLC: 52062906 Update: 20030415. 12 July 2003 http://FirstSearch.oclc .org/WebZ/.

Textblad för söndagsskolan. 14 Oct. 2003 http://websök.libris.kb.se/websearch.

Theological Studies and Issues. OCLC: 32006102 Update: 20011022. 12 July 2003 http://FirstSearch.oclc.org/WebZ/.

Tidskrift för Svensk Ev. Luth. kyrkohistoria i N. Amerika och för teologiska och kyrkliga frågor. OCLC: 23934526 Update: 19950609. 19 July 2003 http://FirstSearch.oclc.org/WebZ/.

Tidskrift för teologi och kyrkliga frågor . . . OCLC: 41054882 Update: 20001214. 14 July 2003 http://FirstSearch.oclc.org/WebZ/.

Tidskrift för teologi och kyrkliga frågor. OCLC: 42340535 Update: 20001222. 12 July 2003 http://FirstSearch.oclc.org/WebZ/.

Tidskrift för teologi och kyrkliga frågor. 3 Oct. 2003 http://websök.libris.kb.se/websearch.

Till werksamhet. 2 Oct. 2003 http://websök.libris.kb.se/websearch.

Ungdoms-vännen. OCLC: 7432696 Update: 20000602. 12 July 2003 http://FirstSearch.oclc.org/WebZ/.

Ungdoms–vännen: illustrerad tidskrift för främjande af sann gudsfruktan och allmänt nyttiga kunskapers spridning. 3 Oct. 2003 http://websök.libris.kb.se/websearch.

Ungdoms–vännen: illustrerad tidskrift för hemmet. 3 Oct. 2003 http://websök.libris.kb.se/websearch.

Ungdomsvännen; illustrerad tidskrift för hemmet . . . OCLC: 40314670 Update: 19981115. 12 July 2003 http://FirstSearch.oclc.org/WebZ/.

The Upsala Alumni Gazette. OCLC: 62294888. Update: 20051117. 21 Oct. 2006 http://FirstSearch.oclc.org/WebZ/

Upsala Alumni Magazine. OCLC: 62289404. Update: 20051221. 21 Oct. 2006 http://FirstSearch.oclc.org/WebZ/

Upsala Alumni News. OCLC: 62724652. Update: 20051221. 21 Oct. 2006 http://FirstSearch.oclc.org/WebZ/

Upsala Gazette. OCLC: 62332539. Update: 20051123. 21 Oct. 2006 http://FirstSearch.oclc.org/WebZ/

Upsala Gazette. OCLC: 62332555. Update: 20051123. 21 Oct. 2006 http://FirstSearch.oclc.org/WebZ/

Upsala Reports. OCLC: 63173834. Update: 20060126. 21 Oct. 2006 http://FirstSearch.oclc.org/WebZ/

The Upsalite. OCLC: 36110676 Update: 19961219. 2 October 2004 http://FirstSearch.oclc.org/WebZ/.

The Upsalite. 11 October 2003 http://websök.libris.kb.se/websearch.

Utah Missionären. 29 October 2004 http://tomos.oit.umn.edu/F/.

Väktaren. 29 October 2004 http://tomos.oit.umn.edu/F/.

Valkyria: Gustavus Adolphus Annual. 11 May 2004 http://mnpals.gustavus.edu.

Valkyrian. OCLC: 45311062 Update: 20001109. 12 July 2003 http://FirstSearch.oclc.org/WebZ/.

Valkyrian; illustrerad månadsskrift. OCLC: 1645949 Update: 20030111. 12 July 2003 http://FirstSearch.oclc.org/WebZ/.

Valkyrian: illustrerad månadsskrift. 11 Oct. 2003 http://websök.libris.kb.se/websearch.

Valkyrian: illustrerad månadsskrift. 30 November 2004 http://tomos.oit.umn.edu/.

Valkyrian, 1897–1909. 30 November 2004 http://tomos.oit.umn.edu/.

Vårt Hem. 14 October 2003 http://websök.libris.kb.se/websearch.

Vart Land. OCLC: 22447201 Update: 20001117. 16 July 2003 http://FirstSearch.oclc .org/WebZ/.

Vårt Land. 11 Oct. 2003 http://websök.libris.kb.se/websearch.

Vart Land. 9 February 2005 http://www.wiscat.net/.

Vestkusten. 11 Oct. 2003 http://websök.libris.kb.se/websearch.

Vestkusten = West Coast. OCLC: 9518417 Update: 20020324. 16 July 2003 http:// FirstSearch.oclc.org/WebZ/.

Vestkusten = West Coast. OCLC: 36139564 Update: 20020714. 16 July 2003 http:// FirstSearch.oclc.org/WebZ/.

Vid Juletid; vinterblommor samlade för de små . . . OCLC: 32916663 Update: 19960314. 16 July 2003 http://FirstSearch.oclc.org/WebZ/.

Vid Juletid; vinterblommor samlade för de små . . . OCLC: 25689605 Update: 20001121. 16 July 2003 http://FirstSearch.oclc.org/WebZ/.

Vid juletid: vinterblommor samlade för de små. 11 Oct. 2003 http://websök.libris .kb.se/websearch.

Vox collegi. 11 May 2004 http://mnpals.gustavus.edu.

Wahoo–bladet. 11 Oct. 2003 http://websök.libris.kb.se/websearch.

Wårt land och folk. OCLC: 26460037 Update: 20001206. 15 July 2003 http:// FirstSearch.oclc.org/WebZ/.

Wårt land och folk. 11 Oct. 2003 http://websök.libris.kb.se/websearch.

The West Central Lutheran. 11 Oct. 2003 http://websök.libris.kb.se/websearch.

The Western Lutheran. OCLC: 1586743 Update: 20011017. 16 July 2003 http:// FirstSearch.oclc.org/WebZ/.

The Western Lutheran. OCLC: 9740193 Update: 20030416. 16 July 2003 http:// FirstSearch.oclc.org/WebZ/.

The Young Lutheran's Companion. OCLC: 11577251 Update: 20011017. 15 July 2003 http://FirstSearch.oclc.org/WebZ/.

The Young Lutheran's Companion. OCLC: 43947294 Update: 20000501. 15 July 2003 http://FirstSearch.oclc.org/WebZ/.

The Young People. OCLC: 52062822 Update: 20030415. 15 July 2003 http://FirstSearch .oclc.org/WebZ/.

ELECTRONIC DATABASE SOURCES FOR AUGUSTANA EVANGELICAL LUTHERAN CHURCH AND CONFERENCE CONVENTION MINUTES/REPORTS

Augustana Evangelical Lutheran Church

Index, Minutes of the Augustana Lutheran Church, 1860–1962. OCLC: 23588494 Update: 20010405. 16 October 2004 http://FirstSearch.oclc.org/WebZ/.

Index, Minutes of the Augustana Lutheran Church, 1860–1962. 11 October 2004 http://lrc.elca.org/WebOPAC/.

Minutes. 1860–1962/Augustana Evangelical Lutheran Church. OCLC: 27863918 Update: 20040224. 16 October 2004 http://FirstSearch.oclc.org/WebZ/.

Minutes. 1860–1962/Augustana Evangelical Lutheran Church. 11 October 2004 http://lrc.elca.org/WebOPAC/.

Minutes of the annual convention/Augustana Evangelical Lutheran Church. OCLC: 7839576 Update: 20030111. 19 July 2003 http://FirstSearch.oclc.org/WebZ/.

Minutes of the . . . annual convention/Evangelical Lutheran Augustana Synod of North America. OCLC: 23807575 Update: 20000403. 19 July 2003 http://FirstSearch.oclc.org/WebZ/.

Minutes of the . . . annual convention/Evangelical Lutheran Augustana Synod of North America. OCLC: 43761531 Update: 20000403. 19 July 2003 http://FirstSearch.oclc.org/WebZ/.

Officielt referat/Scandinavian Evangelical Lutheran Augustana Synod of North America. OCLC: 13356727 Update: 20030111. 19 July 2003 http://FirstSearch.oclc.org/WebZ/.

Officielt referat/Scandinavian Evangelical Lutheran Augustana Synod of North America. OCLC: 43761068 Update: 20030111. 19 July 2003 http://FirstSearch.oclc.org/WebZ/.

Protokoll/Scandinavian Lutheran Augustana Synod of North America. OCLC: 15032498 Update: 20000403. 19 July 2003 http://FirstSearch.oclc.org/WebZ/.

Protokoll/Scandinavian Lutheran Augustana Synod of North America. OCLC: 43760771 Update: 20000526. 19 July 2003 http://FirstSearch.oclc.org/WebZ/.

Protokoll hallet [sic] vid Skandinaviska Ev. Lutherska Augustana Synodens. OCLC: 36034406 Update: 20030111. 19 July 2003 http://FirstSearch.oclc.org/WebZ/.

Referat/Evangelical Lutheran Augustana Synod of North America. OCLC: 35906452 Update: 20000403. 19 July 2003 http://FirstSearch.oclc.org/WebZ/.

Referat/Evangelical Lutheran Augustana Synod of North America. OCLC: 43761321 Update: 20000403. 19 July 2003 http://FirstSearch.oclc.org/WebZ/.

Referat/Scandinavian Evangelical Lutheran Augustana Synod of North America. OCLC: 43761160 Update: 20000403. 19 July 2003 http://FirstSearch.oclc.org/WebZ/.

Referat/Scandinavian Evangelical Lutheran Augustana Synod of North America. OCLC: 43761207 Update: 20000403. 19 July 2003 http://FirstSearch.oclc.org/WebZ/.

Report of the . . . annual convention/Evangelical Lutheran Augustana Synod of North America. OCLC: 32164728 Update: 20000403. 19 July 2003 http://FirstSearch.oclc.org/WebZ/.

Report of the . . . annual convention/Evangelical Lutheran Augustana Synod of North America. OCLC: 43761834 Update: 20000403. 19 July 2003 http://FirstSearch.oclc.org/WebZ/.

Report of the . . . synod. Augustana Evangelical Lutheran Church. OCLC: 7447492 Update: 20000403. 19 July 2003 http://FirstSearch.oclc.org/WebZ/.

Report of the . . . synod. Augustana Evangelical Lutheran Church. OCLC: 43761872 Update: 20000403. 19 July 2003 http://FirstSearch.oclc.org/WebZ/.

Report of the . . . synod. Augustana Evangelical Lutheran Church. 30 October 2004 http://ecco.easterncluster.com/.

Regional Conference Reports

California Conference

Minutes of the . . . Annual Convention/California Conference. OCLC: 54390748 Update: 20040210. 16 October 2004 http://FirstSearch.oclc.org/WebZ/.

Canada Conference

Referat över . . . årsmötets förhandlingar/Canada Conference. OCLC: 56189510 Update: 20040813. 2 October 2004 http://FirstSearch.oclc.org/WebZ/.

Central Conference

Report of the annual convention. Central Conference. OCLC: 42343499 Update: 20030417. 16 October 2004 http://FirstSearch.oclc.org/WebZ/.

Columbia Conference

Minutes [of the] . . . annual convention of the Columbia Conference of the Augustana Evangelical Lutheran Church. OCLC: 48591386 Update: 20011213. 16 October 2004 http://FirstSearch.oclc.org/WebZ/.
Referat öfver förhandlingarna vid Columbia–Konferensens. OCLC: 48591375 Update: 20030111. 16 October 2004 http://FirstSearch.oclc.org/WebZ/.

Illinois Conference

Minutes. 1861–1962. Illinois Conference. OCLC: 28490285 Update: 20020418. 16 October 2004 http://FirstSearch.oclc.org/WebZ/.
Minutes, 1861–1962. Illinois Conference. 11 October 2004 http://lrc.elca.org/WebOPAC/.
Minutes of the annual convention. Illinois Conference. OCLC: 56189727 Update: 20040813. 16 October 2004 http://FirstSearch.oclc.org/WebZ/.
Officielt referat öfver förhandlingarna wid Illinois–konferensens . . . årsmöte . . . OCLC: 49338286 Update: 20040516. 16 October 2004 http://FirstSearch.oclc.org/WebZ/.
Protokoll hållet wid Illinois–konferensens . . . mote . . . OCLC: 49338287 Update: 20040516. 16 October 2004 http://FirstSearch.oclc.org/WebZ/.

Iowa Conference

Minutes of the convention. Iowa Conference. OCLC: 5591336 Update: 20020924. 16 October 2004 http://FirstSearch.oclc.org/WebZ/.
Official minutes of the annual convention. Iowa Conference. OCLC: 42343521 Update: 20030111. 19 July 2003 http://FirstSearch.oclc.org/WebZ/.

Officielt referat öfver förhandlingarna vid Iowa–konferensens . . . årsmöte . . .
OCLC: 49346423 Update: 20040516. 16 October 2004 http://FirstSearch.oclc
.org/WebZ/.
Protokoll hållet wid Iowa–konferensens, årsmöte ... OCLC: 49338285 Update: 20040516.
16 October 2004 http://FirstSearch.oclc.org/WebZ/.

Kansas Conference

Minutes of the . . . annual convention. Kansas Conference. OCLC: 35906757 Update:
20050104. 26 February 2005 http://FirstSearch.oclc.org/WebZ/.
Protokoll hållna vid Kansas–konferensens möten åren . . . OCLC: 49338282 Update:
20040516. 16 October 2004 http://FirstSearch.oclc.org/WebZ/.
Protokoll öfver förhandlingarna vid Kansas–konferensens af Skand. Ev. Luth.
Augustana-synoden . . . årsmöte . . . OCLC: 49338283 Update: 20040516. 16 Oc-
tober 2004 http://FirstSearch.oclc.org/WebZ/.
Referat ofver [sic] forhandlingarna [sic] vid Kansas–Konferensens . . . OCLC:
36022977 Update: 20040328. 16 October 2004 http://FirstSearch.oclc.org/
WebZ/.
Referat öfver förhandlingarna wid Kansas–konferensens . . . årsmöte . . . OCLC:
49338284 Update: 20040516. 16 October 2004 http://FirstSearch.oclc.org/
WebZ/.

Minnesota Conference

Minnesota konferensens protokoll, 1869–1878. 20 October 2004 http://www.
mnpals.net/F/.
Minutes of the . . . Annual Convention . . ./. . . Minnesota Conference. OCLC: 15043548
Update: 20020403. 19 July 2003 http://FirstSearch.oclc.org/WebZ/.
Minutes of the . . . Annual Convention . . ./. . . Minnesota Conference. OCLC: 45071313
Update: 20020507. 19 July 2003 http://FirstSearch.oclc.org/WebZ/.
*Officielt referat öfver förhandlingarna vid Minnesota-konferensens af Ev. Luth. Augus-
tana-synoden . . . årsmöte . . .* OCLC: 15069829 Update: 20000926. 19 July 2003
http://FirstSearch.oclc.org/WebZ/.
*Officielt referat öfver förhandlingarna vid Minnesota-konferensens af Ev. Luth. Augustana-
synoden . . . årsmöte . . .* OCLC: 45069086 Update: 20000926. 19 July 2003 http://
FirstSearch.oclc.org/WebZ/.
Protokoll hållet wid Minnesota-konferensens . . . årsmöte . . . OCLC: 15069755 Update:
20000926. 19 July 2003 http://FirstSearch.oclc.org/WebZ/.
Protokoll hållet wid Minnesota-konferensens . . . årsmöte . . . OCLC: 45063098 Update:
20000926. 19 July 2003 http://FirstSearch.oclc.org/WebZ/.
*Referat/Evangelical Lutheran Augustana Synod of North America [Minnesota Confer-
ence]* OCLC: 15069962 Update: 20030111. 19 July 2003 http://FirstSearch.oclc
.org/WebZ/.
*Referat/Evangelical Lutheran Augustana Synod of North America [Minnesota Confer-
ence]* OCLC: 45069585 Update: 20030111. 19 July 2003 http://FirstSearch.oclc
.org/WebZ/.

Referat af förhandlingarna vid Luth. Minnesota-konferensens af Augustana-synoden . . . årsmöte . . . OCLC: 15069950 Update: 20000926. 19 July 2003 http://FirstSearch.oclc.org/WebZ/.

Referat af förhandlingarna vid Luth. Minnesota-konferensens af Augustana-synoden . . . årsmöte . . . OCLC: 45069453 Update: 20000926. 19 July 2003 http:// FirstSearch.oclc.org/WebZ/.

Referat öfver förhandlingarna vid den Luth. Minnesota konferensens af Augustana-synoden . . . årsmöte . . . OCLC: 15069922 Update: 20000926. 19 July 2003 http://FirstSearch .oclc.org/WebZ/.

Referat öfver förhandlingarna vid den Luth. Minnesota konferensens af Augustana-synoden . . . årsmöte . . . OCLC: 45069216 Update: 20000926. 19 July 2003 http://FirstSearch .oclc.org/WebZ/.

Referat öfver förhandlingarna vid Lutherska Minnesota-konferensens af Augustana-synoden . . . årsmöte . . . OCLC: 15070012 Update: 20000926. 19 July 2003 http://FirstSearch .oclc.org/WebZ/.

Referat öfver förhandlingarna vid Lutherska Minnesota-konferensens af Augustana-synoden . . . årsmöte . . . OCLC: 45069720 Update: 20000926. 19 July 2003 http://FirstSearch.oclc.org/WebZ/.

Referat öfver förhandlingarna vid Minnesota-konferensens af Ev. Luth. Augustana-synoden . . . årsmöte . . . OCLC: 15069814 Update: 20000926. 19 July 2003 http://FirstSearch .oclc.org/WebZ/.

Referat öfver förhandlingarna vid Minnesota-konferensens af Ev. Luth. Augustana-synoden . . . årsmöte . . . OCLC: 45068960 Update: 20000926. 19 July 2003 http:// FirstSearch.oclc.org/WebZ/.

Referat öfver förhandlingarna vid Minnesota-konferensens af Ev. Luth. Augustana-synoden . . . årsmöte . . . OCLC: 15069902 Update: 20000926. 19 July 2003 http:// FirstSearch.oclc.org/WebZ/.

Referat öfver förhandlingarna vid Minnesota-konferensens af Ev. Luth. Augustana-synoden . . . årsmöte . . . OCLC: 45069159 Update: 20000926. 19 July 2003 http:// FirstSearch.oclc.org/WebZ/.

Referat öfver förhandlingarna vid Minnesota-konferensens af Skand. Ev. Luth. Augustana-synoden . . . årsmöte . . . OCLC: 15069804 Update: 20000926. 19 July 2003 http://FirstSearch.oclc.org/WebZ/.

Referat öfver förhandlingarna vid Minnesota-konferensens af Skand. Ev. Luth. Augustana-synoden . . . årsmöte . . . OCLC: 45068869 Update: 20000926. 19 July 2003 http://FirstSearch.oclc.org/WebZ/.

Referat öfver förhandlingarna wid Minnesota-konferensens . . . årsmöte . . . OCLC: 15069785 Update: 20000926. 19 July 2003 http://FirstSearch.oclc.org/WebZ/.

Referat öfver förhandlingarna wid Minnesota-konferensens . . . årsmöte . . . OCLC: 45063134 Update: 20000926. 19 July 2003 http://FirstSearch.oclc.org/WebZ/.

Referat över . . . årsmötets förhandlingar/Evangelical Lutheran Augustana Synod of North America. OCLC: 15070086 Update: 20000926. 19 July 2003 http:// FirstSearch.oclc.org/WebZ/.

Referat över . . . årsmötets förhandlingar/Evangelical Lutheran Augustana Synod of North America. OCLC: 45071214 Update: 20000926. 19 July 2003 http:// FirstSearch.oclc.org/WebZ/.

Referat över förhandlingarna vid . . . årsmöte . . ./Evangelical Lutheran Augustana Synod of North America. OCLC: 15070043 Update: 20000926. 19 July 2003 http:// FirstSearch.oclc.org/WebZ/.

Referat över förhandlingarna vid . . . årsmöte . . ./Evangelical Lutheran Augustana Synod of North America. OCLC: 45071107 Update: 20000926. 19 July 2003 http://First-Search.oclc.org/WebZ/.

Report from the . . . Annual Convention of the Evangelical Lutheran Minnesota Conference . . . OCLC: 15070134 Update: 20020515. 19 July 2003 http://FirstSearch.oclc .org/WebZ/.

Report from the . . . Annual Convention of the Evangelical Lutheran Minnesota Conference . . . OCLC: 45070095 Update: 20020315. 19 July 2003 http://FirstSearch.oclc .org/WebZ/.

Nebraska Conference

Minutes of the annual convention/Nebraska Conference. OCLC: 43769431 Update: 20000404. 16 October 2004 http://FirstSearch.oclc.org/WebZ/.

New England Conference

Minutes of the annual convention/New England Conference. OCLC: 56209287 Update: 20040817. 16 October 2004 http://FirstSearch.oclc.org/WebZ/.

New York Conference

Minutes of the . . . annual convention/New York Conference. OCLC: 42769305 Update: 19991104. 19 July 2003 http://FirstSearch.oclc.org/WebZ/.

Protokoll hållet wid New York-konferensens . . . årsmöte . . . OCLC: 49338289 Update: 20040516. 16 October 2004 http://FirstSearch.oclc.org/WebZ/.

Referat öfver förhandlingarna vid årsmötet. [New York Conference]. OCLC: 49824852 Update: 20030401. 19 July 2003 http://FirstSearch.oclc.org/WebZ/.

Referat öfver förhandlingarna vid New York-konferensens af Ev. Luth. Augustana-synoden . . . årsmöte . . . OCLC: 40662945 Update: 19990122. 19 July 2003 http://FirstSearch.oclc.org/WebZ/.

Pacific Conference

Referat öfver förhandlingarna vid Pacific-Konferensens . . . OCLC: 13028300 Update: 20030111. 16 October 2004 http://FirstSearch.oclc.org/WebZ/.

Red River Valley Conference

Minutes of the . . . Annual Convention/Red River Valley Conference. OCLC: 3506928 Update: 20040515. 16 October 2004 http://FirstSearch.oclc.org/ WebZ/.

Minutes of the . . . Annual Convention/Red River Valley Conference. OCLC: 3507738 Update: 20040515. 16 October 2004 http://FirstSearch.oclc.org/WebZ/.

Superior Conference

Minutes of the annual convention/Superior Conference. OCLC: 43769281 Update: 20000404. 16 October 2004 http://FirstSearch.oclc.org/WebZ/.
Minutes of the . . . annual convention of the Superior Conference. OCLC: 54506509 Update: 20040611. 16 October 2004 http://FirstSearch.oclc.org/WebZ/.

Texas Conference

Minutes of the annual convention . . . Texas Conference. OCLC: 25503334 Update: 20011023. 18 October 2004 http://FirstSearch.oclc.org/WebZ/.
Minutes of the annual convention of the Texas Conference . . . OCLC: 56218158 Update: 20040818. 16 October 2004 http://FirstSearch.oclc.org/WebZ/.

West Central Conference

Minutes of the . . . annual convention. West Central Conference. OCLC: 35906758 Update: 19961113. 16 October 2004 http://FirstSearch.oclc.org/WebZ/.

TYPESCRIPT SOURCES

Augustana College Library Publications Inventory as of 11/03, ts. Augustana College Library, Rock Island, IL. 17 Nov. 2003.
Augustana College Library Occasional Papers Inventory as of 11/03, ts. Augustana College Library, Rock Island, IL. 17 Nov. 2003.
Augustana Historical Society Publications Available: June 2000, ts. 7 March 2003.
Baker, Sharon. Krauth Memorial Library, Lutheran Theological Seminary, Philadelphia, PA. Periodicals Published by Augustana Lutheran Church. February 2003 Working Draft, ts. 14 February 2003.
———. Krauth Memorial Library, Lutheran Theological Seminary, Philadelphia, PA. Periodicals (And Serials) Published by Augustana Lutheran Church. Second List/June, 2003 Working Draft, ts. 24 June 2003.
Doksansky, Iris. Archives, Luther Library, Midland Lutheran College, Fremont, NE. Periodicals Published by Augustana Lutheran Church. February 2003 Working Draft, ts. 12 February 2003.
———. Archives, Luther Library, Midland Lutheran College, Fremont, NE. Periodicals (And Serials) Published by Augustana Lutheran Church. Second List/June 2003 Working Draft, ts. 22 August 2003.

Ebertz, Susan. Reu Memorial Library, Wartburg Theological Seminary, Dubuque, IA. Periodicals Published by Augustana Lutheran Church. February 2003 Working Draft, ts. 23 January 2004.

———. Reu Memorial Library, Wartburg Theological Seminary, Dubuque, IA. Periodicals (And Serials) Published by Augustana Lutheran Church. Second List/June, 2003 Working Draft, ts. 09 June 2004.

Eldevik, Bruce. Library, Luther Seminary, St. Paul, MN. Periodicals Published by Augustana Lutheran Church. February 2003 Working Draft, ts. 16 April 2003.

Hamma Library, Trinity Lutheran Seminary, Columbis, OH. A Selective Union List of Serial Publications issued by the Augustana Lutheran Synod, and its Agencies and Associates: 1855–1962 . . ., ts. 16 November 2004.

Hilker, Pat. List of Serials Held at California Lutheran University, ts. 11 June 2003.

Jenner, Anne. Swenson Swedish Immigration Research Center, Augustana College, Rock Island, IL. A Selective Union List of Serial Publications Issued by the Augustana Lutheran Synod, and its Agencies and Associates: 1855–1962 . . . holdings in the Swenson Center as of Jan. 2005, ts. 28 January 2005.

Jesuit-Krauss-McCormick Library, Lutheran School of Theology, Chicago, IL. Periodicals Published by Augustana Lutheran Church. February 2003 Working Draft, ts. 7 May 2003.

———. Suggestions for titles of Augustana serial publications to be checked in the pre–1979 in–library card catalog, ts. 10 December 2004.

Mummert, Sara. A. R. Wentz Library, Lutheran Theological Seminary at Gettysburg, Gettysburg, PA. Periodicals Published by Augustana Lutheran Church. February 2003 Working Draft, ts. 1 March 2003.

———. A. R. Wentz Library, Lutheran Theological Seminary at Gettysburg, Gettysburg, PA. Periodicals (And Serials) Published by Augustana Lutheran Church. Second List/June, 2003 Working Draft, ts. 24 July 2003.

Roth, Sara Fox. Tri–Synod Archives, Passavant Center, Thiel College, Greenville, PA. Periodicals Published by Augustana Lutheran Church. February 2003 Working Draft, ts. 30 October 2003.

———. Tri–Synod Archives, Passavant Center, Thiel College, Greenville, PA. Periodicals (And Serials) Published by Augustana Lutheran Church. Second List/June, 2003 Working Draft, ts. 30 October 2003.

Strunk, Jeannine. List of Augustana Serials Held at Evangelical Lutheran Church in America Archives, ts. 15 May 2003.

———. List of Lutheran Serials with OCLC #, ts. 23 June 2003.

———. List of Serials with Historical Charts, ts. 23 June 2003.

Thorstensson, Edi. Folke Bernadotte Memorial Library, Gustavus Adolphus College, St. Peter, MN. Periodicals Published by Augustana Lutheran Church. February 2003 Working Draft, ts. 15 April 2004.

———. Folke Bernadotte Memorial Library, Gustavus Adolphus College, St. Peter, MN. Periodicals (And Serials) Published by Augustana Lutheran Church. Second List/June, 2003 Working Draft, ts. 15 April 2004.

———. Folke Bernadotte Memorial Library, Gustavus Adolphus College, St. Peter, MN. Augustana Periodicals Survey, Gustavus Adolphus College [and Archives], ts. 18 February 2005.

ELECTRONIC MAIL SOURCES

Adler, Sharon. "Re: [Infohawk] Ask Staff Request." E-mail to the author. 28 Oct. 2004.

Alt, Marti. "Ask–a–Librarian Ohio State University." E-mail to the author. 09 Oct. 2004.

Anderson, Arvid. "Re: Augustana Heritage Association Newsletter." E-mail to the author. 18 Sept. 2003.

Billesbach, Ann. "Re: Swedish language newspaper." E-mail to the author. 15 Aug. 2003.

Deppe, Ruth Ann. "Augustana Heritage periodicals." E-mail to the author. 17 Oct. 2003.

Dixon, Clay Edward. "Periodical List." E-mail to the author. 12 June 2003.

Doksansky, Iris. "Luther yearbooks." E-mail to the author. 07 July 2005.

Eckhardt, Vicki. "Lutheran Periodicals." E-mail to the author. 26 Feb. 2003.

Eldevik, Bruce. "Augustana Serials Project." E-mail to the author. 30 April 2003.

———. "Re: Augustana Serials Project." E-mail to the author. 9 May 2003.

Forbes, Susan. "Re: Reference question." E-mail to the author. 20 Jan. 2005.

Hilker, Pat. "List of Serials Held at California Lutheran University." E-mail to the author. 2 June 2003.

Jenner, Anne. "Re: Augustana serial publications report." E-mail to the author. 31 Jan. 2005.

Kern, Kathleen. "Re: Referat ofver forhandlingarna." E-mail to the author. 06 Dec. 2004.

Knutsson, Monica. "union list Augustana Heritage Association." E-mail to the author. 28 Aug. 2003.

Krieger, Mary. "Information about archives/library." E-mail to the author. 10 Dec. 2004.

Lohrentz, Kenneth. "Re: Attn: Ref Question." E-mail to the author. 01 Feb. 2005.

Mummert, Sara. "Augustana Periodicals." E-mail to the author. 26 Feb. 2003.

———. "Re: Ask the Librarian Question." E-mail to the author. 30 March 2005.

Nielsen, Steve. "MHS Library holdings for microfilmed newspapers/serials." E-mail to the author. 03 March 2005.

———. "MHS library holdings information." E-mail to the author. 31 March 2005.

———. "Ratta Hemlandet och Augustana." E-mail to the author. 06 April 2005.

———. "Re: MHS Library holdings for microfilmed newspapers/serials." E-mail to the author. 04 March 2005.

———. "The Picayune." E-mail to the author. 07 Oct. 2004.

Peterson, Jean. "Augie Pubs." E-mail to the author. 10 June 2003.

Pfahl, Carla. "Holdings Information for MNCAT Record." E-mail to the author. 09 Nov. 2004.

Seattle Public Library, Reference Services. "Library Question." E-mail to the author. 14 Nov. 2004.

Strunk, Jeannine. "Re: Augustana holdings list." E-mail to the author. 20 June 2003.

Thoreson, Joel. "Augustana Archives." E-mail to the author. 27 Jan. 2003.

———. "Augustana Conference minutes." E-mail to the author. 03 Dec. 2004.

———. "Re: Augustana Conferences." E-mail to the author. 27 May 2003.
———. "Re: Augustana Conferences." E-mail to the author. 03 June 2003.
———. "Re: Augustana Synod convention reports language." E-mail to the author. 12 Jan. 2005.
———. "Re: Augustana Synod Names." E-mail to the author. 6 Aug. 2003.
Thorstensson, Edi. "Augustana Periodicals Survey." E-mail to the author. 18 Feb. 2005.
———. "Re: Augustana Periodicals Survey." E-mail to the author. 14 April 2005.
University of Illinois, Urbana–Champaign, Reference Library. "Re: Ungdomsvän-nen." E-mail to the author. 24 April 2005.
Westly, Travis. "Library Question—Answer [Question #70311]." E-mail to the author. 25 Feb. 2005.
Wiederaenders, Bob. "Augustana Serials." E-mail to the author. 5 June 2003.

MANUSCRIPT SOURCES

Baker, Sharon. Letter to the author. 5 March 2003.
———. Letter to the author. 9 July 2003.
Bergeron, Jeanette M. Letter to the author. 4 March 2003.
Brandelle, Jeannette. Letter to the author. 15 Oct. 2003.
Doksansky, Iris. ELCA Archives Inventory Forms. 12 Feb. 2003.
Etzel, Brent. Letter to the author. 17 Nov. 2003.
Hultgren, Arland J. Letter to the author. 17 Dec. 2001.

Chronological Listing of Titles

Titles from the union list are arranged in the following list by the beginning year of publication.

1854

Svenska Posten

Illinois Conference Minutes of the . . . annual convention

1855

Hemlandet: det Gamla och det Nya

1856

Det Rätta Hemlandet

1857

Minnesota Posten

1858

Minnesota Conference/Minutes of the . . . annual convention

1860

Protokoll hållet wid Skandinaviska ev. Lutherska Augustana-Synodens . . . årsmöte

1863

Det Rätta Hemlandet och Missionsbladet

1868

Augustana

1869

Iowa Conference/Minutes of the . . . annual convention

Det Rätta Hemlandet och Augustana

1870

Kansas Conference/Minutes of the . . . annual convention
Missionären (Chicago, IL)
New York Conference/Minutes of the . . . annual convention

1871

Luthersk Kyrkotidning (Vasa, MN)
Student-Katalog

1872

Luth. Kyrkotidning

1873

Luthersk Kyrkotidning (Red Wing, MN)
Nytt och Gammalt

1874

Augustana
Barnvännen

1875

Evangelisk Luthersk Tidskrift för Kyrkan Skolan och Hemmet
Fridens Härold

1876

Missionären (Moline, IL)
Augustana College Catalog

1877

Catalogue of Gustavus Adolphus College
Minnesota Stats Tidning
Nåd och Sanning

1878

Schibboleth
Skaffaren
Skolvännen

1879

Augustana och Missionären
Kansas Stats Tidning
Ungdoms-Vännen

1880

Evangelisk Luthersk Barntidning
Korsbaneret

1881

Augustana Observer
Bethania

1882

Catalogue of Bethany Academy at Lindsborg, Kansas
Kansas Posten
Skaffaren och Minnesota Stats Tidning

1883

Excelsior
Olive Leaf

1884

Academica
Luther Academy Catalog
Officielt referat öfwer förhandlingarna wid Skandinaviska ev. Luth.
    Augustana-Synodens . . . årsmöte

1885

Pedagogen
Skaffaren
Till Verksamhet

1886

Barnens Tidning
Bethany College Bulletin
Bethany College Catalog
Blommor vid Vägen
Children's Friend
Ebenezer
Vårt Land och Folk

1887

Framåt (Lindsborg, KS)
Hemvännen
Lekkamraten
Nebraska Conference/Minutes of the . . . annual convention
Vestkusten

1888

Catalogue of Hope Academy, Moorhead, Minnesota
Hem-Missionären
Österns Väktare
Pacific Conference/Referat öfwer förhandlingarna vid
    Pacific-Konferensens
Wahoo-Bladet

1889

Augustana
Home Missionary
Utah Missionären

1890

Balder
Julklockorna
Juvelskrivet
Söndagsskolans Textblad
Vårt Land

1891

Annual Messenger
Bethania
Folkvännen
Fosterlandet
Gustaviana
Heimdall
Referat öfwer förhandlingarna wid Skand. Evangelisk-Lutherska Augustana-Synodens . . . årsmöte
Vox Collegi

1892

The Alumnus
Bethany Messenger
För-Gät-Mig-Ej
Framåt (Providence, RI)
Lyceum Annual
Sions Väktare
Ungdomens Tidning
The Young Observer

1893

California Conference/Minutes of the . . . annual convention
Columbia Conference/Minutes of the . . . annual convention
Dorkas
Den Lille Missionären
Upsala College Catalog
Väktaren

1894

Almanack
Augustana Journal
Framåt (Brooklyn, NY)

1895

Bethany's Budbäraren
Canada
Minnesota Stats Tidning
Referat öfwer förhandlingarna wid Evangelisk-Lutherska Augustana-Synodens . . . årsmöte
Ungdoms-Vännen

1896

Bethany Annual
Gustavus Journal
Österns Härold
Sjukvännen

1897

Förgät-Mig-Ej
Lindsborgs-Posten
Valkyrian

1898

Augustana Library Publications
Lille Barnvännen
Tidskrift för Svensk Ev. Luth. Kyrkohistoria i N. Amerika och för
  Teologiska och Kyrkliga Frågor
Vid Juletid

1899

Tidskrift för Teologi och Kyrkliga Frågor

1900

Augustana Theological Quarterly
Axplockerskan
Class Annual
Columbia
Hemåt
Nytt Bibliotek för Barn och Ungdom
Prärieblomman
Runan

1902

Augustana Observer
Bethany Messenger
För-Gät-Mig-Ej
Kansas Missions Tidning

1903

Luthersk Tidskrift för Hednamission och Diakoni
Our Church Messenger
Vår Nya Kyrkotidning

1904

College Calendar/Minnesota College
Kyrkotidning för Cleveland-Distriktet
Luther Academy Visitor
Manhem
Solstrålen
Textblad för Söndagsskolan
Väktaren

1905

Augustana Bulletin
Betania
College Breezes

Församlingsvännen
Garnet and Silver-Gray
Julrunan
Kyrkobladet
Kyrkotidning för Jamestown-Distriktet af Svenska Lutherska New
   York-Konferensen
Upsala Gazette

1906

Almanac
Kyrkosången
Missionären
Missions-Tidning
Runes
Solglimten

1907

Fylgia
Fyrbåken
Kyrkohärolden
Sions-Bladet
Svenska Canada-Tidningen
Young Lutheran's Companion

1908

Daisy
Kansas Young Lutheran
Kina Missionären
Luthersk Kyrkotidning

1909

Luther College Catalog
Luther College Visitor
The Picayune
Stadsmissionären
Tabitha
Valkyria
Vårt Hem

1910

Jubilee
North Star Signal
Superior Conference/Minutes of the . . . annual convention

1911

The Lutheran Companion

1912

Breidablick
Christian Messenger

The Moccasin
The Rockety-I

1913

Calendar/Minnesota College
Canada Conference/Minutes of the . . . annual convention
Guldax
New England Conference/Minutes of the . . . annual convention
Red River Valley Conference/Minutes of the . . . annual convention

1914

Canada Härold
Luther College & Academy Yearbook
Svenska Amerikanaren Hemlandet

1915

BethphageBiblioteket
My Church

1916

God Jul

1917

Gustavian
Inner Mission Herald
Protokoll hållet vid Skandinaviska Ev. Lutherska Augustana
  Synodens

1918

Årsbok/Svenska Litterära Sällskapet De Nio
Luther College Advocate

1919

Canada News

1920

Bible Banner
Bible Study Quarterly
Gustavian Weekly
L.B.A. Bulletin
Lutheran Messenger

1921

Diakoniss-Baneret
Missionary Calendar
Our Church
The Picayune (Annual)

1922

Augustana Quarterly
Honan Glimpses
Luther Bladet
Messenger

1923

Augustana Luther Leaguer
Texas Conference/Minutes of the . . . annual convention
Young People

1924

Bond
Deaconess Banner
Lutheran Publications
Minutes of the . . . annual convention/Evangelical Lutheran
    Augustana Synod of North America
Upsala Gazette

1925

City Missionary
Lutheran Brotherhood
Mission-Tidings

1926

Augustana Foreign Missionary
New England Luther Leaguer
News Bulletin

1927

Columbia Lutheran

1928

Little Folks

1929

Bible Study Quarterly: Student's Edition
Bible Study Quarterly: Teacher's Edition
The Upsalite

1930

Beacon
Church Paper for the Cleveland District

1931

Augustana Historical Society Publications
Kansas Conference Lutheran
Lutheran Beacon
Lutheran Review

1932

Church School Teacher
The Conference Messenger

1935

Challenger

1937

Report of the . . . annual convention/Evangelical Lutheran Augustana
    Synod of North America
Western Lutheran

1938

Saga

1939

Minnesota Lutheran

1940

The Home Altar
Bethphage Messenger
Theological Studies and Issues

1941

Minnesota Conference Charities

1943

Minnesota Conference Advance

1944

Greater Gustavus Quarterly
Pastor's Paragraphs

1945

New England Conference News
Upsala Alumni News

1946

Canadian Crusader
Home Mission News
What's New in Books

1947

Augustana Overseas
Superior Light

1948

Augustana Annual
Augustana-Men
Augustana Missions
New England Lutheran
Report of the . . . Synod/Augustana Evangelical Lutheran Church

1949

The Advance
Augustana Seminary Review
Lutheran Quarterly

1950

All Yours
Augustana Lutheran
Augustana Lutheranen
Reflector
The Uniting Word

1951

Augustana Overseas
One

1952

    A Drop of Ink
    Lutheran Brotherhood Bond
    The Lutheran Companion
    The Social Missions Review

1953

    Upsala Alumni Magazine

1954

    Augustana Churchmen
    Bethany College Bulletin/Alumni News
    Junior Life
    Teen Talk
    'Til 8 Stories

1955

    Bulletin/Lutheran Bible Institute
    Views

1956

    Augustana
    Augustana Missions
    Lutheran Social Service News
    Newsletter/Board of World Missions

1957

    Augustana Library Publications, Occasional Paper
    Augustana Lutheran Churchmen
    The Quarterly Release

1958

    From Luther
    Lutheran Libraries
    Newsletter of Augustana Brotherhood
    West Central Lutheran

1959

    Bethanian
    Central Conference/Report of the annual convention
    Lutheran Women's World
    Occasional Paper/Augustana College Library
    Resource
    West Central Conference/Minutes of the . . . annual convention

1960

    Augustana College Bulletin
    Lutheran Women
    Thru 8 Stories

1962

    The Seminary Review

1963

Publication/Augustana Historical Society

1965

Bethany College Bulletin/Bethany Magazine
The Immanuel Banner

1969

The Upsala Alumni Gazette

1971

Immanuel Medical Center Banner
Junction

1972

None of the Above
The Observer

1973

Banner (Omaha, NE)
The Gustavian Weekly

1974

Upsala Reports

1979

Arkivfynd
Augustana College Magazine

1981

Swedish American Genealogist

1983

Newsletter/Augustana Historical Society

1984

Bethany Magazine

1986

Augustana College Library Occasional Paper
Swenson Center News

1988

Bethany College Messenger

1991

The Gazette

1992

Augustana College Library Publications

1995

Augustana Heritage Newsletter
Gustavus Quarterly

1999

The Augustana Heritage Newsletter

Geographical Index

Titles from the union list are arranged in the following list by the geographical location at which first publication occurred. Subsequent places of publication are not included. The name of the state is followed by the publication title and then the name of the city of publication.

California
    Ebenezer: San Francisco
    Hemåt: San Francisco
    Luther Bladet: Escalon
    Lutheran Review: Modesto
    Vårt Hem: Oakland
    Vestkusten: San Francisco

Canada
    Canada: Winnipeg, Manitoba
    Canada Härold: Calgary, Alberta, and Winnipeg, Manitoba
    Canada News: s.l.
    Canadian Crusader: Saskatoon, Saskatchewan
    Sions Väktare: Winnipeg, Manitoba
    Svenska Canada-Tidningen: Winnipeg, Manitoba
    Väktaren: Winnipeg, Manitoba
    Views: Haney, British Columbia

China
    Honan Glimpses: Shekow & Hankow

Väktaren
Vårt Land och Folk

Illinois (Rock Island)
Almanac
Almanack
Alumnus
Augustana (1874)
Augustana (1889)
Augustana (1956)
Augustana Annual
Augustana Bulletin
Augustana Churchmen
Augustana College Bulletin
Augustana College Catalog
Augustana College Library Occasional Paper
Augustana College Library Publications
Augustana College Magazine
Augustana Foreign Missionary
Augustana Historical Society Publications
Augustana Journal
Augustana Library Publications
Augustana Library Publications, Occasional Paper
Augustana Lutheran
Augustana Lutheran Churchmen
Augustana Lutheranen
Augustana Men
Augustana Observer (1902)
Augustana Quarterly
Augustana Seminary Review
Augustana Theological Quarterly
Balder
Beacon
Betania
Bible Study Quarterly
Bible Study Quarterly: Student's Edition
Bible Study Quarterly: Teacher's Edition
Blommor vid Vägen
Calendar
Challenger
Church Paper for the Cleveland District
Church School Teacher
Class Annual

Protokoll Hållet wid Skandinaviska Ev. Lutherska Augustana-Synodens
. . . *Årsmöte*
Publication / Augustana Historical Society
Referat öfwer Förhandlingarna wid Evangelisk-Lutherska Augustana-
Synodens . . . *Årsmöte*
Referat öfwer Förhandlingarna wid Skand. Evangelisk-Lutherska
Augustana-Synodens . . . *Årsmöte*
Report of the . . . *Annual Conventiion/Evangelical Lutheran*
Augustana Synod of North America
Report of the . . . *Synod/Augustana Evangelical Lutheran Church*
The Rockety-I
Runan
Saga
The Seminary Review
Skolvännen
Solglimten
Solstrålen
Söndagsskolans Textblad
Swenson Center News
Teen Talk
Textblad för Söndagsskolan
Theological Studies and Issues
Thru 8 Stories
Tidskrift för Svensk Ev. Luth. Kyrkohistoria i N. Amerika och för
Teologiska och Kyrkliga Frågor
Til 8 Stories
Vårt Hem
West Central Lutheran
What's New in Books
Young Lutheran's Companion
The Young Observer
Young People

Iowa

L.B.A. Bulletin: Des Moines

Kansas (Lindsborg)

Academica
Bethania
Bethanian
Bethany Annual
Bethany College Bulletin
Bethany College Bulletin/Alumni News

Bethany College Bulletin / Bethany Magazine
Bethany College Catalog
Bethany College Messenger
Bethany Magazine
Bethany Messenger (1892)
Bethany Messenger (1902)
Bethany's Budbäraren
Catalogue of Bethany Academy at Lindsborg, Kansas
Christian Messenger
Daisy
Förgat-Mig-Ej (1902)
Framåt (Lindsborg, KS: 1887)
Kansas Conference Lutheran
Kansas Posten
Kansas Stats Tidning
Kansas Young Lutheran
Lindsborgs-Posten
Nytt och Gammalt
Pedagogen

Massachusetts

Evangelisk Luthersk Tidskrift för Kyrkan Skolan och Hemmet: Boston
Missionären: Worcester
New England Luther Leaguer: Worcester

Minnesota

Catalog of Hope Academy, Moorhead, Minnesota
    Ev. Luthersk Tidskrift: Red Wing
Folkvännen: Moorhead
Luth. Kyrkotidning: Vasa
Luthersk Kyrkotidning: Red Wing
Luthersk Kyrkotidning: Vasa
Minnesota Posten: Red Wing
North Star Signal: Warren
Skaffaren: Red Wing

Minnesota (Minneapolis)

Advance
All Yours
Augustana Missions (1948)
Augustana Missions (1956)
Augustana Overseas (1947)
Augustana Overseas (1951)
Bible Banner

Bulletin / Lutheran Bible Institute
Calendar / Minnesota College
College Calendar / Minnesota College
Förgät-Mig-Ej
Home Mission News
Inner Mission Herald
Kyrkosången
Lutheran Brotherhood Bond
Lutheran Libraries
Messenger
Minnesota Conference Advance
Minnesota Conference Charities
Minnesota Stats Tidning (1877)
The Moccasin
News Bulletin / Lutheran Brotherhood of America
Newsletter / Board of World Missions
Pastor's Paragraphs
The Picayune
The Picayune (Annual)
Reflector
The Social Missions Review

Minnesota (St. Paul)

Kina Missionären
Kyrkohärolden
L.B.I. Bulletin
Luthersk Tidskrift för Hednamission och Diakoni
Minnesota Lutheran
Minnesota Stats Tidning (1895)
Skaffaren (St. Paul, MN: 1885)
Skaffaren och Minnesota Stats Tidning
Tabitha
Ungdoms-Vännen

Minnesota (St. Peter)

Annual Messenger
Arkivfynd
Breidablick
Catalogue of Gustavus Adolphus College
College Breezes
Excelsior
Greater Gustavus Quarterly
Gustavian
Gustavian Weekly (1920)

The Gustavian Weekly (1973)
Gustaviana
Gustavus Journal
Gustavus Quarterly
Heimdall
Junction
Manhem
None of the Above
Runes
Valkyria
Vox Collegi

Nebraska

Bethphage Messenger: Axtell
BethphageBiblioteket: Axtell
Guldax: Axtell

Nebraska (Omaha)

Axplockerskan
Banner (Omaha, NE)
Deaconess Banner
Diakoniss-Baneret
Dorkas
The Immanuel Banner
Immanuel Medical Center Banner
Den Lille Barnvännen
Sjukvännen

Nebraska (Wahoo)

From Luther
Luther Academy Catalog
Luther Academy Visitor
Luther College Advocate
Luther College & Academy Yearbook
Luther College Catalog
Luther College Visitor
Till Verksamhet
Wahoo-Bladet

New Jersey

Årsbok/Svenska Litterära Sällskapet de Nio: Kenilworth and East Orange
The Gazette: East Orange
The Upsala Alumni Gazette: East Orange

Upsala Alumni Magazine: East Orange
Upsala Alumni News: East Orange
Upsala College Catalog: Kenilworth & East Orange
Upsala Gazette: Kenilworth & East Orange
Upsala Reports: East Orange
The Upsalite: East Orange

New York
Barnvännen: New York
Framåt (Brooklyn, NY: 1894)
Fridens Härold: Brooklyn
Österns Härold: Brooklyn
Österns Väktare: Jamestown
Valkyrian: New York
Vårt Land: Jamestown

Ohio
One: Columbus

Pennsylvania
Augustana Observer (Philadelphia, PA: 1881)
Församlingsvännen: Duquesne
Lutheran Quarterly: Gettysburg
Resource: Philadelphia

Rhode Island
Framåt: Providence
Vår Nya Kyrkotidning: Pontiac

Utah
Utah Missionären: Salt Lake City

Washington
Columbia: LaConner
Columbia Lutheran: Tacoma
Sions-Bladet: Tacoma
Western Lutheran: Olympia

Personal Name Index

Personal names included in the narrative essays in the titles lists are included in this personal name index. The full name and birth and death dates, when verified, are shown for further identification. Titles of publications with which each individual is associated are also indicated. Refer to title entry for additional information.

Abrahamson, L. G. (Laurentius Gustav), 1856–1946
Augustana (1889)
Augustana Historical Society Publications
Augustana och Missionären
Ungdomens Tidning

Adolphson, Gilbert
The Lutheran Companion (1911)

Alexis, J. E. A. (Joseph Emanuel Alexander), b. 1885
The Garnet and Silver-Gray

Almer, A. F. (Axel F.)
Augustana Foreign Missionary
Augustana Quarterly
Kina Missionären
Luthersk Tidskrift för Hednamission och Diakoni

Andeer, C. W. (Carl Wilhelm), 1870–1949
Julrunan
Ungdomens-Vännen (1895)
Valkyrian

Ander, O. Fritiof (Oscar Fritiof), 1903–
Augustana Historical Society Publications
Augustana Library Publications
Publication/Augustana Historical Society

Anderson, A. G.
Prärieblomman

Anderson, A. J. (Anders J.), 1877–1912
The Garnet and Silver-Gray

Anderson, A. V. (Agnes V.)
The Garnet and Silver-Gray

Anderson, Arvid
The Augustana Heritage Newsletter

Anderson, B. (Berndt)
Skaffaren och Minnesota Stats Tidning

Anderson, G. B.
Lutersk Kvartalskrift

Anderson, George
The Daisy

Anderson, Nancy
The Augustana Heritage Newsletter

Anderson, Reuben C.
Iowa Conference Minutes

Anderson, Richard C. (Richard Charles), 1930–
Augustana College Library Publications

Andreen, G. A. (Gustav Albert), 1864–1940
Augustana Bulletin
Augustana Historical Society Publications

Augustana Library Publications
Augustana Observer (1902)

Andren, F. N. (Fritz Nathanael)
Österns Väktare

Andrews, George G. (George Gordon), 1887–1938
Augustana Historical Society Publications

Ankarfelt, Signe
Förgät-Mig-Ej

Arbaugh, George B. (George Bartholomew), 1905–
Augustana Library Publications

Arbaugh, George E. (George Evans), 1933–
Augustana Library Publications

Ardahl, O. H.
Korsbaneret

Arden, G. Everett (Gothard Everett), 1905–1978
Illinois Conference Minutes
Publication/Augustana Historical Society

Armstrong, N. P.
Hemlandet det Gamla och det Nya

Auslund, J. (Jonas), 1843–1878
Ev. Luthersk Tidskrift

Bäckman, C. A.
Hemvännen
Korsbaneret
Lutersk Kvartalskrift
Ungdoms-Vännen (1879)

Baglo, Ferdinand Eugene, 1926–
Canada Conference Minutes

Barton, H. Arnold (Hildor Arnold), 1929–
Publication/Augustana Historical Society

Beckman, Peter
Publication/Augustana Historical Society

Belan, Judith A.
Publication/Augustana Historical Society

Bengston, C. J. (Carl Johan), 1862–1937
Augustana (1889)
Korsbaneret
The Lutheran Companion (1911)
Ungdoms-Vännen (1895)

Bengtson, John Robert
Augustana Library Publications

Bergendoff, C. J. I. (Conrad John Immanuel), 1895–1997
Augustana College Library Occasional Paper
Augustana Historical Society Publications
Augustana Library Publications
Lutheran Quarterly
Occasional Paper/Augustana College Library
Publication/Augustana Historical Society

Berger, V. (Vilhelm), 1867–1938
Valkyrian

Bergin, A. (Alfred), 1866–1944
Lindsborgs-Posten
Ungdoms-Vännen (1895)

Bergman, G. (Gustaf)
Columbia

Bergren, E. F. (Emil F.)
Almanac
Almanack
Kyrkobladet

Bergstrom, L. P.
Canada Härold

Bersell, A. O. (Anders Olof), 1853–1903
Augustana och Missionären
Hemvännen

Breck, John
The Bible Study Quarterly
The Bible Study Quarterly: Student's Edition
The Bible Study Quarterly: Teacher's Edition

Brolander, Glen E., 1929–
Publication/Augustana Historical Society

Brunström, D.
Kansas Missions Tidning

Burke, Rudolph C.
Augustana Missions (1956)

Cantor, Gordon N.
Occasional Paper/Augustana College Library

Capps, F. Herbert (Finis Herbert), 1920–
Publication/Augustana Historical Society

Carlberg, G. (Gustav), 1884–
Honan Glimpses

Carlson, C. Emanuel (Carl Emanuel)
Publication/Augustana Historical Society

Carlson, Edgar M. (Edgar Magnus), 1908–
Publication/Augustana Historical Society

Carlson, E.W. (Ernest W.), 1884–1923
The Garnet and Silver-Gray

Carlson, J. S. (John S.), 1857–1925
Lutersk Kvartalskrift

Carlson, S. A. (Samuel Augustus), 1868–
Vårt Land

Carlsson, E. (Erland), 1822–1893
Augustana och Missionären
Hemlandet det Gamla och det Nya
Missionären (Moline, IL: 1876)
Rätta Hemlandet

Svenska Posten
Tidskrift för Svensk E. Luth. Kyrkohistoria i N. Amerika och för
Teologiska och Kyrkliga Frågor

Carlton, C. G. (Carl G.)
Class Annual

Cederberg, William E. (William Emanuel)
Augustana Library Publications
Class Annual

Cervin, A. R. (Anders Richard), 1823–1900
Augustana och Missionären
Hemlandet det Gamla och det Nya
Missionären (Moline, IL: 1876)
Rätta Hemlandet
Rätta Hemlandet och Augustana
Rätta Hemlandet och Missionsbladet

Chillen, O.
Församlingsvännen

Chinlund, E. G. (Emil G.)
Deaconess Banner

Christenson, A. A. (Arthur Alvin), 1891–
Guldax

Cramer, C.H. (Clarence Henley), 1905–
Augustana Library Publications

Croonquist, A. P.
Skaffaren och Minnesota Stats Tidning

Dahl, K. G. W. (Kjell Gustav William), 1883–1917
Guldax
Julrunan
Ungdoms-Vännen (1895)

Dahl, P. M., d.1944
Canada
Svenska Canada-Tidningen

Dahlberg, J. G. (John G.)
Augustana Theological Quarterly
Korsbaneret

Dahleen, J. A.
Evangelisk Luthersk Tidskrift för Kyrkan Skolan och Hemmet
Fridens Härold

Dahlstedt, N. E.
Bethania

Dahlstrand, A. (Axel)
Minnesota Stats Tidning (1877)

Dorf, G. A. (Gustav Alfred), 1871–1943
Lindsborgs-Posten

Dowie, James I. (James Iverne), 1911–2005
Augustana Historical Society Publications
Augustana Library Publications
Publication/Augustana Historical Society

Ebb, N.
Församlingsvännen

Eckman, F. M. (Frans M.)
Ungdoms-Vännen (1895)

Edmund, Rudolph William
Augustana Library Publications

Edwins, A. W. (August William), 1871–1942
Kina Missionären
Luthersk Tidskrift för Hednamission och Diakoni

Eklund, Emmet E. (Emmet Elvin), 1919–
Publication/Augustana Historical Society

Emberg, D. (Duane)
Views

Enander, J. A. (Johan Alfred), 1842–1910
Hemlandet det Gamla och det Nya
Prärieblomman

Ungdoms-Vännen (1879)
Valkyrian

Engberg, J. (Jonas)
Hemlandet det Gamla och det Nya

Englund, M. J.
Augustana (1889)
Österns Väktare

Engstrom, S. (Sigfrid Emanuel), 1907–1955
Augustana Annual
Pastor's Paragraphs

Erickson, C.
Augustana Library Publications

Erickson, Edgar L. (Edgar Lewis), 1902–1968
Augustana Library Publications, Occasional Paper

Erlander, J. E.
Bethania

Erling, Bernhard
Publication/Augustana Historical Society

Erling, Maria (Maria Elizabeth), 1955–
Publication/Augustana Historical Society

Esbjörn, C. L. E. (Charles Linus Eugene), 1862–1938
Augustana Journal
Hemvännen
*Tidskrift för Svensk. Ev. Luth. Kyrkohistoria i N. Amerika och för
Teologiska och Kyrkliga Frågor*

Esbjörn, C. M. (Constantinus Magnus), 1858–1911
Augustana och Missionären
Korsbaneret
Lutersk Kvartalskrift
Ungdoms-Vännen (1879)

Esbjörn, L. P. (Lars Paul), 1808–1870
Barnvännen
Hemlandet det Gamla och det Nya
Svenska Posten

Espelie, Ernest M.
Publication/Augustana Historical Society

Evald, C. A. (Carl Anderson), 1849–1909
Barnvännen
Nåd och Sanning
Ungdoms-Vännen (1895)

Evald, E. (Emmy Carlsson), 1857–1946
Calendar
Missions-Tidning

Fahlund, G. A. (George Alvin), 1876–1956
Almanac
Almanack
Korsbaneret

Farley, Ruth L. Swanson
Augustana Synod Minutes

Fjellman, Burnice
Mission-Tidings

Flanagan, J. T. (John Theodore), 1906–
Augustana Library Publications

Fleming, K.
Canada
Väktaren

Fogelström, E. A. (Erik Alfred), 1850–1909
Dorkas
Lille Barnvännen
Ungdoms-Vännen (1879)

Fors, A. P. (Andrew Peter)
Augustana Journal
Väktaren

Forsander, N. (Nils), 1846–1926
Augustana Theological Quarterly
Bethania
Hemvännen

Gustavson, Reuben G. (Reuben Gilbert), 1892–
Occasional Paper/Augustana College Library

Gyllander, H. (Hugo), 1868–1955
Vid Juletid

Haff, J. L.
Ungdoms-Vännen (1895)

Hägglund, S. G. (Sven Gustav), 1874–1943
Augustana Observer (1902)
Korsbaneret

Hall, George F. (George Fridolph), 1908–
Publication/Augustana Historical Society

Hallberg, C. A.
Kyrkobladet

Hallquist, A.L. (Alfred L.)
Class Annual

Hamming, Edward, 1915–
Augustana Library Publications

Hansen, Marcus Lee, 1892–1938
Augustana College Library Occasional Paper
Augustana Historical Society Publications

Hansen, Olga Wold
Augustana Historical Society Publications

Hasselmo, Nils, 1931–
Publication/Augustana Historical Society

Hasselquist, T. N. (Tufve Nilsson), 1816–1891
Augustana (1868)
Augustana (1874)
Augustana och Missionären
Hemlandet det Gamla och det Nya
Luthersk Kyrkotidning
Minnesota Posten
Missionären (Chicago, IL: 1870)

Rätta Hemlandet
Rätta Hemlandet och Augustana
Rätta Hemlandet och Missionsbladet
Svenska Posten
Tidskrift för Svensk Ev. Luth. Kyrkohistoria i N. Amerika och för
  Teologiska och Kyrkliga Frågor
Ungdoms-Vännen (1879)

Highland, Augusta
Mission-Tidings

Hill, S. M. (Samuel Magnus), 1851–1921
Lutersk Kvartalskrift
Till Verksamhet
Ungdoms-Vännen (1895)

Hoff, H. J. (Hans J.)
Lindsborgs-Posten
Kansas Conference Lutheran

Hoglund, A. W. (Arthur William), 1926–
Augustana Library Publications

Holmes, L. (Ludvig), 1858–1910
Julrunan
Österns Väktare
Ungdoms-Vännen (1895)
Valkyrian

Holmgrain, O. V. (Oscar Vindician), 1852–1930
Augustana Journal
Textblad för Söndagsskolan
Ungdoms-Vännen (1895)
Young Lutheran's Companion

Horberg, Leland, 1910–1955
Augustana Library Publications

Hult, A. (Adolf), 1869–1943
Augustana Journal
Augustana Theological Quarterly
Theological Studies and Issues

Hult, A. (Anders), 1833–1913
Barnvännen
Väktaren

Hultkrans, C. A. (Carl A.)
Kina Missionären
Luthersk Tidskrift för Hednamission och Diakoni
Ungdoms-Vännen (1895)

Hutchinson, E. P. (Edward Prince), 1906–1938
Augustana Library Publications

Indebetou, H. (Hedvig), 1844–1933
Vid Juletid

Jackson, Gregory Lee
Publication/Augustana Historical Society

Jacobson, R. A.
The Jubilee

Jarvi, Raymond, 1942–
Publication/Augustana Historical Society

Johansen, C. K. (Charles K.)
Valkyrian

Johansen, H. (Håkan)
Valkyrian

John, Erwin (Erwin E.)
Lutheran Libraries

Johnson, A. E.
Hemlandet det Gamla och det Nya

Johnson, Emeroy, 1899–
Arkivfynd
Augustana Historical Society Publications
Minnesota Conference Minutes
The Young People

Johnson, H. P.
Korsbaneret

Johnson, Richard A. (Richard Abraham), 1910–
Augustana Library Publications

Johnston, L. A. (Lawrence Albert), 1855–1918
Bethania
Ungdoms-Vännen (1895)

Joranson, Einar
Augustana Library Publications

Kempe, J. W.
The Bible Study Quarterly: Student's Edition
The Bible Study Quarterly: Teacher's Edition

Kerfstedt, A. (Amanda), 1835–1920
Vid Juletid

Kjellgren, J. E.
Luthersk Tidskrift för Hednamission och Diakoni

Kjellgren, J. T. (Johan Theodor), 1859–1917
Ungdoms-Vännen (1895)

Kraft, C. (Carl), 1870–1941
Augustana (1889)
Julrunan

Krantz, J. A.
Ungdoms-Vännen (1895)
Utah Missionären

Lagerström, R. (Reinhold), 1861–1936
Kyrkosången

Larson, J. Edor (John Edor), 1885–1963
Nebraska Conference Minutes
Red River Valley Conference Minutes

Lawson, Eben (Eben Ezer), 1873–1951
Gustavian
Valkyria

Lawson, Evald B. (Evald Benjamin), 1904–1965
Augustana Historical Society Publications

Leaf, J. P.
Lindsborgs-Posten

Lindahl, Elder M., 1926–
Publication/Augustana Historical Society

Lindahl, J. (Josua), 1844–1912
Ungdoms-Vännen (1879)

Lindahl, S. P. A. (Sven Peter August), 1843–1908
Augustana (1889)
Barnens Tidning
Barnvännen
Blommor vid Vägen
Hemvännen
Korsbaneret
Schibboleth

Lindberg, C. E. (Conrad Emil), 1852–1930
Augustana Observer (1881)
Nåd och Sanning

Lindberg, J. E. (Johannes E.)
Canada News

Lindberg, Luther E. (Luther Eugene), 1933–
New England Conference Minutes

Lindberg, P. M.
Ungdoms-Vännen (1895)

Lindberg, Paul M. (Paul Martin), 1905–1993
Publication/Augustana Historical Society

Lindblad, A. J.
Österns Väktare

Lindeblad, H. O.
Hemvännen
Väktaren

Lindell, C. O. (Carl Oscar), 1847–1905
Barnvännen
Evangelisk Luthersk Barntidning

Nåd och Sanning
Ungdomens Tidning

Linder, F. A.
Deaconess Banner

Linder, Oliver A. (Oliver Anderson), 1863–1939
Svenska Amerikanaren Hemlandet

Lindevall, C. A. (Carl August), 1863–1952
Korsbaneret

Lindquist, A. W. (Albert William), 1873–1944
Korsbaneret

Lindquist, Emory K. (Emory Kempton), 1908–
Augustana Historical Society Publications
Publication/Augustana Historical Society

Linner, J. E.
Luthersk Tidskrift för Hednamission och Diakoni

Lofgren, D. A. (David Amandus), 1868–1939
Betania

Lönnquist, C. A. (Carl Adolph), 1869–1937
Guldax
Julrunan

Lugn, Alvin L. (Alvin Leonard), 1895–1976
Augustana Library Publications

Lund, Doniver A. (Doniver Adolph), 1919–
Publication/Augustana Historical Society

Lund, E. (Emil), 1850–1942
Augustana Theological Quarterly
Iowa Conference Minutes

Lund, Emil F. S. (Emil Ferdinand Svitzer), b. 1858
Minnesota Conference Minutes

Lundeen, A. (Anton Mander), 1892–1968
Augustana Foreign Missionary

Lundholm, A. T. (Algot Theodore), 1875–
Augustana (1889)
Augustana (1956)
Korsbaneret

Lundquist, E. (Emil)
Kansas Stats Tidning

Lundquist, M. L. (Merton L.)
Texas Conference Minutes

Lunnow, M. (Magnus)
Minnesota Stats Tidning (1877)

Magnuson, A. A.
Österns Väktare

Malm, G. N. (Gustav Nathaniel), 1869–1928
God Jul

Matson, T. E. (Theodore E.)
Augustana Missions (1956)

Mattson, H. (Hans), 1832–1893
Minnesota Stats Tidning (1877)

Maurer, Sherry C. (Sherry Case)
Publication/Augustana Historical Society

Mauritzson, J. G. U. (Jules Gothe Ultimus), 1868–1931
Ungdoms-Vännen (1895)
Vid Juletid

Melin, P. R. (Peter R.)
Kyrkosången

Mellander, May
Missions-Tidning

Mowrer, Orval Hobart, 1907–1982
Occasional Paper/Augustana College Library

Naeseth, H. C. K. (Henriette Christiane Koren), 1899–
Augustana Historical Society Publications
Augustana Library Publications
Saga

Nelander, E. (Edward), 1855–1915
Kansas Posten
Lutersk Kvartalskrift
Pedagogen

Nelson, C. E. (Carl E.)
Augustana (1889)
Kina Missionären

Nelson, Carl L. (Carl Leonard)
Publication/Augustana Historical Society

Nelson, Harry E.
Augustana Library Publications
Publication/Augustana Historical Society

Nelson, N. J. W. (Nels Johan Wilhelm), 1867–1954
Columbia

Nelson, P.
Canada Härold

Nelson, R. S. (Robert S.)
The Bible Study Quarterly: Student's Edition
The Bible Study Quarterly: Teacher's Edition

Nelson, Vincent E. (Vincent Edward), 1913–
Augustana Library Publications

Nibelius, F. (Fredrik), 1850–1897
Nåd och Sanning

Nilsson, Betty A., 1878–1963
Missions-Tidning

Nolan, Michael
Publication/Augustana Historical Society

Norberg, P. G.
Hemlandet det Gamla och det Nya

Nordstrom, O. L. (Oscar Leonard), 1880–
Augustana Historical Society Publications

Norelius, E. (Eric), 1833–1916
Augustana (1874)
Augustana (1889)
Augustana Theological Quarterly
Ev. Luthersk Tidskrift
Hemlandet det Gamla och det Nya
Korsbaneret
Luthersk Kyrkotidning
Minnesota Posten
Missionären (Chicago, IL: 1870)
Skaffaren
Tidskrift för Svensk Ev. Luth. Kyrkohistoria i N. Amerika och för
   Teologiska och Kyrkliga Frågor
Ungdoms-Vännen (1879)
Ungdoms-Vännen (1895)

Norling, J. E.
Fosterlandet

Norman, C. G. (Carl Gustaf), 1861–1916
Framåt (1894)
Framåt (1887)
Framåt (1892)

Nothstein, I. O. (Ira Oliver), 1874–1962
Augustana Historical Society Publications
Augustana Library Publications
My Church

Noyd, M. (Martin)
Till Verksamhet
Väktaren

Nyquist, J. P. (Jonas Petter Nilson)
Missionären (1870)

Nystrom, D. (Daniel), 1886–1982
My Church

Olsson, A. (Alexander), 1868–1952
Vestkusten

Olsson, A. (Anna), 1866–1946
Julrunan

Olsson, Karl A., 1913–
Publication/Augustana Historical Society

Olsson, Nils William, 1909–
Swedish American Genealogist

Olsson, O. (Olof), 1841–1900
Augustana (1874)
Augustana Journal
Augustana och Missionären
Hemvännen
Korsbaneret
Lille Missionären
Luthersk Kyrkotidning
Missionären (Chicago, IL: 1870)
Nytt och Gammalt
The Olive Leaf
Skolvännen
Ungdoms-Vännen (1879)

Olsson-Seffer, Pehr (Pehr Hjalmar), 1873–1911
Augustana Library Publications

Osborn, J. E. (Joseph Esbjörn), 1843–1932
Barnvännen

Östenson, H. (Harald) (Pseud. for P. M. E. Pettersson)
Vid Juletid

Palmquist, Donovan J., 1928–2004
Augustana Heritage Newsletter

Palmquist, Ethel D.
Mission-Tidings

Parkander, Dorothy J., 1925–
Publication/Augustana Historical Society

Reynolds, Maynard C. (Maynard Clinton), 1922–
Occasional Paper/Augustana College Library

Rinell, J. A.
Kyrkobladet

Rodabaugh, J. H. (James Howard), 1910–1985
Augustana Library Publications

Rodell, A. (Albert), 1853–1897
Augustana (1889)
Augustana Journal
Augustana Observer (1881)
Hemvännen
Lille Missionären

Rosander, C. A. (Carl A.)
The Young Observer

Runbeck, Dolores
The Quarterly Release

Runeberg, J. L. (Johan Ludvig), 1804–1877
Ungdoms-Vännen (1895)

Rydberg, Per Axel, 1860–1931
Augustana Library Publications

Ryden, E. E. (Ernest Edwin), 1886–1981
Augustana Annual
The Jubilee
The Lutheran Companion (1911)
The Lutheran Companion (1952)

Rydholm, C. P. (Carl Peter), 1843–1902
Augustana och Missionären
Missionären (1876)

Rystrom, Lauree Nelson
The Olive Leaf

Sahlstrom, L. A.
Förgät-Mig-Ej

Saloutos, Theodore, 1910–1980
Augustana Library Publications
Occasional Paper/Augustana College Library

Sandahl, Charles F. (Charles Frederick), 1871–1944
Nebraska Conference Minutes

Sandell, E. (Eric)
Förgät-Mig-Ej

Sandell, J. A.
Textblad för Söndagsskolan

Sandgren, C. H. (Carl H.)
Columbia Conference Minutes
My Church

Sandzen, B. (Birger), 1871–1954
God Jul

Schersten, Albert F. (Albert Ferdinand), 1889–
Augustana Historical Society Publications
Augustana Library Publications

Schön, A. (Anders), 1864–1930
Hemlandet det Gamla och det Nya
Prärieblomman
Ungdoms-Vännen (1895)

Schroeder, David A. (David Alan), 1949–
Augustana College Library Publications

Schroeder, Phil
Publication/Augustana Historical Society

Seaborg, Glenn T. (Glenn Theodore), 1912–1999
Occasional Paper/Augustana College Library

Sebelius, S. J. (Sven Johan), 1874–
My Church

Seedoff, J. F. (Johan Fr.)
Ungdoms-Vännen (1895)

Sorensen, W. Robert
Publication/Augustana Historical Society

Staack, Henry F.
Augustana Historical Society Publications

Stark, G. K. (Gustaf Knut), 1867–1947
Väktaren

Stephenson, George M. (George Malcolm), 1883–1958
Augustana Historical Society Publications
Publication/Augustana Historical Society

Stockenström, H. (Herman von), 1853–1902
Skaffaren

Stolpe, M. (Mauritz), 1858–1938
God Jul

Stomberg, A. A. (Andrew Adin), 1871–1943
Ungdoms-Vännen (1895)

Strömberg, L. (Leonard—i.e., Oscar Leonard), 1871–1941
Förgät-Mig-Ej
God Jul

Sundelius, P. A.
Hemlandet det Gamla och det Nya

Sundell, E. (Edward), 1859–1929
Valkyrian

Swan, G. N. (Gustaf Nelson), 1856–1938
Augustana Historical Society Publications
Ungdomens Tidning
Ungdoms-Vännen (1895)

Swanbeck, J. W.
Väktaren

Swanberg, F. N. (Fredrik Nikolaus), 1853–1913
Bethphage Biblioteket

Swanson, C. A. (Charles A.)
Österns Väktare

Swanson, D. Verner
Augustana Synod Minutes

Swanson, Richard A.
Publication/Augustana Historical Society

Swanson, Roland
The Bible Study Quarterly: Student's Edition
The Bible Study Quarterly: Teacher's Edition

Swanson, S. Hjalmar (Swan Hjalmar), 1886–
Augustana Overseas (1947)

Swärd, A. A. (Axel August), 1854–1891
Valkyrian

Swenson, B. (Birger), 1895–
Almanac
Almanack
Augustana Annual
Publication/Augustana Historical Society

Swenson, C. Vernon (Carl Vernon), 1898–1957
Augustana Overseas (1947)

Swenson, Mrs. C. Vernon
Little Folks

Swenson, Frank Albert, 1912–
Augustana Library Publications

Swensson, A. (Alma Lind), 1859–1939
Missions-Tidning

Swensson, C. A. (Carl Aaron), 1857–1904
Bethany Messenger (1892)
Förgät-Mig-Ej (1892)
Förgät-Mig-Ej (1902)
Fosterlandet
Framåt (Lindsborg, KS: 1887)
Kansas Posten
Korsbaneret
Lindsborgs-Posten

Lutersk Kvartalskrift
Pedagogen: Kristlig Skoltidning
Ungdomens Tidning
Ungdoms-Vännen (1879)
Ungdoms-Vännen (1895)

Tegner, E. (Esaias), 1782–1846
Ungdoms-Vännen (1895)

Telleen, Jane
Augustana College Library Occasional Paper

Tengwald, V. J. (Victor Johan), 1860–
Canada Härold

Thander, Gunnar Erik Axel
Valkyrian

Thelander, P.
Korsbaneret
Ungdoms-Vännen (1895)

Thorsell, Elisabeth, 1945–
Swedish American Genealogist

Tilberg, Frederick, 1896–
Augustana Library Publications

Towley, Carl K. (Carl Kahrs)
Minnesota Lutheran

Tredway, J. Thomas (John Thomas), 1935–
Publication/Augustana Historical Society

Tweet, Roald D. (Roald Dahl), 1933–
Augustana College Library Occasional Paper
Publication/Augustana Historical Society

Udden, J. A. (Johan August), 1859–1932
Augustana Library Publications
Hemvännen
Kansas Posten
Ungdoms-Vännen (1879)

Udden, S. (Svante), 1853–1937
Canada
Canada Härold
Sions Väktare
Väktaren

Van Doren, Mark, 1894–1972
Occasional Paper/Augustana College Library

Vibelois, J.
Nåd och Sanning

Wahlström, M. (Matthew)
Ungdoms-Vännen (1879)

Wald, Arthur
Augustana Historical Society Publications

Wallin, J. E. Wallace (John Edward Wallace), 1876–
Augustana Library Publications. Occasional Paper

Wallin, R. (Ralph)
Views

Wallmark, O. (Otto)
Skaffaren och Minnesota Stats Tidning

Weber, Erwin, 1921–
Occasional Paper/Augustana College Library

Weisenburger, F. P. (Francis Phelps), 1900–
Augustana Library Publications

Wendell, C. A. (Claus August), 1866–1950
The Lutheran Companion (1911)

Wersell, Thomas W.
Augustana Missions (1956)

Westberg, Lael
Church School Teacher

Westin, Gunnar, 1890–1967
Publication/Augustana Historical Society

Publications Issued by Augustana Evangelical Lutheran Church Institutions

Titles in the union list which were issued by an Augustana Evangelical Lutheran Church academic or social service institution are arranged in alphabetical order in the following list under the name of the parent institution.

ACADEMIC INSTITUTIONS

Augustana College (Rock Island, Illinois)
Augustana Bulletin
Augustana College Bulletin
Augustana College Catalog
Augustana College Library Occasional Paper
Augustana College Library Publications
Augustana College Magazine
Augustana Library Publications
Augustana Library Publications, Occasional Paper
Augustana Observer (1902)
Augustana Story (see *Augustana College Bulletin*)
Balder
Catalogue (see *Augustana College Catalog*)
Class Annual
The Garnet and Silver-Gray
The Jubilee
Julrunan
Lyceum Annual
The Observer

Observer (see *Augustana Observer* (1902); *The Young Observer*)
Occasional Paper/Augustana College Library
The Rockety-I
Runan
Saga
Skolvännen
Student-Katalog
Swedish American Genealogist
Swenson Center News
The Young Observer

Augustana Theological Seminary (Rock Island, Illinois)
Augustana Seminary Review
The Seminary Review
Theological Studies and Issues

Bethany College (Lindsborg, Kansas)
Academica
Bethania
Bethanian
Bethany Academy Catalogue (see *Catalogue of Bethany Academy at Lindsborg, Kansas*)
Bethany Annual
Bethany College Bulletin
Bethany College Bulletin/Alumni News
Bethany College Bulletin/Bethany Magazine
Bethany College Catalog
Bethany College Messenger
Bethany Daisy (see *Daisy*)
Bethany Magazine
Bethany Messenger (1892)
Bethany Messenger (1902)
Bethany's Budbäraren
Budbäraren (see *Bethany's Budbäraren*)
Catalogue of Bethany Academy at Lindsborg, Kansas
Daisy
För-Gät-Mig-Ej (1902)
Forget-Me-Not (see *För-Gät-Mig-Ej* [1902])
Messenger (see *Bethany Messenger* [1902])
Pedagogen

Gustavus Adolphus College (St. Peter, Minnesota)
Annual Messenger
Arkivfynd

Breidablick
Catalogue of Gustavus Adolphus College
College Breezes
Excelsior
Greater Gustavus Association Quarterly (see *Greater Gustavus Quarterly*)
Greater Gustavus Quarterly
Gustaf Adolfs Journalen (see *Gustavus Journal*)
The Gustavian
Gustavian Weekly (1920)
The Gustavian Weekly (1973)
Gustaviana
Gustavus Adolphus College Catalog (see *Catalogue of Gustavus Adolphus College*)
Gustavus Adolphus Journal (see *Gustavus Journal*)
Gustavus Journal
The Gustavus Quarterly
Heimdall
Junction
Manhem
None of the Above
Runes
Valkyria
Vox Collegi

Hope Academy (Moorhead, Minnesota)

Catalogue of Hope Academy, Moorhead, Minnesota
Folkvännen

Luther Academy and College (Wahoo, Nebraska)

Advocate (see *Luther College Advocate*)
Anchor (see *Luther College & Academy Yearbook*)
From Luther
The Key (see *Luther College & Academy Yearbook*)
Luther Academy Catalog
Luther Academy Visitor
Luther College Advocate
Luther College & Academy Yearbook
Luther College Catalog
Luther College Visitor
Luther Visitor (see *Luther Academy Visitor; Luther College Visitor*)
Till Verksamhet
The Triangle (see *Luther College & Academy Yearbook*)
Viking (see *Luther College & Academy Yearbook*)

Lutheran Bible Institute (Minneapolis, Minnesota)
Bible Banner
Bulletin/Lutheran Bible Institute
L.B.I. Bulletin
Let's Be Intercessors (see *Bulletin/Lutheran Bible Institute*)
Lutheran Bible Institute Bulletin (see *L.B.I. Bulletin*)
Reflector

Minnesota College (Minneapolis, Minnesota)
Calendar/Minnesota College
College Calendar/Minnesota College
Messenger
The Moccasin
The Picayune
The Picayune (Annual)

North Star College (Warren, Minnesota)
North Star Signal
Skolvännen: North Star Signal (see *North Star Signal*)

Upsala College (East Orange, New Jersey)
Årsbok/Svenska Litterära Sällskapet de Nio
The Gazette
Nios Årsbok (see *Årsbok/Svenska Litterära Sällskapet de Nio*)
The Upsala Alumni Gazette
Upsala Alumni Magazine
Upsala Alumni News
Upsala College Catalog
Upsala Gazette
Upsala Reports
The Upsalite

SOCIAL SERVICE INSTITUTIONS

Bethesda Hospital and Bethesda Deaconess Home (St. Paul, Minnesota)
Tabitha

Bethphage Mission (Axtell, Nebraska)
Bethphage Messenger
Bethphage Biblioteket
Guldax
Mosaic: Opening Doors to Extraordinary Lives (see
   Bethphage Messenger)

Immanuel Deaconess Institute (Omaha, Nebraska)
(Later: Immanuel Medical Center)
  Axplockerskan
  Banner (Omaha, Nebraska)
  Deaconess Banner
  Diakoniss-Baneret
  Dorkas
  The Immanuel Banner
  Immanuel Medical Center Banner
  Kalender för Qvinlig Diakoni och Barmhertighetsverksamhet (see *Dorkas*)
  Lille Barnvännen
  Sjukvännen

Subject Index

Titles from the union list are arranged in the following list in broad subject categories. This subject index does not include any publications issued by Augustana Evangelical Lutheran Church institutions. Those titles are indicated in a separate "Publications Issued by Augustana Evangelical Lutheran Church Institutions" list.

Children

Olive Leaf
Solglimten
Solstrålen
Söndagsskolans Textblad
Thru 8 Stories
'Til 8 Stories
Vid Juletid

Christmas
God Jul
Julklockorna
Vid Juletid

Devotional
The Home Altar
Bethania
Nåd och Sanning
Nytt och Gammalt
Rätta Hemlandet
Uniting Word
Vårt Land och Folk

General
Almanac
Almanack
Augustana (1868)
Augustana (1874)
Augustana (1889)
Augustana (1956)
Augustana Annual
Augustana Journal
Augustana Lutheran
Augustana Lutheranen
Augustana Observer (1881)
Augustana och Missionären
Canada
Canada Härold
Canada News
Ev. Luthersk Tidskrift
Förgät-Mig.Ej
Fosterlandet
Fylgia
Gamla och Nya Hemlandet

Hemlandet det Gamla och det Nya
Hemvännen
Korsbaneret
Lutheran Companion (1911)
Lutheran Companion (1952)
My Church
Rätta Hemlandet och Augustana
Svenska Amerikanaren Hemlandet
Vårt Hem
Vårt Land

Literary

Augustana Journal
God Jul
Prärieblomman
Ungdoms-Vännen
Ungdomsvännen
Valkyrian

Men

Augustana Churchmen
Augustana Lutheran Churchmen
Augustana Men
Bond (1924)
L.B.A. Bulletin
Lutheran Brotherhood Bond
News Bulletin/Lutheran Brotherhood of America
Newsletter of Augustana Brotherhood

Miscellaneous

A Drop of Ink
Lutheran Libraries
Lutheran Publications
Schibboleth
Swedish American Genealogist
What's New in Books

Missions

Augustana Foreign Missionary
Augustana Missions (1948)
Augustana Missions (1956)
Augustana Overseas (1947)
Augustana Overseas (1951)

Nebraska
Wahoo-Bladet

New England/New York
Beacon
Church Paper for the Cleveland District
Evangelisk Luthersk Tidskrift för Kyrkan Skolan och Hemmet
Församlingsvännen
Framåt (Brooklyn, NY: 1894)
Framåt (Providence, RI: 1892)
Fridens Härold
Fyrbåken
Kyrkobladet
Kyrkotidning för Cleveland-Distriktet
Kyrkotidning för Jamestown-Distriktet af Svenska Lutherska New
  York-Konferensen
Lutheran Beacon
Lutheran Social Service News
Luthersk Kyrkotidning
Missionären
New England Conference News
New England Lutheran
Österns Härold
Österns Väktare
Vår Nya Kyrkotidning

Pacific Northwest
Columbia
Columbia Lutheran
Lutheran Messenger
Sions-Bladet
Western Lutheran

Swedish Language Text
Almanack
Augustana (1868)
Augustana (1874)
Augustana (1889)
Augustana (1956)
Augustana Lutheranen
Augustana och Missionären
Barnens Tidning
Barnvännen

Betania
Bethania
Blommor vid Vägen
Canada Härold
Ebenezer
Ev. Luthersk Tidskrift
Evangelisk Luthersk Barntidning
Evangelisk Luthersk Tidskrift för Kyrkan Skolan och Hemmet
Förgät-Mig-Ej
Församlingsvännen
Fosterlandet
Framåt (Brooklyn, NY: 1894)
Framåt (Lindsborg, KS: 1887)
Framåt (Providence, RI: 1892)
Fridens Härold
Fylgia
Fyrbåken
Gamla och Nya Hemlandet
God Jul
Hem Missionären
Hemåt
Hemlandet det Gamla och det Nya
Hemvännen
Julklockorna
Juvelskrinet
Kansas Missions Tidning
Kansas Posten
Kansas Stats Tidning
Kina Missionären
Korsbaneret
Kyrkobladet
Kyrkohärolden
Kyrkosången
Kyrkotidning för Cleveland-Distriktet
Kyrkotidning för Jamestown-Distriktet af Svenska Lutherska New York-
  Konferensen
Lekkamraten
Lille Missionären
Lindsborgs-Posten
Lutersk Kvartalskrift
Luth. Kyrkotidning
Luther Bladet
Luthersk Kyrkotidning

About the Author

Virginia P. Follstad, a retired librarian, began her professional career as research assistant to Dr. Reuben K. Youngdahl at Mount Olivet Lutheran Church in Minneapolis, Minnesota. After earning her master of arts in library science at the University of Minnesota–Minneapolis, she was a reference librarian at the Walter Library, the main library at the University of Minnesota–Minneapolis. Subsequent professional positions were reference librarian at the Fresno County Library in Fresno, California; reference librarian and cataloger at Bradley University in Peoria, Illinois; and cataloger at the Andersen Library at the University of Wisconsin–Whitewater. She was director of the Irvin L. Young Memorial Library in Whitewater, Wisconsin, for the last twenty-two years of her career.

She holds a certificate of professional development in library administration from the University of Wisconsin; a bachelor of arts in English from Bethany College in Lindsborg, Kansas; and an associate of arts in liberal arts from Luther College in Nebraska.

Memberships include the Augustana Heritage Association, American Library Association, and Wisconsin Library Association. She is also an elected member of Beta Phi Mu, the national library science and information studies honor society.

A native of Oakland, Nebraska, mother of two and grandmother of two, she lives at rural Whitewater, Wisconsin, with her husband, Dr. Merle N. Follstad. She began research for this book immediately following retirement, when the Augustana Heritage Association commissioned her for this project.